1993

THE EMERGENCY EVACUATION
OF CITIES

THE EMERGENCY EVACUATION OF CITIES

A Cross-National Historical and Geographical Study

Wilbur Zelinsky
Leszek A. Kosiński

Rowman & Littlefield Publishers, Inc.

ROWMAN & LITTLEFIELD PUBLISHERS, INC.

Published in the United States of America
by Rowman & Littlefield Publishers, Inc.
8705 Bollman Place, Savage, Maryland 20763

British Cataloging in Publication Information Available

Library of Congress Cataloging-in-Publication Data

Zelinsky, Wilbur, 1921-
The emergency evacuation of cities : a cross-national
historical and geographical study / Wilbur Zelinsky,
Leszek A. Kosiński.
p.   cm.
Includes bibliographical references and index.
1. Evacuation of civilians.   2. Emergency management.
3. Natural disasters—Social aspects.   I. Kosiński,
Leszek A.   II. Title.
HV554.Z45 1991
363.3' 48—dc20   91–23165 CIP

ISBN 0–8476–7673–0 (hardcover : alk. paper)

Printed in the United States of America

Contents

List of Tables

List of Illustrations

Foreword

This study originated several years ago during a period when there was a lively discussion going on in both the popular press and professional literature concerning the practicality of the mass evacuation of urban populations as a civil defense strategy in the event of nuclear warfare or the imminent prospect thereof. The problem was (and is) of considerable concern to the senior author as a private citizen, but it also roused the interest and professional curiosity of both of us as human geographers. The central question became obvious enough: What can we learn from the historical record, scholarly literature, and existing theory that might shed light on the efficacy of the evacuation strategy if the world were to find itself on the verge of a nuclear holocaust—or in the event of other unprecedented catastrophes? Or is it conceivable that past experience may be irrelevant in coping with major disasters— nuclear, industrial, or "natural"—in the decades ahead?

A search for relevant publications on emergency evacuations, other forms of disaster response, and similar topics revealed the scarcity and weakness of whatever existing scholarship might be brought to bear upon the question. There are, it is true, some worthwhile isolated studies of particular events, some in-depth analyses of the sociology and social psychology of evacuations in certain parts of the First World, and some thoughtful, but hypothetical, treatments of what could take place during some future military crisis, but no attempt at a comprehensive view of disasters and the evacuation phenomenon. More particularly, there was a dearth of studies attempting to draw lessons for the present out of the historical experience of past disasters. In light of this situation and the increasing salience of disasters of all sorts and the responses thereto for students of human society (as discussed in Chapter 1), it seemed sensible to consider initiating a general study involving all important accessible events, with special attention to the geographical and demographic aspects of these disasters, in an effort to derive whatever generalizations might be distilled from the historical record.

We might note in passing that we have one advantage that is somewhat unusual for historical geographers. All twenty-seven events treated in this study occurred during our lifetimes, and, in greater or lesser degree, we were aware of them as they were taking place. In fact, we were personally involved, at least marginally, in two of the disasters—the Warsaw evacuations and Three Mile Island.

Whatever the shortcomings of this volume it can claim a certain value by virtue of uniqueness. This is the very first attempt to examine the topic of emergency evacuations on a worldwide scale across the entire range of disasters and to do so in some time depth as well. As such, we believe it will be useful to students and practitioners at all levels in a variety of fields, including disaster studies and management, urban studies, planning, demography, military science, history, and geography. Our fondest hope is that our efforts will stimulate other scholars into delving more deeply into the questions we have raised and into going well beyond the limits of an exploratory venture. Our successors will enjoy an advantage that eludes us at this time. Unfortunately for humanity at large, but as a kind of devilish blessing for the analyst, there is every reason to expect that the years to come will produce an ample supply of fresh disasters with which to fill up many of the gaps in our current knowledge and understanding.

ACKNOWLEDGMENTS

We owe major debts to many persons and organizations, but first and foremost to the National Geographic Society (NGS) whose generous research grant made this enterprise possible. In that connection, the advocacy of two NGS officers, Drs. Harm De Blij and Barry Bishop, on behalf of a risky proposal was particularly important, and we shall not soon forget their partisanship. We are also grateful for the working facilities and secretarial assistance provided by our two university departments, and are especially appreciative of the expert cartographic services provided by Messrs. Geoffrey Lester (supervisor) and Michael Fisher of the University of Alberta's Department of Geography.

Listed below are the many individuals who provided information, counsel, and moral support. We thank them all and hope that, despite the obvious imperfections of our efforts, they will not be too disappointed by the results. We look forward to receiving their comments and indeed to hearing from any of our readers. We still have much to learn.

Prof. David E. Alexander, University of Massachusetts; the librarians of the American Red Cross, Washington, D.C.; Mr. Mariano Bahamonde R., Cruz Roja Chilena; Prof. Jürgen Bähr, Universität Kiel; Mr. Harry G. Barnes, Jr., Chargé d'Affaires, U.S. Embassy, New Delhi, India; Prof. Jacqueline Beaujeu-Garnier, Université de Paris; Mr. François Bédarida, Institut d'Histoire du Temps Présent, Paris; Ms. Biegle, Document Librarian, UN High Commissioner for Refugees, Geneva; Ms. Blum, Bibliothèque de Documentation Internationale Contemporaine, Nanterre; Edmund Booth, Ove Arup & Partners, London; Mr. Jean Bourgeois-Pichat, Comité International de Coopération dans les Recherches Nationales en Démographie, Paris; Prof. Harold C. Brookfield, Australian National University; Mr. Gérard Calot, Institut National d'Etudes Démographiques, Paris; Ms. Campregher, Librarian, Bundesanstalt für Landeskunde und Raumforschung, Bad Godesburg; Prof. Adolf Ciborowski, Politechnika Warszawska, Warsaw; Dr. Françoise Cribier, Centre National de la Recherche Scientifique, Paris; Dr. Marian Marek Drozdowski, Instytut Historii, Polska Akademia Nauk, Warsaw; Gerald Dunn, UN Disaster Relief Office, Geneva; Prof. Kazimierz Dziewoński, Instytut Geografii i Zagospodarowania Przestrzennego, Polska Akademia Nauk, Warsaw; Prof. John Erickson, University of Edinburgh; Dr. Joachim Fischer, Archivist, Staatsarchiv Frankfurt; Dr. K. H. Frank, Chief Archivist, Weltwirtschafts-Institut, Kiel; Prof. Werner Fricke, Universität Heidelberg; Prof. Hiromu Futagami, Toyama University; Mr. Gaschignard, Direction de la Securité Civile, Paris; Dr. Andrzej Gawryszewski, Instytut Geografii i Zagospodarowania Przestrzennego, Polska Akademia Nauk, Warsaw; Prof. Maria Luisa Gentileschi; Prof. Pierre George, Institut de France, Paris; Ms. M. Hanne, Librarian, League of Red Cross Societies, Geneva; Dr. Karl Haubner, Akademie für Raumforschung und Landesplanung, Hannover; Ms. Jacqueline Hecht, Institut National d'Etudes Démographiques, Paris; Dr. Susanna Hecht, University of California, Los Angeles; Ms. Heimo, International Committee of the Red Cross, Geneva; Mr. B. Helfer, Das Hessische Hauptstaatsarchiv, Wiesbaden; Dr. Wolfgang Herden, Universität Heidelberg; Prof. Kenneth Hewitt, Wilfrid Laurier University; Jeanne X. Kasperson, Clark University; Dr. Hiroshi Kawabe,

Research Institute for Population Issues, Tokyo; Mr. Kepelman, UN Disaster Relief Office, Geneva; Dr. Krystyna Kersten, Instytut Historii, Polska Akademia Nauk, Warsaw; Ms. Kinder, Archivist, Bundesarchiv, Koblenz; Dr. Hans K. Kullmer, Statistisches Bundesamt, Wiesbaden; Dr. W. Linke, Bundesinstitut für Bevölkerungsforschung, Wiesbaden; Ms. Traute Lüders, Weltwirtschafts-Institut, Kiel; Mr. U. Mammey, Bundesinstitut für Bevölkerungsforschung, Wiesbaden; Ms. Tatiana Ivanovna Mandzhurina, Gosudarstviennyi Muzei Istorii Leningrada, Leningrad; Mr. Jacques Maron, Henry Dunant Institut, Geneva; Mr. George T. McCloskey, Office of the U.S. Foreign Disaster Assistance, Agency for International Development, Washington; Ms. Mercier, Institut d'Histoire du Temps Présent, Paris; Dr. Stanislaw Misztal, Instytut Geografii i Zagospodarowania Przestrzennego, Polska Akademia Nauk, Warsaw; Mr. Ward Morehouse, Council on International and Public Affairs, New York; Prof. Debnath Mookherjee, Western Washington University; Mr. T. K. Moulik, Indian Institute of Management, Vastrapur; Prof. Daniel Noin, Université de Paris; Ms. Françoise Perret, International Committee of the Red Cross, Geneva; Mr. Heinrich Platz, Bundesamt für Zivilschutz, Bad Godesberg; Prof. E. L. Quarantelli, University of Delaware; Mr. René Remond, Fondation Nationale des Sciences Politiques, Paris; Mr. Everett M. Ressler, Institut Henry Dunant, Geneva; Mr. Harrison Salisbury, New York *Times*; Mr. Philip E. Schambra, Science Attaché, U.S. Embassy, New Delhi; Mr. Theodore Shabad, New York *Times*; Dr. W. Strubelt, Bundesanstalt für Landeskunde und Raumforschung, Bad Godesberg; Mr. P. Tanghe, Librarian, Weltwirtschafts-Institut, Kiel; Mr. Haroun Tazief, Commissariat à l'Etude et à la Prévention de Risques Naturels Majeurs, Paris; Mr. Hans Toelle, Bundesamt für Zivilschutz, Bad Godesberg; Prof. Jean Vidalenc, Paris; Mr. Roger Walon, Intergovernmental Committee for European Migration, Geneva; Dr. Hilde Wander, Weltwirtschafts-Institut, Kiel; Mr. Steven R. Weisman, New York *Times*; Prof. Gilbert F. White, University of Colorado; Mr. Ralph Winstanley II, Counselor Embassy for Economic Affairs, U.S. Embassy, Bogotá; Dr. Grigori Vladimirovich Yoffe, Institut Geografii, Akademia Nauk SSSR, Moscow; Ms. York, Librarian, International Committee of the Red Cross, Geneva; Ms. Micheline Zéghouani, Reference Librarian, UN Disaster Relief Office, Geneva.

Wilbur Zelinsky
Leszek A. Kosiński
August 1990

Chapter 1

Introduction

BACKGROUND AND AIMS

If the emergency evacuation of a city is a relatively unusual event, it has come to pass, nonetheless, in many places under widely different circumstances, and has disrupted the lives of tens of millions of persons during the present century alone and uncountable numbers in earlier periods. Taken as a whole, this exceptional form of human mobility constitutes an important phenomenon, but one that remains poorly understood and whose theoretical and practical implications have yet to be explored adequately. Our intention here is to describe and analyze the accessible evidence for a number of relatively recent evacuations on a comparative, cross-national basis, with special attention to their geographic and demographic dimensions, and then to consider the larger lessons inherent in this material for students of human societies and urban places.

Perhaps the best way to begin is by defining the class of events being scrutinized in this study. Our concern is with the outward movement to presumably safe localities of a substantial portion (but almost never the entirety) of the residents of a city when they are confronted with an actual, potential, or imagined natural or human disaster that is perceived to be a serious threat to life and property—and their eventual return. A major qualification is that the actors in question regard the evacuation as a temporary expedient and, whether they actually do so or not, that they intend to return to their customary residences as quickly as is prudent. In a few cases, the actors in question believed that the community would be reconstituting itself at a new, physically safer site. Although we do not deal with them in detail, for purposes of comparison or control, we are also interested in those documented instances when urban populations considered the option of evacuating in the face of imminent danger but decided to remain in place. We include not only events where the decision-making process was highly centralized, and movement (or non-movement) was directed by official authority, but also cases where individuals or households acted spontaneously on their own and still others where both modes of choice came into play.

There is more than one reason for concentrating on urban populations. First it is usually easier to document the centrifugal movements of concentrated city dwellers and their subsequent return than the more complex paths of diffusely distributed rural folk. Moreover, the relevant statistics are generally somewhat more plentiful for the urban than for the rural case. There is also the obvious fact that because of relatively high population densities disasters with quite limited spatial impact are likely to affect many more persons in cities than in the countryside. But perhaps a more compelling consideration is the fact that urbanization is now such a universal, rapidly progressing phenomenon, that so many countries are now highly urbanized, and that, from all indications, the majority of the world's population will be living in urban settings by the end of this century. Consequently, our knowledge in matters of urban evacuation will become increasingly pertinent to the generality of humankind. We have been especially interested in places that might be called metropolitan, that is, those with populations exceeding 50,000; however, in at least three instances we have found it worthwhile to deal with cities falling below that threshold.

We do not suggest that emergency evacuation of rural persons is not worthy of study (and some of our case studies do involve rural as well as urban communities). Ultimately, of course, any definitive treatment of evacuation phenomena will embrace the residents of every type of settlement; however, given our limited resources, it seemed sensible to confine ourselves to the city-based cases in order to achieve the largest immediate return for our finite efforts.

As it happens, a few essentially rural episodes of evacuation have received detailed treatment. Most notable perhaps is the thorough account of the Holland Flood Disaster of 1953 (NAS/NRC Committee on Disaster Studies 1955), during which farm and village residents were transferred into the relative safety of nearby cities, and Robert Geipel's (1982) admirable geographical and sociological work on the temporary redistribution of the inhabitants of a large, essentially rural/ small town section of Friuli in northeastern Italy following a major earthquake in 1976. Similarly, there appears to have been much dislocation of village populations—duly noted in the scholarly literature—caused by recurrent earthquakes in southern Italy in 1980 and 1981 (Alexander 1981, 1984; Stratta 1981), and as a result of even more catastrophic seismic events in Guatemala (Bates et al. 1977) and in eastern Turkey several times in the recent past; but we have little information on the spatial aspects of the human responses to such disasters.

Tempting though it may be to consider the emergency evacuation of cities as a form of forced migration, such temporary transfers of population cannot be fully equated with the involuntary movements of political or ethnic refugees or expelees, convicts, prisoners of war, slave laborers, and other such unfortunates. Although a certain degree of compulsion appears in many of the events analyzed in this study, in the majority of instances the potential evacuee enjoyed some measure of freedom in choosing whether to stay or go; and as already noted, he or she would leave with the hope and intention of resuming the previous place and mode of existence within a relatively short period of time—two characteristics absent in the story of the genuine forced migrant. An even more basic consideration is the fact that the rationale for the temporary depopulation of the city, in the minds of the responsible parties, is the preservation of community and, more immediately, of course, the saving of lives.

A wide array of disasters can generate the temporary emptying of a city, and we have been cognizant of all of them in this investigation. Within the natural realm, they include: major storms, floods, earthquakes, and volcanic eruptions. (Not infrequently, one type of physical disaster is linked with another.) Among human disasters, the approach of hostile armies and actual or threatened aerial bombardment or artillery shelling may trigger urban flight, and many of a growing variety of industrial and freight traffic accidents can prompt evacuation of densely settled areas. Mercifully, one recurrent horror that depopulated cities in premodern times, namely, major epidemics of infectious disease (most notably bubonic plague), has effectively vanished in recent times and so will not be dealt with here.

The inclusiveness of our study universe sets it apart from previous items in the literature on evacuations. Obviously, every disaster, and thus every resultant evacuation, is unique in some fashion. However, we must agree with Perry and Mushkatel (1984:45) that

> The goal . . . is to demonstrate that there are no significant conceptual or theoretical reasons for treating natural and man-made disasters as funda-

mentally different, such that they must be separated and studied using different frameworks for social scientific analyses.

But we venture further than other students of disaster or evacuation who have managed to find common ground for events generated by natural forces and human beings in that we see no logical excuse for excluding evacuation resulting from warfare. Only one writer on the subject (Kreps 1984:326) even hints that military phenomena might fall within the realm of disaster research. Indeed John Western and Gordon Milne state categorically that "Cyclones and warfare are not comparable events and the strategies used in warfare and in the control, direction and protection of civilians under the threat of armed attack have little applicability in civil life, no matter the drama that is occasionally experienced" (1979:502). Looking even further afield, it is a sad fact, as David Heer reports (1978:475), that "The study of the demographic effects of warfare is a topic which has been relatively neglected by demographers."[1] However, a moment's reflection should suffice for the realization that evacuations inspired by warfare often bear a close resemblance to other types.

But whatever the specific cause for such extraordinary movements, the student of the emergency evacuation of cities must deal with a daunting number of variables. Most obvious are questions of timing, duration, and distance. These events may be quite brief, beginning and ending within just a few hours or days, or they may last for several years. The trip may occur before, during, or just after the disaster, but in some cases in anticipation of a catastrophe that fails to materialize. The evacuees may remain within commuting range of their normal action-space, but, in other instances, they may find themselves shifted hundreds or thousands of kilometers from familiar surroundings, and possibly even into a foreign country. Another primary variable is the number of evacuees in absolute terms and as a percentage of total population at risk. The spectrum of volition and organization runs all the way from the totally spontaneous, unorganized exodus to tightly controlled movements signaled and orchestrated by governmental authorities, and with every gradation between these extremes. Equally variable is the decision-making unit, which can range from the household or individual upward to the relevant municipal, regional, or national agency. There is also much variety in levels of preparedness. In addition, we find interesting expressions of selectivity in the kinds of people who choose to evacuate as opposed to those who remain. The means of transport run the full gamut from travel on foot to aircraft.

In this study we pose several questions, some of which have already been hinted at. Under what circumstances do mass evacuations of cities occur, and when and why do they fail to materialize? How many of what sorts of people evacuate, just when, how rapidly, how far, and in what direction by what means to what sorts of destinations? When and how do the evacuees return? What are the short- and long-term impacts upon the places evacuated and the host areas? Are there meaningful differences in evacuation behavior among different national cultures and ethnic and racial groups within and among countries and between communities classified by level of socioeconomic development? What other differences and similarities can we detect among events when they are viewed in the perspective of other significant variables? But the ultimate questions are: What contribution can the study of such past events make toward a general theory of human mobility and our understanding of urban places—and thus toward our unraveling of the deepest problems concerning the nature of human society? On a more mundane level, will the knowledge gained through an analysis of historic evacuations help mitigate the effects of future calamities?

The changing conditions of twentieth-century life and, possibly, a certain amount of ethnocentrism have helped shape the design of this study. Despite the spottiness of the documentary record, there is reason to believe that the incidence of emergency evacuation of cities has increased markedly during recent decades. The simple reality that the number of cities has grown so rapidly, along with their populations and territorial extent, has meant more people and more places at risk. Advances in industrial and transportation technology and a remarkable proliferation of synthetic hazardous substances have exposed greater numbers of city dwellers to the possibility of death or injury from industrial mishaps and accidents involving trucks, ships, barges, pipelines, freight trains, and aircraft (Gilmore 1980:191). Equally significant is the fact that, by chance or design, military operations in the major conflicts of this century have been directed increasingly against industrial and population centers (Hewitt 1983a, 1987) and partial or complete evacuation of the target cities has often become the most sensible countermeasure.

Whether or not the actual number or frequency of evacuations has increased in recent times, our awareness and knowledge of them certainly has, especially as record and communication systems have improved. Until well into this century, statistics of any kind are lacking for virtually all the various urban evacuations we believe to have occurred over the past several hundred years. Thus we may never be able to reconstruct the details of such celebrated events as the evacuation of Moscow in 1812 (Gerrare 1903:290), and the evidence for the panic flight from various plague-ridden cities in Western Europe from the early Middle Ages through the seventeenth century is almost entirely anecdotal. There is scarcely a documentary trace of the many evacuations from premodern Asian cities prompted by military events and natural disasters, an especially unfortunate situation given the fact that the Asian civilizations seem to have been particularly susceptible to the latter (Jones 1981:22–41).

It is disconcerting to learn how poor or inaccessible are the source materials, even today, for disaster-related events in the Third World. Thus we are unable to include here any discussion of the evacuation of Nanking and other large Chinese cities during the war with Japan that began in 1931, the emptying of Vietnamese (Thrift and Forbes 1986), Kampuchean, or Korean cities during the long wars that racked those nations, or precisely what happened to Dhaka during Bangladesh's struggle for independence (Hewitt n.d.:5–6; Kamaluddin 1985). We can mention only in passing the evacuation of perhaps 700,000 of Tangshan's 1,000,000 residents following a horrendous earthquake in July 1976 (New York *Times* 1976),[2] and say nothing at all about possible recent evacuations caused by floods, earthquakes, volcanic eruptions, social unrest, or warfare in such countries as India, Indonesia, the Philippines, Peru, Nigeria, Armenia, Iraq, or Lebanon. (But it may be worth noting that newspaper accounts suggest that no fewer than 250,000 to 300,000 residents of Beirut had fled that metropolis by early 1989, an exodus that continues at the time of writing.)

Although data can be unearthed, given enough effort, for virtually all the important recent evacuations caused by natural disaster in the advanced countries of the First World, trying to trace the ebb and flow of urban populations in Belgium, northern France, northern Italy, and much of Eastern Europe during World War I may be a hopeless task. The situation may be better for the many dislocations of urban folk during World War II, but even there many blanks still remain. In any case, it is clear enough that the set of events we are able to treat in any detail is not a random selection from the universe of such items, but rather is probably biased toward those events that are closer in time and social space to the more advanced communities of the contemporary "West." But one can still hope that our array of cases is sufficiently broad and diverse to provide the basis for some general insights into the phenomenon of the emergency evacuation of cities.

Even though we begin finding exploitable records, however region-
ally biased, from the mid-1930s onward, we still encounter difficulties
in terms of the completeness, reliability, and detail of the reports. "In
a truly rigorous scientific sense . . . our knowledge base about human
system responses to disaster events is embryonic at best" (Drabek
1986b:13). The explanation for our epistemological dilemma has to do
with the nature of the event itself and, equally, with institutional
arrangements and human reactions. Among all the significant topics
handled by the demographic analyst, migration and mobility have
always been the most poorly documented, even in the most normal of
periods. But disasters are, by definition, extraordinary occurrences,
and in even the most advanced of countries with the most sophisticated
of statistical systems and specialized, experienced disaster relief organizations, officials are almost never equipped to cope with the
statistical complexities of short-term transfers of population or the
attributes of the persons in question (Belcher and Bates 1983:118).
Moreover, the nature of the emergency may be such as to strain the
capabilities of any regular record-keeping system or even cause its
temporary breakdown. Thus warfare, floods, fire, or earthquake may
mean suspension of normal data-gathering activities and the displacement or destruction of past and present files.

As a result, we are obliged to rely mainly on a variety of ad hoc
sources that usually offer only approximate and partial material that
can be of questionable value. These include: newspaper accounts;
reports by national and international relief agencies or special commissions; military surveys; narratives by participants; the occasional
retrospective scholarly survey; museum displays (as in Leningrad);
and the writings of historians, who, for the most part, have been
remarkably oblivious to natural and industrial disasters or their consequences.

In partial compensation for all these glaring lacunae in our knowledge, we do have a few instances in which urban evacuations have
received intensive publicity and detailed scholarly scrutiny. Such was
the case for the officially administered relocation of women, children,
invalids, and other nonessential personnel from the major cities of
Great Britain during the Phoney War period of 1939–40. The uniqueness and newsworthiness of the process combined with the proximity
of a large corps of curious scholars and the abundance of records
prepared by a diligent bureaucracy made it possible to report on these
transfers in great and credible detail. Quite comparable in intensity has
been the coverage by both journalists and social scientists accorded

the nuclear power plant accident at Three Mile Island (TMI) in March 1979 and its resulting exodus of residents. The location of the event and thus its proximity to the central channels of mass communication along with its uniqueness and troubling technological and policy implications resulted in a near-saturation level of comment and analysis. Paradoxically, however, another dramatic disaster, the Agnes flood of June 1972, which afflicted the very same section of the country—the valley of the Susquehanna and its tributaries in Pennsylvania and New York—and indeed the worst flood on record for the eastern United States, caused many temporary dislocations from streamside cities, but has received almost no systematic attention from students of disasters or emergency evacuations. Rather similar to the case of TMI has been the impact of the 1974 Darwin hurricane disaster on Australia's social science community. The unparalleled severity of the crisis, at least by national standards, and a substantial volume of detailed information from those actively involved have provided excellent opportunities for careful analysis. The same statement applies to the evacuation prompted by the derailment of chemical tank cars in Mississauga, Canada in November 1979.[3]

The traditions and attitudes of journalists, historians, and other scholars have contributed to our data-gathering difficulties. In their almost total preoccupation with the military and political aspects of major civil and international conflicts, the chroniclers of such have almost nothing to tell us about the whereabouts or wanderings of mere civilians. Thus, for example, in the multivolume official history of the Korean War, 1950–53 (Appleman 1961), every battle and skirmish, however small, is described in excruciating detail, but the one or two one-line mentions of civilian refugees treat them only as nuisances impeding the movement of troops. Out of the incredible welter of literature on World War II—literally tens of thousands of books and articles—only a few dozen have any substantive material on urban evacuations. Although we do manage to treat such events in Great Britain, France, the Low Countries, Germany, Poland, and the Soviet Union in this study, we are unable to piece together a coherent account of the exodus of inhabitants from major Italian cities that undoubtedly did occur (Bonacina 1970; Gentileschi 1983; *Corriere Milanese,* June 5, 1983; Vinci 1944) or the flight from a good many cities in North Africa, China, and Burma. Similarly, the available information is totally inadequate for such war-related urban evacuations as those that most certainly took place during the Spanish Civil War (1936–39) or of Nicosia during the unpleasantness involving Greek and Turkish Cypriots in 1974, or, as already noted, in Southeast Asia, Bangladesh, Basra, and Beirut.

Another factor deepening the information gap and general scholarly neglect in some instances may well be a collective sense of shame. Thus the French have not gone out of their way to commemorate or seek to understand l'Exode, that pellmell flight southward of many hundreds of thousands of persons just hours in advance of the invading troops in 1940, although contemporary German writers, for example, Gerber (1941), had a propaganda field day with the material.[4] Likewise the postwar Japanese and Germans have taken little public notice of the massive removals of urban residents during the latter stages of World War II; and none of their historians have tried as yet to assemble a coherent account of these remarkable episodes from scattered, incomplete, but still useful archival sources. On the other hand, the Poles seem to be much more eager to ensure remembrance of the complex population shifts within their country during World War II. Thus Professor Marek Drozdowski of the Polish Academy of Sciences' Institute of History has compiled a four-volume study of the 1944 depopulation of Warsaw (designated Warsaw II in our treatment), scheduled for publication under the titled *Exodus Warszawy* in late 1989. Unfortunately, we have not yet gained access to this publication.

We must note that the principal reason for the marked differences in length among the presentation of the twenty-seven case studies is the amount of relevant information at hand. These differences do not necessarily reflect the relative importance of the various events.

With some reluctance, we have omitted from our roster of case studies a number of situations in which mass evacuation was an obvious, arguably prudent response to an actual or potentially catastrophic event, but where no substantial movement materialized (see Table 1-1). Such has been the case, for example, in Chile, a country stricken all too frequently with destructive earthquakes, but where residents have chosen to sit things out within their partially ruined cities (Booth 1985; Kennedy 1982). Evidently, the Chileans have developed an "earthquake culture," one involving both protective modes of building construction and psychological resignation to the inevitable. Somewhat similar was the situation in Thessaloniki, Greece in response to the earthquake of June 20, 1978 (Fournier d'Albe and Agnanostopoulos n.d.; Karakos et al. 1983; Metaxa et al. 1979).

Elsewhere city dwellers faced with the very real prospect of a sudden, massive eruption of a historically active volcano, accompanied by earth tremors, have chosen, with some exceptions, to remain in

Table 1-1. Relevant Disasters Not Treated in This Study

Evacuation	No Evacuation or No Relevant Information

A. Urban Areas

Agnes Flood, Susquehanna Valley, Pennsylvania and New York, 1971	Basra and Baghdad, Iraq, bombardment, 1987
Armenia, earthquake, 1988	Beirut, Lebanon, civil war, 1983–
Dacca, Bangladesh, civil war, 1971 (Kamaluddin 1985)	Chile, earthquakes, 1965, 1985 (Booth 1985; Kennedy 1982)
Date and Abata, Hokkaido, Japan, volcanic eruption, 1979 (Hirose 1979)	Jerusalem, Israel, war, 1948 (Joseph 1960)
Hamburg, Germany, flood, 1962 (Bericht des vom Senat . . . 1962)	Madrid and Barcelona, Spain, civil war, 1936–39 (Thomas 1977)
Hanoi, Vietnam, war, 1965–73 (Thrift & Forbes 1986:96, 145–46)	Nicosia, Cyprus, civil war, 1974 (International Committee of the Red Cross 1974)
Milano, Italy, aerial bombardment, 1943 (*Corriere Milanese* 1983; Gentileschi 1983; Vinci 1944)	Popayán, Colombia, earthquake, 1983 (U.S.AID 1986)
Moscow, Russia, war, 1812 (Simon 1964:169)	Rabaul, New Britain, imminent volcanic eruption, 1984 (Brookfield 1984; Kuester & Forsyth 1985)
Nanking, China, war, 1937	Tehran, Iran, bombardment, 1987
Naples, Italy, earthquake, 1980 (Geipel 1982:184)	
Pozzuoli, Italy, imminent volcanic eruption, 1983–84 (Gore 1984; Kamm 1983; Twomey 1984)	
Seoul and other cities, Korea, war, 1950–53 (Appleman 1961)	
Tangshan, China, earthquake, 1976 (New York *Times*, July 29, 1976)	
Thessaloniki, Greece, earthquake, 1978 (Fournier d'Albe & Agnanostopoulos n.d.; Karakos et al. 1983; Metaxa et al. 1979)	

B. Rural and Nonmetropolitan Areas

Friuli region, Italy, earthquake, 1976 (Geipel 1982)	Cyprus, civil war, 1974 (International Committee of the Red Cross 1974)
Netherlands, flood, 1953 (NAS/NRC 1955)	Nevado del Ruiz, Colombia, volcanic eruption, 1985 (Voight 1988)
	Southern Italy, earthquakes, 1980, 1981 (Alexander 1984)

place. Such was the decision made by the great majority of the citizens of Pozzuoli on the shores of the Bay of Naples when alarming signs of an imminent catastrophe threatened the habitability of the city for many months beginning in late 1983 (Gore 1984; Kamm 1983; Twomey 1984). As a compromise solution, some persons took to sleeping outside the danger zone, then returning to work inside the city during the day. An almost identical dilemma confronted the inhabitants of Rabaul, New Britain, which claims the dubious distinction of being the world's largest town actually built inside the crater of a historically active volcano. Unmistakable symptoms of an impending major eruption were seen and felt in early 1984, causing widespread anxiety but only a minor trickle of departures, mostly of dependents of workers (Brookfield 1984; Kuester and Forsyth 1985). Fortunately, the anticipated calamity has not materialized to date. The most tragic example in recent years in which warning signals were not acted upon—mainly because of administrative ineptitude—is that of the November 13, 1985 eruption of Nevado del Ruiz in Colombia (Voight 1988). More than 20,000 persons perished in or near their homes.

There have been other types of non-events (in evacuation terms) under circumstances where prudent decision makers might have urged most residents of a city to leave, perhaps most obviously places about to undergo military siege. A classic example is that of Jerusalem during the Arab–Israel War of 1948. Although there were heavy military and civilian casualties, as well as much property damage, at no time did the Israeli commanders facilitate or condone the departure of a hard-pressed population (Joseph 1960). In this and similar instances, the retention of the civilian population may have been a potent political weapon.

PREVIOUS SCHOLARSHIP

If the methodical study of evacuations is still at a rudimentary stage, incomplete or defective data are not entirely to blame. The vagaries of disciplinary history and the sociology of knowledge are equally culpable. Insofar as there is any scholarly tradition focusing on the general topic in question, it involves the weak convergence of two schools of disaster studies: one comprising a relatively small group of geographers and another based in a loose cluster of sociologists and social psychologists.

The geographic study of hazards, largely centered in the United

States and energetically pioneered by Gilbert F. White, has generated a large body of work on the physical and social causes and consequences of a variety of destructive events that is both useful and intellectually impressive (Burton et al. 1978). Although this literature has treated certain classes of problems comprehensively and analytically as well as offering detailed accounts of individual calamities, it has largely ignored, or slighted, the question of evacuation. Moreover, only a few isolated geographers, such as Heinrich Müller-Miny (1959) and Kenneth Hewitt (1983a, 1987, n.d.) have considered the general social and physical effects of military disasters.

Beginning in the 1950s, and roughly contemporaneous with the geographic school, has been the rise of another primarily American scholarly enterprise: the sociological study of disaster (Perry and Mushkatel 1984:17–18). Its participants have given a good deal of attention to evacuation behavior, and, although they have often concentrated on particular cases, they have also tried to extract universal generalizations from their materials (Drabek 1986b; Quarantelli 1980). Some investigators have advocated a comparative approach (Roth 1970), and a few have actually adopted the practice, examining groups of events within the United States or, cross-nationally, among three or more countries. However, the author of the most comprehensive and useful review to date of findings concerning disaster behavior admits that ". . . nearly all the findings recorded in this book originated within a single society and have never been subjected to cross-national testing" (Drabek 1986:416). Unfortunately for our purposes, the sociologists, along with the psychologists and political scientists engaged in this tradition have displayed only a casual interest in the spatial and demographic aspects of evacuation, or none at all. Instead they have focused on such matters as nonspatial coping strategies and tactics, the perceptions of the population at risk, psychological effects and aftereffects, community relations, economic impacts, communication problems, and other questions of concern to the crisis manager. We must stress again another major shortcoming in this literature: the failure to take note of evacuations induced by past military events. Perhaps the best way to grasp current sociological thought concerning evacuation behavior is to consult the two diagrams presented by Perry (1985:75, 93).

Another rather scattered literature, one clearly pragmatic in intent, has been developing recently around a related subject: the effectiveness of the evacuation strategy in dealing with *future* contingencies, most specifically nuclear warfare or major accidents at nuclear power plants. This approach often involves the playing out of speculative scenarios, a sort of applied spatial engineering. Oddly enough, and unlike the work referred to above, these projections pay little or no attention to historical experience, so that it is not difficult to challenge their credibility. One of the principal purposes of this study is to address this obvious deficiency, but in terms of applying the lessons of the past to the full range of emergency evacuations, not solely to those of a nuclear character.

There has been a deafening silence in the demographic community on the subject of emergency evacuations. Thus, for example, a bibliography on forced migration (Donnermeyer 1975) does not contain a single reference to the emergency evacuation of cities or rural localities. Aguirre's (1983) bold programmatic statement, a manifesto that explores this scientific vacuum and indicates the salience of evacuation studies for the full, meaningful appreciation of population mobility, stands in solitary splendor. (The programmatic proposals by Kunz [1973] and Foucher [1982] bear only tangentially on evacuation behavior.) Evidently, demographers and the majority of mainstream geographers and other social scientists tend to be wary of unique events, the traditional domain of historians, who, as we have seen, have somehow overlooked emergency evacuations. The dominating impulse in contemporary social science has been toward the formulation of at least middle-range theory. For that purpose, routine, repetitive phenomena are much more comfortable to work with than are extraordinary, idiosyncratic occurrences. Thus one will search in vain for even the barest mention of emergency evacuations in geography or demography textbooks.

A strong case can be made, however, for the peculiar value of data derived from disasters and other unusual events in formulating general or middle-range theory (Eichenbaum 1970). In contrast to the working conditions prevailing for researchers in the physical and biological sciences, both financial and ethical considerations prevent students of human society from performing realistic experiments with their subjects, and practice drills involving the wholesale evacuation of cities or even just neighborhoods are inordinately expensive and most awkward politically. Thus not only do "Disaster studies provide rich data for addressing basic questions about social organization—its origins, adaptive capacities, and survival" (Kreps 1984:310), but "Disaster events represent unique laboratories; they are in this sense ethically acceptable natural experiments" (Drabek 1986b:420).

If one examines only the normal range of events, it is possible to

Table 1-2. Events Analyzed in This Study

Event	Place	Date of Disaster	Definition of Actual or Perceived Disaster
Anchorage	Alaska, U.S.A.	Mar. 27, 1964	Major earthquake
El Asnam	Algeria	Oct. 10, 1980	Major earthquake
Belize	Belize	Oct. 30–31, 1961	Tropical hurricane (and flood)
Bhopal I	India	Dec. 2–3, 1984	Large accidental release of lethal chemical
Bhopal II	India	Dec. 16–17, 1984	Deactivation of remaining chemicals perceived as potential disaster
Chernobyl[1]	USSR	Apr. 26, 1986	Major accidental release of radioactive materials
Darwin	Australia	Dec. 25, 1974	Tropical hurricane
France I	French–German frontier zone	Sept. 3, 1939 (declaration of war)	Threat of German military action
France II (l'Exode)	Northern France, Belgium, Luxembourg, and portions of the Netherlands	May 10, 1940	German invasion and occupation
Germany I (evacuation of children)	German–French frontier zone	1939	Expected ground hostilities
Germany II	Germany	1943–45	Allied bombing campaign
Gulf Coast hurricanes (7 storms)	U.S. Gulf Coast from western Florida to Texas	June 27, 1947; Sept. 25–26, 1953; Sept. 11–12, 1961; Sept. 9–11, 1965; Aug. 17, 1969; Sept. 23, 1975; Sept. 12, 1979	Tropical hurricanes and floods

Japan	Japan	1943–45	U.S. bombing campaign
Leningrad	USSR	Aug. 27, 1941 to Jan. 1945	Siege and bombardment of city
Managua	Nicaragua	Dec. 22, 1972	Major earthquake
Mississauga	Ontario, Canada	Nov. 10, 1979	Railroad accident resulting in release of lethal chemicals
Ohio River flood	Ohio River from Wheeling, W.Va. to Cairo, Ill., U.S.A.	Jan.–Feb. 1937	Major flood
Skopje	Yugoslavia	July 26, 1963	Major earthquake
La Soufrière	Guadeloupe, French West Indies	Mar.–Dec. 1976	Threat of major volcanic eruption
Three Mile Island	Pennsylvania, U.S.A.	Mar. 29, 1979	Nuclear power plant accident and threat of major release of radioactive material
United Kingdom I (spontaneous evacuation)	Great Britain	Sept. 1938–45	Threat of German bombing campaign
United Kingdom IIa	Great Britain	Sept. 1939–Aprl. 1940	Threat of German bombing campaign
United Kingdom IIb	Great Britain	May 1940–May 1945	German bombing campaign and threat of invasion
USSR	Western Soviet Union	June 22, 1941–early 1944	German invasion and occupation
Warsaw I	Warsaw, Poland	Sept. 8 to Oct. 1, 1939	Battle and siege of Warsaw
Warsaw II	Warsaw, Poland	Aug. 1 to Oct. 2, 1944	Warsaw uprising
Winnipeg	Manitoba, Canada	May–June 1950	Major river flood

[1]Nearby city of Kiev was also affected and is included in the present analysis.

apply not one but a multiplicity of models or other theoretical devices to explain their operation; but the rare extreme case toward the furthest edge of the observable may offer the test than can separate the probable explanation from the more spurious alternatives. This argument applies with exceptional force to the construction of valid theory covering human mobility. Graeme Hugo's observations on the utility of information derived from the study of famine, another exploration of human adaptation to extreme conditions, applies equally well to work on evacuations.

> Closer examination of the conditions under which particular types of population mobility survival strategies are and are not adopted as responses to environmental stress thus should be rewarding not only in context of the study of famine but in furthering our understanding of population movement generally. (Hugo 1984:27)

Consequently, aside from whatever intrinsic interest the emergency evacuation of cities may have for the scholar or crisis manager, it and other varieties of extraordinary spatial behavior confront us with exceptional opportunities. Do existing concepts of migration and mobility accommodate the unusual or extreme cases? If not, how must they be modified to cover both the usual and the exception? And, if there is any need for further argument in support of studying individual disasters and their attendant evacuation, there is the fact that such happenings may irreversibly alter reality or our perception thereof. Such has been the case, for example, with the atomic bombing of Hiroshima and Nagasaki and the accidents at Three Mile Island, Bhopal, and Chernobyl.

What follows is the first study of its kind. It differs quantitatively from related investigations by virtue of the number, range, and variety of events being treated comparatively and cross-nationally over a span of fifty years, but also qualitatively by concentrating on the spatial and demographic aspects of the events. Given a difficult data situation and various strictures concerning which events are admissible for analysis and which are not, we found ourselves able to examine a total of twenty-seven case studies using published and unpublished materials (see Table 1-2). In Table 1-3 we have offered our best judgments as to the adequacy of the documentation for each of these events in terms of both quantity and quality. Some of the incidents consist of a single evacuation from a single city; others involve a more complex train of events and/or more than a single locality caught up in crisis. Our

Table 1-3. General Adequacy of Available Documentation for Evacuations*

Excellent	Good	Fair	Poor
Mississauga	La Soufrière	Germany II	Warsaw II
Three Mile Island	Leningrad	Chernobyl	Belize
United Kingdom IIa	Germany I	Gulf Coast hurricanes	United Kingdom I
United Kingdom IIb	France I	Managua	El Asnam
Darwin	Japan	Ohio River flood	Bhopal I
Anchorage	Winnipeg	France II	Bhopal II
		Warsaw I	
		USSR	

*Events are arrayed within columns in approximate order of quantity and quality of documentation.

universe of events spans a half-century period (1937–86), and includes cities located within eighteen countries in all (see Figure 1-1). In keeping with our general strategy of casting a wide geographical and categorical net and seeking meaningful generalization through cross-national analysis, the countries and cities in question differ considerably in level of socioeconomic attainment and many of their social and demographic characteristics. Since this is a pioneering venture, it is too much to expect that we can offer more than the most tentative of answers, but we do hope that we have begun to ask the right questions in the right ways.

PREEXISTING HYPOTHESES

A reading of the literature reveals the existence of a number of hypotheses concerning evacuation behavior. Some are quite explicit, but others are unmistakably present below the surface of these writings. Empirical evidence, however limited in range, undergirds some of the statements that follow, while others seem to be little more than shared assumptions, matters of faith. In any case, none of these hypotheses have previously been tested using the fullest possible array of cross-national materials.

We have selected for review here only twenty-two hypotheses that bear directly on the concerns of this study, that is, those having something to do with the spatial and demographic aspects of evacuation. A principal objective of this investigation is, insofar as we can, to test the validity of these concepts against our empirical and analytical findings. Although we shall not engage in such an exercise until the closing section of the book, it seems sensible to set forth the various

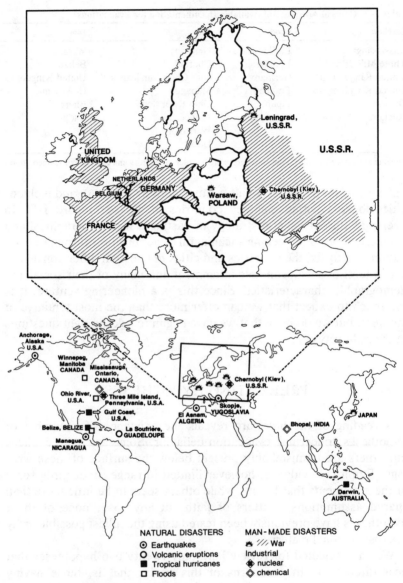

Figure 1-1. Location of case studies

hypotheses at this point and prior to presenting the individual case studies, so that the reader may keep them in mind as the evidence accumulates.

The hypotheses appear in approximate order of plausibility, beginning with those most inherently credible and/or best supported in the literature produced by other writers, and proceeding to the least likely and/or most speculative in terms of available fact. Where appropriate, we have also added short explanatory comments to the hypotheses; but it is important to realize that we are simply relaying the conventional wisdom at this point, not passing critical judgment.

1. *The propensity to evacuate, or the likelihood of being advised to evacuate, varies inversely with actual or perceived distance from the site of a disaster.*

Such a principle should hold whether such a site is a specific point or an extended zone.

2. *The distance-decay principle generally applies to the movements of evacuees, so that the number temporarily residing at a given point will be inversely proportional to distance from disaster site or zone of actual or perceived danger.*

Since there is usually a tract of land surrounding the disaster site that is deemed hazardous, a map registering the location of the evacuees should display a kind of "doughnut effect," that is, a vacant central zone encircled by a halo of evacuees, one relatively dense toward the edge of the evacuated territory but progressively thinner with increasing remoteness from that area.

3. *Evacuees tend to move in whatever direction(s) are believed to minimize or cancel the effects of the disaster.*

Thus, if the physical impact of the disaster is directional in nature, for example, a flooding stream, a flow of fresh lava, wind-driven clouds of lethal substances, or an advancing hostile army, the resulting dispersion of residents will be directionally skewed, with maximum numbers moving in the direction(s) deemed safest.

4. *The risk of death or injury during evacuation is less than that incurred by remaining in place during the disaster period.*

There seems to be general agreement that the evacuation strategy, whatever its economic and social costs, has proved to be effective and benign in terms of protecting life and limb and, specifically, that the hazards incurred during these emergency journeys are relatively minor except possibly in war-related evacuations.

5. *Social relationships and previous travel experience can markedly affect choice of destination by the evacuee.*

Thus, given freedom of choice and opportunity, an evacuee will frequently seek temporary refuge with relatives or friends or in places previously visited if past experiences there were positive or, at worst, neutral.

6. *Whatever the nature of the emergency, the great majority of human beings are inherently reluctant to leave their home localities voluntarily. Consequently, voluntary evacuations tend to be smaller and/or later than would be reasonable, or officially desired, given the actual or expected magnitude or dangerousness of a disaster.*

A corollary of this statement is the well-documented existence of a hard-core group of persons who are not willing to leave their homes even in the face of the sternest official directives.

7. *It follows from the foregoing that evacuees will return home as quickly as they are able to do so physically and administratively.*

A contributing factor, especially in wartime movements, can be the social friction and material discomfort in the temporary location. One consequence of this urge is that emergency managers often experience great difficulty in preventing residents from returning prematurely to their customary localities.

8. *Disasters usually generate some convergence toward the disaster zone as well as evacuation from it.*

Such a countermovement, consisting largely of the idly curious as well as officials, technicians, and relief workers with specific disaster-related tasks, may be smaller in volume than the outward surge, but is a widely noted phenomenon.

9. *Causative factors having to do with evacuation and the various attributes of such movements are associated in multivariate fashion, so that rarely, if ever, do we find a simple direct correlation between any single variable and evacuation behavior.*

This is simply one way of restating the obvious: the very large difficulties in working out cause-and-effect relationships for any aspect of individual or social performance.

10. *Nuclear families tend to evacuate as a unit.*

The exceptions are most likely to occur when governmental authorities decree otherwise or when there are attractive alternatives for individual family members.

11. *Women, children, and the infirm are more likely to evacuate than able-bodied males of working age.*

12. *Families with children are more likely to evacuate than childless families or single individuals.*

13. *Unless they are institutionalized, the elderly tend to be less likely to evacuate than is the case with younger persons.*

The reasons advanced for such reluctance are: stronger attachment to place; impaired mobility; greater conservatism in general; and less interest or emotional investment in the future.

14. *A positive correlation exists between socioeconomic status within the community and the propensity to evacuate.*

This statement implies that individuals possessed of greater wealth, status, and education have superior access to information, are more mobile, have more options in terms of destinations, and perhaps are more responsive to official announcements.

15. *The effectiveness of an evacuation is a function of preplanning, quantity and quality of administrative or managerial resources, and the effectiveness of the communication and transport systems.*

16. *Emergency evacuations simply facilitate or accelerate redistributional trends already under way that would have been consummated eventually even in lieu of any disaster.*

17. *Evacuations have no discernible long-term effects on the demographic characteristics of the population at risk or that of the host area.*

Phrased in alternative fashion, this hypothesis asserts that, given two cities of similar size and social makeup, the occurrence of an emergency evacuation in one but not in the other would result in no significant divergence in their attributes after the passage of, at most, a few years.

18. *Prior experience with similar disasters, whether in the area in question or elsewhere, increases the probability that an individual or family will evacuate.*

Some division of opinion on this point exists in the literature, but most analysts subscribe to this belief.

19. *Panic evacuations have never been observed or are extremely rare.*

The literature stresses the principle that individuals and groups behave rationally and with reasonable decorum—or at least as much so as possible given available information—when confronted with a disaster.

20. *Evacuation behavior is essentially invariant with respect to class of disaster, that is, other things being equal, human beings will respond in very much the same way when faced with evacuation decisions whatever form the disaster might take.*

Such a statement is based largely on the experiences of North Americans involved with technological and natural disasters.

21. *War-related evacuations have little in common with peacetime evacuations caused by technological or natural disasters.*

This axiomatic belief (which tends to contradict Hypothesis 20) is seldom stated outright, but is implied by the avoidance of war-related events in studies dealing with evacuations in any sort of comprehensive fashion and by the customary accounts of wartime evacuations, which treat them as isolated phenomena with no reference to other types of evacuation.

22. *Evacuation behavior is essentially invariant among ethnic groups within a given country or among the inhabitants of different countries if allowances are made for differences in demographic, social, economic, and other standard variables.*

Such a hypothesis documents the belief that observed interethnic or cross-national differentials in evacuation behavior are exclusively products of such attributes as education, income, age, mobility history, family, and residential attributes rather than any essential ethnic or other cultural factors.

DEFINITIONS

For many of the terms used in this study the standard definitions in any good dictionary will do quite nicely. However, some of the key terms in the pages that follow have special meaning or connotations in the context of emergency evacuations, and should be specified at the outset.

We are obviously concerned with the ways in which various communities respond to *disasters*. We find the following definitions offered by specialists in disaster research helpful in grasping the concept:

> [Any event] . . . concentrated in time and space, in which a society . . . undergoes severe danger and incurs such losses to its members and physical appurtenances that the social structure is disrupted and the fulfillment of all or some of the essential functions of the society is prevented. (Perry 1985:16)
>
> . . . disasters are: *events, observable in time and space, in which societies or their larger subunits (e.g., communities, region) incur physical damages or losses and/or disruption of their routine functions.* (Kreps 1984:312) [Emphasis in original]

But we must modify these definitions in one significant way by noting that disasters that never take place or are deferred long past the date at which they are anticipated can still be regarded as genuine disasters if they generate substantial social disruption, including emergency evacuations. In the case of two events treated here—Bhopal II and La Soufrière—the dreaded physical catastrophe never did materialize. In four other instances—France I, Germany I, United Kingdom I and IIa—the expected calamity did not arrive until a good many months after major transfers of population. In still another situation, that of the Three Mile Island episode, the question of whether the accidental release of radiation was great enough to justify evacuation remains controversial.

We have earlier defined *emergency evacuations* and thus, by implication, *evacuees,* with some precision; but it is important to keep in mind the basic distinction between evacuees and *refugees.* The latter are essentially one-way migrants, in most instances crossing international borders, who find it necessary to abandon their homes because of actual or imminent physical danger or, quite frequently, threats to their social integrity, and do so with little or no prospect of return within the foreseeable future. On occasion, refugee movements may result from *expulsion,* that is, the forced displacement of either individuals or entire categories of persons by some agency of an antagonistic government as experienced, for example, by so many national communities in Eastern Europe just before, during, and immediately after World War II. Although refugees may wish or hope for an eventual return to their place of origin, such repatriation cannot be planned for within the foreseeable future, unlike the expectations of the normal evacuee. We have no quarrel with the general definition of refugee presented by the *Multilingual Demographic Dictionary* (1982): "A person who has usually migrated on his own volition, though there may have been strong pressure on him to migrate because his continued stay in his country of origin may have exposed him to danger of persecution,"—except to add "and physical harm" to the end of the phrase.

Neither term—evacuee or refugee—should be confused with *homeless* as that term is currently used by social scientists although, obviously, evacuees and refugees may temporarily lack shelter. Homeless persons are, for the most part, long-term residents of a particular locality who suffer the misfortune of having no indoor space in which to sleep on a regular basis or a place to receive mail.

Whether movements of evacuees or refugees should be subsumed under the general category of *forced migration* is a question to which we shall return at a later point. But there can be little doubt that emergency evacuations can be classified as a special form of *circulation*. The term covers cyclical, often repetitive journeys—outward and eventual return movements—of variable duration (a matter of hours to years) and distance (from a few kilometers to thousands) performed for a variety of personal, social, or economic purposes. What distinguishes circulation from migration is the matter of intentionality. The circulator intends to return to the point of origin, and normally does so, while, on the other hand, the migrant experiences what is meant to be lasting change of residence and community. Taken together, migration and circulation account for the entirety of the phenomenon we call *spatial mobility*. (The existence of other nonspatial forms of mobility need not concern us here.)

One phenomenon that *may* be observed in emergency evacuations and other extraordinary situations is *panic*. In this case, we accept the standard definition: sudden, overpowering fright, whether justified or not, that results in frantic, unreasoning efforts to seek safety. For our purposes, we need add only the note that such efforts mean hasty flight away from the perceived source of danger even if no destination or logical escape route has been selected, and that such flight may involve distinctly antisocial behavior (Quarantelli 1954:272).

ORGANIZATION OF STUDY

Following this introductory chapter, our report consists of three major sections. In Chapters 2 to 5, which are essentially expository, we present such relevant material as we have managed to assemble concerning twenty-seven emergency evacuations of predominantly urban populations (see Table 1-2). We have arrayed these discussions, or case studies, within the four chapters, each embracing a particular class of disasters, as follows: (1) floods and storms; (2) earthquakes and volcanic eruptions; (3) war-related evacuations; and (4) industrial accidents. Each set of chronologically ordered case studies is preceded by a brief introductory statement.

It is worth noting that in five instances—those of war-induced evacuation in Warsaw, Great Britain, France and the Low Countries, Germany, and the two triggered by the industrial accident at Bhopal—we have segmented our treatment temporally. That is, the two or three episodes of evacuation may have affected much the same populations inhabiting the same localities, but occurring as they did sequentially and in quite distinctive fashion, each deserves, and has received, separate treatment. In one other case, that of the Soviet Union, we have detached the treatment of the Leningrad evacuation from the larger national experience because its characteristics and the related materials are so special.

In Chapter 6 we engage in a comparative analysis of the twenty-seven events by taking account of whatever attributes lend themselves to some form of quantitative or methodical treatment, whether numerical or otherwise. This analysis is then followed by our seventh and final chapter, which begins with a critical review of the twenty-two hypotheses set forth above and their acceptance, rejection, or modification. The concluding pages present (but not entirely in the suggested sequence): (*a*) our broader findings, that is, the more general theoretical and practical implications of the historical record of these selected emergency evacuations of urban populations as we have best been able to interpret them; and (*b*) some unfinished business for future students of such phenomena.

NOTES

1. In a series of remarkable essays, Kenneth Hewitt (1983a, 1987, n.d.) has demonstrated why geographers and other scholars must take aerial warfare into account in their work on the modern city. One of his counterintuitive contentions that has yet to be tested empirically has to do with the general effect of prolonged hostilities on population distribution and the possibility of an in-gathering of the displaced into cities rather than their dispersal (Hewitt n.d.:26).

2. A recent monograph treats the seismological aspects of the Tangshan disaster in considerable detail, along with an account of the physical havoc of the built-up area, but devotes only a single sentence to the evacuation of the population: "Although 105,589 patients were transferred to surrounding provinces and cities, 20,700 were moved out of the district by planes, trains, and trucks" (Chen et al. 1988:69).

3. If we were to begin this study all over again, we would not hesitate to include the Armenian earthquake of December 1988 and the resulting organized evacuation of many of the survivors from the devastated cities. Given the likelihood of relatively detailed information, it would have been a valuable addition to our inventory of events, but our work was much too far along by that date to consider any such last-minute addition.

4. But we must recognize the value of three important, if isolated, studies—

those by Vidalenc (1957), Ollier (1970), and Vanwelkenhuyzen and Dumont
(1983) that deal with l'Exode from the French (in the case of the first two) and
Belgian perspectives respectively. The Vidalenc volume has long since been
out of print.

Chapter 2

Evacuations Caused by Floods and Storms

River valleys, lake shores, and the coastal zones of islands and continents offer many advantages in terms of physical resources and ease of access to places far and near. Consequently, it is hardly surprising to discover that human populations have tended to cluster in such favored locations since the dawn of history. But such an affinity for lowlying areas with fertile soils and inviting marine resources as well as strategic siting for commerce can carry with it a heavy price in human suffering. These are also the places most obviously susceptible to devastating floods from rain-swollen streams and, in certain regions, to the havoc wrought by the winds and high seas or storms originating in oceanic reaches far from land. For thousands of years, humanity has tried to reduce the risks of coastal or riverine locations by erecting dikes and dams; but such safety measures, rarely absolutely dependable, required costly efforts possible only in high-density zones. Consequently, much of the population in such locations is exposed to a considerable degree of risk and uncertainty.

If such meteorological disasters have bedeviled the rural population of such lands as China, India, and Bangladesh, among many others, for millennia, the problem has taken on something of a new twist in recent decades. The populations of most older cities in sites vulnerable to storms and floods have expanded remarkably and new cities have materialized, in part because of the rise of manufacturing. Moreover, the subtropical littorals of North America, once so thinly settled, have attracted dense crowds of vacationers and permanent settlers, while much the same phenomenon has developed in seaside locales in the

27

West Indies, Hawaii, Mexico's Pacific Coast, and other tracts where the occasional hurricane or typhoon can destroy life and property on a grand scale.

The obvious strategy for safeguarding the potential victims of floods and storms has come into play only in recent times: their temporary removal to safer localities. And that indeed is what has occurred, before, during, or after the crisis, in the five case studies presented here. They have been selected in part because of the availability of at least minimal documentation (a genuine rarity for the majority of such disasters) but also because these events illustrate different degrees of preparedness and success in coping with meteorological emergencies in widely separated urbanized regions of the world. We should also note that we have purposely ignored the scores of disasters in which there was no urban evacuation of any consequence as well as many others where only rural inhabitants were at risk.

THE OHIO RIVER FLOOD OF 1937

The flood that devastated the entire valley of the Ohio River during January and February 1937 may well have been the most destructive in American history in terms of property damage and the extent of territory and number of communities affected. It also resulted in the temporary dislocation of record numbers of both urban and rural inhabitants. The only comparable precedent may have been the 1927 flood in the lower Mississippi Valley, one whose worst effects were confined mostly to farmland and rural folk.

The 1937 disaster was the outcome of a highly unusual meteorological situation. Following a series of minor floods in the spring of 1936, the Ohio River Basin experienced a wetter-than-average December. With temperatures somewhat above normal, the rains (but no snow) continued during early January increasing in intensity and reaching their climax during a steady downpour from the 17th through the 25th. As luck would have it, the stationary front that produced the deluge hovered almost directly over the course of the Ohio River. While all monthly records for January precipitation were shattered for weather stations along the stream, with readings of twelve to twenty-four inches, the situation was much less extreme along the Ohio's tributaries, so that flooding was confined largely to the Ohio itself and the lower stretches of its tributaries. Nonetheless, some outlying cities,

Table 2-1. Selected Evacuations Caused by Floods and Storms

	Ohio River Flood	Winnipeg	Gulf Coast Hurricanes	Belize	Darwin
Date	Jan.–Feb. 1937	May–June 1950	1953–79	Oct. 30–31, 1964	Dec. 25, 1974
Nature of disaster	Major river flood	Major river flood	Series of tropical hurricanes and floods	Tropical hurricane and flood	Tropical hurricane
Urban population at risk (in 1,000s)	1,179	330	Variable	40	45–47
Number evacuated (in 1,000s)	294–421+	65–107	2,576–2,776	<10	34.5–36.5
Percent of population at risk	25–36	20–32	n.a.	<25	75–79

such as Frankfort, Kentucky and Nashville, Tennessee did suffer serious difficulties.

By January 18, flood stage had been reached from Cincinnati to Cairo, but the stream waters did not achieve their highest level until the week of the 24th when all previous flood records from around Point Pleasant, West Virginia to Cairo were exceeded. By the beginning of February, clearing weather and lower temperatures eased conditions somewhat, but much land remained flooded and many places were uninhabitable for several weeks after the worst had passed. All during the flood period, there had been extreme apprehension about the prospects for disaster in the lower Mississippi Valley, and preparations for an emergency went forward in portions of Missouri, Arkansas, Tennessee, and Mississippi, including some evacuations of rural inhabitants. Fortunately, despite some minor local flooding, the levees and other protective measures prevailed, and the Ohio flood waters reached the Gulf without serious incident.

In addition to much rich farmland, the banks of the Ohio are punctuated at frequent intervals by scores of urban places ranging in size from the barely urban to such notable metropolises as Pittsburgh, Cincinnati, and Louisville. With only two important exceptions—Owensboro, Kentucky, and Pittsburgh, the latter lying beyond the zone of maximum rainfall—all these towns suffered serious damage and were partially or almost entirely evacuated in late January 1937. In one case, that of Steubenville, Ohio, no evidence has been found as to the severity of the situation.

As might have been expected, the disaster received enormous press, radio, and newsreel coverage. Despite that fact, it is difficult to obtain reliable statistics bearing on evacuation or other social aspects of the event. News accounts frequently carried wildly different numbers from day to day, an understandable situation given the frantic conditions under which officials and reporters had to operate. Subsequently, there seems to have been only a single extended retrospective account of the flood, the one produced by the American Red Cross (1938), which, though indispensable, is written from that organization's perspective and does not provide adequate coverage of some topics. Because of the thinness of documentation, all the data cited here derive from the American Red Cross (ARC) report and newspaper stories of the period.

Two factors that contributed to the toll of human misery in 1937 would be less operative today. The art or science of weather and flood \recasting was less advanced a half-century ago than it is today; and the United States of 1937 was neither nationally nor locally equipped with anything like the kinds of emergency planning and organization for the routine handling of disasters that are available today. As the magnitude of the 1937 flood became apparent, various ad hoc measures were adopted to handle rescue, relief, evacuation, and other emergency matters. Although leading officials of various federal agencies and the Red Cross coordinated their activities as best they could in Washington, with the active participation of the president, there was much improvisation at the local and regional level. In addition to the Army, Coast Guard, National Guard, Public Health Service, Civilian Conservation Corps, and Works Progress Administration, the Salvation Army and other church groups, veterans' organizations, railroad companies, and the governors, mayors, and sheriffs of the affected states, cities, and counties devoted whatever resources they could to alleviate human distress.

The areal extent of the flooding was enormous, some 196 counties in 12 states being affected. Approximately 1.5 million persons were directly endangered by the flood and were evacuated; and, rather surprisingly, only 137 deaths (almost certainly an undercount) and 544 injuries were attributed to it (American Red Cross 1938:21). According to the statistics assembled by the Red Cross for the approximately 1 million persons (287,739 families) rural and urban to which they extended some form of aid (see Table 2-2), Kentucky was the most severely afflicted state, with Ohio, Arkansas, Indiana, Illinois, West Virginia, Missouri, and Tennessee following in that order. The number and percentages of city dwellers forced from their homes varied considerably from one locality to another. The dominant factor was the topography of the city site and thus the amount of lowlying land swept by flood waters. In the cases of Paducah and Cairo, nearly all the inhabited terrain was actually under water or in imminent danger (American Red Cross 1938:100–01). Likewise, roughly half of Louisville's surface was covered by the swollen Ohio. In contrast, only a small fraction of Cincinnati experienced inundation, since most of the city rests upon a rolling hilly upland.

It is not feasible to ascertain what portion of the 1.5 million persons displaced by the flood are classifiable as urban, but it was certainly substantial. Table 2-3 assembles such figures as were reported by three major daily newspapers for cities of significant size. It incidentally illustrates the wide range in estimates of evacuees or the homeless in some instances. (Because there was such minor change in population numbers for all these places during the 1930s, we have used only 1940

Table 2-2. Ohio River Flood, 1937: Emergency Relief Under American Red Cross Management

State	Families Affected by Flood	Camps and Concentration Centers	Maximum No. of Families in Camps and Concentration Centers	Families Under Care Outside Concentration Centers and Camps	Total Families Cared For
West Virginia	17,615	55	5,767	2,296	8,063
Ohio	54,641	238	7,568	5,565	13,133
Kentucky	85,381	771	81,771	31,583	113,354
Indiana	32,312	102	10,643	24	10,667
Tennessee	11,800	93	20,624	9,563	30,187
Mississippi	7,773	31	3,060	1,738	4,187
Louisiana	6,001	15	1,055	2,364	3,419
Alabama	—	5	856	37	893
Illinois	18,313	109	3,627	9,020	12,647
Missouri	12,600	77	7,887	5,852	13,647
Arkansas	40,916	75	11,968	5,775	17,743
Pennsylvania	54	4	308	—	308
Misc. Midwestern	333	—	—	—	—
Total	287,739	1,575	155,134	73,817	228,951

Source: American Red Cross 1938:197.

Table 2-3. Ohio River Flood, 1937: Reported Number of Urban Evacuees*

| | | Evacuees | |
Location	1940 Population	Maximum Estimate	Minimum Estimate
Cairo, Ill.	14,407	10,500	9,000
Cincinnati, Ohio	455,610	41,500	41,500
Evansville, Ind.	97,062	25,000	2,000
Frankfort, Ky.	11,492	5,600	5,600
Huntington, W.Va.	78,836	28,000	28,000
Jeffersonville/New Albany, Ind.	36,907	4,000	1,500
Louisville, Ky.	319,077	230,000	150,000
Paducah, Ky.	33,765	33,000	24,000
Parkersburg, W.Va.	30,103	2,000	2,000
Portsmouth, Ohio	40,466	21,000	21,000
Wheeling, W.Va.	61,099	20,000	10,000
Total	1,178,824	420,600 (35.9% of pop.)	294,600 (25.2% of pop.)

*As reported by New York *Times,* Chicago *Tribune,* and Pittsburgh *Press.*

Census data.) We do not have any statistics for the many smaller urban places within the flood area. It would appear that Louisville witnessed the largest exodus of any of the affected cities, with some 50 to 70 percent of its citizens displaced. On a percentile basis, Paducah and Cairo were even more extreme victims of the disaster. In all, somewhere between one-quarter and rather more than one-third of the population of the eleven cities tabulated left their homes during the emergency.

As far as can be ascertained from the limited information available, the evacuees seemed to have left their homes and workplaces at the last possible moment—and to have returned as soon as possible. Insofar as there was any selectivity in the process, women, children, the elderly, and the infirm tended to depart first leaving behind some able-bodied males for the heavy work of flood protection and rescue and the maintenance of essential services.

It is safe to surmise that, in lieu of any master plan, the degree of control over the movements of refugees ran the full gamut from spontaneous evacuation by single families to the forced removal of large numbers by local governmental edict. The distances and directions varied considerably. Some flood victims chose to move upstairs to the second or higher story of their building, temporarily or for the duration. Many others simply headed for the nearest high ground, which, in the case of nearly every city in question, would be within the city itself or its suburbs. But in some instances the homeless were transported as far as Atlanta, Georgia or Birmingham, Alabama. Tables 2-3 and 2-4 summarized such numerical and place-specific data as are available. As Table 2-3 indicates, the Red Cross operated no fewer than 1,575 "camps and concentration centers," mostly in the drier portions of the flood-stricken states, but also some in Louisiana, Alabama, Mississippi, and Tennessee at some remove, presumably, from the flood zone. These places accommodated 155,134 families at one time or another, or approximately 750,000 individuals, while another 73,817 families (ca. 360,000 persons) registered by the Red Cross found refuge in other (presumably private) facilities. Another half-million persons not handled by the Red Cross probably found accommodations with friends or relatives, whether locally or at some distance from their flooded homes. The organized facilities included tent cities, schools, church buildings, and auditoriums. It is interesting to note that "separate sections of the [tent] cities were assigned to whites and negroes" (American Red Cross 1938:114). As is typically the case in flood emergencies, there was little or no convergence by outsiders except for relief workers and journalists.

Modes of transport for the evacuees were quite varied. Many walked, of course, carrying whatever they could. Those traveling significant distances relied mainly on the railroads, whose rolling stock, including boxcars as well as regular passenger cars, was used to the limit. Others used buses, trucks, boats, and private autos. The automobile was of less importance in this emergency than it as to be in later American mass evacuations when a much larger percentage of

Table 2-4. Ohio River Flood, 1937: Selected Origins and Destinations of Urban Flood Evacuees*

Destination	Origin/Numbers
Atlanta, Ga.	Louisville, Ky.
Birmingham, Ala.	5,000 to 10,000 (origin unspecified)
Benton, Ky.	Paducah, Ky., 3,000
Charleston, Mo.	Cairo, Ill., 3,000; 6,000 refugees and levee workers
Charleston, W.V.	Huntington, W.V.
Columbus, Ohio	Portsmouth, Ohio, 5,000
Fort Knox, Ky.	1,500 (origin unspecified)
Golconda, Ill.	Paducah, Ky.
Indianapolis, Ind.	2,500 (origin unspecified)
Mayfield, Ky.	Paducah, Ky., 500
Memphis, Tenn.	50,000; 60,000 cleared through station
⌐wensboro, Ky.	2,500 (origin unspecified)

⌐eported by New York *Times*, Chicago *Tribune*, and Pittsburgh *Press*.

families owned their own vehicles. Movement via any means was hampered not only by the weather but also by the fact that many bridges were impassable and many roads and rail lines were temporarily out of commission.

The migration homeward from tent cities, concentration centers, and other facilities began as soon as the waters subsided, and was less orderly than the outward movement (American Red Cross 1938:122–24). Although the process was in full swing during the early days of February, many localities, especially in western Kentucky and southern Illinois, were not fit for habitation for some weeks after the Ohio itself approached normal levels. Even where standing water was no longer a problem, essential services and materials may have been lacking or in short supply. The upstream localities seemed to have recovered most rapidly; thus the last of Huntington's possibly 28,000 evacuees reached their homes by February 7.

The economic costs of the disaster were massive, but it is difficult to assess the long-term demographic impact of the 1937 flood. In all probability, it was slight or nonexistent if we set aside the local resettlement of some communities previously inhabiting especially hazardous sites. Over the long term, however, emergency planners and managers learned valuable lessons from a disaster that in terms of magnitude of area and affected population has been unmatched before or since in the United States. These lessons have been applied effectively in the logistics of a latter generation of flood and hurricane emergencies.

WINNIPEG FLOOD, 1950

Winnipeg, Manitoba suffered a major spring flood in May 1950, one that caused the evacuation of much of the population of the Canadian prairie city. One result of this event was a substantial engineering project designed to protect the city from flooding in later years.

The present study is based on press reports from the daily Winnipeg *Tribune,* a government report published a few months after the disaster (Clark 1950), and a rather popular account by Frank Rasky (1961). Apparently, the literature generated by this flood was rather limited; the city bibliography lists only eight items under the subheading "Floods" (Sloane et al. 1974).

The flood in the Red River Basin (in whose lower portion Winnipeg is situated) was caused by an unusual combination of several factors:

the relatively high water content of the snow; a sequence of cold and warm temperatures; and heavy rainfall during the flood. The possible flood hazard was recognized as early as February, and by end of March run-off at or above the minimum flood level was certain (Clark 1950:16). The upper parts of the Red River Basin in North Dakota and Minnesota suffered some flooding, and on April 11, 1950 Winnipeg citizens were warned about the high probability of flooding as severe as that two years earlier. In many communities, work began to reinforce the existing dikes, sandbag some areas, and mobilize equipment and crews for emergency activity.

Large areas south of Winnipeg were under water by early May, and various small communities, including the towns of Emerson and Morris, were evacuated. On May 6 the flood hit Winnipeg. After an all-night rainfall and extremely heavy winds, two dikes failed (Wildwood Dyke and Riverview Dyke) and evacuation began (Clark 1950:17).

On May 6, the Canadian Army took over the direction of relief work, and Flood Control Headquarters, under the command of Brigadier Ronald E. A. Morton (a veteran of the D-Day landing), was set up in the Manitoba Legislature Building (Rasky 1961:175). The army relinquished command on May 31. On May 7, an interagency committee meeting resulted in establishing a system of data-gathering and forecasting that operated quite effectively during the flood. By May 10, sufficient data existed to predict that a crest stage of 31 feet would be reached on May 15. This forecast was later revised a number of times. In fact, the crest, recorded on May 19, reached a level of 30.3 feet, but a near-peak stage (about 30 feet) lasted from May 14 to May 20 (Clark 1950:26). A flood stage of 18 feet continued for fifty-one days. The availability of forecasts, fairly accurate for three to four days in advance, reduced the danger and facilitated emergency relief operations.

Relief work was carried out by armed forces personnel (some 5,000 troops) and some 100,000 volunteers (Rasky 1961:176). Various organizations were extremely active, particularly the Canadian Red Cross (CRC Society, Manitoba Division 1950). The work included building and maintaining the dikes, pumping of water, organizing evacuations, and also feeding the needy, medical services, and so on. Rasky reports:

As in a war, food was stockpiled; emergency passes and ration cards were printed. . . . The radio stations went on twenty-four-hour flood duty. . . Ten thousand people daily were inoculated against typhoid. And emergency flood centers feeding cocoa and sandwiches to evacuees and dike workers were set up in the Y.M.C.A.s, Canadian Legion Posts and the University of Manitoba buildings. The city auditorium itself was converted into a vast Red Cross dormitory. (1961:176)

Help was arriving by air and by train from all over Canada and from the United States. More than two hundred reporters from throughout Canada, the United States, and England had arrived. Not all their reporting was accurate. According to the Red Cross file, a Los Angeles newspaper apparently reported "that the flood has washed away the entire city and a New York correspondent announced that every inhabitant had fled Winnipeg" (Rasky 1961:185).

In fact, about one-tenth of the city area was inundated by May 14. Some 8,200 homes in Greater Winnipeg were flooded, including 5,500 in which water reached above the first floor (Clark 1950:22). The areas most seriously affected by river flood and sewer backups were the ones situated along the Red River, particularly the community of St. Vital.

Evacuation of patients from four hospitals began on May 6. On May 10, voluntary evacuation of some 20,000 women and children, mostly from St. Vital, was under way. The Winnipeg *Tribune* reported that the number of evacuees reached 40,000 by May 11; 60,000 by May 12; 75,000 by May 13; and over 100,000 by May 17. The total number of evacuees reached 107,000 out of a total population of 330,000 (Rasky 1961:167). Their origin is given in Table 2-5. Among the evacuees there were 1,500 patients of six hospitals, old age homes, and nursing homes. Of these 1,200, stretcher and walker cases were transferred to Calgary, Regina, Saskatoon, and closer points; 200 were sent to fourteen Alberta hospitals (Winnipeg *Tribune,* May 15, 1950). The last patients to leave the unheated King George Isolation Hospital were nine polio-stricken Inuit children (Rasky 1961:185).

Table 2-5. Origin of Population Evacuated from Greater Winnipeg During 1950 Flood

Location	Friday May 12, 1950	Monday May 15, 1950
St. Boniface	8,000	15,000
West Kildonan	3,500	4,500
Fort Garry	5,000	5,000
East Kildonan	2,500	3,500
St. Vital	20,000	20,000
Other Areas (Riverview, Pt. Douglas, Scotia St.)	20,000	n.a.
Total	ca. 60,000	n.a.

Source: Winnipeg *Tribune,* May 12 and 15, 1950.

Most of the evacuees were sheltered locally, but long-distance moves, not limited to sick and aged, also occurred. Some 36,000 persons were placed in Manitoba (including 17,350 through the Red Cross), and 10,500 in Saskatchewan (including 7,250 through Red Cross), and 11,000 in Ontario (Winnipeg *Tribune*, May 19, 1950). Placements were made in both public buildings and private homes. Apparently thousands of telegrams came from throughout Canada offering shelter. Owners of summer cottages outside Winnipeg mailed keys to the Red Cross requesting that their places be used for the homeless (Rasky 1961:185). Evacuation was carried out by both public transportation (trains, buses) and private cars.

When the high crest of the flood (30.3 feet) reached Winnipeg on May 18, two plans were being prepared at Flood Headquarters. Plan "Blackboy" was a disaster plan providing for the evacuation of the entire city should the Red River rise by another two feet. "Operation Rainbow" was a provision for termination of the emergency and the rehabilitation of Winnipeg (Rasky 1961: 186). On May 20, the water level began to decline, evacuation was halted, and "Operation Rainbow" went into effect. By May 30, hospital and old age home patients began to be sent back (Winnipeg *Tribune*, May 25 and 30, 1950).

The evacuation of Winnipeg affected almost one-third of the population in a process that was gradual and spread through a weeklong period. About one-half of the 107,000 evacuees were accommodated locally, the other half being placed elsewhere within the Province of Manitoba and in the two neighboring provinces of Saskatchewan and Ontario. The emergency lasted for about three weeks, and evacuation was over after approximately twenty-five days (May 5–30). Emergency relief, including evacuation, was coordinated by military command and the troops were used along with the volunteer organizations (particularly the Red Cross). There was a very sympathetic and massive public response to the disaster both locally and nationally and even internationally.

The Manitoba Flood Relief Fund, which collected $8.7 million in cash and goods, was used to assist victims of the flood. The recommendations of a Royal Commission of Enquiry resulted in construction of a major overflow system of canals nine years later (Rasky 1961:187), a costly system ($57 million) but one that was to prove its worth in subsequent years.

In many ways, the management of the Winnipeg Flood of 1950 was exemplary demonstration of societal response to a natural disaster. dition to a record of commendable efficiency, what makes this event memorable is its magnitude. There have been many other flood emergencies in North America that have been handled more or less efficiently, but none involving a larger population in the history of Canada or even in the annals of the United States, aside perhaps from the 1927 Mississippi Flood, the 1937 Ohio River Flood, and the 1972 Agnes Flood that afflicted much of the Middle Atlantic region. In any case, the story of Winnipeg in 1950 illustrates how much had been learned from the past and how useful this particular crisis proved in preparing for future disasters and possible evacuations.

GULF COAST HURRICANES, 1953–79

During the warmer months of most years, several tropical storms of hurricane force originate in the Caribbean or the nearby portion of the Atlantic, and some may work their way westward or northward to ravage the Gulf or South Atlantic coasts of the United States (U.S. National Oceanic and Atmospheric Administration 1973). Until the twentieth century, such violent bouts of weather had little or no impact on the location of coastal populations, either temporarily or permanently. In recent decades, however, actual evacuation of large numbers of residents or visitors just before or during major storms has occurred frequently, or has been considered seriously, as cities have flourished along the littoral of a boom region and much of its shoreline has been developed for tourists and pleasure-seekers. Fortunately, in dramatic contrast to the Galveston disaster of 1900 or the New England hurricane of 1938, this strategy has greatly reduced the death toll (although it has had only minimal impact on property damage) as Americans have benefited from a veritable revolution in mass communications, advances in the science or art of weather prediction and the tracking of storms, and growing skill and sophistication of disaster managers.

As experience has accumulated and bitter lessons have been learned from past mistakes, as governmental authorities and relief organizations at every level have evolved and implemented increasingly effective disaster plans, and as the general public has learned to regard the hazards of hurricanes quite seriously, a more or less standard pattern of response has developed. Thus the massive evacuation of both urban and rural residents from localities in or near the path of approaching hurricanes has become routinized, something that could not have been said a generation ago. Consequently, it would be redundant to discuss each significant hurricane individually and in detail, even if adequate information were available.

The approach we have adopted is to analyze seven important hurricanes occurring between September 1953 and September 1979 that prompted significant evacuations and for which relatively abundant data have been found. Although each storm had its distinct personality meteorologically, all share some basic commonalities in terms of human response, as will soon become evident. There have been other major hurricanes since 1979 with resulting evacuations, but the only available accounts, which are journalistic, would add little to what can be derived from the events listed in Table 2-6.

The reason for restricting attention to the Gulf Coast and Florida is that it was there that the major evacuations have taken place, partly as a matter of chance but at least equally because of the facts of physical geography. Memorable hurricanes have indeed swept northward along the Atlantic Coast to threaten the Carolinas and points beyond. Such events as the phenomenal Agnes Flood of June 1982 that drenched portions of Virginia, Maryland, Pennsylvania, and New York after the inland passage of the hurricane, or Hurricane Gloria, which ravaged New England in September 1985, readily come to mind. But neither these nor any of the other hurricanes moving north beyond the subtropics prompted any serious nonlocal evacuations. On the contrary, the coastal cities of Florida, Alabama, Mississippi, Louisiana, and Texas (and extensive rural tracts) are located on vulnerable sites, some indeed, like Galveston, on lowlying barrier islands. Thus, they can receive the full brunt of hurricanes as they make their first landfall; high seas can inundate all or much of the built-up areas of the cities; and flooding streams can endanger the many sea-level municipalities that lie at their mouths. The presence of heavy ship traffic poses additional perils, as happened at Baton Rouge after Hurricane Betsy caused the sinking of a chlorine barge in the Mississippi. During its raising two months later (November 1965), the Red Cross was prepared to evacuate and shelter upwards of 70,000 persons, but in the end actually moved only hospital patients (American Red Cross files).

One of the principal problems in coping with the hurricanes that traverse the Gulf of Mexico—or any body of water for that matter—is forecasting their course and rate of forward movement with any precision, even given the most elaborate technologies meteorologists now have at their command. Hurricanes have been known to exhibit the most bizarre sorts of locational behavior, sometimes following zigzag or circular paths, while changing direction suddenly, sometimes

Table 2-6. Major Gulf Coast Hurricanes, 1953–79

Hurricane	Date	Affected Area	Principal Cities Evacuated	Estimated No. of Evacuees	Principal Destinations
Florence	Sept. 25–26, 1953	Florida Panhandle	Panama City, Fla.	10,000	Other portions of county
Audrey	June 27, 1957	Galveston, Tex. to Alabama	None	41,000+	Lake Charles, La.; Port Arthur, Tex.
Carla	Sept. 11–12, 1961	Louisiana and most of Texas coast	Corpus Christi, Galveston, Port Arthur	500,000 to 750,000	Inland Texas and Louisiana and Arkansas, inc. Dallas, Houston, Texarkana, Little Rock
Betsy	Sept. 9–11, 1965	Louisiana and Mississippi	New Orleans, La.; Biloxi and Gulfport, Miss.	800,000 to 1,000,000	New Orleans and local inland towns
Camille	Aug. 17, 1969	Alabama to Louisiana	Biloxi and Gulfport, Miss.	200,000+	Inland Mississippi towns, including Laurel
Eloise	Sept. 23, 1975	Ft. Walton Beach to Panama City, Fla.	Panama City, Fla.	100,000	Tallahassee, Fla.; southern Georgia
Frederic	Sept. 12, 1979	Alabama and Mississippi	Mobile, Ala.; Pascagoula, Miss.	375,000	Inland localities in Alabama, Mississippi, Florida, and Louisiana

Sources: American Red Cross 1962a, 1962b; Baker et al. 1976; Bates et al. 1963; Drabek et al. 1981; Forrest 1965; Huff & Carroll 1962; Killian 1954; McLuckie 1977; Moore et al. 1963; Windhan et al. 1977; American Red Cross files.

advancing hundreds of miles in a day and at other times dawdling for days over the same locality. The result has been the occasional mass evacuation when the storm fails to arrive at the predicted point, as happened at Panama City, Florida when it seemed imperiled by Hurricane Florence. After about 10,000 of some 40,000 residents responded to urgent advisories by moving to safer localities within the county, the storm suddenly altered course during the night of September 25–26, 1953 and hit the coast some 90 to 100 miles west of the anticipated landfall.

The vagaries of hurricane dynamics have generated many problems for disaster managers and other government officials. Although, as already suggested, there has been much progress in recent years in planning and executing evacuations, each specific storm situation still makes for difficult decisions. Should the inhabitants be encouraged to leave? If so, with what degree of urgency? Should the movement be purely voluntary? If not, what amount of compulsion is to be applied? When is the proper time to begin and end the movement? Precisely which areas should be evacuated? When should the residents be allowed to return to their homes? And at what governmental level should these decisions be made and implemented? Is it up to the governor, mayor, or sheriff? There are not only the uncertainties of storm path and severity to contend with but also the economic, social, and political costs of wrong guesses.

Two quite different case histories help illustrate these difficulties. When Hurricane Audrey attacked the Gulf Coast from the vicinity of Galveston to Alabama on June 17, 1957, it encountered a population that had not suffered from such storms for a considerable period. Nowhere was this more tragically true than in those twenty parishes of southwest Louisiana where winds and flooding were at their worst (Bates et al. 1963; American Red Cross files). Evacuations—in this instance almost entirely from rural areas—did eventually materialize, and *into* such urban places as Port Arthur, Texas and Lake Charles, Cameron, and Crowley, Louisiana, but whether from lack of adequate warnings or administrative shortcomings, most of these frantic movements of at least 41,000 individuals, by boat, helicopter, and automobile, occurred *after* the storm had passed. The immediate result was 305 confirmed deaths, quite apart from an indeterminate number of bodies never recovered, and serious losses of livestock and other property. A longer-term result was the traumatic impact on the attitudes of the inhabitants not only of Louisiana but of the entire Gulf region, the maturing of a "hurricane culture" such that subsequent evacuations were handled in a timelier, more effective fashion.

Just four years later, an even more vicious storm, Hurricane Carla, visited the same general area and generated one of the largest, most successful evacuations in American history (American Red Cross 1962a, 1962b; Huff and Carroll 1962; Moore et al. 1963; Treadwell 1962). Originating off the coast of Central America on September 4, 1961, this unusually severe storm moved northward, then stalled off the Texas coast for three days before making its landfall at Port Lavaca, roughly midway between Galveston and Corpus Christi, on September 11. With gale force winds as far outward as 300 miles initially, Carla headed northward, then northeastward across the central United States before finally expiring near Lake Ontario on September 15.

With abundant advance warning, most of the urban and rural residents of the seriously affected coastal areas had left their homes for inland havens comfortably in advance of the storm, many departing as early as September 9. All told, as many as 750,000 persons may have taken part in this exodus. The total included most of the residents of Port Arthur, 52,000 of Galveston's 67,000 inhabitants, 25,000 of the 32,000 in Texas City, and a goodly fraction of Corpus Christi. Significant numbers also evacuated some inland towns where the danger of serious storm damage was minimal. In quantitative terms, the Carla evacuation was remarkable not only for volume of movement but also for distance traveled, almost entirely by means of private vehicles. The American Red Cross set up no fewer than 656 shelters in Texas and Louisiana that accommodated a total of 206,103 evacuees. Many were situated in relatively accessible places, such as Houston or Beaumont, but the most remote was in Fredericksburg, Texas, some 335 miles from Galveston. Many persons found temporary lodgings in Arkansas, Oklahoma, or the far west of Texas, several hundreds of miles from the danger zone. Although the Texas authorities had established an emergency plan (specifically for military crises) with designated evacuation routes and tried to implement them with the advent of Carla, the motorists largely ignored the official directives and worked out their own routings. The entire outward movement was remarkably smooth and orderly, not a single serious traffic accident being reported. For a storm of its magnitude, Carla claimed a surprisingly small total of deaths: forty-five.

Leaving aside the rather aberrant case of Hurricane Audrey, the six storms selected for study (and others not documented here) fall into a repetitive pattern in terms of evacuation, one from which we can extract some interesting generalizations.

In recent years there has been relatively little difficulty in inducing most of the residents of endangered areas to evacuate to safer localities in advance of approaching hurricanes. Given the intense coverage of storm information over radio and television and vivid memories or mass media images of previous disasters, it has seldom been necessary to invoke police powers to get residents out of their homes. Departure has normally occurred one day to a few hours before the arrival of high wind or waves. In a region reasonably well supplied with paved highways, the overwhelming majority of people have traveled in their own (or neighbor's) automobiles and trucks, with only a minimum of congregate bus or railroad transport or pedestrian traffic. For obvious reasons, there is no resorting to coastal shipping, and the literature fails to record any movement by air, which is understandable in a period when many airports would be shut down or operating on a limited basis.

The movement has involved both urban and rural residents, but the major destinations seem to be totally urban in character, ranging in size from small towns to such metropolises as Dallas, New Orleans, or Houston. The distance-decay effect seems to apply, except for those going to distant friends or relatives or their own second homes. As official shelters, hotels, and motels, private homes, and other facilities within close range of the points of origin fill up, the travelers move on to the next nearest set of facilities until the outward surge of evacuees has spent itself. In many cases, safe shelter is available on higher ground or within the more substantial public buildings within the cities under siege by the storm, so that far-ranging movement is at a minimum. Movement into cities from the rural hinterland has been common in several instances, not just Hurricane Audrey. In any case, when space is not available in the city for its residents or persons from the nearby countryside, the rule has been to search out the next closest locality providing shelter. As has been the general experience in other American disasters, roughly one-third of the evacuees utilize the Red Cross or other official shelters, while probably at least half the remainder avail themselves of their own second home or of the hospitality of friends or kin. Hospitable strangers and commercial facilities account for the remainder.

Although there have been several retrospective studies of the social, demographic, and psychological attributes of evacuees and stayers (e.g., Baker et al. 1976; Bates et al. 1963; Carter et al. 1983; Killian

1954; Moore et al. 1963; Wilkinson and Ross 1970; Windhan et al. 1977), much remains to be learned on these topics. The few safe generalizations that emerge seem to apply to other North American evacuations as well. Thus the tendency for evacuees to move in family groups and for families with young children to have the greatest propensity to leave, for females to be readier to move than males, and for the elderly to be less likely to evacuate. There is some evidence that renters and recent settlers will be more mobile under emergency conditions than homeowners or longtime residents (Killian 1954). The various surveys report mixed results as to the effect of previous hurricane experience on willingness to evacuate.

These evacuations are truly temporary with a probable modal duration of only two or three days. In some instances, of course, extensive damage to homes and inadequate utilities or protective services have prevented residents from returning as quickly as they would like. In fact, the single greatest operational problem in managing hurricane-induced evacuations may be controlling the return movement. Traffic tends to be less orderly than during the exodus, and the police may have great difficulty in persuading anxious homeowners and plant and store managers not to return before it is safe to do so. Unpleasant confrontations at highway barricades are a frequent occurrence. Convergence by nonresidents is much less of a problem. Aside from relief workers and journalists, not many of the curious or other persons are attracted to the sites of hurricane damage; and whatever labor is needed for reconstruction is normally available from the predisaster work force.

It seems safe to assume that the demographic effects of Gulf Coast and other American hurricanes have been wholly temporary (excepting the small number of fatalities) whether one examines the places visited by the storm or the localities furnishing refuge for the evacuees. Residents return as rapidly as possible to their homes, and none who had not been planning to migrate in any event remain behind. Within a matter of days or weeks at the most both population size and composition have returned to their prehurricane patterns. Yet, in a sense, the evacuation strategy has had a meaningful impact on the population— by preserving the status quo. Had it not been put into effect, many persons would have died or been injured. As things have turned out since the 1960s, evading hurricanes by means of evacuation has reduced deaths to a minimum, and has done so at a reasonable social and economic cost.

BELIZE CITY, 1961

Tropical storms, sometimes of hurricane force, have frequently punctuated the history of Belize (formerly British Honduras). None has been more disastrous or had greater demographic and political impact than Hurricane Hattie, which ravaged the western shores of the Caribbean on October 30–31, 1961.

Meteorologists had given adequate warning of the approach of this major storm, but initially they had anticipated a landfall some ninety miles north of Belize City. As so often happens in the evolution of tropical storms, the forecast was inaccurate and Hattie veered in a southwesterly direction during the night of October 30, so that its eye passed close to the capital city, with devastating results. It was a storm of exceptional ferocity. Maximum wind velocities exceeded 150 mph, and gusts up to 200 mph lashed the town (Gregg 1968:114). Even more damaging than the wind were the flooding streams and the rising sea water that reached a level some twelve feet above normal. Since the elevation of Belize City's surface is only a foot or two above sea level, the combined effect of water and wind was catastrophic; and approximately half the structures in the city were destroyed or rendered unusable.

The storm wrecked or badly damaged many of the smaller settlements in rural Belize, but since the capital contained about 40,000 of British Honduras's total population of 93,000 in 1961, it was only there that a large number of inhabitants were affected. The possibilities of evasive action just before or during the storm were limited. In any case, disaster planning would seem to have been rudimentary at best, and the organization, financial resources, and physical facilities for evacuating large numbers of people were simply inadequate. It is not known whether any townspeople attempted to leave by air; evacuation by ocean-going vessels as of October 30 or 31 was impossible as was movement via whatever roads paralleled the coast. However, "All those who had cars loaded them up with their families and most prized possessions and wended their way inland to the higher ground, even as far as San Ignacio, 72 miles west of Belize City" (Gregg 1968:114).

The scanty documentation covering the Hattie disaster affords no hint as to how many Belizeans sought refuge inland; but, given the shortage of vehicles, the thinness of settlement in the hinterland, and the lack of accommodations, the number fleeing westward via the single available highway cannot have been large. Approximately 10,000 of those trapped inside the city sought shelter in the more substantial public buildings (Palacio 1982:126), while most of the others simply moved upstairs to the second or third floors, or roofs, of residential structures to wait out the storm. Recorded deaths, caused mostly by the rising sea water, totaled 262 (Gregg 1968:115). Because of severe shortages of housing and food—compounded by serious looting (Gregg 1968:118; Palacio 1982:126) during the immediate aftermath—a significant, but indeterminate, number of Belizeans took up temporary residence elsewhere, especially in Jamaica and the United States. Thus, a British freighter that managed to ride out the storm anchored within sight of the city of Belize, departed on November 2 with its cargo of fruit and a few of the destitute townspeople for an American Gulf port (Eustace 1977:14).

The consequences of Hattie are of greater interest to students of emergency evacuations and their sequelae than the immediate circumstances of the disaster. Thanks to substantial international relief efforts and major subsidies from the British and local governments, most of the storm damage was repaired in a matter of months, virtually all evacuees had returned, and by the early 1960s few traces of the disaster remained visible (Gregg 1968:119–20). Today the size of Belize's only substantial urban center equals or exceeds the predisaster level.

The storm prompted at least three significant official efforts at redistributing the coastal population of Belize. The most immediate, and probably most successful, of the programs was the construction of Hattieville within four weeks of the hurricane on a site sixteen miles west of Belize City in order to provide adequate interim housing for many of the 3,000 persons still left in public shelters a month after the storm. Given the provision of a hospital, school, police station, and, at least initially, free food, clothing, and shelter, Hattieville fulfilled the expectations of both government and evacuees (Palacio 1982:126–27). One of the positive factors working in its favor was the feasibility of daily commuting for the men laboring on the reconstruction of Belize City. Current maps of the country indicate the persistence of the settlement, but no information concerning its population is available.

The devastation wrought by Hattie provided the government with some leverage to expedite preexisting intentions to shift some of the coastal population inland into what were to become self-sustaining agricultural communities. The resettlement of the affected coastal folk to three new colonies—New Mullins River, Silk Grass, and Georgetown—was voluntary in nature but poorly planned and executed, so that despite substantial governmental investment none seem to have survived the formative period (Palacio 1982:127–31).

The most important and durable of the resettlement schemes spawned by Hattie was the creation of Belmopan, the new capital city some fifty miles west of Belize City (Palacio 1982:131–34). In a manner reminiscent of Brasilia and Canberra, but with a much shorter lead time and less effective advance planning, the government decided in 1962 to shift its base of operations to an inland site for the two purposes of averting the almost certain recurrence of hurricane damage in Belize City and the stimulation of hinterland development. The actual transfer of offices and personnel began in 1970, and, with a population of 3,000 in 1975, Belmopan has become a viable community, in effect, the product of a delayed evacuation inspired by a natural disaster. But, as is the case in other nations with synthetic capitals, the new urban center cannot challenge the economic or demographic supremacy of the primate city. What remains certain is the inevitability of another Caribbean hurricane that will once again make Belize uninhabitable.

DARWIN, 1974

Cyclone Tracy, the tropical storm that devastated Darwin during the early hours of December 25, 1974, was the worst natural disaster experienced by Australia during its 200-year history of European settlement. Darwin, the administrative center for the Northern Territory and its only significant urban settlement, other than Alice Springs, is located along Australia's northern coast, and is separated from other significant clusters of population by enormous distances, that is, on the order of thousands of kilometers.

The storm was unusually severe, with maximum wind velocity estimated at 250 km/h, and Darwin lay directly in its path. Of the rather more than 8,000 dwellings in the city, approximately 5,000 were destroyed or damaged beyond repair, while only 500 remained intact and completely habitable. The number of known dead was 49, but many others were listed as missing and presumed dead; 112 injured persons were admitted to hospitals on Christmas day; and at least 1,000 outpatients were treated. The larger public buildings and schools suffered relatively little damage. Water, electric power, fuel, and sanitary facilities were unavailable, or strictly rationed, during much of the following week and probably beyond; and communications with the outside world were totally cut off during the first few hours, and quite limited and difficult thereafter.

Property damage and casualties might have been significantly lower if the local authorities and general population had lent greater credence to the official weather forecasts, which proved, in this instance, to be quite accurate. The Meteorological Bureau had been issuing a series of storm warnings that began four days before the actual event. However, a combination of circumstances led to a low level of preparedness. Darwin does not seem to have had a carefully organized disaster management plan; "Tracy" had been preceded only a few days earlier by a cyclone that had veered away from the coast when almost within striking distance of the city, and that recent experience was so off-putting that few persons were inclined to worry about the threat of another storm. "In addition, it was Christmas Eve and Darwin, a hard-drinking town at the best of times, was 'well away' on Christmas Eve" (Western and Milne 1979:492).

> There is little evidence to show that emergency headquarters were fully manned, extra personnel rostered for duty, a meeting of the Emergency Services Committee called, emergency communications deployed and tested, or other precautionary measures taken. In view of the adequate warning period, there would have been time to move a portion of the population into the more substantial buildings that had a greater chance of survival. (Stretton 1979:504)

At dawn on Christmas day, the survivors faced a desperate situation. By nightfall, General Alan Stretton, director–general of Australia's Natural Disasters Organization, had arrived on the scene from Canberra and immediately assumed emergency powers to manage and coordinate rescue and relief operations. This he proceeded to do promptly, briskly, and with surprising effectiveness, with the assistance of a number of committees staffed by local volunteers and some 1,000 priority personnel flown in from other Australian localities.

Among other urgent decisions, it was deemed essential to evacuate as many nonessential inhabitants as possible as quickly as possible. Vital supplies and facilities were available for only a small fraction of the normal population; the threat of epidemic disease was a serious one; and the temporary surplus number of Darwinians might well have impeded efforts at recovery and rehabilitation during the first days and weeks following the disaster. Another consideration was the difficulty of policing a larger-than-necessary population, for, despite the general statements in the American literature to the contrary, looting did prove to be a problem in the Darwin case (Chamberlain et al. 1981). The result was by far the largest evacuation Australia has ever known. The circumstances were such that the statistics on the exodus are far more complete than is usually the case for events of this type. One might observe that even if the authorities had fully accepted the prestorm warnings, it is most unlikely they would have considered large-scale evacuation as a viable option before the storm, in contrast to the standard strategy of the coastal cities of the southeastern United States. Darwin's geographical situation precludes any such relatively routine operation.

The total number of persons present in Darwin on Christmas Eve 1974 is variously estimated at between 45,000 and 47,000. Because of the holiday season, it may be assumed that this number included very few tourists, business visitors, or visiting government officials. It is worth noting that, given the character of its economy, an exceptionally large fraction of Darwin's population consists of short-term employees, essentially a transient population.

On Christmas day, even before the official evacuation drive had begun, and for some days thereafter, a large number of residents left Darwin on their own initiative, driving their automobiles along the single highway leading southward toward Adelaide, the nearest metropolitan destination, some 3,000 [sic] kilometers distant and, presumably, to other larger cities as well. A consideration usually neglected in the disaster literature is worth noting here: the fact that many people are most reluctant to be parted from household pets. Given the option of a free airplane ride to a safe haven, but without their animals, many families chose the long, difficult, relatively costly drive with pets in tow and presumably a relatively large load of household effects during the hot Australian summer. Approximately 11,000 Darwin residents, or a third of the evacuees, exited by road. We lack data as to their specific destinations.

> Those who chose to drive to Brisbane from Darwin were checked through Mount Isa . . . some 1,000 miles from Darwin. . . . From Mount Isa to Brisbane the evacuees were given the choice of 1) continuing the road journey, 2) loading their auto on a train and making the trip by train, or 3) loading their car onto a train and flying on to Brisbane. (Haas et al. 1974:19)

It would be interesting to learn about the problems of food, lodging, and fuel for the thousands of wayfarers, but the literature is silent on the subject.

Under Stretton's direction, a nominally voluntary evacuation took place by air, one involving some 25,628 persons over a period of five days. The following priorities were laid down (Stretton 1976:2):

- Priority One—Sick and injured; pregnant women
- Priority Two—Women and children only, unless father was to be essential for well-being of the group
- Priority Three—Elderly people
- Priority Four—Married couples
- Priority Five—Single people

Although some leading citizens of Darwin proposed immediate, compulsory removal of the aborigines—a significant minority of the city's population—because of their presumed propensity to spread disease, all racial and ethnic groups were accorded equal treatment and given the same options of leaving or staying. Each adult was asked to indicate to which of several large cities in Australia he or she wished to be flown.

> Selection of final destination was based on a variety of reasons: 1) location of family (parent, brothers, sisters); 2) familiarity as a result of prior residence there; 3) climate; 4) anticipated similarity between school programs in Darwin and schools in final destination. The vast majority did have a preference and so far as we know all eventually got to their preferred city, even though it may have been as much as 24 hours from departure at Darwin airport until arrival at final destination for those who evacuated by air. Those who drove took from four days to two weeks to reach their destination. (Haas et al. 1974:23)

In effect, then, the residual population of 10,500 to 11,000 on New Year's day would have become quite abnormal demographically, with a strong preponderance of young single males and husbands temporarily separated from spouse and children. The removal of so many individuals with a certain amount of baggage in so brief a period required heroic measures in terms of both equipment and logistics. Since the capacity of the military fleet was inadequate, most of the country's commercial aircraft were recruited for the dramatic mass movement. The fact that the airlift was technically voluntary created certain difficulties for the managers. Despite strenuous propaganda, not everyone was eager to see his or her family temporarily divided or deposited in temporary quarters in an unfamiliar locale. At one critical juncture, when far fewer passengers were presenting themselves at the collection points than had been scheduled, the crisis managers met their quota by announcing free transportation (to be financed by the federal government) not only for the outward but for the eventual return to Darwin.

Specific data are lacking as to the destinations of the evacuees. As already suggested, the huge empty spaces of the Northern Territory provided no suitable habitations, even temporarily. Retrospective surveys indicate that some 61 percent of the evacuees found shelter with extended family members or friends. Given the highly urbanized character of the Australian population, such temporary relocations must have been predominantly in the half-dozen state capitals, plus Canberra and the lesser cities. The same statement probably applies to those roughly 10,000 persons accommodated in emergency, barrack-like quarters. Evidently, no one seriously considered such relatively accessible foreign destinations as Singapore or the larger Indonesian metropolises.

The problem of convergence developed as soon as news of the disaster reached the rest of the world. Fortunately, the unusual isolation of the site eliminated all but the hardiest of sightseers. Nevertheless the number of persons with plausible reasons for traveling to Darwin was quite large. The list included members of parliament and the cabinet and other government officials, diplomats, journalists, representatives of welfare and philanthropic organizations, business people with branch offices in Darwin, technical specialists, and volunteer workers. Since food, shelter, and water were at a premium in the stricken city, and much of the space in incoming aircraft was reserved for urgently needed supplies, a strict embargo was imposed as of December 27 on all inbound passengers lacking entry permits. It was not lifted until June 30, 1975; but it is likely that administration of the embargo had been greatly relaxed long before, since Darwin contained somewhere between 33,000 and 42,500 inhabitants by that date according to various estimates. Thus, if the disaster and the subsequent evacuation drastically reduced the number of persons present within the space of a week, the rebound in Darwin's population was quite vigorous. It is likely that within a year the disaster had left few traces, at least in terms of population size. The story is rather different when other demographic attributes are considered.

All during its history, Darwin has been characterized by high rates of in- and out-migration, by a vigorous circulation of a population containing a relatively high percentage of young adults and their young children. The Tracy disaster, in effect, accelerated the departure of persons who would have been leaving fairly soon, in any event, at the end of their tours of duty. The disaster served as a catalyst, prompting many to return to their original homes elsewhere and resume earlier lifestyles amidst familiar surroundings. Thus a considerable portion of the evacuees did not return and had no intention of doing so. The short-term impact on Darwin's demographic structure, with the large influx of construction workers and other persons associated with rehabilitation efforts, was to increase the relative number of persons between the ages of twenty-five and thirty-nine, and especially males from twenty-five to thirty.

The Tracy episode provided Australian social psychologists with an unprecedented opportunity to measure the impact of such traumas on a sizable sample of their population, and several researchers did exploit the possibility. Most of their detailed findings are not relevant to this study, but one major conclusion does seem applicable: that when respondents are grouped into three classes—stayers, returned evacuees, and nonreturning evacuees—there are significant differences in level and duration of psychological stress among them. Those who did not return suffered most socially and mentally, while those who remained in Darwin throughout the crisis seem to have incurred the least injury to their social–psychological well-being.

The immediate hardships endured by the evacuees, as well as the less visible but longer-lasting personal scars, generated a controversy among Australians that has never been satisfactorily resolved (Western and Doube 1978). Two of the scholarly investigators (Western and Milne 1979) argue strongly against mass evacuation of the sort enforced in Darwin, stating that

> Data from both the present study and the Brisbane flood study suggest that the victims of natural disasters are far from resourceless, and to treat them as such and as manipulable objects is to impede rather than encourage their recovery from atypical, unusual and very probably a once-in-a-life-time event. (Western and Milne 1979:502)

But remaining unanswered is the question as to whether the gain in mental and social health that might have resulted from allowing or encouraging the Darwin residents to remain in their shattered city would have outweighed the cost of the illnesses, injuries, and physical deprivations that were almost certainly avoided by means of the evacuation strategy.

Chapter 3

Evacuations Related to Earthquakes and Volcanic Eruptions

If we detect a certain worldwide correlation between denser human populations and damaging floods and storms, there is also a certain parallelism in the level or risk of catastrophic earthquakes or volcanic eruptions and the location of heavily populated areas, at least in the lower and middle latitudes. Among other possible explanations, zones of recent vulcanism or diastrophic activity often offer superior agricultural opportunities. Furthermore, in tropical lands the slopes of volcanic mountains offer the inhabitants superior climatic conditions and protection against malaria. Be that as it may, the potential victims of major seismic or volcanic episodes must live under a severe handicap: the difficulty, indeed the virtual impossibility at the present time, of forecasting the timing or severity of such events, or even whether they will occur at all. Given the fact that the incidence of destructive earthquakes is rather low in most areas, there is a natural tendency to believe that the next disaster cannot occur during one's lifetime.

As a result, of the five case studies offered here, only one includes evacuation in anticipation of disaster. And the story of La Soufrière, like that of the partial evacuation of Pozzuoli, Italy or Rabaul, New Britain, is one of a calamity that never quite came to pass. In the remaining four events, evacuation occurred immediately after a major earthquake and largely because of difficult housing and general living conditions in a shattered city. Because of the lack of any warning, there was a significant loss of life and property in Skopje, Anchorage, Managua, and El Asnam.

We trust that a comparison of the characteristics of the four seismic events and their evacuations will prove instructive. But it is important

55

Table 3-1. Selected Evacuations Caused by Earthquakes and Volcanic Eruptions

	Skopje	Anchorage	Managua	La Soufrière	El Asmam
Date	July 26, 1963	Mar. 27, 1964	Dec. 22, 1972	Mar.–Dec. 1976	Oct. 10, 1980
Nature of disaster	Major earthquake	Major earthquake	Major earthquake	Threat of major volcanic eruption	Major earthquake
Urban population at risk (in 1,000s)	170	49	400	75	80
Number evacuated (in 1,000s)	100–150	1.5–2.1	200–300	38–72	52
Percent of population at risk	59–88	3–4	50–75	51–96	65

to point out that even though evacuation, whether spontaneous or organized, is becoming a much more common response to earthquakes and volcanic eruptions in or near urban areas than was true in the past, for the most part residents of many earthquake-prone metropolises or those within range of volcanoes in such countries as Chile, Mexico, Colombia, the Philippines, Italy, and Japan still prefer to remain within the confines of their cities when disaster strikes. Subsequently, these city dwellers rarely abandon their high-risk locations, but tend to reconstruct and occupy buildings on the same sites.

SKOPJE, 1963

The 1963 earthquake in Skopje generated considerable interest in the international community. Generous and immediate help to the surviving population, long-term interest and aid in reconstruction of the city, and a relatively substantial literature on the subject are all expressions of this interest and empathy. One should add that the creation in 1985 of a Permanent Coordinating Committee on Earthquake Risk Reduction in the Balkan Region, sponsored by the United Nations Educational, Scientific, and Cultural Organization (UNESCO), had its origin in a regional seminar held in October 1984 in Skopje on the initiative of the government of Yugoslavia and UNESCO to examine the studies devoted to the Skopje earthquake carried out during the preceding year (M'bow 1985).

The sources used in this report include: a study by N. N. Ambraseys (1966), of the Imperial College of Science, London, which concentrates on technical aspects of the event but also gives a valuable day-by-day account of developments after the quake; a brief study by J. Fisher (1964), who worked for a time in Macedonia and was present at the site five days after the disaster; another brief study by C. D. Dacy and H. Kunreuther (1969); and a most valuable personal interview with A. Ciborowski (1983), who played an important role during reconstruction on behalf of the United Nations Organization. A study by the United Nations Development Programme (1970) and by Polservice (1965?), the latter prepared for the UN in collaboration with the Institute of Town Planning and Architecture in Skopje, have also been consulted.

Skopje, a major city and capital of the Yugoslav Republic of Macedonia, is situated on a fertile plain dissected by the river Vardar and surrounded by mountains on all sides. During its history of more than 2,000 years, it has developed as a major communication hub and regional center in this part of the Balkans, and the acquisition of political functions after World War II only increased its importance. This was reflected in the growth of its population, which more than doubled prior to the quake (see Table 3-2), and in the concentration of investments, including a new steel mill, the location of which was considered by some as a major planning blunder (Fisher 1964:46). By the time of the quake, the city accounted for 40 percent of Macedonian industry and 80 percent of its commerce (Fisher 1964:46) but only 14 percent of its population.

The population of the city has been rather diversified, and by 1953, Albanians, Turks, and Gypsies, most of them Moslems, accounted for one-third of the total. Subsequently, the Turkish element decreased substantially due to emigration to Turkey. Between 1951 and 1962, 37,700 Turks apparently left Skopje, which acted as a collection center for the southern portion of the country (Fisher 1964:46).[1] On the other hand, there was a substantial influx of Albanians (Shiptars) who were gradually taking over the slum areas abandoned by the Turks.

The Skopje Valley has had a long history of seismicity and local earthquakes. The earliest known occurrence was in A.D. 518 and was probably responsible for the desertion of old Skupi in 519. A strong earthquake shook the city in 1555, and major tremors occurred not far from Skopje in 1890 and 1921 (Ambraseys 1966:63). The most recent major quake came during the early morning (5:17 A.M.) of Friday, July 26, 1963. The shock, registering 6.0 on the Richter Scale and with a focal depth of 4 km ± 2 km, lasted less than five seconds. It left many

Table 3-2. Population of Skopje, 1890–1965

Year	Myers and Campbell	Vogelnik	Ambraseys	Statistical yearbooks	Other Sources
1890			32,000		
1921	40,700	44,666			
1931	68,300	68,334	64,000		
1945			70,000		
1948	87,700	87,654			91,257[1]
1953	121,600	122,143	122,000		
1961			172,000	165,529[2]	161,983[1]
1963			173,000		
1965				228,000[3]	

[1]V. Blašković 1967, *Ekonomska Geografija Jugoslavije,* 2nd ed., Zagreb, Informator, 82–83.
[2]UN Statistical Office, *UN Demographic Yearbook 1963: 255.*
[3]*Statistical Pocketbook of Yugoslavia 1968: 118.*
Source: P. F. Myers and A. A. Campbell 1954, *The Population of Yugoslavia.* Washington, Bureau of the Census, International Population Statistics Reports, Series P-90, No. 5, p. 120; Vogelnik 1961:281; Ambraseys 1966:2.

buildings shattered, but subsided before it had sufficient time to produce total collapse among the majority of structures. Aftershocks continued for two days and caused further damage. Altogether some 1,070 deaths and over 3,000 injuries can be attributed to this disaster (Ambraseys 1966:64, 81).[2] Between 20 and 25 percent of the city was affected slightly or not at all; the remainder was either totally destroyed or damaged but repairable (see Table 3-3). Ambraseys (1966:64) estimates the total loss at 41 percent of the value of the entire housing stock.[3] Immediately after the quake, some 150,000 people were made homeless out of a total population for Greater Skopje estimated at 200,000 (Ciborowski 1983).[4]

Immediately after the quake the city was cut off from the rest of the country since telephone lines and even radio transmitters had been put out of action. By 10:00 A.M., contact with the outside world was reestablished and Belgrade was notified about the details of the disaster. Prearranged emergency plans were immediately activated and rescue operations began. Later on Friday, 180 seriously injured persons were evacuated to hospitals in various cities throughout Yugoslavia. On Saturday, the decision was taken to evacuate the city, and by midday actual evacuation of women and children had begun.[5]

Groups of children were taken to various parts of the country, where they stayed with private families or in hotels. By Saturday, supplies and rescue and medical teams began to arrive from abroad. On Sunday, July 28, evacuation of children seven to fourteen years of age continued, while a considerable number of destitute families began to move out on foot or using carts and trucks. Some of these evacuees stayed in the suburbs of Skopje, others moved further away to the villages and towns assigned to them. The outgoing convoys created traffic jams causing considerable delays and complications for the arrival of supplies and incoming heavy trucks and machines.

By Monday, July 29, over 100,000 people had apparently left the city

Table 3-3. The Destruction of Skopje, 1963*

Extent of Structural Damage	Apartments and Other Residences	Built-Up Area	Affected Population
Collapse	8.2	7.0	8.5
Condemned	33.6	29.9	36.4
Repairable	36.6	39.9	30.6
Slight damage	19.0	19.8	20.3
Not damaged	2.6	3.4	4.2

*In percent.
Source: Ambraseys 1966:81.

(all these details according to Ambraseys 1966:67–71). The total number of evacuated persons was probably close to 150,000 (Davis 1975:661), and it appears that only badly injured adults (as well as children) were moved long distances away, while other adults remained in the tent cities surrounding Skopje (Ciborowski 1983). Apparently, various ethnic groups reacted differently.[6] Gypsies, who had a tradition of urban living dating back some 200 years, lived in a compact area just north of the city center. Their substandard houses were badly damaged but they were relatively easy to repair and the Gypsies set about doing it immediately. The authorities allotted them the area further north, where the land was promptly subdivided, and they were given the right to use material salvaged from the ruins. Almost all families have eventually moved to this area, so that the Gypsy community retained its sense of identity and social cohesion, and the new, relatively uniform area, though modest enough, represents a great improvement over the old slum, which was converted to other uses (Ciborowski 1983).

The initial return of evacuees in September was slow, but by early October the influx had become quite heavy. In addition, laborers, mostly unskilled and mainly from the surrounding areas, were pouring into the city to find jobs in construction and repair work.[7] The population, which initially declined to 60,000 (Fisher 1964:46), including 30,000 able-bodied persons helping in rescue operations (Davis 1975:661), increased to 150,000 in early October (including, presumably, a number of newcomers) (Ambraseys 1966:72). The return of evacuees was completed in October 1963 (Davis 1975:661). This was also the case for schoolchildren, whose stay in other linguistic areas posed a difficult problem of adjustment and contributed to a universal demand by parents to have them returned home (Ciborowski 1983).

Careful analysis of these statistics poses some problems. If the population of Skopje before the disaster had been 200,000, and some 140,000 to 150,000 persons were evacuated (leaving behind 60,000 including some people from outside), their total return together with the influx from outside would swell the city size to over 200,000. If, on the other hand, the population before the earthquake was closer to 170,000, and 60,000 remained after evacuation, then the evacuation involved 100,000 to 120,000, rather than 150,000, during a two-month period.[8]

Temporary shelters were provided in tents, but very quickly the repair of recoverable houses and construction of prefabricated houses in nine suburban sites began. Some 14,000 units of the latter were built on the principle of neighborhood units complete with services, and from the beginning it was assumed that they would be incorporated into the new master plan. Initially they were intended to last five to ten years, but after being sold to their occupants and being greatly improved and expanded, these houses are still in use and remain in very good shape. The decision to rebuild the city on the same site was made almost immediately after the disaster, even before various studies were completed. Evidently the attitudes of the local population and officials of the Macedonian Republic were instrumental in reaching this decision. There may have been some inclination to eliminate the "oriental" character of the city by transferring the Gypsies, Turks, and Albanians elsewhere (Fisher 1964:48). Fortunately, while the city was fully rebuilt and substantially expanded, this impulse was resisted, and Skopje retains some of its ethnic heterogeneity.

ANCHORAGE, 1964

At 5:36 P.M., March 27, 1964, southcentral Alaska experienced the most severe earthquake in recent North American history, one estimated to range between 8.3 and 8.6 on the Richter Scale. The most populous community to be seriously affected, within a generally lightly settled region, was Anchorage, situated some eighty miles WNW of the epicenter. With a combined civilian and military population approximating 49,000 at the time, Anchorage was also the largest urban place within the entire state.

Because of the timing of the event, occurring as it did after business hours and the close of schools on the eve of the Easter weekend, loss of life (115) was less than might have been anticipated, but property damage was quite extensive in Anchorage and other nearby communities. The Anchorage quake may well have been the best documented and most thoroughly studied earthquake in history, in part because of the valuable lessons to be learned in terms of disaster planning and management, but also because of its great technical interest for geophysicists. Fortunately for our purposes, the massive official report (National Research Council, Committee on the Alaska Earthquake 1970) accords a good deal of attention to the demographic and economic aspects of the event, and it has been our principal source of information; but valuable material was also found in Dacy and Kunreuther (1969), Kunreuther and Fiore (1966), Anderson (1969), and Bowden (1982).

Although Anchorage lies within one of the most active seismic zones in the world, there were no advance warnings of an earthquake of the magnitude of the one occurring in March 1964. But in this respect the Anchorage case is scarcely unique in the annals of disaster history. Despite the lack of any elaborate predisaster planning or organization, relief efforts at the local, state, and federal levels were prompt and effective. With adequate transportation and communication facilities, ample financial aid, and volunteer assistance from many organizations and individuals, rescue work and reconstruction began quickly, and within a year or so, the Anchorage area could be regarded as having fully recovered. Stimulated to some degree by the aftershocks that persisted for hours after the main event, a significant evacuation of civilians materialized. There is no evidence that governmental authorities intervened in any significant way to plan, direct, or control the movement, or to encourage or dissuade potential evacuees. Nor is there any indication in the literature that anything like panic followed the disaster.

The Anchorage case is perhaps singular, at least within the North American context, by virtue of the relative isolation of the city and its remoteness from the main body of the American population. This fact has enabled analysts to estimate postdisaster movements with greater precision than is normally feasible by referring to vehicle counts along the single highway connecting Alaska with the "Lower 48" and also by considering the volume of traffic through the Anchorage airport and the monthly school registration figures as a surrogate measure for total population. The values so derived place the total exodus in the days and weeks following the earthquake in the 1,500 to 2,070 range, or roughly 3 to 4 percent of the total population.

The fact that such a relatively small fraction of the population felt impelled to leave means that the remaining residents were able to find shelter in the city despite the damage to many structures. During the critical period, there was an excess of approximately 8,000 passengers recorded at the Fairbanks airport, as compared to the same time periods in other years, but there is no way of determining how many of these travelers were regular residents fleeing the locality for the duration—or for good. By far the greater portion of the evacuees were women and children; and we can assume that there were few male members of the military, if there were any, who left the scene. The motives for leaving are not noted in the literature, but we may guess that fear of a major recurrence of seismic activity and/or the physical inconveniences of life in a damaged city may have prompted departure.

The pattern of dispersal was atypical for North American evacuations. Nearby communities lacked facilities for accommodating a sudden influx of evacuees, and it is unlikely that many of the leavers had close personal connections with Fairbanks or Juneau, the closest towns of any size beyond the stricken area. Thus nearly all the outward movements seem to have been to relatives or friends many hundreds or thousands of miles distant in the Lower 48. We have no information at all as to specific destinations.

It is possible, even likely, in view of the dependent status of the great majority, that virtually all the evacuees had returned by late summer or early fall 1964. But, given the relatively high rate of transience among Anchorage's inhabitants, even during seismically quiet periods, it is impossible to determine how many of the evacuees would have been leaving permanently for other localities if the earthquake had not happened. What is truly unusual about the counterflow of persons *into* Anchorage from April 1964 onward is the scale of convergence by outsiders. Despite efforts by the governor to dissuade the in-movement of jobseekers, they did arrive in considerable numbers. (Because of distance and cost, we can assume few of the merely curious.) Thus the inbound traffic received by Anchorage in April 1964 exceeded normal volume by some 69 percent. School enrollment in September 1964 was about 150 above the level of the previous year, and there was an additional increment of 1,500 in the number of pupils during the following twelve-month period. By far the greater part of this increment can be attributed to construction and government workers and their families, but what proportion was produced by earthquake-induced activity, as opposed to the vigorous long-term growth Anchorage had come to expect, we have no way of telling. In any event, whatever physical scars may have been left by the earthquake, within two years after the event, at most, the demography of the Anchorage area revealed no signs of disaster; and the same can be said about the economy and occupational structure.

Did the evacuation of a relatively small fraction of the city's inhabitants serve any useful purpose? It is quite doubtful whether the exodus averted any deaths or injuries, and perhaps the most that can be claimed for it is that the temporary removal of nonessential persons facilitated the management of life under emergency conditions and the rapid physical rehabilitation of the community. If the authorities never gave any methodical thought to ordering and overseeing an evacuation, in actuality any such program may have been unnecessary.

MANAGUA, 1972

The earthquake that struck Managua, Nicaragua's capital and primate city, during the night of December 22–23, 1972 was extraordinarily destructive. It should have come as no surprise since the metropolis is built over several active faults in that portion of Central America most susceptible to major and minor seismic activity, and Managua had already experienced a long series of such events. However, this particular disaster was unprecedented in scope. The foreshocks that began around 10 P.M., December 22, were followed by three violent tremors between 12:30 and 1:20 A.M. The result was the reduction to rubble of some 600 blocks in central Managua, about 60 percent of the city, at least 10,000 persons killed, 20,000 injured, and over 300,000 left homeless with the destruction or damaging of most of the housing stock in a city with about 400,000 inhabitants at the time. Moreover, nearly all small businesses were wiped out, the utilities severely disrupted, hospitals and most school buildings rendered inoperable, and 70 percent of government facilities put out of commission.

Despite its seismic history and vulnerability, Nicaragua in general and Managua in particular were almost completely lacking any disaster preparedness program or organization. There were many reports of presumably responsible officials and public employees failing to assume their emergency duties until they had looked after the welfare of their own families. The consequence was something approaching chaos before aid from external sources began to arrive and General Somoza began to assert some control over the situation a few days after the event. Indeed, looting began immediately and by December 27 had reached epidemic proportions.

The only logical response to the crisis for most of the survivors, after doing what they could for the dead or wounded, was to seek shelter, food, and water outside the zone of destruction. Thus a massive outward movement began spontaneously on December 23 and continued for some days threafter, mostly by bus and on foot. It is conservatively estimated that 200,000 evacuees left Managua, possibly as many as 300,000, for only 100,000 persons were left in the central city by December 28.

Much of the usual need for planned emergency shelter for the homeless was obviated by the extended family system. An estimated 75 percent of the refugees went to live in or around the homes of relatives. An enormous, spontaneous, self-reliant evacuation and relocation to cities up to 80 kilometers away took place in the immediate aftermath, only later to be organized and enforced by governmental services. (Kates et al. 1973:987)

In effect, then, the food and other supplies available among private residences filled the gap until official emergency measures could be instituted, thanks to substantial aid from agencies and individuals in foreign countries.

The rapid removal of so many individuals so quickly was made possible by a fortunate conjunction of circumstances. It can be attributed to

Managua's simplified one-level road transport system, its large pool of public transport equipment, and a minimum of private autos obviating traffic jams that would have clogged the escape routes. Also, the oil refinery survived the earthquake and its initiative in distributing gasoline to suburban stations helped keep evacuating vehicles moving. (U.S. Agency for International Development n.d.:3).

By December 30, most, if not all the residents of the downtown area had moved out. An estimated 180,000 remained in other parts of the city or camped on the outskirts. Some 35,000 moved on to Granada and 30,000 to Leon. Tens of thousands of others sought shelter in Masaya, Esteli, Rivas and small towns and villages surrounding Managua. Of the victims left homeless, an estimated 80% found shelter with relatives; 10% were housed in schools and another 10% were eventually sheltered in tent cities. (U.S. Agency for International Development n.d.:3–4).

Quite obviously, no one attempted a careful count of the evacuees or their pattern of dispersal since the (arithmetically suspect) figures reported by the Nicaraguan Red Cross (200,000 evacuees) vary substantially from those suggested by the U.S. Agency for International Development (AID), namely, 60,000 persons going to Granada, 40,000 to Leon, 40,000 to Masaya, and 30,000 to Carazo, while "another 90,000 [sic] persons sought refuge in various cities and villages within the interior and also in neighboring countries" (Cruz Roja Nicaraguense 1973:15). Yet another source indicates a doubling of Masaya's population from 35,000 to 70,000 (Mallin 1974:17–18).

The first official refugee camp was established on December 28 about a half-hour drive from the city. On January 3, a tent city was erected on a site previously used for a Boy Scout jamboree at which water, sewage, and other facilities were available. In early February, a consortium of government and private agencies began building 11,000 low-cost housing units in Managua's outskirts to shelter returning employees and workers engaged in rebuilding the city. Although the project was completed on May 21, 1973, no direct information is available on the occupancy rate. (Table 3-4 suggests a temporary population somewhere between 10,000 and 30,000.)

Within a few weeks, Managuans had begun to return to relatively undamaged portions of the city; and, as Table 3-4 demonstrates, population size had recovered to its predisaster level by early 1975, then continued the vigorous growth that had characterized the recent past, for example, a doubling between 1950 and 1963.

We lack information as to how many Managuans may have decided to remain indefinitely in other communities rather than return to their previous locality, but at least one city may have retained a significant number of evacuees. Anecdotal evidence suggests that the unusually rapid recent growth of Masaya, a city within commuting range of Managua, can be attributed, in part, to the December 1972 evacuation of its neighbor.

Although General Somoza declared the city would be rebuilt (after advising its citizens not to return for six months or more), neither his regime nor the subsequent Sandinista government was able or willing to undertake the immense job of reconstructing the dead center of Managua. It is not at all clear whether this is a matter of financial difficulties, political or bureaucratic ineptitude, or some other factors. In any event, what had been the densely occupied commercial, administrative, and residential core of the metropolis remains a rubble-strewn wasteland containing only a half-dozen or so office buildings and hotels and a few families of squatters living in some partially

Table 3-4. Population of Managua, 1972–76

Date	"Ciudad Compacta"	"Barrios Perifericos"	City of Managua: Total	Municipio of Managua
Dec. 22, 1979	398,503	10,693	409,196	457,396
Dec. 31, 1972	157,249	12,560	169,809	217,189
Jan. 28, 1973	195,721	16,800	212,561	286,355
May 30, 1973	219,207	27,399	246,606	300,036
June 30, 1973	227,772	29,220	256,992	310,453
Dec. 31, 1973	313,408	39,027	352,435	407,925
June 30, 1974	336,505	27,832	364,337	424,219
June 30, 1975	402,252	19,665	421,917	463,218
June 30, 1976	449,259	19,881	469,140	509,805

Source: Bähr 1980:14.

ruined structures. The situation is unique among the major cities of the Third World, indeed among metropolises anywhere: a doughnut-shaped urban agglomeration whose rapidly growing periphery surrounds a void. It is also a city in which there is now a much stronger areal segregation of the socioeconomic groups that had been spatially mixed to a considerable degree before the disaster. "The wealthy were quickly rehoused within eighteen months and the middle class within three years. Large numbers of the lower class are still waiting in cramped quarters for promised housing" (Bowden 1982:120).

In summary, there was no viable alternative to the massive reshuffling of most of Managua's population after December 23, 1972 that occurred with little effective assistance from governmental authorities and was rendered feasible by the strong family ties that characterized a society as yet only partially modernized. The result was that the survivors of the earthquake did indeed survive and that most, if not all, were eventually able to return to some sector of the Managua metropolitan area. But in geographic and demographic terms it was a radically restructured city to which they returned, one literally turned inside out by its shattering experience. The long-term impact of the disaster upon the remainder of Nicaragua's urban system is not at all clear, but the growth of at least one of its secondary centers may have been stimulated. Although it is tempting to draw analogies between the Managua experience and the major earthquakes that will inevitably afflict the cities of California, the contrasts between the Nicaraguan and American social, economic, and technological situations are so great that such an exercise may be futile.

LA SOUFRIÈRE, 1976

A disaster that never quite came to pass on the West Indian Island of Guadeloupe during the latter half of 1976 precipitated a series of events of considerable theoretical and practical interest to students of emergency evacuations.

Relatively minuscule Guadeloupe (1,780 km²), an overseas department of the French Republic, is located toward the northern end of the Lesser Antilles (see Figure 3-1); and, like other islands in the chain, it is essentially the product of volcanism during very recent geological time. Its configuration is rather peculiar, assuming as it does the shape of a butterfly, with its two peninsulas of virtually equal extent joined together by a narrow isthmus traversed by a single road and bridge.

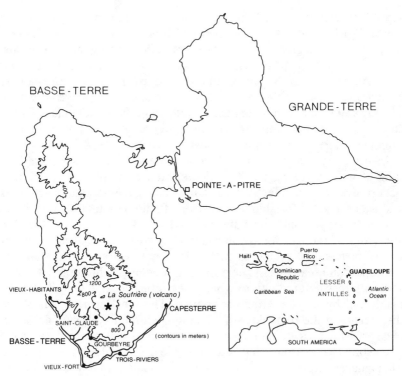

Figure 3-1. Guadeloupe: Location map

Grande-Terre, the eastern segment, is a tract of relatively subdued terrain containing the majority of Guadeloupe's 317,000 to 350,000 inhabitants as of 1976, many of them (ca. 147,000) in Pointe-à-Pitre and environs, the largest urban agglomeration on the island. The western section, Basse-Terre, consists of a rugged mountainous spine, essentially a row of volcanic peaks, flanked by a coastal plain of irregular width. La Soufrière, the highest of these peaks (1,467 meters), has been the most active during historic times. Physical evidence suggests a major eruption occurring around 1550 A.D., while lesser activity has been observed in 1797, 1836, and 1956.

The specter of Mount Pelée haunts officials in Guadeloupe and France. When that volcano on nearby Martinique suddenly exploded cataclysmically in 1902, approximately 30,000 persons perished from fumes, ash, and lava, the worst catastrophe of its kind in modern history. Although La Soufrière has been quiescent in recent years, the government initiated precautionary measures in the early 1970s. They included the installation of a well-equipped seismic station during the period 1972–74 and a series of conferences by technical experts and government officials in 1974–75 leading to the drafting of a comprehensive emergency plan carrying the acronym ORSEC, one which included provisions for mass evacuation. The plan was fully in place by March 1976, with extensive briefings of local functionaries and considerable general publicity—and none too soon.

We are fortunate in having detailed narratives of the events of 1976 in official reports (Guadeloupe Information Service 1977; Guadeloupe Prefecture 1977), journalistic dispatches (New York *Times* 1976) and B. de Vanssay's (1979) doctoral thesis, a document concerned primarily with the social, medical, and psychological aspects of those traumatic months. It is from these materials that the following account has been fashioned.

It appears that from July 1975 onward there was a progressive, if irregular, increase in seismic disturbances in the neighborhood of La Soufrière along with other indications that the volcano was beginning to reawaken. In the face of this ominous intensification of abnormal activity, many meetings and consultations took place between November 1975 and April 1976, some involving scientists and officials from overseas, and special efforts were made to disseminate the details of ORSEC to the general population. So great was the level of apprehension that President Giscard d'Estaing paid a special visit to the island on May 22 to assure the inhabitants that they enjoyed the moral and material support of the homeland. At least one brief, local spontaneous evacuation did occur, that of the residents of Saint-Claude, a community on the slope of the volcano, probably during the "Crisis of March 24."

The first truly frightening episode took place on the morning of July 8 when La Soufrière emitted a huge black cloud and a considerable amount of fine ash to the accompaniment of a major tremor. The prefect declared a "pre-alert" situation, but, without waiting for formal orders, approximately 20,000 to 25,000 residents of the peninsula left Basse-Terre for Grande-Terre within a period of just a few hours. By July 13, the total number of evacuees approximated 30,000, and some 6,850 had found shelter in the school buildings of Grande-Terre. About half the evacuees were received by friends and relatives. The Guadeloupean officials did bestir themselves late on the morning of the 8th, arranging as they did the prompt removal of some 1,400 hospital patients from Saint-Claude by sea and air to facilities in the Pointe-à-Pitre area. Although the able-bodied evacuees left their homes in a condition approaching panic, the police and security forces were able to control traffic so effectively along the two-lane coastal highway that there were no casualties. Because of major congestion at the single bridge connecting the two peninsulas, the army hastily put in place a second emergency "Bailey Bridge" to facilitate the eastward flow.

From July 1976 until the end of the year, the volcano and its environs were subjected to constant and intensive monitoring using state-of-the-art instruments, many of them flown in from foreign laboratories. There also ensued a long series of public and private meetings among technical experts from a number of governmental agencies and research institutions in a variety of countries, the main purpose of which was to ascertain the likelihood and timing of a life-threatening eruption of La Soufrière during the latter half of 1976. No one disputed the possibility that a volcano of its type might very well explode in cataclysmic Peléean or Vesuvian fashion some day. The immediate question, however, was whether the detectable signals implied an imminent massive upwelling of magma with a consequent explosive lethal discharge of lava, gases, and solid matter or, rather, simply the venting of a good deal of steam and fine ash without any serious threat to the well-being of the neighboring inhabitants. On that point there was bitter, acrimonious disagreement among some highly reputable scientists and uncertainty and waffling among others.

In the course of events, the noncatastrophic interpretation of La Soufrière turned out to be the correct diagnosis of its restiveness. In the short run, the local authorities accepted the more optimistic of the prognoses, so that on July 10 the prefect suggested that all the evacuees—excepting hospital patients—should return home, and most complied with his request. The administration took some pains to calm the population, and, among other measures, publicized the fact that various holidays and festivals would go on as planned during the weeks to come. At the same time, however, they redoubled their vigilance, intensified their disaster planning program, and soon were to request additional public safety personnel from overseas.

The volcano refused to cooperate. Following several days of relative quiet, on July 25 La Soufrière belched forth a considerable quantity of dust and ash, and sharp tremors were felt four days later. The residents of two nearby villages found the situation so disturbing that they chose to evacuate. During the ensuing days, the indications of an imminent disaster began to multiply. Thus on August 9 there was considerable seismic activity and another ominous cloud rising from the volcano, resulting in more spontaneous evacuation. The 347 shocks recorded on August 12 prompted officials to urge the evacuation of Saint-Claude. On the following day, officials decided to evacuate the aged and ill from Basse-Terre and all other nonessential personnel were also invited to leave the area, all this in response to the opinion of one team of volcanologists that the immediate future might witness the greatest crisis in the history of the Caribbean.

The climatic episode began on August 15 when the prefect ordered the evacuation of the entire imperilled zone, with the sole exception of the town of Vieux-Fort, which is relatively immune to any immediate assault by the volcano by reason of its topographic situation. Blessed with the wisdom of hindsight, we now realize that the evacuation was not necessary; but, given the immediate circumstances, there was no prudent alternative to a prompt transfer of the population at risk, even in lieu of scientific consensus. Indeed, in the days that followed, all the portents of approaching disaster became more numerous and alarming. The frequency of violent tremors increased, as did the venting of dark gases, especially during the period August 23–26. A major ash fall occurred on August 19–21, while the maximum number of tremors (1,257) was recorded on August 24. The prefect had already ordered the residents of Vieux-Fort to leave on August 17.

The elaborate precautions taken by the administration paid off. The exodus of an officially reported 72,000 urban and rural persons, predominantly by auto, bus, and ship, and various vehicles provided by the government, proceeded rapidly and smoothly with no outbreak of panic, and once again without a single casualty. The evacuation of livestock occurred on August 18 while fishing boats were transferred on the 20th. Just how complete the depopulation of the evacuation zone may have been is far from certain. De Vanssay (1979:109) suggests that of the 73,243 persons enumerated within the area in question in 1974, including the residents of the city of Basse-Terre and vicinity (1967 population, 31,469), only 37,862 were actually enumerated in reception areas, but she also notes evacuation rates varying between 70 and 78 percent among communities. She also claims that the rate of response to the official order varied inversely with the distance from the volcano. Obviously, given the urgency of the situation, it would have been impractical for the security forces to enter and search every dwelling in order to rout out the more reluctant citizens. There is some evidence that females substantially outnumbered males among those leaving the peninsula on August 15. In her retrospective survey of the event, de Vanssay (1979:128) found that 53 percent of the 470 responding evacuees identified themselves as females as against 30 percent male and 17 percent who failed to note gender. What is certain is that the security forces effectively sealed off the evacuation zone, so that only those with special permits were allowed to enter briefly, chiefly persons who had left behind certain material necessities. Thus the only convergence toward the endangered zone or Guadeloupe in general involved emergency personnel, scientists, and journalists. All the while, it is important to note, there was a full and constant flow of information, by radio and other means, from the authorities to the general population.

The evacuees found safe havens within the peninsula of Grande-Terre. As of August 15, 18,500 individuals were housed in public shelters, and by the end of the month their number had grown to 20,500. They were distributed among ninety-eight centers in eighteen communities. Fortunately, since 90 percent of the shelters were school buildings, the evacuation occurred during the summer school holiday. It is quite apparent that, once again, many of the evacuees availed themselves of the hospitality of friends and kinfolk, while many others sought commercial facilities instead of resorting to official shelters. De Vanssay's survey of 470 evacuees (1979:125) suggests a distribution somewhat at variance with the official data. Some 30 percent of her sample group stayed with relatives, 14 percent with friends, 52 percent in rented lodgings, and 4 percent on their own property. There was some shifting about after the initial bedding down, including some movement from friends and relatives to camps, and from camps to rental units. There were also some efforts, not totally successful, to shift evacuees from the relatively accessible locations in western Grande-Terre to remoter sites. In any case, by mid-September some 33,000 "rationnaires" were being fed—and probably most of them sheltered as well—by the government.

The authorities went to extraordinary lengths to maintain the welfare of the evacuees. In addition to flying in beds and other emergency gear, they carefully supervised feeding, health, sanitation, security, and leisure activities. They also coped valiantly with the problems of educating the large school-age cohort among the evacuees, improvising facilities as needed with the onset of the school year.

The size of the refugee population remained relatively stable throughout September 1976. Although the anticipated volcanic disaster had not materialized, La Soufrière did not cease rumbling and venting unpleasant gases and dust. By the end of the month, however, the pressures for a return to normal existence became increasingly compelling. Beyond the problem of getting pupils back to school, there was the deteriorating economic situation of most of the adult evacuees, their plight only partially alleviated by governmental aid. The strain upon governmental resources had also begun to tell.

Thus, as the abnormal activity of the volcano gradually subsided during the final quarter of 1976, the authorities allowed a piecemeal, stage by stage, return of the residents of the evacuated zone whenever and wherever they deemed the risk tolerable. The process began by allowing certain workers to make day-trips to their workplaces but to return to their temporary homes for the night, hardly a difficult feat within a small island where the straight-line distance between the cities of Pointe-à-Pitre and Basse-Terre is only 36 km. Subsequently, the residents of one community after another were permitted to return full-time, the usual pattern being for the father to move back first, with spouse and children following some days later as the various schools began to reopen. Thus the number of rationnaires in Grande-Terre declined steadily during October and November, from 29,000 on October 8, to 25,000 on October 15, 16,000 as of November 4, and only 10,000 by November 29. By mid-September normal economic activities were resumed in about two-thirds of the evacuation zone. No looting had occurred during the period of absence. The reactivation of the final tract of the evacuated zone began on December 1. Although a few stragglers remained behind after the beginning of the new year, for all practical purposes the temporary evacuation of a substantial fraction of Guadeloupe's population had become history when 1976 came to a close. There was general concurrence with governmental policy—both to evacuate and then to return the population at risk—on the part of the technical experts. At a conference held in Paris on November 15–18, 1976, the consensus among scientists who had been monitoring the situation was that the time of immediate danger was past, but that constant, sophisticated surveillance of the volcano would be needed for the indefinite future.

The net result of what might seem to have been an exercise in futility and an absorbing case study of the politics of disaster management was the installation of improved seismic and volcanological stations and a thorough testing of the official emergency plan. At a considerable financial cost to the local and national government and at a large social, psychological, and economic cost to the evacuees and their hosts, the Soufrière episode of 1976 did demonstrate that with careful planning, preparation, and handling of information, and the allocation of adequate resources, it is possible to remove large numbers of persons from disaster-prone areas quickly and safely and then restore the pre-emergency pattern of existence reasonably well even in a Third World community. How widely applicable the lessons of La Soufrière may be is another question. Neither is it entirely clear whether, given the absence of a catastrophic eruption in 1976, the Guadeloupeans will respond to any future volcanic crisis with the same degree of patience and cooperation.

EL ASNAM, 1980

The earthquake that hit El Asnam on October 10, 1980 measured 7.2 on the Richter Scale, and was apparently the strongest ever recorded in North Africa. It was followed by several aftershocks over a period of about a week and resulted in some 75 to 80 percent destruction of the city. The hardest hit were administrative buildings, sociocultural centers, schools, and large apartment blocks while industrial areas suffered only minor damage (see Table 3-5). According to initial reports, the epicenter was located near the village of Beni Rached north of the city; later it was agreed that it was located some 10 km east of El Asnam, at a depth of some 10 km. Not only was the city of El Asnam destroyed but also villages in a large surrounding area covering 15,000 km^2 and having a population of 1,600,000.

In preparing this section two sources were used: (a) a manuscript submission by S. Misztal (Polish geographer on contract in Algeria, 1981–84) based on his own field work, several documents, and press

Table 3-5. Results of Preliminary Damage Survey of El Asnam, Mid-November 1980

| | Level of Damage in Percent | | |
Structure Use	No Damage to Light Damage	Moderate to Major Damage	Condemned or Collapsed Buildings
Administrative	5	55	30
Multifamily housing	5	50	45
Single-family housing	20	70	10
School	5	25	70
Industrial	80	15	5
Commercial	10	75	15
Hospital	10	60	30
Water reservoir	50	40	10
Recreation	30	60	10
Socio/cultural	5	60	35
Overall	22	52	26

Source: Leeds 1983:3–2.

coverage ("El Moudjahid"); and (b) a report prepared by a team organized jointly by the Committee on Natural Disasters of the U.S. National Research Council and the Earthquake Engineering Research Institute and coordinated by V. Bertero and H. Shah. The report, edited by Arline Leeds (1983), deals mainly with the geological and engineering aspects of the disaster.

El Asnam is situated in the Mediterranean zone of North Africa between the principal cities of Algeria: Algiers and Oran. It lies in a zone of narrow valleys separated by parallel ranges of the Atlas Mountains some 60 km away from the sea. This region, with a farming tradition dating from Roman times, is located in an area of high seismicity, and the city and surrounding villages have been frequently damaged by earthquakes.

The present-day city of El Asnam dates from 1843 when the French General Bugeaud established a city under the name Orleansville on the ruins of the Roman city of Castellum Tringitanum. Orleansville was devastated by an earthquake on September 9, 1954, when some 1,500 persons were killed. Thereafter French authorities rebuilt the city, but apparently no antiseismic codes were observed, an oversight that resulted in wholesale collapse of post-1954 buildings in the 1980 quake. Renamed El Asnam after Algerian independence (1962), the city changed its name again in 1981 and is now known as Ech-Cheliff (Leeds 1983:P-1).

The first destructive tremor occurred at 1:25 P.M. Friday, October 10 and lasted thirty-five to forty seconds. It apparently came without warning. Since it was the Islamic sabbath, most people were at home while many others were outside, strolling in the streets and parks. However, many people were gathered in the Grand Mosque, and many casualties were recorded in Cité An Nasr, an apartment–cafe–market complex with 3,000 inhabitants. The total number of victims was estimated at 25,000 persons killed and 41,000 injured (including 4,000 seriously). The number of homeless exceeded 400,000. All these figures relate to the region (vilaya) of El Asnam and several districts in other vilayas, but, according to local information, most people killed and injured were residents of the city (Misztal 1984:2). Apparently, according to the 1978 census, the municipality of El Asnam had 106,000 inhabitants, including 76,000 within the city proper.[9] Rescue activities started immediately after the quake and were organized spontaneously by the survivors and local authorities. On the next day, a Central Coordinating Council (Commission Nationale de Coordination pour la Zone Sinistré) had been established by the president of the republic, and by the fifth day the army was in charge of all operations.

Considering that no earthquake contingency plan was available, an effective response materialized surprisingly quickly and efficiently. According to the authors of the American report, "Authoritarian rule and discipline imposed by the military administrators helped return the city of El Asnam to some semblance of order within two weeks of the destructive 10th October, 1980 earthquake" (Leeds 1983:5-3). The vilaya of El Asnam was immediately closed for nonemergency vehicles. All civilian population was evacuated from the city proper (built-up area) and orders were given to shoot looters. By the second day, foreign rescue teams with specialized sonar equipment arrived on the scene, and both national and international medical teams were present within a few days (400 Algerian physicians and more than 300 foreign doctors in addition to several hundred assistant personnel).

The survivors were evacuated locally beyond the built-up area and four tent cities were erected: (1) Chatia, (2) Lalla Aouda, (3) Sidi Ali Bahlouf, and (4) Ouled Mohamed. These were divided into sections and "islands" (ilots), the latter including ten to fifteen families, and all units were headed by People's Committees, which were responsible for keeping records, formulating requests, and distributing tents, food, and supplies made available by the Croissant Rouge Algerien (Misztal 1984:3). In addition, some homeless persons began constructing shanty towns using local materials. It appears that a weekly newspaper, *Algérie Actualité,* reported on a debate as to whether morale was higher in shanty towns or in tent cities (Leeds 1983:5-2). The difficult housing situation in Algeria as well as unwillingness on the part of survivors to leave the city, obviated long-distance evacuation. Only a very few individuals were moved beyond the devastated area, mainly to recreational centers (to Vilaya Mostagem, 10 families or 76 persons; to Vilaya Mascara, 59 families or 364 persons). On the other hand, in spite of the hasty replacement of destroyed school buildlings, where 150,000 primary school students and 19,500 secondary school students from the general region could continue their studies, another 15,000 secondary school students were dispersed all over the country, for example, to Vilaya Mascara, 1,024 persons, Blida, 537 persons, and Saida, 183 persons (Misztal 1984:5).

The total extent of the evacuation from the city can be estimated at about 52,000 persons, including some 3,000 heavily injured. Only some 18,000 moved into distant areas (3,000 injured and 15,000 high school children). This estimate is based on the following reasoning:

- The total population of the city proper was about 80,000 at the time of the quake (76,000 in early 1978 plus 2 percent growth during the following period)
- Some 10 percent, or 8,000 remained at home (20 percent of single-family and 5 percent of multi-family housing escaped damage altogether)
- Some 20,000 were killed (most of the total 25,000 for the region) and 3,000 heavily injured (most of the total of 4,000)
- All seriously injured were flown to distant hospitals in northern Algeria (Misztal 1984:4)
- All evacuated high school children were transferred to distant locations

Construction of light replacement houses (some donated from abroad) began within a few months, and these, together with "bidonvilles" provided provisional shelters to the survivors. Within the first three years, some relatively lightly damaged buildings were repaired and new ones were constructed. The decision was made to reconstruct the city (but this time adopting antiseismic standards), and, according to the physical plans prepared by the Agence Nationale d'Aménagement du Territoire, the population of the municipality is expected to increase substantially from 120,000 in 1981 to 160,000 by 1990 and 215,000 by the year 2000 (Misztal 1984:6).

As of 1983, most of the evacuated population were still living in prefabricated, temporary housing. Farming activities in the region had been resumed; all roads, bridges, and other lifelines were functioning. However, full reconstruction of the city was far from over.

NOTES

1. The Yugoslav–Turkish agreement of 1954 provided for emigration of Turks from Yugoslavia. According to the Turkish data, 161,200 such persons were admitted into Turkey from 1954 to 1962 (Turkey, State Institute of Statistics 1928–. *Statistical Yearbook of Turkey*, 1959, 1971).

2. The number of persons killed was estimated at 1,000 by Ciborowski (1983) and 1,070 by Ambraseys (1966). Fisher (1964) gives a higher and probably exaggerated number of 2,000.

3. According to Ciborowski, 65 percent of the city was destroyed. Later estimates were apparently higher than the initial ones.

4. According to Dacy and Kunreuther (1969:153), some 170,000 had their homes destroyed or badly damaged.

5. Some children were already away from the city on various trips and in summer camps. Their number is not known, however.

6. A social survey that showed different behavior of various ethnic communities (Polservice 1965?) was classified by the Yugoslav government, but some details were reported by Ciborowski (1983).

7. According to Ciborowski (1983), many newcomers were Albanians from neighboring Kosovo who took over the old Turkish quarter (replacing Turks who had left even before the earthquake) and part of the old Gypsy area.

8. Ambraseys (1966:69) reported that by Monday, July 29 more than 100,000 had left the city.

9. These figures were given by Misztal (1984:2). According to Leeds (1983:1-3), the population of the city was estimated at 125,000 and the loss of life was reportedly 5,000 to 20,000.

Chapter 4

War-Related Evacuations

It seems safe to claim that over the course of history the number of persons evacuated from cities because of military events far exceeds the total sum of evacuees generated by all other causes. If we happen to limit ourselves here to the movements associated with World War II, it is not only because they were the most massive of their kind but also, as explained in Chapter 1, on account of the inadequacies of data for evacuations during other conflicts.

But even in the case of World War II we are handicapped by problems of data availability and quality, a reflection in large part of a persistent mind-set among scholars and officials. In the words of Kenneth Hewitt (1987:468):

> . . . the fascination which we scholars, no less than the popular studies, have with leaderships, weapons, battles, spying and such, dominates the literature. Not only does this distract attention from the plight of national civilian majorities, but also it has tended to make them, and their roles and needs, appear pathetic, if not banal. Their problems appear as unfortunate side-effects, if not boring irrelevancies in the clash and decision of "great forces."

Yet, however minute a percentage of this veritable mountain of World War II documentation may deal with civilian concerns, it is still substantial in absolute terms. Indeed, quantitatively it compares favorably with our materials on evacuations unrelated to warfare.

If it is true, as we suspect, that the great majority of large war-related urban evacuations are twentieth-century affairs, there are two obvious explanations: the recent robust growth of many older cities and the proliferation of new ones; and the changing character of modern warfare. Among its other innovations, World War I introduced the world to the aerial bombardment of cities and the use of poison gas on the battlefield (and potentially against city dwellers). The various localized wars during the interwar period strengthened the belief that civilian residents of cities were no longer immune from enemy assault by air as well as by ground attack. From its very beginning, World War II confirmed these apprehensions as civilian casualties and suffering rivaled, or perhaps exceeded, the misfortunes of military personnel. As was the case with World War I, the later conflict brought with it to-and-fro surges of large armies, this time not only across much of Europe but also North Africa and major portions of East Asia to the accompaniment of unprecedented streams of civilian refugees and evacuees.

We analyze these movements as best we can for Great Britain, France and the Low Countries, Germany, Poland, the Soviet Union, and Japan working under the handicap of patchy data. To our regret, the important urban evacuations taking place in Italy, China, and perhaps other countries during the same period have left too few documentary traces for treatment here. It is even more disappointing that we are unable to discuss any of the numerous urban evacuations resulting from post-1945 regional conflicts, for example, the Korean War, Nigeria's civil war, Bangladesh's war for independence, the prolonged hostilities in Vietnam, Kampuchea, and Laos, the war between Iraq and Iran, the ongoing struggle in Lebanon, or Cyprus's civil war.

Despite these omissions, our set of six events—subdivided into two episodes in the cases of Warsaw, France, and Germany and three for Great Britain—does provide a wealth of useful information. Interesting as they may be in and of themselves or as contributions to a fuller understanding of modern warfare, the insights furnished by these wartime movements also help illuminate the general nature of emergency evacuations. Certain family resemblances surface among all such disturbances of the demographic status quo, whatever the immediate inspiration for the exodus.

As is the case for the other series of case studies, the ordering of events in this chapter is temporal. The rationale behind the positioning of the Germany I and II presentation as next to last in the sequence is that the major evacuations did not take place until the final two years of World War II.

Table 4-1. Emergency Evacuation of European and Japanese Cities Related to World War II (1939–45)

Types of Evacuation	Organized	Spontaneous
Evacuations from zones/centers threatened by enemy actions (air raids, naval, or ground attacks)	Evacuation from frontier zones in France and Germany, 1939; coastal areas of Britain, 1939–40	Individuals leaving on their own, especially in Great Britain
Partial or complete evacuation from areas threatened by the advancing enemy	Evacuation from Warsaw, 1939; beginning of the 1940 exode in Belgium and France; evacuation of various Soviet cities; East German cities, 1944–45	Panic flight from Warsaw, Sept. 1939; continuation of Belgium and French exode
Evacuation from bombed-out areas	British children and mothers, 1939–45; children and women from various German cities, 1943–44; Japanese children and mothers, 1943–45	Milan, 1943; Germany, 1943–45; Japan, 1944–45
Evacuation from a city under siege	Leningrad, 1941–43	
Partial or total eviction from conquered areas/centers	Evictions from various western Polish cities in 1939–40; from Warsaw in 1944	

GREAT BRITAIN, 1938–46
(UNITED KINGDOM I, IIA, AND IIB)

The evacuation of a significant fraction of Great Britain's city dwellers just before and during World War II, and their subsequent return, was a phenomenon that offers unusually rich research opportunities to the student of human mobility. It is not simply a matter of sheer volume of movement, ample though that may have been, but rather the exceptionally rich documentation of many aspects of the episode, the extent of preparatory planning, its long duration (by far the most prolonged of all the events treated in this study), and the striking dissimilarities between the British experience and that of the contemporary Germans and Japanese.

The explanation for the large, detailed literature on Britain's wartime evacuations lies in the existence of a considerable corps of social scientists who personally witnessed the comings and goings of the evacuees, were intrigued by the implications of such a vast, unique social experiment, and had access to the voluminous records kept by the multitudinous national and local bureaucracies—records that suffered only relatively minor physical damage or loss during the conflict—and, of course, had access also to the population in question. At least 229 separate local or specialized reports had appeared by 1950 (Titmuss 1950:179–80) along with several book-length studies, including Padley and Cole (1940), Isaacs (1941), Boyd (1944), and, most comprehensively, Richard Titmuss's (1950) admirable account. Regrettably, however, there still remain some large lacunae in the statistics and descriptive literature on certain significant aspects of the redistribution of the British population between 1938 and 1946, deficiencies that will be pointed out in due course. Moreover, there was no single, central agency within the government responsible for overseeing and documenting all phases of the various evacuations, so that there are discrepancies (on the order of several percent) among the sets of figures emanating from various offices (Padley and Cole 1940:42). These caveats aside, no other body of war-related evacuation data rivals that of the British for quantity, reliability, or detail.

Prewar Preparations and Population Movements
(United Kingdom I)

One of the most remarkable aspects of the British story was the amount of time and effort lavished on planning and preparing for mass evacuation whenever warfare became a reality (Stanford Research Institute 1953:193–94; Titmuss 1950:23–44). The introduction of poison gas and aerial bombardment during the 1914–18 conflict had aroused much apprehension within governmental and other circles in Great Britain concerning the horrific disasters that could decimate the civilian population in the event of another major war. Serious studies of civil defense measures began as early as 1931, and the level of anxiety and intensity of work on protective strategies increased as the decade wore on, stimulated no doubt by the tragic fate of many urban and rural residents in China, Manchuria, Ethiopia, and Spain.

The guiding assumption throughout all such prewar preparations (based upon a minimum of historical experience) was that the anticipated war with the Third Reich could well begin with a massive aerial assault by the formidable Luftwaffe, and that such an attack would set off a panic flight of unprecedented proportions from London and other large urban centers. The logical consequence of such thinking was the imperative need to transfer several million of the most vulnerable, but dispensable, persons, that is, children and their mothers, the aged, and the infirm, to presumably safe localities elsewhere within the British Isles, and to do so in methodical, predetermined fashion as calmly as possible just as soon as it became clear that an outbreak of hostilities was inevitable and imminent. To that end a multiplicy of governmental agencies involved in transportation, housing, education, fiscal matters, medical and other social services, and other functions at all levels from the national down to the most local worked out detailed schemes for just such a massive redistribution. In spite of much bureaucratic and parliamentary squabbling, revision of details, transfers of responsibilities among agencies before and during the war—and despite the failure of evaluation to develop on the expected scale—the government adhered to this basic plan throughout the years of crisis.

A second central decision was that the decision to evacuate would be voluntary in nature although every medium of public persuasion was brought to bear. And, surprisingly, once again, the government never deviated from this principle, although it was sorely tempted to do so during some of the darker moments of the war. On the other hand, the authorities did apply compulsion at the other end of the exodus, albeit with much adjustment to local circumstances. Designated households in reception areas were required to accommodate evacuees, however reluctantly, and received payments to cover the costs of their hospitality. As it turned out, this feature of the plan was the one occasioning the greatest social and political unhappiness.

A final principle that also remained unaltered throughout the crisis was that nearly all evacuees were to be billeted in private homes within the reception areas. The exceptions were generally minor or temporary: persons requiring hospitalization or special social or physical care. The reasons were quite practical. During a period of extraordinary strain upon national resources, there was neither enough money nor workers for the construction of livable camps and hostels for hundreds of thousands of evacuees. When mass housing was resorted to, for some thousands of displaced persons, schools, church buildings, and other public structures were commandeered.

As 1938 arrived, the eventual waging of another war against Germany seemed inevitable, and work on evacuation planning escalated from the theoretical or speculative to the working out of real and practical details. The planners designated three sets of zones within the island of Great Britain: (1) areas scheduled for evacuation, that is, major urban and industrial centers, with an aggregate population of about 13,000,000 (Padley and Cole 1940:44); (2) neutral areas, containing some 14,000,000 inhabitants, that were neither to generate nor receive evacuees; and (3) the reception areas, largely rural and small city in composition, with a prewar population of about 18,000,000 that were to accommodate a predicted influx of 4,000,000 evacuees (see Figure 4-1). Figure 4-1 identifies these territorial categories in England and Scotland.

Within the reception areas, local authorities carried out field surveys, of varying degrees of reliability, to ascertain the availability and characteristics of emergency housing space within private dwellings. Transportation, school, and other officials drew up elaborate plans and schedules for assembling and promptly transporting the following classes (Titmuss 1950:33–34).

1. Schoolchildren, removed as school units under the charge of their teachers
2. Younger children, accompanied by their mothers or by some other responsible person
3. Expectant mothers
4. Adult blind persons and cripples whose removal was feasible

Unfortunately, there was a basic weakness in the scheme, one that became obvious as soon as this official evacuation began in September 1939. "This dominating concern to get mothers and children out of London [and other cities] at all costs, and as quickly as possible, meant

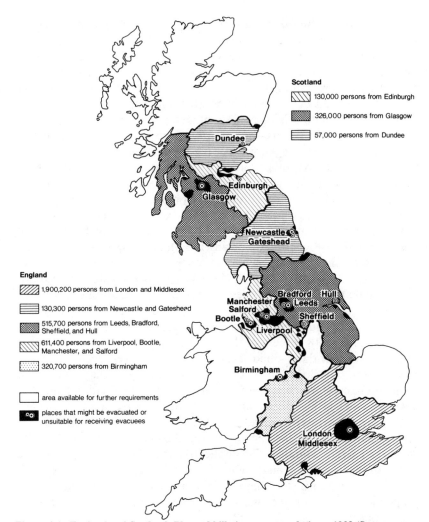

Figure 4-1. England and Scotland: Planned billeting accommodations, 1938 (Source: Titmuss 1950:39)

that problems at the other end—of reception, billeting and welfare—
were obscured and neglected'' (Titmuss 1950:40).

Although the official evacuations to nonmetropolitan tracts of Great
Britain did eventually account for a large number of persons, two other
categories of population transfer, private and mostly unofficial, may
well have equaled or exceeded them in volume. For purposes of this
study, we designate this pair of spontaneous movements, events that
unfolded during the twenty-four-month period beginning with September 1938, as United Kingdom I. All the evacuations treated here must
be distinguished from other forms of war-related mobility with which
we are not concerned, such as the movement of troops and workers in
war industries or the influx of refugees from foreign countries.

First and earliest was the spontaneous exodus of relatively well-to-
do Londoners and other residents of likely target areas that was well
under way in 1938, especially during the Munich Crisis in September,
when there was a panic scramble observable at the London rail
terminals (Padley and Cole 1940:69). During this premature migration,
some 150,000 departed for Wales and there was a ''continuous rush of
cars from London'' (Stanford Research Institute 1953:193). By February 1939, a considerable portion of the surplus accommodations in
receiving areas—18 percent of those in England and Wales, 21 percent
of those in Scotland—had been ''privately'' reserved (Titmuss
1950:37–39). The location of these reserved facilities is a matter of
some interest. Those who were preparing for self-evacuation tended to
favor the five southwestern counties (Cornwall, Dorsetshire, Somerset,
Wiltshire, and Herefordshire) and Scotland, especially seaside and
resort districts (Boyd 1944:54–55), while showing relatively little interest in the eastern counties. The implication is that most of these private
reservations were not made with friends or relatives. ''In general,
private reservations were highest in those counties with the largest
proportions of big houses, and lowest in the counties containing more
small houses'' (Titmuss 1950:38).

In addition to the families and individuals who eventually sought
safety in outlying areas, there was also a large-scale migration of
private and public institutions, including schools, universities, nursing
homes, a variety of charitable organizations, and many business firms
and their personnel (Titmuss 1950:101). The results of a series of
ingenious calculations performed by Titmuss (1950:101–02, 546–49)
suggests that with the approach and outbreak of hostilities, that is, the
end of June 1939 through the first week of September, approximately
2,000,000 persons privately evacuated themselves to safer areas in

England and Wales, quite apart from the significant number who left
for Scotland, Ireland, or abroad. It was reported from Southampton
that 5,000 persons left for America in forty-eight hours (Calder
1969:36).[1] In any event, the estimated total of private evacuees is
greater than the aggregate of 1,500,000 to 1,750,000 persons participating in the officially assisted program.

In May 1940, with the German sweep through the Low Countries
and France and the imminent prospect of an invasion of Great Britain,
many offers of hospitality for British children arrived from the Com-
monwealth countries and the United States. In short order, a governmental interdepartmental committee established the Children's Overseas Reception Scheme and began to process some 211,000
applications for children aged five to sixteen to be sent overseas (Boyd
1944:36–37; Calder 1969:128–30; Titmuss 1950:246–47; Stanford Research Institute 1953:198). Altogether, 24,514 of the applications were
approved, and the number of children who actually arrived safely in
the dominions under the scheme (none being directed to the United
States) was 2,664, of whom 1,532 went to Canada, 576 to Australia,
353 to South Africa, and 203 to New Zealand. In addition, approximately, 11,000 to 14,000 children left for overseas destinations under
private arrangements, over 5,000 of them finding temporary homes in
the United States. Such evidence as we have suggests that most of the
families involved in this operation, the second phase of United Kingdom I, could be categorized as middle class or higher. The program
came to an abrupt and tragic end when the *City of Benares* was sunk
on September 17, 1940 with the loss of 73 children and 6 accompanying
adults—and the realization that the British Navy could not provide
adequate protection. Presumably all, or nearly all, of the youngsters
who spent five years in foster homes overseas returned to their British
parents at the end of the war.

The Official 1939 Exodus (United Kingdom IIa)

With the declaration of war on September 1, 1939, the official
evacuation scheme was fully activated (an episode designated here as
United Kingdom IIa), and over a period of three days all those children
and mothers who were willing to leave the evacuation areas did so,
accompanied by teachers and other adult helpers. They arrived by
bus, subway, or other appropriate means at the designated railroad
depots, where special trains, and, then frequently, total buses, spirited

them away as rapidly as possible to predetermined destinations in the hinterland. In a few cases, parties from London's eastern suburbs proceeded to ports in East Anglia by boat (Calder 1969:38).

Despite all the elaborate preparations, two problems were immediately apparent. Because of the exigencies of railroad schedules, there were many instances of individuals directed to the wrong train and ending at the wrong destination, of school classes intending to travel together being scattered among two or more trains, and of the wrong number of the wrong sorts of evacuees arriving at many stations to the bewilderment and confusion of the receiving officials. Later attempts at spatial resorting were only partially successful. What was equally dismaying was a major shortfall in volume of evacuees. The authorities had anticipated, or hoped for, a total of around 4,000,000. Even after a massive propaganda campaign, only about 40 percent of that number materialized during September 1939 (quite apart from those making private arrangements for evacuation) for reasons that were not immediately apparent. As it turned out, this initial exodus of some 1.5 to 1.7 million persons represented the high-water mark of the entire six-year emergency period, and attrition was to be rapid and massive during the weeks and months that followed.

In terms of source regions for those officially evacuated and counted in early September 1939, we find that the Greater London area was far in the lead, accounting as it did for nearly half the total. As indicated in Table 4-2, the other English evacuation areas and the Scottish contributed around 40 and 12 percent of the evacuees respectively. In analyzing the response at the local level to official entreaties to leave,

Table 4-2. England and Scotland: The Official Evacuation, September 1939; Source Areas

	Source Areas			
Evacuee Group	London and Metropolitan Area	Other Evacuation Areas in England	Evacuation Areas in Scotland	Total
Unaccompanied schoolchildren	393,700	371,200	62,059	826,959
Mothers and accompanied children	257,000	169,500	97,170	523,670
Expectant mothers	5,600	6,700	405	12,705
Handicapped people and those with special needs	2,440	2,830	1,787	7,057
Subtotal	658,740	550,230	161,421	1,370,391
Teachers and helpers	89,355		13,645	130,000
Total	1,298,325		175,066	1,473,391

Source: Adapted from Titmuss 1950:103.

some wide disparities appear that defy easy explanation (Titmuss 1950:550–51). Thus we find that only 15 percent of the eligible school-children in Sheffield left home unaccompanied by parent, and only 20 percent in Coventry and 22 percent in Nottingham, while the figure was 70 percent in the Manchester area and 71 percent in Newcastle.

Incomplete, but useful, information is available concerning the destinations of the official evacuees (Titmuss 1950:103, 553). In mapping the counties, or major subdivisions thereof, in which unaccompanied children were billeted within England during the initial wave of evacuation, we find a relatively complex pattern, but one that seems largely explainable in terms of friction of distance (see Figure 4-2). Thus we see the concentration of displaced children in the southeastern counties adjacent, or close, to Greater London and the bunching of evacuees among the rural tracts of Lancashire and Cheshire within hailing

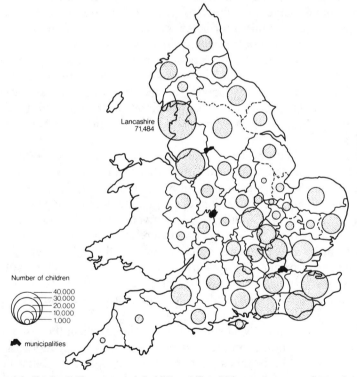

Figure 4-2. England: Unaccompanied children billeted in reception areas, September 1939 (Source: Titmuss 1950:550–51)

distance of Midland metropolises. A smaller, but significant, fraction of the evacuees moved westward into Wales, a reported 56,987 under official auspices in addition to some 120,000 of the individuals participating in the private exodus (Titmuss 1950:547, 553). In evident contrast to the spatial choices of private evacuees, who tended to combine comfort with the out of the way, relatively few children were dispatched to the remoter counties, such as Cornwall or Westmoreland. We can assume a similar spatial array for the half-million or more mothers and offspring traveling together. Once again, there was considerable unevenness from place to place in the level of mobility among the evacuable mothers-cum-children. Although only 7 and 9 percent of the eligibles in Grimsby and Hartlepool, respectively, availed themselves of the opportunity to seek safety elsewhere, 66 percent of those in Bootle were so inclined (Titmuss 1950:552).

The official bodies concerned with the evacuation program had ample reason to be deeply disturbed about its shortcomings well before the month of September drew to a close. Not only had the actual turnout of evacuees fallen far below the projected level, but an alarmingly large proportion of the persons in question elected to return home shortly after arriving at the reception areas. Indeed some observers reported the bizarre spectacle of trains loaded with urban youngsters and accompanying adults arriving at one platform of a rural station while groups of disgruntled evacuees stood on the opposite platform waiting for the next city-bound train to return them to their regular abodes.

By January 1940, no fewer than 61.1 percent, or about 900,000, of the official evacuees had abandoned their temporary billets and returned home (Titmuss 1950:172). In England only 55, 13, and 9 percent of the unaccompanied schoolchildren, mothers and accompanied children, and expectant mothers, respectively, remained in reception areas. The attrition rates in Scotland were even higher, for only some 28 percent of the September evacuees were still domiciled away from their places of origin. These figures may understate the actual volume of cross-traffic since there was a trickle of out-movement during the final quarter of 1939, followed by the return of most of the persons in question.

The available data reveal some spatial differentials in the propensity to return. Thus defections tended to be higher among mothers and children billeted in localities relatively close to London or other major source areas and in the eastern counties where the fear of bombing raids was especially strong, while retention rates were higher in the west and in remoter localities in general (Padley and Cole 1940: 55; Titmuss 1950:173–74). Another nonspatial consideration was size of family: "Parents with only one or two children were less likely to send them away, and swifter to bring them back, than those with five or six; the smaller the family, the more it clung together" (Calder 1969:40).

In any event, of a total of somewhere between 3.5 and 4 million residents of England and Scotland who voluntarily moved to presumably safe havens just before or during the opening phase of World War II, the majority abandoned this strategy by winter and had streamed back home. A word of caution may be in order about statements concerning the volume of evacuation. Many individuals participated more than once, so that a good deal of double-counting must have occurred.

A combination of factors accounts for the dismal execution of the official redistribution of the more vulnerable and/or expendable members of British society. The most obvious of these was the failure of the enemy to oblige by initiating the dreaded bombing campaign on schedule. In fact, there was a notable dearth of military action, by land, sea, or air in Western Europe during the first seven months of the war, the so-called Phoney War period, but loud, intense criticism of the evacuation scheme reverberated throughout virtually every sector of British society.

Adding to this absence of any immediate peril were the inadequacies of the physical and social arrangements in the reception areas following what for many were physically and psychologically traumatic journeys. It was difficult, sometimes impossible, to reassemble splintered classes of pupils; and both the quantity and quality of schooling for the relocated students was minimal. Homesickness certainly played a role, but even more important was a powerful sense of family solidarity and, consequently, the reluctance to separate spouses for extended periods, or older from younger siblings. Social services and cultural amenities in the countryside generally fell below the meager standards enjoyed by even the most deprived of city folk. But quite likely the fact that proved most damaging to the official evacuation program was the profound sociocultural gulf between hosts and guests. They had been strangers to one another, for, unlike the situation in a belatedly modernized Japan, most of the large urban population had lost their ancestral rural roots and any vital connection with the extra-urban world had shriveled and died for this majority of Britons. Moreover, a disproportionate share of the evacuees were not only residents of crowded metropolises but dwelled within the lower strata of a strongly class-conscious society. The simple fact that fertility levels among the poor were markedly higher than among the middle and upper classes (who were overrepresented among those evacuating privately) contributed to the disproportionate share of slum children among evacuees. In this collision of two worlds that had been so largely sealed off one from the other, there was much unhappiness over almost every aspect of behavior, including clothing, dietary practices, personal hygiene, sleeping arrangements, etiquette, language, and, quite often, religion. The problems of adjusting to a strange environment and often an increasingly unfriendly host population were especially acute for mothers with young children, so that their rate of departure was much greater than for the unaccompanied children.

Despite all the qualitative and quantitative disappointments of the earliest phases of the official evacuation program, it did yield some positive benefits. The existence of a mechanism for escaping cities under heavy enemy attack, whether or not the option was ever resorted to, was undoubtedly a psychic asset. Whatever the unspoken intent of the planners (and the point is not at all clear), the temporary absence of significant numbers of persons did reduce the pressures, in terms of workers and funds, for providing social and other services in cities that were hard pressed to function effectively during crucial periods of the war. Furthermore, mothers freed from the burdens of child care could be recruited into war-related industries in dire need of personnel. But it may be argued that the greatest good generated by the mass reshuffling of what was mainly an underprivileged population was unplanned, long term, and educational. Forced fraternization across class, regional, and cultural boundaries meant revelations for all concerned and ultimate consensus that remedial change was essential. Although it is hardly feasible to document the claim in rigorous fashion, it is altogether reasonable that the major innovations and advances in British social policy effected in the postwar period came about, in part at least, because of that vast social experiment, the government-induced redistribution of a substantial section of the population.

The 1940–46 Evacuations (United Kingdom IIb)

The evacuation of September 1939 was only the first of a series. Confronted with the obvious failings of the initial exodus, the government intensified its publicity efforts during the fall and winter of 1939–

40, but with paltry results. Only a minute fraction of the parents living in evacuation areas registered their children for unaccompanied residence elsewhere, and even fewer actually delivered them to the designated reception centers. It was only in spring 1940, with the German conquest of France and the Low Countries, that evacuations began to outpace returns (and we enter the phase of British evacuation we have labeled United Kingdom IIb). Titmuss has ably summarized the subsequent events:

> This great uprooting of human beings from their homes took place in three big waves of diminishing strength, each connected by a slender, continuing trickle. The first, which accounted for about 1,450,000 people, was carried through within a few days at the outbreak of war. In the spring and early summer of 1940 a further 300,000 or so were moved to safer inland districts from London, certain towns on the coast and other areas. This was the prelude to the second big wave which moved about 1,250,000 people. It spread itself over a much longer period of time than the first; for the number evacuated rose and fell largely in response to changes in the weight and geographical distribution of air attacks. As the enemy withdrew his bombers the flow of evacuees subsided until, by 1942, only a small trickle was reaching the reception areas. The third wave, affecting around 1,000,000 people within two months, irrupted violently in the summer of 1944 when flying-bombs were flung at London and southeastern England. (Titmuss 1950:355)

Table 4-3 and Figure 4-3 summarize the available data and estimates for the entire war period.

It is noteworthy that the magnitude of official (and, presumably, private) evacuations declined irregularly over time, even though the level of risk tended to increase from 1939 onward. This rather paradoxical situation, this mass adjustment to abnormal living and working conditions, developed in spite of greater sophistication and flexibility on the part of the evacuation managers, and stronger inducements, including the use of travel and subsistence subsidies and improved living facilities, in reception areas.

The geography of the diaspora also changed in the course of the war, although area-specific numbers are lacking. The threat of invasion in 1940 and, a good deal later, the flying bombs and rockets afflicting the southeastern portions of Great Britain prompted strenuous efforts to remove children from the eastern and southeastern counties, including some evacuees who had been billeted there. The complex shifting about of offices, war industries, and their work forces also meant that

Table 4-3. British Government Evacuation Scheme, 1939–45*

	England and Wales					Scotland					Total for Great Britain
Date	Unaccompanied Children	Mothers and Children	Teachers and Helpers	Other Adults[1]	All Classes	Unaccompanied Children	Mothers and Children	Teachers and Helpers	Other Adults[1]	All Classes	All Classes
Sept. 1939	765,000	426,500	89,000	18,000	1,298,500	62,000	99,000	13,000	1,000	175,000	1,473,500
Jan. 1940	420,000	56,000	43,400	3,380	522,780	37,600	8,900	3,100	200	49,800	572,580
Aug. 1940	421,000	57,000	27,000	14,000	519,000	17,900	7,400	1,600	100	27,000	546,000
Feb. 1941	480,500	571,000	25,000	262,000[2]	1,338,700	11,800	15,700	1,000	1,500	30,000[3]	1,368,700
Sept. 1941	435,700	450,000	21,000	157,000	1,063,700	25,600	85,000	1,300	29,700	141,600[4]	1,205,300
Mar. 1942	332,000	279,000	18,000	109,000	738,000	18,400	47,400	1,400	13,400	80,600[4]	818,600
Sept. 1942	236,000	196,000	13,000	85,000	530,000	13,600	31,500	1,200	8,200	54,500[5]	584,500
Mar. 1943	181,000	148,000	9,000	68,000	406,000	9,500	23,000	1,000	6,500	40,000[6]	446,000
Sept. 1943	137,000	124,000	6,400	55,000	322,400	7,800	18,800	900	5,500	33,000[7]	355,400
Mar. 1944	124,000	132,000	5,400	58,000	319,400	6,000	15,700	700	7,600	30,000[8]	349,400
Sept. 1944	284,000	601,000	6,800	121,000	1,012,800	5,100	15,900	400	6,000	27,400[9]	1,040,200
Mar. 1945	132,000	243,000	4,000	59,000	438,000	1,700	11,200	100	3,200	16,200[10]	454,200
Sept. 1945	13,250	—	—	—	13,250	150	3,500	—	1,800	5,500[11]	18,750

*Total number billeted in all areas.

[1]Includes homeless persons, expectant mothers, children in nurseries, camps, and hostels, invalids, old people, handicapped persons, civil defense personnel, emergency medical service staff, and war workers up to April 1942. The last three groups are excluded thereafter.

[2]Mainly homeless people; including 66,200 such people billeted in evacuation areas.

[3]Including 11,700 evacuees from English areas billeted in Scotland.

[4]Including an unknown number of evacuees from English areas billeted in Scotland.

[5]June 1942. Including an unknown number of evacuees from English areas billeted in Scotland.

[6]December 1942. Including an unknown number of evacuees from English areas billeted in Scotland.

[7]June 1943. Including an unknown number of evacuees from English areas billeted in Scotland.

[8]December 1943. Including 4,300 evacuees from English areas billeted in Scotland.

[9]June 1944. Including 5,100 evacuees from English areas billeted in Scotland.

[10]April 1945. Including 10,600 evacuees from English areas billeted in Scotland.

[11]October 1945. Including 850 evacuees from English areas billeted in Scotland.

Source: Titmuss 1950:567.

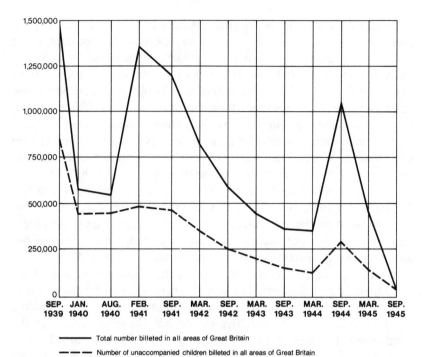

Total number billeted in all areas of Great Britain

— — — Number of unaccompanied children billeted in all areas of Great Britain

Figure 4-3. British government evacuation scheme, 1939–45 (Source: Titmuss 1950:356)

many provincial communities were no longer capable of sheltering evacuees. Up to June 1941 about 5,100 mothers and children went to Eire and Northern Ireland from evacuation areas, but after the bombing of Belfast in May 1941 the movement was suspended (Titmuss 1950:367fn).

The summary material in Table 4-3 and Figure 4-3 suggests two generalizations. First, despite the best efforts of the authorities, eligible evacuees responded effectively only to actual or anticipated enemy attacks and indifferently to governmental persuasion. During many, perhaps most, months of the war, the volume of persons returning home exceeded those exiting under the official, but consistently voluntary, evacuation scheme. Second, even during the most intense episodes of bombing, the morale of British city dwellers did not crack; and the great majority made a conscious decision to risk death or injury and to undergo other tribulations in familiar settings while keeping family and neighborhood ties intact rather than take refuge elsewhere. One can only speculate what might have happened if the

scale of urban destruction in Great Britain had equaled that experienced by the inhabitants of Japan's and Germany's metropolises in
1944–45. Fortunately, despite the considerable havoc wrought by the
Luftwaffe and by rocket assaults, such near-obliteration never came to
pass, nor did the cities suffer wholesale depopulation. Although the
cities were far from deserted, they did experience significant temporary loss of residents. Nowhere was this more evident than in London,
where the combination of official and private evacuations, conscription
into the armed forces, and outward shifts of government and industrial
workers reduced the population of the inner portions of the metropolitan area approximately 40 percent below its 1939 level (Iklé 1950a:30).
As Table 4-4 indicates, the losses suffered by the core of Greater
London were partially balanced by the influx of evacuees and others
into the suburban periphery; but the total metropolitan area had not
fully regained its former population size even as late as 1947.

In one respect the British story does parallel the ordeal of German
and Japanese city dwellers. For some days or weeks after the destruction of much of the housing stock in several provincial cities, including
Plymouth, Coventry, Bristol, Merseyside, and Clydebank, many of the
bombed-out residents took to "trekking," that is, commuting every
evening by bus, foot, or other conveyance to the open countryside
where they would sleep in barns or other structures or in the fields
before returning to work in the morning (Calder 1969:205, 212; Titmuss
1950:307–08, 313). Statistics are not available for this form of short-
term evacuation, but undoubtedly it involved many tens of thousands
of individuals.

Well before the end of the war, government officials had begun
planning an orderly reversal of the evacuation (Stanford Research
Institute 1953:204–05; Titmuss 1950:431–35). Ironically, September 8,

Table 4-4. Population of Greater London, 1931–47*

Area	1931	1939	1941	1945	1947
County of London	4.4	4.0	2.3	2.5	3.2
Inner Urban Ring	1.5	1.5	1.0	1.1	1.4
Suburban Ring	2.0	2.7	2.4	2.5	2.9
Green Belt	0.8	1.1	1.2	1.2	1.3
Outer County Ring	0.9	1.0	1.2	1.1	1.1
Total	9.6	10.3	8.1	8.4	9.9

*In millions.
Source: Iklé 1950a:30.

1944, the day the government announced suspension of general evacuation facilities, was also the very day the first rocket fell on London. It was decided to operate the "evacuation in reverse" with London, Hull, and other east coast towns receiving the last of the returnees. But, as had happened so often during the war, the official plan went by default. With the certainty of Germany's defeat apparent by summer 1944, the majority of the evacuees used their own devices to return well ahead of the official schedule during the winter of 1944–45. The only major deterrent was the shortage of housing in the battered cities. Thus, in the end, only 75,000 persons returned home in organized parties under government auspices out of the 1,000,000 still billeted in September 1944. Nevertheless, and despite an enormous eagerness to resume a normal existence, a residual population of evacuees remained in their wartime billets for some months after the German surrender. On July 31, 1945, 76,000 persons were still being accommodated under the evacuation scheme in England and Wales and 5,499 in Scotland, largely because of housing problems in the cities (Titmuss 1950:434). By March 1946 the number had fallen to 38,000. Thus it was only by slow, painful degrees that the evacuation scheme came to an end quietly, sometime in 1946.

What had been accomplished by the evacuation of large numbers of civilians from British cities during World War II? It was clearly another affirmation of the near impossibility of inducing an optimal number of persons to leave their homes during wartime except under the direst of circumstances—a lesson to be drawn from the experience of other combatant nations. On a practical demographic level, there can be no doubt that a certain number of deaths and injuries were avoided by dispersing potential victims. If the official total of civilians in Great Britain killed by enemy action was between 60,000 and 63,000 and the number of injured at least 200,000 (Titmuss 1950:559–60), these values would probably have been several thousand higher in lieu of evacuation. But such savings were purchased at enormous economic, social, and psychological cost. What is certain is that after 1947 the spatial array of the British population no longer displayed any impact attributable to the evacuation. Except perhaps for a slight depression of fertility caused by separation of spouses and a lowering of educational attainment among a sizable segment of the urban young, the long-term demographic effects may have been negligible. Much more important was the psychic impact of the experience, and its role in restructuring British society and its attitudes.

WARSAW, 1939–44 (WARSAW I AND II)

Warsaw represents a prime example of a city experiencing all the varieties of population movements caused by the changing fortunes of war and ruthless policies imposed by foreign occupiers. These movements began at the very outset of World War II, in September 1939, continuing until the almost complete destruction and depopulation of the capital city in 1944, and then persisted even later as the liberated city began to draw back many of the survivors dispersed in various parts of the country and elsewhere in Europe.

At the outbreak of war on September 1, 1939, the German thrust into western Poland sent waves of refugees hurrying eastward, some of whom reached Warsaw; subsequently, the threat to the capital prompted a short-lived official as well as spontaneous evacuation. During the siege of Warsaw, the Nazis offered to evacuate civilians— an offer that was not accepted. Finally, after the city's surrender on September 28, 1939, there was an outflow of some refugees, along with an outflow of some of the natives of the city.

During the Nazi occupation of Warsaw (September 30, 1939 to January 17, 1945), considerable movement took place both within and outside the city. The anti-Jewish policies of the German administration led to the creation of a Jewish ghetto in November 1940, eventually sealed off from the rest of the city and finally destroyed in the spring of 1943. During its brief existence, the population of the ghetto swelled as a result of the forced influx of Jews from other parts of Poland as well as other countries of Europe. On the other hand, very high mortality, deportations to extermination camps (especially Treblinka), and finally losses during the desperate uprising reduced and eventually totally eliminated the ghetto population. During the war there was also an influx of German adminstrative and military personnel and some movement of the Polish civilian population into and out of the city.[2]

Finally, the ill-fated general uprising in August and September of 1944 culminated in a wholesale eviction of whatever population still remained on the west bank of the Vistula, then still under German control. The return of survivors after January 17, 1945 represented the last stage in this epic drama of the destroyed capital, which then began its repopulation and an eventual return to something approaching normalcy.

Obviously not all of the movements noted above fall into the category of emergency evacuations. The short-term evacuation of 1939, which was both planned and executed, would certainly qualify. (We designate it as Warsaw I.) The removal of the Jewish population was final in every respect, a phenomenon hardly to be defined as an evacuation. On the other hand, the removal of the remaining population in 1944 was intended to be final but turned out to be temporary, an evacuation that we label Warsaw II. Some comments on this latter movement will be included in the discussion that follows.

Sources

The Second World War has generated an enormous literature in Polish as it has in other languages. Since the selection and analysis of events by Polish authors has had obvious political implications, the authorities of the People's Republic of Poland exerted tight control over research and publications in the past, using every sort of instrument from approval of research priorities and funding to censorship. This explains the uneven development of this literature and a relatively late "explosion" of studies in which previously unacceptable topics or approaches finally won some tolerance. It is quite clear that the 1944 uprising and associated events and the role played by various nationalist participants belonged to this category of sensitive topics.

The considerable body of literature in Poland dealing with World War II ranges from personal diaries and memoirs through collections of reprinted documents to analytical studies based on data made available long after the events. Polish military historians, not unlike their counterparts in other countries, tend to stress military strategies and actions and the fate of civilians was discussed only marginally, if at all. Books dealing specifically with Warsaw devote more space to the movements of population in this city, and these were of much greater value for the present study.

The sources used here can be divided into several categories:

- General historical accounts of war (Rawski et al. 1966) and of Warsaw (Drozdowski and Zahorski 1975)
- Studies concerned with Warsaw during the war (Bartelski 1968; Landau 1962; Ratyńska 1982) or, more specifically, with the first siege of Warsaw in September 1939 (Bartoszewski 1959; Beczkowicz 1972; Cieplewicz 1969; Drozdowski 1975, 1976; Instytut Historii 1964; Porwit 1959) or the Warsaw uprising in 1944 (Madajczyk 1974)
- Studies of a demographic character devoted to the population of

Warsaw (Lipowski 1970: E. Strzelecki 1972; Z. Strzelecki 1984; Szczypiorski 1976), or, more specifically, the Jewish population and the Warsaw ghetto (Berenstein and Rutkowski 1958; Sakowska 1975)

• Reports of foreign observers (Biddell 1976; Carton de Wiart 1950)

Such documents provide both factual information and results of analyses that can be used to reconstruct the complicated set of events affecting the city's population. The Institute of History, Polish Academy of Sciences has initiated several major projects, some of which were published and used in the present study. The results of one very relevant project on the 1944 exodus of Warsaw's population were expected to be published only toward the end of 1989. The text was not available to the authors, but an interview with its editor provided interesting insights (Drozdowski 1989).

Evacuation in 1939 (Warsaw I)

The German attack on September 1, 1939, and the successes of the invading armies advancing from different directions, resulted in the rapid occupation of the western and northern areas of Poland. These setbacks prompted the evacuation of government offices and employees with their families as well as the flight of the general population from a number of endangered cities. Great streams of refugees trying to escape used all available means of transportation ranging from special trains and private cars to bicycles or simply walking generally eastward. Warsaw became a destination for many of these western evacuees, but at the same time the capital city was affected quite early by evacuations that were both planned and spontaneous. The various population movements involving Warsaw are shown diagrammatically in Figure 4-4.

On September 3, 1939, a decision was made to evacuate agencies of the central government; and on September 5 the newly appointed Minister of Information M. Grażyński declared during a press conference that Warsaw would be evacuated. That evening President of the Republic L. Mościcki, who had moved his official residence from the centrally located castle to the suburbs four days earlier (Błota, near Falenica), left for Lubartów and later Ołyka in the east. During the next two days, organized and spontaneous evacuations, the latter characterized by chaos and panic, paralyzed the city. On the night of

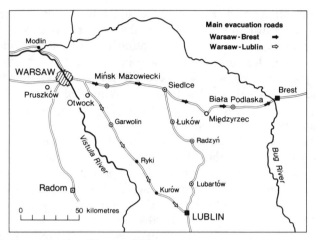

Figure 4-4. Evacuation from Warsaw, 1939

September 6–7, railway transports were leaving for eastern and south-eastern cities from stations packed with people who were not accurately informed about the time of departure. As a result, there were apparently some cases of death, the victims having been pushed under moving trains or suffocating in the crowds (Landau 1962:5).

Various government agencies were evacuated by trains, trucks, and cars, mainly in the direction of Lublin. The first to go were the Ministry of Foreign Affairs, with part of the diplomatic corps, and the Ministry of Defense. The prime minister announced the departure of his cabinet shortly after midnight September 6–7 and by 2:00 A.M. they had actually left, initially for Lublin, later moving to Łuck (diplomats were stationed in Krzemieniec), and after September 17 crossed over into Romania. The High Command left during the same night, initially to Brest. On September 11 it moved again to Młnów; and on September 18, after the Soviet troops entered Polish territory, the commander-in-chief with his entourage crossed via Kuty into Romania (Rawski et al. 1966:157, 161). The military situation of Warsaw deteriorated after some of the anti-aircraft units as well as the remainder of the fighter brigade of the air force were pulled out. The evacuation panic resulted in the disappearance of the police (creating a need for the formation of people's militia), some of the firefighters, personnel of two major hospitals, and so on. Some government officials were fleeing with their families, but, on the other hand, there were also reports that some employees, particularly women and older men, refused to join the evacuation. Rapid and unexpected evacuation of some offices (see Figure 4-5), destruction of files, and the withdrawal of some troops (including heavy artillery) created an atmosphere of anxiety and panic.

On top of all this, in a radio appeal broadcast about midnight that fateful night of September 6–7, Colonel R. Umiastowski, then the chief of propaganda in military headquarters, requested all young men to leave the city in order to join the army somewhere in the interior. This evacuation order was rescinded almost immediately. Although this cancellation was announced via radio at 3:00 A.M. and posters to the same effect were distributed in the city on September 8, Colonel Umiastowski's appeal led to a massive departure that very night, not only of young men but also of many others (Instytut Historii 1964:xiv–xv). Various personal accounts include comments on this evacuation, which affected so many people. By that time, railways were paralyzed, and most people simply walked, some pushing prams, while others were lucky enough to get hold of horse cabs, horse-drawn carts, or even cars. This panicky wave of evacuees included employees of important services such as power stations, the telephone system, and the like (Instytut Historii 1964:168, 382). Not all young people followed the initial order, however. Some simply waited for a day or two until the mood had changed, others were persuaded by women who argued that some men should stay and take care of their families (Instytut Historii 1964:175). It is difficult to estimate the size of this evacuation. Poniatowski and Zelwiański (1972:9) talk about more than 50,000 young men, Landau (1962, vol. 1:10) quotes his friend, a former senior official of the statistical office, who made a rough count of the flow on the main evacuation route to Garwolin and came up with an estimate of some 100,000. In view of constant air attacks, bombing and strafing along the road, as well as fires raging in bombed-out towns (Garwolin, Ryki, Kurów), movement of such a mass of people was extremely slow and painful. No supplies were available and later reports mention rapid depletion of all food on the way or even water in the wells (Landau 1962, vol. 1:10).

On the whole, the city administration resisted the panic, and the mayor, S. Starzyński, who on September 8 was appointed civil commissioner by the Military Command of Warsaw, made the first of his influential radio appeals not to leave the city but to prepare for defense. He and Commanding General W. Czuma became heroic leaders in the siege of Warsaw, which ended in capitulation of the devastated city by the end of September. According to many personal accounts, the decision to defend the city and the radio appeals heard on the way

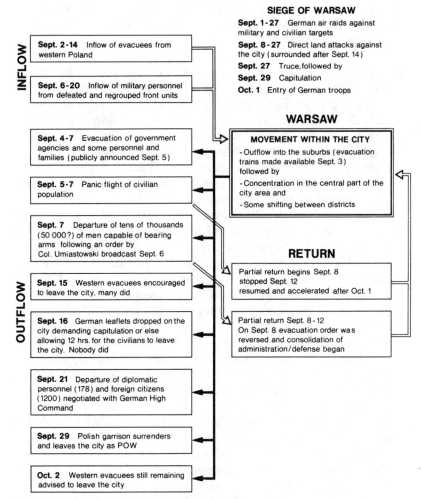

Figure 4-5. Population movements in Warsaw, 1939

prompted many people to return to Warsaw. Here are some examples, all taken from a collection published by the Institute of History (Instytut Historii 1964).

- F. Bożek, who obeyed Umiastowski's order, went to Lublin via Garwolin and Kurów (2 days?) and returned in three days (p. 154)
- M. Dębski evacuated with the personnel of a League of Antiaircraft Defense on September 6 together with a dozen or so other officials and their families (they had a truck and two sedans at their disposal) and reached Lublin, but on September 9 started his return journey by car and returned to Warsaw September 10 at dawn after a difficult drive against the main current of walking refugees (mostly young men) (p. 160)
- A. Nowakowski left Warsaw on September 7, immediately after Umiastowski's appeal (without even saying goodbye to his family) but returned by September 9 from Garwolin, where he heard Starzyński's broadcast. Together with a friend, he walked back overnight and returned to his work in the power plant (p. 170)
- J. Gebethner saw off an evacuation convoy of his publishing company on September 4 (they left for Lwów) but remained himself in Warsaw (p. 177)
- Z. Sosnowski left on September 7 before dawn in a convoy of trucks and cars carrying some 120 persons from the city telephone offices (some could not be notified, others refused to go), and via Ryki reached Lublin with great difficulties caused by traffic jams on roads clogged with pedestrians and horse-drawn carts. Having heard about the decision to defend Warsaw, nearly all decided to return. They took another route via Radzyń, Łuków, Siedlce (bombed and burned out) and reached Warsaw on September 9. The road west of Siedlce was jammed with refugees. Rumors about the destruction of Warsaw and its partial occupation by the Germans prompted some of Sosnowski's comrades to change their minds again and return to Lublin (pp. 382–83)
- W. Zawadzki left on September 7, prompted by Colonel Umiastowski's appeal. Together with a dozen or so fellow city hall employees, they walked via Wawer, Mińsk, and Stoczek to Łuków. There on a city square they heard Starzyński's appeal broadcast over the loudspeakers and decided to return to Warsaw, which they reached on September 10. They hurried as much as they could in spite of heavy counter-traffic of refugees (including city police) and the military in order not to be cut off in the city by

the German column, supposedly moving from the southeast (p. 481)

Apparently Garwolin marked the end of a trek for many evacuees who at that point decided to return (Landau 1962, vol. 1:8). The peak of evacuation occurred on September 7, and September 9 was the day of massive return; but some returnees were getting back as late as September 12, just before the German ring was closed around Warsaw on September 14–15 (Bartoszewski 1959:101, 105). It should also be noted that on September 12 the Warsaw Military Command issued an order not to allow any more evacuees returning from directions of Modlin and Mińsk into the city, but directing them instead to the southeastern periphery in the direction of Otwock (Cieplewicz 1968:76–77).

On the basis of these accounts, one can reconstruct the timing and geographic pattern of short-term evacuation and return (see Figure 4-5). Three other developments related to the September evacuation deserve mention. On September 16, 1939, German dropped leaflets requesting capitulation of the Warsaw garrison and in case of refusal threatening an all-out attack against the city. According to these leaflets, they were prepared to allow twelve hours for civilians to leave in the directions of Siedlce and Garwolin (Cieplewicz 1968:567–68). Evidently hardly anyone took advantages to this offer, although on the same day the officer commanding the eastern section (Praga) issued an order to allow anyone to leave the city who wished to do so but not to admit anybody from the outside (Cieplewicz 1969:77). Apparently the reason for that order was the deteriorating supply situation, and some evacuees from the west did in fact leave the city (Drozdowski and Zahorski 1975:403; Instytut Historii 1964:82).

On September 17, 1939 the German command gave instructions to its units concerning negotiations for the evacuation of the diplomatic corps and civilian population. The latter was never to take place but evacuation of diplomatic corps did occur on September 21. Apparently, after an initial evacuation of diplomats on September 5, several embassies still remained, including the Norwegian, Finnish, and Danish. The dean of the diplomatic corps, Norwegian ambassador Dietleff, negotiated the evacuation, which included 178 diplomats and 1,200 other foreign citizens (Instytut Historii 1964:xxiii, 354).

From the very beginning of the war, Warsaw was also a destination for refugees and evacuees arriving from the west. The first evacuation trains arrived on September 2 (Drozdowski 1975:90), and on September 4 the first civilian refugees from western Poland, from the areas of Częstochowa and Łodź, appeared in the capital (Instytut Historii 1964:xiii). An influx of western evacuees estimated at some 50,000 (Porwit 1959:204) continued and created an additional burden for the city administration. Shelters, food, and medical care for the refugees were organized by a committee of self-help appointed on September 5. Within a few days, 83 evacuation points were established and soon after 269 were active. The number of refugees/evacuees, including local Warsaw residents, registered in these centers exceeded 200,000 by September 8, and shelter was offered to 42,000. Many, however, were still homeless (Beczkowicz 1972:290). Many squatted in apartments abandoned by residents of Warsaw who had left. Some of the new arrivals left with the evacuation wave on September 6–7, some left later, encouraged by the city administration and the remainder apparently left after the capitulation of the city.

The influx of military personnel represented another type of migration. German victories over the Polish armies were followed by arrival of remnants of various units into the city, resulting in the strengthening of its garrison from several thousand on September 4 to some 120,000 after September 20 (Drozdowski 1989).

One should also note considerable movement of population within Warsaw. Even before the outbreak of war, affluent families moved to their suburban cottages or simply extended their vacations there (Podkowa Leśna, Zalesie). There was also some organized evacuation into suburban areas. On the other hand, when fighting was raging in the closer suburbs for nearly two weeks during the siege, many people moved to central parts of the city to stay with their friends or relatives or simply to squat in available space, whether public or private. Apparently all those persons went back to their homes at the end of the siege (Landau 1962, vol. 1:14). Refugees from bombed-out sections of the city were also on the move. Their difficulties continued even later.

All types of movements are presented in Figure 4-5. The total size of the outflow can be estimated at close to 100,000, including: organized evacuation of government agencies with family members, estimated by Drozdowski (1989) at 25,000 to 30,000; evacuation of young men following the appeal of Colonel Umiastowski, probably numbering some 50,000; and outflow of other civilians, including foreigners, rather limited in size, perhaps ca. 10,000. In view of the threat of approaching German armies, the general direction was east and southeast. Trains and trucks were used in the early stage but large masses of people went simply on foot. The distances ranged from a few to several hundred kilometers.[3]

The return began very soon, in some cases after two or three days. Drozdowski (1989) estimates that one-third of those who followed Umiastowski's order returned almost immediately, others became part of the massive flow of refugees. Other evacuees were returning during the month of October 1939 (Landau 1962, vol. 1:31). Probably most of the evacuees eventually returned, but some who managed to leave the country and join the Polish armed forces organized abroad (Middle East, France, later Britain) were to spend several years, if not their entire lives, outside the country.

Demographic Developments in Warsaw, 1940–43

During some four and a half years between the September 1939 campaign and associated events (termed here Warsaw I) and the final exodus of 1944 (Warsaw II) the city's population underwent dramatic changes in every respect, including its size and distribution. Although they can hardly be classified as evacuations, they will be discussed briefly here since the knowledge of this interlude is important for understanding the tragic finale of Warsaw at war.

After the upheavals of September–October 1939, the population of the city began to increase as a result of several factors:

- Return of evacuees and demobilized soldiers, certainly in the tens of thousands
- Influx of persons expelled from western provinces incorporated into the Greater Reich. Their number could be estimated at some 40,000 by mid-1940 (Ratyńska 1982:60)
- Spontaneous influx of Jews from small towns in the area followed by forced transfers into the ghetto, officially created in November 1940. According to Gilbert (1982:55) their number could have exceeded 70,000; he estimates the Western European influx at over 40,000
- Forced transfers of some Western Polish, German, and Belgian Jews into the ghetto

On the other hand, there were considerable outflows of population including:

- Deportations of Jews to annihilation camps (mainly Treblinka). Several waves of these forced moves occurred between July 22 and September 21, 1942 and could have totaled 300,000[4]
- Deportations for forced labor into the Reich estimated at 86,500 from October 1, 1939 to June 10, 1944 (Ratyńska 1982:84)
- Deportations to concentration camps. Apparently some 18,500 were shipped during the period October 1942 to February 1944 (Ratyńska 1982:64)

The total population for Warsaw may have reached a maximum of 1.4 million by the end of 1941/beginning of 1942 (Szarota 1988:70). Its subsequent decline was mainly due to the destruction of the ghetto and extermination of its population. Apparently the population of the ghetto changed as follows: 410,000 in January 1941; 460,000 in March 1941; 380,000 in July 1942; and 60,000 in October 1942 (Berenstein and Rutkowski 1958:78). The last figure is based on official data from the Jewish Council (35,000) augmented by an estimate of those concealed in various bunkers and hideouts.[5] In addition, some 20,000 were hiding on the "Aryan" side (Ratyńska 1982:63).

After the suppression of the uprising of the ghetto, which began April 19, 1943, this part of the city was completely destroyed (after having been thoroughly looted) and depopulated, and its ruins were later used for executions of resistance fighters. According to German sources, during the liquidation of the ghetto some 7,000 perished in the ruins and 56,000 were shipped away to their death. Some survivors apparently managed to sneak away to the "Aryan" side (Drozdowski and Zahorski 1975:441). By the end of July 1944, when the general uprising began in Warsaw, its population had declined to about 1 million, including 950,000 Poles.[6]

Finally, one should mention intracity movements induced by German attempts to segregate the population. From the first days of occupation, attempts were made to create a purely German residential enclave. Officially proclaimed on January 10, 1942, it was implemented, at a reduced scale only, in the spring of 1944, but it caused considerable dislocation of Polish residents evicted from their apartments if they happened to be located in the "wrong" area. By May 1943, some 20,000 had been evicted, but expulsions continued until a year later (Szarota 1988:280, 442–46). Much more extensive were the migrations caused by creating the Jewish ghetto. During approximately six weeks, October to mid-November 1940, 130,000 Jews and 113,000 Christians were forced to change residence (Szarota 1988:62).

All these movements, which affected about one-fifth of the total population, caused considerable hardship and usually led to deterioration of housing conditions. They represented only one of many instruments of humiliation and terror unleashed by the Nazis during five years of occupation. The uprising in 1944 was a desperate attempt by the population of Warsaw to take revenge on the invaders.

Uprising in 1944 and Exodus of Population (Warsaw II)

The 1944 uprising resulted in the almost complete destruction and depopulation of the city. It began on August 1 in all parts of Warsaw and lasted two months. In spite of initial successes, the rebels were never able to control the whole city, and after the initial shock the Germans gradually recovered most of the contested area and forced the rebels to capitulate. The situation was somewhat different on the eastern bank of the Vistula River (Praga), where the uprising was stopped after only three days and German rule reestablished until September 13, when the Red Army moved in.

In view of the approaching battle front, the German administration had panicked in late July, and their trepidation produced a hasty evacuation of some offices and personnel. But the Nazi grip over the city had not been broken yet, as evidenced by the suppression of the uprising. Massacres of both fighters and civilians occurred as a matter of course, particularly in the earlier phase.[7] The civilian population was caught in the fighting and suffered heavy losses, estimated at some 150,000 dead. The survivors were involved in an unprecedented migration, one seen as final by the enemy but as a temporary evacuation by Poles.

Apparently some civilians left the city in the last days of July, either taking vacation in the exurban resorts or simply leaving the city for security reasons in view of the approaching Red Army and the expectation that the river would become a line of German defense. The size of the outflow was estimated by German sources at 100,000 (Madajczyk 1974, vol. 2:698). After the uprising had started, there was considerable movement within the city and eventually outside it. Civilians were trying to escape from areas reconquered by German troops into the areas still held by rebel forces. The largest of these flows, estimated at 60,000, went to Old Town by mid-August (Madajczyk 1974, vol. 1, pt. 1:453). The German military also occasionally forced people to move locally before evicting them. In general, however, the German command decided to remove survivors from the areas under their control. This included residents of the suburbs, where the uprising never succeeded, and from the districts conquered in various stages. Residents of Wola were evicted after August 6, those in Ochota from August 8 to 12; Poles living in Praga were marched across the bridge on August 11 and 24. They were removed from Old Town after its fall on September 2, from Mokotów after September 24, and from Żoliborz after September 30. People were initially concentrated in centers established for this purpose within the city area and later forced to march toward the suburbs or taken by train to transition camps southeast of the city, the largest of which was located in abandoned railway repair yards in Pruszków (known as Durchgangslager or Dulag 121) established as early as August 6. The general policy was to move evacuees through the systems as quickly as possible in order to either ship able-bodied men and women to labor camps in the Reich or dump them in various areas of the General Government still under German control.[8] Some sick and disabled persons were released locally, while many escaped from the marching columns, although the guards shot at escapees, all too often with tragic results.

In early September, the German command offered civilians a chance to leave the beleaguered city. Leaflets dropped from planes were not very specific or reassuring but some people left during the two-day period, September 8–9. Their number was given by Polish sources at 9,000, by Germans at 27,000 (Madajczyk 1974, vol. 1, pt. 1:8), or even more (Korboński 1978:202).

The final evacuation was carried out on the basis of the capitulation agreement signed on October 2. It provided orderly evacuation of both military personnel (guaranteed the right of prisoners of war according to the 1929 Geneva Convention) and civilians, freedom from any prosecution or legal harassment for previous activities, and evacuation of objects with artistic, cultural, or religious importance (Madajczyk 1947, vol. 2:352, 353).

There was considerable difference of opinion as to the size of the expected evacuation. Germans expected 150,000 to 250,000; the Polish Welfare Council (known as RGO) expected 280,000 to 300,000; and the Polish command estimated the likely outflow at 400,000 (Madajczyk 1974, vol. 2:613, 698).

In fact, the outflow after capitulation was much smaller. The log of the German 9th Army recorded 153,519 persons between October 1 and 9 (Korboński 1978:203).[9] In the final report on the uprising prepared by F. Gollert for Governor General H. Frank, the number of civilians who left Warsaw after the capitulation is given as more than 100,000; in addition, there were 17,500 fighting men and women (Madajczyk 1974, vol. 2:698). According to the same source, the camps in Pruszków and Ursus (the latter active only a few days) handled 350,616 persons, who were divided up as follows: 153,810 shipped to Germany for labor (in fact, some ended up in concentration camps); 167,752 distributed throughout General Government (Warsaw, Radom, Cracow districts); 25,926 released locally as sick and disabled; and 3,129 kept in the camp for local work.

Dr. Gollert provided additional data on the distribution of evacuees. Apparently 33,089 were located in Cracow District; 107,224 in Radom District; and 51,554 in the neighboring areas of Warsaw District. However, the actual concentration of Warsaw residents in the three counties closest to the abandoned city was much higher. Including 100,000 persons who left the city prior to the uprising, several tens of thousands who left in the early days before Warsaw was sealed off, and those who returned from Cracow and Radom districts, Gollert estimated the total at 200,000 in Warsaw, Łowicz, and Sochaczew counties (Madajczyk 1974, vol. 2: 700).

In addition, the president of the RGO, K. Tchórznicki, prepared a report based on his contacts with German authorities from October 1 to 6 (Madajczyk 1974, vol. 2:367). In it he mentioned plans made by the Germans for unloading evacuation trains (each carrying 4,000). Cracow District was to receive 52,000 to be unloaded at ten stations; Radom District was scheduled for 52,000 to be unloaded at seven stations; and, in addition, Miechów County was to receive 20,000. Presumably it was only a partial plan since many important destinations were not even mentioned (Częstochowa, Cracow, and areas around Warsaw). Information based on these reports is presented in Figure 4-6. It is obvious there were considerable discrepancies between plans and reality.

The total number of evacuees from Warsaw, whether spontaneous or organized, was much higher than the official German figures. In Polish sources it is usually given at 500,000 to 550,000 (Madajczyk 1974, vol. 1, pt. 1:366; vol. 1, pt. 2:468). This figure seems somewhat closer to the truth, as indicated by the following calculations:

Polish population of Warsaw in summer 1944:	950,000
Of whom the right bank, Praga (assuming same number as in January 1945) accounted for:	140,000
Remaining on the left bank in summer 1944:	810,000

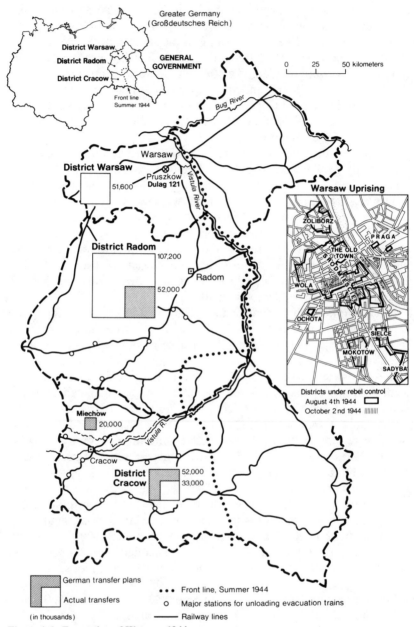

Figure 4-6. Evacuation of Warsaw, 1944

Still present in January 1945:	20,000
Estimate of deaths during the uprising	
(Bartoszewski in Madajczyk 1974, vol. 3:504):	150,000
Implied evacuation, flight, and deportations:	640,000

Should the number of deaths be smaller, as some authors postulate (Strzelecki 1972:357), then the number of evacuees would have been correspondingly higher.

The 1950 *Census* showed 909,000 persons who had lived in Warsaw as of September 1939. Since this number included children born after 1939 (classified according to the responses of their mothers) and excluded those who died after October 1944, one should adjust the total. Subtracting 14 percent (for the children born after 1944) and adding 5 percent (for the subsequently deceased) we arrive at some 820,000 former Warsaw residents presumably alive in January 1945. Of them only 160,000 were found in Warsaw at that time, which leaves 660,000 elsewhere. Since some people may have left before the uprising (including over 100,000 persons deported to camps and forced labor), the estimated evacuation should be reduced correspondingly. On the other hand, there were wartime in-migrants to Warsaw who ended up as evacuees. In addition, some evacuees were still abroad during the *Census*. Consequently, the figure of 600,000 may represent a reasonable approximation.

Immediately after the liberation of Warsaw in January 1945, its survivors began to return. Although the city was hardly habitable, its population began to grow rapidly. In fact, increases, mainly concentrated on the left bank, were estimated at 312,000 in 1945; 65,000 in 1946; 37,000 in 1947; 29,000 in 1948 (see Table 4-5). Nevertheless, a

Table 4-5. Population of Warsaw, 1939–50*

Year	Population	Year	Population
1939	1,310,000	1945	474,000
1940	1,334,000	1946	539,000
1941	1,350,000	1947	576,000
1942	1,027,000	1948	605,000
1943	965,000	1949	638,000
1944	162,000	1950	672,000[1]

*End of year estimates.
[1]According to the census of December 3, 1950, the population of Warsaw was 659,400 of whom 520,000 resided in Warsaw in August 1939. In addition, some 409,000 of former Warsaw residents were enumerated in other parts of Poland. (Children born after 1939 were classified according to previous residence of their mothers.)
Source: Mirowski 1968:49, 64, 75.

large number of former inhabitants did not return. According to the *Census* of December 6, 1950, there were 409,000 such persons enumerated in other parts of Poland. After adjustments for subsequently born children and presumed postwar deaths, the number can be reduced to 373,000, a value that represents slightly more than half the evacuees (calculated by the same method). Admittedly, some of them may have left Warsaw before 1944, others may have returned to Warsaw after the war but left subsequently; but even if the proportion is reduced by half it still shows a very considerable long-term consequence of the 1944 evacuation.

One can speculate as to how much the dispersal of Warsaw's population contributed to a certain social homogenization that has occurred in postwar Poland. Former residents of Warsaw were conspicuously present in many areas of the country in both the old and the newly repopulated northern and western provinces.

Conclusion

Among the many demographic events affecting Warsaw's population during World War II, two can be defined as evacuations. Comparing them reveals both similarities and differences.

Size. Warsaw II (550,000) was at least five times greater then Warsaw I (up to 100,000). In relative terms, Warsaw II affected 58 percent of the population at risk, whereas Warsaw I involved only 8 percent.

Direction. Both were biased by war-related events. Warsaw I was directed east–southeast, whereas Warsaw II was skewed south–southwest.

Duration. The Warsaw I evacuation occupied several days, while the return lasted several weeks; the Warsaw II exodus extended over two months, and the first returnees were able to come back after only a three-month absence.

Degree of spontaneity. In the case of Warsaw I, decisions were made essentially by individuals, even if in some cases official orders were given; in Warsaw II extreme danger and physical force all but eliminated freedom of decision.

Transportation means. In Warsaw I, trains, trucks, and cars were used, but in many instances people walked, particularly those who returned early. In Warsaw II, people were marched to assembly points (sometimes a distance of several kilometers) and later shipped by trains.

Demographic consequences. The impact of Warsaw II was obviously much larger and of much greater duration of both city and host areas than was the case for Warsaw I.

FRANCE (AND THE LOW COUNTRIES), 1939–40

The early stages of the Second World War had a unique impact upon French society by causing massive flows of population that affected virtually the entire country. Past experience, including the First World War and growing international tensions in Europe during the late 1930s, prompted the French government to prepare an elaborate evacuation plan that was partially implemented in 1939–40. This episode is treated here as France I. The German invasion in May and June 1940 caused a huge outflow of population from areas threatened or occupied by enemy forces. Known as "l'Exode," this movement involved not only the French but also Belgians and, to a much smaller extent, the Dutch and Luxembourgeois. It will be discussed here under the code name France II. Most evacuees returned relatively quickly in late summer/early fall 1940.

The literature on this subject is relatively limited, but the interested reader can rely on a few major works. An early study by J. Vidalenc (1957) deals with both the early evacuation and the "Exode" proper. It was based on extensive interviews with both decision makers and participants. Over a decade later, another weighty volume appeared (Ollier 1970) in which the author made extensive use of archival materials. The specific case of Brittany, which was one of the principal destinations, has been treated by A. Meynier (1950), who relied on an extensive network of informants. In addition, we have consulted several other important documents: an early study published as an appendix to a book by Padley and Cole (1940); a provisional summary of Vidalenc (1951); a case study of a specific southern commune (Laurens 1980); a chapter in Sauvy's book on the occupation (1978); and an article on repatriation by Lagrange (1977). E. Gerber (1941) presented a contemporary German view, and a dispassionate analysis appeared after the war in a periodical devoted to civilian anti-air raid protection ("Dokumentarischer Bericht" 1956–57). Examples of journalistic accounts are booklets in French (De la Hire 1940) and German (van Wehrt 1941). The Belgian exode, partially overlapping the French flight, was described in a book derived from a series of programs aired by the Belgian radio and television network RTBF (Vanwelkenhuyzen and Dumont 1983).

French Evacuation Plan

The French planners considered the possibility of evacuating civilians, but only in anticipation of artillery bombardment or, to some extent, air raids, not a retreating French army. Although various instructions were issued from time to time, planning and preparation had to be done very discreetly so as not to create unnecessary panic.[10] Nevertheless, as early as 1930–31, preparation began for long-distance and long-term evacuations, including identification of destination areas. The list of départements to be evacuated was compiled in 1935 and revised in 1938. In addition, the list of destination départements was modified in the latter year and areas of departure matched with those of arrival (Vidalenc 1957:17–18). In total, eighteen départements with an aggregate population of 12.6 million were to be completely or partially emptied of nonessential population, and forty-one départements were identified as possible places of temporary asylum. In addition, evacuation of the principality of Monaco was envisaged (see Figure 4-7). The largest block of eleven départements, extending to both coasts, was reserved for residents of the Paris metropolitan area. Brittany was to accommodate evacuees from the northernmost frontier areas. Evacuees from the remainder of the frontier zone were to be directed to southwestern France.

The evacuation plan contained instructions on routing. For example, evacuees from the Nord were supposed to concentrate in the neighboring Pas-de-Calais before being dispersed among various destinations in Brittany. Aisne was to serve as a transit area for evacuees from Ardennes, even though Aisne itself was to be evacuated as well. Special attention was devoted to the Paris region (Seine Département), whose inhabitants were to be dispersed among eleven départements. In this case, various districts of Paris and its suburbs were matched with specific départements elsewhere. For example, evacuees from east-central Arrondissements 4 and 5, as well as the rather distant suburbs of Colombes, Puteaux (both in the north), and eastern Vincennes, were to go to maritime Calvados. The Département of Maine-et-Loire, accessible from the Austerlitz and Montparnasse stations, was to accommodate inhabitants of the relevant contiguous Arrondissements 13 and 15. Département Eure was reserved for the wealthy 16th Arrondissement.

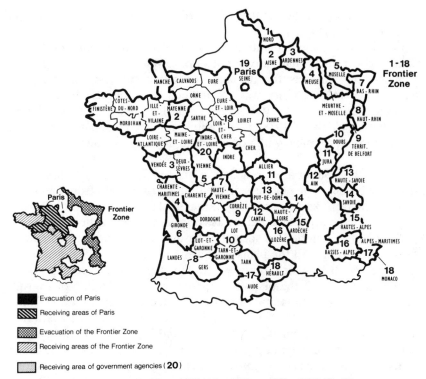

Figure 4-7. French evacuation plan, 1939 (Adapted from Ollier 1970:38–40)

In discussing this plan, Vidalenc (1957:22–25) pointed out its rather abstract character. For example, no notice was taken of a concentration of recent in-migrants from Brittany, who, instead of being sent back to their native region, were assigned to the Loire area. Similarly, there was no provision for sending people originating from Auvergne, concentrated around the Lyon and Austerlitz stations and Place de la République (Arrondissements 3, 4, and 5), to their native Massif Central. Furthermore, neighbors from across the street may have ended up in widely separated destination areas.

Evacuation was to have been principally by those trains used to bring military personnel to Paris before sending them on to the frontier zone. A total of 232 trains were to leave the Paris region every day, including 81 regular trains, 113 additional, and 38 special ones. All planning was based on the assumption that evacuation would be orderly and uninterrupted. There was to be flexibility in train destinations depending on the number of tickets sold for different directions (Vidalenc 1957:25).

Finally, one should mention a special evacuation plan for those central government institutions that were to relocate to Indre-et-Loire Département, famous for its chateaux along the river Loire. For example, Foreign Affairs was to proceed to Langeais, Finance to Chinon, Education to Azay-le-Rideau, and Parliament to Tours. After the Munich Crisis of 1938, preparations for accommodating various institutions were made with considerable urgency (Vidalenc 1957:26–27).

Within the frontier area, evacuation was to affect places up to 20 km from the border. The planners divided this territory into front and rear zones. The front zone (potentially threatened by actual hostilities) was to be automatically evacuated in case of general mobilization. The rear zone would be emptied on special order and only after the evacuation of the front zone. All the plans were worked out by the Service de la Défense Passive, which reported to the Ministry of Defense. An important aspect of the planning process was the selection of transit camps with adequate sanitary facilities located 20 to 30 km away from the border, not very far from the railway stations. These camps were actually strips extending some 7 to 8 km and included several villages capable of accommodating 10,000 to 15,000 evacuees each. A German source discusses evacuation procedures, as well as actual evacuation of the frontier belt in 1939 ("Dokumentarischer Bericht" 1956–57).

Evacuation in 1939 (France I)

Mounting political tensions in Europe in 1938 produced the first waves of spontaneous evacuation. In September of that year both the stories in the alarmist press and a statement by the minister of Public Works warning residents of the frontier region to leave while trains were still operating normally encouraged many people to travel west. Even though the Munich agreement calmed the atmosphere, at least temporarily, by the spring of 1939 apprehension was growing again.[11] Apparently quite a number of people from the Lille area rented apartments in Brittany, or, when leasing vacation homes for the summer of 1939, inquired about the possibility of extending the lease through the winter of 1940, or shipped some of their more valuable furniture to friends in the West (Meynier 1950:11). The immediate crisis may have subsided, but the inhabitants of the frontier area remained jittery. In any case, such early preoccupation with safety provided some knowledge that was undoubtedly helpful in the days to come.

The German invasion of Poland on September 1, 1939 and a subsequent declaration of war by France and Britain on September 3 increased the level of anxiety even though actual hostilities were taking place only on the Polish front. Nevertheless, a massive evacuation of the frontier belt began September 2, the same day that general mobilization was proclaimed throughout France.[12] The area affected extended along the entire French–German border, that is, in the three départements of Alsace-Moselle, Bas-Rhin, and Haut-Rhin. The number of people requiring evacuation was estimated at 365,000, which meant the use of 304 trains ("Dokumentarischer Bericht" 1956–57:48).

The first measures were implemented at 4:00 A.M., and within six hours all posts were apparently occupied. Evacuation proceeded rapidly and, on the whole, very smoothly, with no interference by the enemy. People first assembled in transit camps where, in some cases, they had to wait until the next day for evacuation trains departing key stations. For example, for Moselle Département, the initial concentration in Metz came from Delme, Hampont, Bourdonnay, Axandge, Pfalzburg, and Moyeuver, and, subsequently, 130 evacuation trains carrying some 160,000 persons left that city. Inhabitants of Bas-Rhin evacuated from Saverne (162,500 in 138 trains), and 42,000 persons (36 trains) left Haut-Rhin from Colmar. They reached their initial destinations, located 550 to 750 km away, the same day or the next, and shortly thereafter they arrived at the host communities using local trains for the final leg of the journey ("Dokumentarischer Bericht" 1967–57:48). Evacuation of Strasbourg's 250,000 inhabitants was accomplished in twenty-four hours (Vidalenc 1957:35).[13] Nearly all evacuees went to the départements assigned to them in the evacuation plan (see Figure 4-7). There is no doubt that, despite some problems, the compulsory evacuation of Alsace was a success; but one should keep in mind a number of favorable factors, including the exceptional awareness of inhabitants (going back to the experience of the First World War), the favorable season of the year, the substantial presence of the military, and the absence of hostilities.

Alsace was not the only region affected in the fall of 1939. Some 550,000 people left the Paris region on a voluntary basis, and some government services were also dispersed into three départements along the Loire River (Vidalenc 1957:38,40). Evacuation proceeded in two major waves. Initially, between September 2 and 12, evacuation trains carried mainly women and children. It should be remembered that the time of the year did much to simplify evacuation, as many children, who were away on holidays, simply did not return to Paris. The number of schoolchildren who stayed away was estimated at 112,000 (Padley and Cole 1940:289). The second exodus occurred around September 20–22. For example, on September 25, a special evacuation train conveying radio personnel brought some 700 Parisians, including 350 musicians and singers along with the famous director D. E. Inghel-brecht, to Rennes (Meynier 1950:13–14).

The decision to suspend all classes of upper secondary schools preparing candidates for so-called *grandes écoles,* the elite post-secondary establishments, prompted another type of evacuation. They were to be closed in an area located to the north and east of the line extending from Le Havre, running south of Paris to Dijon, Lyon, and the Rhone River. At the same time, the University of Paris introduced restrictions whereby only residents from the region could enroll. The net result was the movement of a considerable number of students, their parents, and some of the teachers to the west, particularly Brittany (Meynier 1950:13–14). Various cities experienced local disper-sion of population, even some relatively small ones. Thus, some 11,000 persons evacuated from Lille to Hesdin and Montreuil, 90 to 110 km away (Vidalenc 1957:41).

It appears that somewhere between 1,000,000 and 1,250,000 persons evacuated during September 1939. Their lengthy stay caused all sorts of problems, including cultural conflicts with the local populations, unemployment, and overcrowding. On the other hand, the expected hostilities and bombardments did not materialize during the winter of *"drôle-de-guerre"* and many people drifted back. For example, on October 1, 1939 the number of evacuees in the Département of Loire-Inférieure was estimated at 82,000, including 22,000 from the Paris region and 60,000 from elsewhere. By May 1, 1940 only 13,000 evacu-ees remained, including 12,000 from Paris (Meynier 1950:13). Presum-ably the proportion of returnees was much lower among the Alsatians since their area was closed by the army. Only some 5,000 persons remained in Strasbourg throughout the winter of 1939–40 ("Dokumen-tarischer Bericht" 1956–57:72).

Even if the majority of evacuees had returned home by October (Ollier 1970:31), there was still a considerable number in temporary lodgings when the winter of 1939 set in. Schools evacuated from the north or from Paris stayed on and with them their students, some parents, and teachers. The presence of large numbers of evacuees stimulated the level of economic activity, the circulation of people, goods, and information, and influenced prices, as well as increasing demand for space, both residential and institutional (Meynier 1950:19–20).

Evacuees, particularly those who stayed longer, fell into several categories. The more affluent among them were able to buy or lease decent accommodation, and they undoubtedly contributed to the local economy, even though shopping trips to Paris or frequent visits by heads of households who remained behind indicated that some evacuees still operated within their customary activity space. Apparently many treated evacuation as an extension of vacations, and there are reports of a rather lively social life in various western cities and resorts (Ollier 1970:149). Persons evacuated with their factories or those directed to garrison cities or centers of military production were usually well taken care of. Those at the lower end of the socioeconomic scale competed for scarce jobs in local markets. The hard-working local population resented public assistance payments received by evacuees. Shared accommodations and overcrowding could hardly contribute to harmonious relationships. There are stories of unreasonable demands and complaints on the part of the newcomers, alleged damage to housing space, growing "compassion fatigue," and the indifference or hostility on the part of the hosts. It is interesting to note that the 1939 evacuees did not move very much in the spring of the following year and had little sympathy for the participants of the great exodus of 1940 (Ollier 1970:149).

L'Exode 1940 (France II)

The uneasy quiet prevailing throughout the winter of 1939–40 was shattered in the spring when Germany launched a sudden attack against her western neighbors and after a relatively short campaign forced them to capitulate. Some key dates relevant for our discussion are worth noting.

10 May	German offensive begins
15 May	The Netherlands capitulates
17 May	Germans enter Brussels
29 May–	Remnants of the British Expeditionary Force and
2 June	some French and Belgian survivors are evacuated
	from besieged Dunkerque

4 June	Belgium capitulates
10 June	Italy declares war on France
10 June	French government leaves Paris for Tours
14 June	French government moves from Tours to Bordeaux
14 June	Paris taken by the Germans
22 June	Armistice signed between France and Germany
24 June	Armistice signed between France and Italy
25 June	Demarcation line between occupied and unoccupied France established (see Figure 4-9)
25 June	New French government moves from Bordeaux to Vichy
3 July	Exclusion zone introduced in northeastern France (see Figure 4-9)

The Western campaign involved not only massive movements of troops but also of civilians who at first were trying to escape from the advancing German armies and later to return home or, in some cases, to continue their trek in search of safe haven. The total number of evacuees, both spontaneous and organized, is estimated at close to 15 million.

Belgians and Luxemburgeois were the first to take to the road, along with some Dutch. The French joined the exodus a little later, but their numbers were significantly higher. Luxembourg was overrun almost immediately; nevertheless some 70,000, or almost 25 percent of its population, managed to escape to France, partly through Belgium.

In the Netherlands there were hardly any planned evacuations, even though there existed a Dutch Committee for Evacuation of Civilian Population. The French troops who entered Netherlands territory at the very beginning of hostilities did evacuate the population of Breda, moving them to Antwerp, but this is the only known case of compulsory evacuation. In addition, there was some spontaneous evacuation, particularly Jews from Amsterdam. In total, some 100,000 people are said to have left their homes, of whom one-third were overtaken by the German troops and returned home by May 14 (Vidalenc 1957:63–70). Some Dutch evacuees crossed into France, but any sizable movement was impossible since evacuation routes were cut off by the swift thrust of German armies into Belgium. Their number was estimated at 50,000, or less than one percent of the Dutch population at the time.[14]

In Belgium, many substantial movements occurred and the majority of them spilled across the borders. Most happened spontaneously but some were initiated by the authorities, even though earlier discussions and war games persuaded Belgian authorities that any attempt to evacuate large numbers on short notice would be futile, and a statement to this effect was issued in February 1940 (Vanwelkenhuyzen and Dumont 1983:18). Evacuation and flight began in Belgium at the very outset of the invasion on May 10, and the situation kept changing rapidly. On the very next day, the question of separating streams of civilians from counter-streams of the armies (Belgian as well as French and British coming to the rescue) was raised. In addition, problems of a dwindling food supply quickly developed, while the matter of inadequate housing and maintaining law and order became critical, and remained so for the rest of the campaign.

Most evacuation was spontaneous but some was ordered by the military (Belgian as well as Allied); some was precipitated by the government appeal to men sixteen to thirty-five years of age to retreat behind the lines. The fate of this so-called *"réserve de recrutement"* will be discussed separately. In addition, various government agencies—personnel together with family members—were evacuated. The rapid deterioration of the military situation was reflected in the sequence of evacuations (see Table 4-6). A growing wave of evacuees soon spilled over into France, ultimately reaching its southernmost areas, and a trickle thereof continued later via Spain and Portugal to the Belgian Congo, Britain, and elsewhere. A segment of this fleeing mass was cut off by the Germans in the Flanders pocket, and, apart from those very few who succeeded in crossing over to Britain, began returning home after hostilities ended. Repatriation of Belgian evacuees from France took more time. The entire process was chaotic and panic was widespread with many cases of looting and violence. In addition, Belgians, especially with Flemish, often faced harassment and arrest by the French authorities, particularly after Belgium's capitulation.

Any initial confidence on the part of the Belgian government quickly evaporated with the realization that the capital was no longer safe, and evacuation of its agencies began on May 12. Oostende and Ypres were the initial destinations; on May 18–19 the government left for France with the intention of establishing itself in Le Havre, but a few days later Poitier became the virtual capital of Belgium for the duration of hostilities. Some members of the cabinet escaped via Dunkerque but later returned to the Continent to join their colleagues in Paris on May 25 (Vanwelkenhuyzen and Dumont 1983:82). The king remained in Belgium but the royal children were evacuated first to France (near Bayeux) and eventually on June 22 to Spain, but on August 4 returned

Table 4-6A. Chronology of Evacuation in Western Europe, May 1940

May 1940	The Netherlands	Belgium	France
10	Arnhem, Nijmegen, Maëstricht, Amsterdam	Verviers	
11	Tilburg, Leiden, Utrecht	Liège, Antwerp	Sedan
12	Rotterdam, Breda, Dordrecht	Namur, Charleroi	Charleville, Mézières
13	South Rotterdam	Brussels, Mons	Avesnes, Maubeuge, St. Quentin, Hirson
14	Middleburg, Walcheren, Vlissingen	Oostende, Gent	Cambrai, Douai, Vervins, Montmédy
15		Courtrai, Ypres	Calais, St. Omer, Hazebrouck, St. Pol, Laon
16			Dunkerque, Lille, Arras, Montreuil, Amiens
17			Boulogne, Abbeville
18			St. Amand-les-Eaux, Le Quesnoy
19			Aulnoy
20			Valenciennes
21			
22			Thionville, Lens, Béthune
23			
24			Armentières

Source: Ollier 1970:292–93.

Table 4-6B. Chronology of Evacuation in France, June 1940

June 1940	France		
4	Poix-sur-Somme, Péronne, Montdidier, Soissons	13	Chartres/Caen/Verdun
5	Ham, Creil	14	Orléans/Le Mans, Cherbourg Nancy, Bar-le-Duc, Lunéville
6	Roye, Elbeuf	15	Tours, Poitiers/Rennes, St.-Malo, Nantes/Besançon, Epinal, Autun, Clamecy
7	Forges-les-Eaux, Meulan, Pontoise/Senlis	16	Sully-sur-Loire, Saumur/Metz, Toul, Pontarlier
8	Chantilly, Paris/Dieppe, Yvetot, Vernon, Les Andelys/Château-Thierry	17	Guéret, Moulins/La Rochelle/ Jura, Lyon
9	Fécamp, Saint-Valery-en-Caux	18	Limoges, Clermont-Ferrand, St.-Etienne/Angoulême
10	Beauvais/Reims/Italian frontier zone between Menton and Cannes	19	Grenoble
11	Rouen	20	Bordeaux, Marseille
12	Le Havre, Evreux, Honfleur/ Troyes, Commercy		

Source: Ollier 1970:292–93.

to Belgium accompanied by a courteous German escort (Vanwelken-huyzen and Dumont 1983:147, 288).

Young men were ordered on May 14 to assemble at various points in western Flanders, including Binche, Ypres, and Roulers, to form a reserve force for the army. Some 500,000 to 600,000 men were in-volved, and in many cases whole families followed as well. The changing fortunes of war affected this particular category of evacuees, some of whom were evacuated to France, while others were directed to Oostende, where there was an attempt to create a reception center between May 21 and 23, with the hope of evacuating the young men via Dunkerque. After Belgian capitulation, the centers lost their pur-pose and potential recruits returned home. However, radio appeals encouraged those in France to reach Toulouse where a new organiza-tion called *Centres de Recrutement de l'Armée Belge* (CRAB) came into being. The first trains with young men arrived on May 22 and their number had greatly increased by May 25, 18,700 being enumerated in Toulouse and 30,000 in Nîmes. French sources suggest the following distribution as of June 27: Gard, 40,000; Hérault, 20,000; Haute-Garonne, 40,000; Ardèche, 40,000.

CRAB was organized into companies of 250, some of which were immediately used as labor battalions that were relatively well treated by their employers. Others languished in very poor conditions, in camps that had been hastily established for earlier refugees of the Spanish civil war. After Belgium's capitulation, the attitude of the French authorities changed and there were attempts to intern the CRAB members or their officers. On the other hand, some were sent as labor battalions to work on fortifications in the last desperate moments of the campaign. Finally, after France's collapse, CRAB members were to be considered civilian refugees and returned to Belgium (Vanwelkenhuyzen and Dumont 1983:121, 217, 224, 254).

The massive evacuation flows from Belgium, of which government officials and CRAB members were but a small part, included millions of persons. At least 2 million of them crossed into France (about one-quarter of the country's population).[15] On May 12, the Belgian government demanded and obtained the right of open entry to France for its citizens upon presentation of a simple identity card, and the massive influx started the next day. Evacuation of various cities and regions began on May 10 and continued for the rest of the month (see Table 4-6). Trains were initially used, even though they were increasingly unreliable, as many ended up in unexpected places. On May 19, train movement finally stopped. At the same time, all sorts of vehicles, including pushcarts and bicycles, were used and many people simply went on foot. A massive outflow from the capital city began on May 13 and continued with increasing intensity and apprehension for several days. The main directions were: Gent-Brugge-Oostende, Mons-Paris, and Ninove-Courtrai-Lille (Vanwelkenhuyzen and Dumont 1983:33).

The first evacuation trains reached Paris on May 10 and preparations began immediately for assistance and relief. Medical personnel were stationed in the Gare du Nord and Gare de L'Est stations. At that point 800,000 evacuees were expected, of whom 200,000 would be directed to England. The number was four times higher than that mentioned in April in secret talks carried out in Paris by a Belgian deputy, Ernest Adam, with the French deputy minister in charge of refugee services, Robert Schuman (Vanwelkenhuyzen and Dumont 1983:145, 153). The actual total turned out to be much much higher. The number of evacuation trains reaching Paris increased after May 13; the first train reached Angers on May 14, Toulouse on May 15, and Poitiers on May 16 (Vanwelkenhuyzen and Dumont 1983:153–54). The concentration of government services in Poitiers, which quickly became overcrowded, influenced distribution of Belgian evacuees in France.

On May 25 the prefect of Vienne introduced regulations allowing Belgians to reside in his département without special permission, but by that time many offices were already established in its capital, Poitiers, and Toulouse had become a Belgian university center (Ollier 1970:273). Initially, Belgian authorities advised refugees that six départements were reserved for that purpose, while the Département of Côte-d'Or was to accommodate Luxembourgeois. At the same time the French announced that only three départements were reserved for Belgians, Côte-d'Or was to be shared by Belgians and Luxembourgeois, and Belgians were advised to leave the neighboring départements of Gironde, Charante-Inférieure, Landes, Haute, and Basses-Pyrénnées (Vanwelkenhuyzen and Dumont 1983:189). These contradictory instructions seem to imply some confusion, inevitable under the circumstances, among the authorities, both Belgian and French. To make matters worse, the French minister of interior, quoting reasons of security, introduced compulsory registration of all Belgians, Dutch, and Luxembourgeois who arrived after May 10. Registration was to take place between May 27 and 31, and any unregistered foreigners were threatened with internment (Vanwelkenhuyzen and Dumont 1983:190). Confusion increased after the king surrendered the Belgian army on May 28. Although the Belgian government in France declared its willingness to continue the fight, the French did not hide their contempt for their northern brothers, who were often victimized by local authorities or private citizens (Vanwelkenhuyzen and Dumont 1983:213).

During the next three weeks, Belgians were affected by the general confusion and gradual collapse of France. The transfer of the French government, first to Tours (June 10) and subsequently to Bordeaux (June 14), provoked further redistribution of refugees and evacuees. For example, on June 10 the prefect of Gironde ordered all refugees, Belgian as well as French, to vacate the capital city of Bordeaux and the area 20 km around it as well as other cities and their surroundings within three days (Vanwelkenhuyzen and Dumont 1983:247). On June 15, the Belgian government was ordered to vacate Poitiers within twenty-four hours. Instead, the cabinet went to Bordeaux and, upon learning about the imminent capitulation of France, decided to stop further resistance against German forces, to organize repatriation of Belgian evacuees, and to return to Belgium. Only one member of the cabinet, Marcel-Henri Jaspar, left for England to continue the struggle (Vanwelkenhuyzen and Dumont 1983:251–53).

The great exodus of French population began on May 10. The military situation influenced its magnitude, timing, and direction. Since the invasion bypassed the fortifications along the Franco–German border, known as the Maginot Line, the first areas affected were the northern départements: Nord, Ardennes, Meuse, and Aisne, with an aggregate population of ca. 4 million. Evidently some 2 million French were on their way during the first week (Gerber 1941:14). The scale of evacuations can be seen from the figures for the Lille agglomeration. The population of Lille proper declined from 200,000 to 20,000, that of Roubaix from 122,000 to 15,000, and Tourcoing was reduced from 82,000 to 7,000 (Vidalenc 1957:100). This implies the departure of 90 percent of their inhabitants from these three urban centers. Evacuation trains were funneled through Paris where 123 reception centers with a capacity of 25,000 places were established for the transients. From May 15 onward they were always full, but hardly anyone stayed in Paris for any length of time since connections with the rest of the country still functioned well (Ollier 1970:124). Other evacuees took coastal routes toward Rouen and Le Havre. Some of them returned home briefly when the German offensive stalled and the action concentrated around Dunkerque.[16] A great wave of evacuees crawling along the roads hit Paris on May 17, and this alarmed the capital's population, particularly since the smell of burning government documents had been hanging over the city since the previous day (Vidalenc 1957:123; Ollier 1970:122). Although the French government was advised about the threat to the capital as early as May 16, evacuation was considered but not yet implemented (Ollier 1970:117).

The French government used the period between May 20 and June 4 to reduce the confusion and assure the population that premature evacuation was unnecessary and sometimes, in fact, provoked by the enemy (Vidalenc 1957:162). Apparently some evacuation trains were even sent back. By the end of the lull, only a small part of France had been occupied by the Germans.

The final German offensive began on June 5, and within a few days their successful breakthrough prompted a second, much more massive phase of the exodus (see Figure 4-8). Its most important component was the evacuation of Paris. By May 27, small posters appeared in apartment houses advising residents about recommended destinations in case anyone would wish to leave. They only identified the départements, thus were rather general, but did contribute to the feelings of

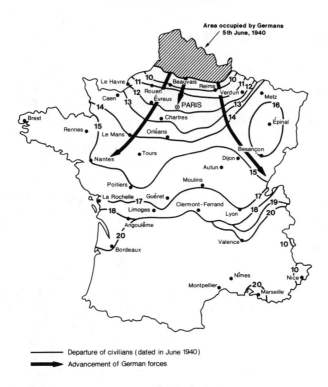

Figure 4-8. Average date of departure during the French exode in 1940 (Source: Vidalenc 1957–173)

apprehension. The gradual process of emptying the city began, objects from the museums were removed, government offices evacuated, more and more shops were closed. Until the end of May, trains ran on schedule, and although sleeping cars as well as first- and second-class cars were full, third-class seats were available (Ollier 1970:124, 131). Post offices closed on June 1, telegraph services on June 5; a day later it became difficult to travel by train to Normandy; on June 8, St. Lazare Station was closed. In the first serious air attack against Paris on June 3, 254 persons lost their lives.

On June 9, the minister of information assured the public that the government would stay in Paris no matter what might happen; the next day the government left for Tours. A shock wave resulted and panic-stricken people started leaving en masse. During the June 10–12 period, some 2 million persons left Paris and the surrounding Département of Seine (Ollier 1970:139). Within four days, forty-five special trains evacuated government personnel and 7,000 tons of records. Extra trains became available to the public but they could not meet the demand.[17] Roads were jammed as masses of vehicles and people moved south at a snail's pace. On June 13, Paris was declared an open city, and the next day German troops entered the capital. The same day the French government left Tours for Bordeaux, having ordered the prefects to try stopping any further exodus (Vidalenc 1957:301).

Panic-stricken, masses of evacuees tried to reach the Loire and cross the river. The bridges could not handle the traffic, and for the next four days pandemonium continued, further aggravated by repeated air attacks by Italian planes, Italy having declared war against France on June 10. The rolling surge of the exodus continued, government restraining orders notwithstanding. At that point the number of people on the road had probably reached its maximum, estimated by Gerber (1941:18) at 12 million.

Apart from the main wave pushing southward in advance of the German armies, another stream of evacuees was moving westward toward Brittany. The speed of the German advance and continued fighting at various points made civilian movements particularly hazardous. Interestingly enough, initial fears regarding the behavior of German troops subsided and hatred was redirected toward those French and Allied troops who continued doing their soldierly duty by fighting the invaders. Not infrequently, mayors clashed with military commanders or tried to surrender their cities without consulting the army (Ollier 1970:163). Finally, one should mention a relatively small evacuation movement along the French–Italian border following the Italian attack against France (Vidalenc 1957:230).

On June 17, Marshal Pétain, who had succeeded P. Reynaud as head of state, announced cessation of military action and entered negotiations with the Germans, which resulted in an official end of hostilities on June 25. The exode ended officially on June 18, when all urban centers over 20,000 were delcared "open cities," and all prefects received appropriate instructions from the minister of interior (Ollier 1970:164).

Most people who participated in the 1940 exodus went by train, at least part of the way, but evacuees also used roads or even went by sea. There were three categories of evacuation by train (Meynier 1950:43):

- Voluntary evacuation, taking place not less than four days before arrival of the enemy, in which passengers who traveled by regular

trains, having paid full fare, were able to check in their luggage, and arrived on time
- Compulsory evacuation in special trains without any charge
- Evacuation that began as voluntary but because of the speed and direction of the enemy advance became compulsory in the sense that trains changed their routing and schedules

In the latter two cases, one could expect various inconveniences, including hasty embarkation, the need to walk long distances to reach the train,[18] limitation of baggage to 30 kg, slow travel, uncertain route and destination, the need to change trains, and the ever-present danger of bombing.

In the case of evacuation by road, municipal buses or commercial trucks and vans were used for organized movements. Otherwise people availed themselves of private cars, horse-drawn carts, motorcycles, and bicycles, or simply went on foot, sometimes pulling or pushing a small cart. Although car owners were less restricted in terms of baggage and route, they often crawled slowly on jammed roads, risking breakdowns and lack of fuel. Meynier quotes cases where twenty-four hours were needed to cover a distance of 14 km (Versailles to Chevreuse). Frequent document controls at numerous checkpoints and controlled routing caused additional delays. Whatever roads were open for traffic were often jammed, while parallel routes were restricted or not utilized at all. Since military convoys and civilians were allowed to share the same routes, increased danger and confusion were the results. Perhaps those traveling by motorcycle or bicycle were relatively fortunate since their mobility was not restricted by traffic jams, but, on the other hand, their payload was rather limited.

People who walked usually continued doing so only for a relatively short distance, hoping to reach an assembly point or an operating train station. There are, however, stories of long-distance hikes, such as from Rouen to Rennes, 300 km in eight days (Meynier 1950:60). In a very few cases, evacuees boarded ships along the northern coast or elsewhere in order to escape to Britain or Africa. Such expatriation, however, meant the beginning of a longer absence that can hardly be treated as a temporary evacuation.

Since the weather was on the whole excellent, the problem of accommodation was not critical. On the other hand, food and water were often at a premium, and there were cases of looting and stealing as well as excessive profiteering. One reads about exorbitant prices demanded by the locals for a glass of water.

Urban dwellers were involved in evacuation to a much greater degree than rural residents and there was an overrepresentation of women and children. All social classes were affected, but there was an interesting pecking order in terms of timing. As noted earlier, the trains leaving Paris prior to the mass exodus had their first- and second-class sections fully occupied, while third-class seats remained available (Ollier 1970:124). A similar hierarchy was visible on the roads, as witnessed by more than one observer, particularly in the earlier days. Large chauffeur-driven cars of the rich were followed by smaller cars (which broke down more often); trucks and vans came later with their mixture of civilians, soldiers, and all sorts of baggage; after a further interval, bicycles, and then people on foot completed the unprecedented procession (Vidalenc 1957:140).

The distances covered by evacuees varied, but in many instances they amounted to hundreds of kilometers. For example, road distances between major cities in question are as follows: Lille to Paris, 219; Lilles to Rennes, 565; Paris to Bordeaux, 559; Brussels to Toulouse, 968.

The studies treating this exodus mention disorganization and panic over and over again.[19] Attempts by the government to control the flow and, in the latter stages, to arrest it were not successful. In fact, Meynier argues that contradictory and poorly timed (either too early or too late) evacuation orders contributed to the chaos along with premature evacuation or flight by those responsible for orderly removal of people from risk areas (1950:36). Bombing and strafing by enemy planes, particularly by the Italian air force after June 10, caused loss of life and contributed to the general disorder (Ollier 1970:50, 127, 60; Vidalenc 1957:286).

Attitudes toward evacuees covered a wide spectrum of behavior, from helpful empathy to economic exploitation to hostile indifference. It seems that, on the whole, people in the west (Brittany) were less sympathetic than those in the south. On the other hand, evacuees were often guilty of aggressive behavior, including break-ins, stealing, and pillaging, in both areas abandoned by inhabitants who fled earlier and those places that were inhabited (Ollier 1970:161, 174).

It is next to impossible to establish with certainty how many people participated in the 1940 exodus. A maximum figure of 12 million at any given date (around June 14) is offered by Gerber (1941:18). Alfred Sauvy, a foremost demographic authority in France and witness to the event, also estimates the total number of persons who left their domicile in France in May–June 1940 at 12 million. The *Census* taken in unoccupied France in mid-August 1940 yielded a sizable 2.5 million of evacuees still awaiting repatriation (see Table 4-7), but this residual figure must be regarded as inadequate, reflecting as it does the situation after a large number of evacuees had returned home. German sources mention 4 million evacuees awaiting repatriation in the unoccupied zone alone by mid-August (Gerber 1941:121). Sauvy feels that the maximum number in the unoccupied zone was more like 10 million, as compared to a prewar population in this area of 13 million (Sauvy 1978:121). In his address announcing the armistice, Pétain spoke of 10 million (Ollier 1970:260). The figure of 12 million is accepted by Ollier (1970:14).

In discussions held on July 8, 1940 between German and French functionaries charged with organizing repatriation, the figure of 8 million was mentioned, including 7 million French (equally divided between the occupied and Vichy zones), 1 million Belgians, and 150,000 Dutch and Luxemburgers. The figure of 7 million appears again in a note prepared by the French directorate for refugees dated March 7, 1941 (Lagrange 1977:49). J. Vidalenc estimates the total number of evacuees at 6 million in addition to another 6 million directly affected by the exodus (1957:359). For the purposes of this study, the figure of 12 million French evacuees is accepted.

Also worthy of note are various estimates of the number of evacuees sojourning in different parts of France. Meynier indicates 1 million in Brittany (1950:70); Bordeaux and its environs are said to have accommodated 800,000 to 1 million (or even a grossly exaggerated 3 million) as compared to the city's 1936 population of 250,000 (an estimate quoted critically by Ollier 1970:239); and the southern city of Pau increased from 38,000 to 150,000 (Ollier 1970:273).

Repatriation

The exodus ended officially on June 18, but some movements continued for a few more days. Furthermore, a number of persons left France by sea, mostly for the African colonies, particularly from Bordeaux and Marseille. If the end of hostilities made return possible, repatriation, assisted or otherwise, was affected by newly created boundaries, including a demarcation line (established June 25) separating the German-occupied zone from a free zone administered by the reconstituted French government led by Pétain. Within the occupied zone, four départements (in Alsace and Lorraine) were unilaterally

Table 4-7. Evacuees in France, Summer 1940*

Départements	1936 population (1,000s)	Evacuees (1,000s)	Percentage of Prewar Population
Unoccupied Zone (Census of Aug. 13, 1940)			
Creuze	202	304	150.5
Dordogne	387	220	56.8
Corrèze	262	210	80.2
Haute-Vienne	334	169	50.6
Hérault	502	132	26.3
Tarn-et-Garonne	165	109	66.1
Puy-de-Dome	486	100	20.6
Haute-Garonne	459	98	21.4
Indre	246	83	33.7
Lot	163	80	49.0
Aveyron	315	75	24.0
Gers	192	72	37.5
Allier	369	70	19.0
Cantal	191	60	31.4
Hautes-Pyrénées	189	60	31.7
Tarn	299	54	18.0
Ardèche	273	52	19.0
Vienne[1]	307	50	16.3[1]
Loire	650	43	6.6
Lot-et-Garonne	253	42	16.6
Basses-Pyrénées[1]	413	35	8.5[1]
Gard	395	33	8.3
Haut-Loire	245	30	12.2
Lozère	98	30	30.6
Ariège	155	24	15.5
Ande	285	23	8.1
Charente[1]	309	20	6.5[1]
Cher[1]	289	20	6.9[1]
Pyrénées-Orientales	233	20	8.6
Rhône	1,028	16	1.6
Isère	573	13	2.3
Remaining twelve départements[3]	4,386	56	1.5
Unknown	—	73[4]	—
Total	14,653[5]	2,486	7.0

continued

Occupied Zone (Estimates for July 15, 1940)

Mayenne	251	200	79.7
Loire-Inférieure	659	194	29.4
Finistère	757	160	21.1
Morbihan	542	144	26.6
Ille-et-Vilaine	566	141	24.9
Côtes-du-Norde	532	112	21.1
Total	3,307	951	28.8

*Incomplete estimate.
[1]Départments divided by demarcation line.
In this table total population is shown even though some of it was in occupied zone.
[2]Census undertaken by "Vichy government" included both French citizens and foreigners. It did not include demobilized soldiers, residents of Alsace and Lorraine being repatriated then, or people at the edge of exclusion zone.
[3]Number of evacuees did not exceed 10,000 in any of these départements.
[4]Difference between the total as given by the sources and the sum of departmental figures.
[5]The total includes population of divided départements. Only part thereof was in the unoccupied zone. Total population of the free zone was given at 13 million by A. Sauvy (1978:72).
[6]Estimates provided by A. Meynier for Brittany may contain some double counting, but on the other hand they are certainly incomplete.
Source: Meynier 1950:69–70; Ollier 1970:254–55 (two départements are missing in her listing—Cantal and Drôme); Vidalenc 1957:425–26.

incorporated into Germany on June 22. On July 23, 1940 the occupiers created an exclusion zone that embraced twelve départements (see Figure 4-9). Part of this exclusion zone came under the direct control of the military command in Brussels (Ollier 1970:260; Sauvy 1978:74). Movement across these various lines was controlled and their permeability changed over time.

The uprooted population had gravitated to southern France, where, as late as mid-August, following a massive repatriation, it still represented at least 17 percent of the local population. In many départements the figure was much higher (see Table 4-7). In spite of early efforts to direct the flows, in reality the refugee population was very mixed, and each département, or even locality, hosted compatriots originating from a variety of mainly northern areas, as well as some foreigners (see Figure 4-9).

The first few days of repatriation proceeded rather smoothly. Short-distance returns, especially those not involving passage across the demarcation line, were simple and quite rapid, and they took place within both zones. Long-distance repatriation required a certain degree of planning and organization, with both German and French authorities involved in managing the flows (Lagrange 1977).

Within the occupied zone, those evacuees residing in Brittany had to cover relatively long distances. The German military authorities regulated traffic quite strictly. They allowed movement only along

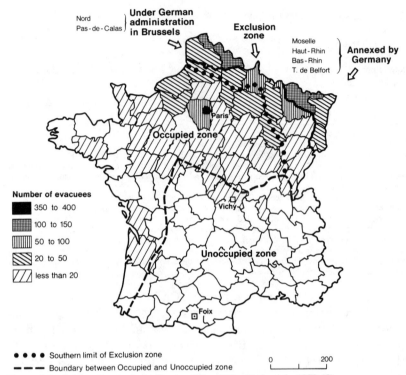

Figure 4-9. Origin of evacuees in Canton Foix, 1939–40 (Source: 1980:48)

certain routes, and routing depended on the destination. Repatriates going to Belgium were obliged to travel from Rennes to Chateaudun, and later north via Chartres and Amiens. Others continued to Orléans where the routes separated as they led to the five regions identified for repatriation purposes by the Germans (Meynier 1950:93 map). Departures for Paris and northern districts were authorized on July 19. The majority of returnees boarded trains, which were initially available free of charge. Meynier lists a number of special trains from July 1 to September 20, 1940 (1950:94). Return to the exclusion zone was prohibited except for certain categories, such as farmers or qualified workers, but in practice other persons managed to filter back. For example, as of November Rennes retained only 1,100 of the 10,000 evacuees from this zone who had been there earlier (Meynier 1950: 96). The final repatriation into the exclusion zone began as late as spring 1942, with special trains running from April 24, 1942 to March 15, 1943 (Laurens 1980:50).

Most evacuees had sought refuge in the unoccupied zone south of the demarcation line. The new French government, alarmed by enormous congestion in this area and its limited capacity to support such a population, was interested in sending as many back as soon as possible. Thus the Vichy regime created a special office of "General Secretary for Refugees," whose main responsibility was to organize repatriation (Lagrange 1977:44). Despite various problems and misunderstandings, the return from the free zone was organized during the next several months in cooperation with German authorities.

Return by auto was possible in July, but fuel was rationed and many repatriates found themselves stranded on their return trip (Ollier 1970:261). By July 1, special permits were needed and procuring them took quite some time.[20] Certain categories of people were not allowed to enter the occupied zone, including "Poles, Czechs, Jews, Negroes and people of mixed blood" (Laurens 1980:50).

Massive returns were feasible in August after direct train service was reestablished in a south–north direction. By August 15, 1,000 trains were said to have crossed the demarcation line and the flow continued thereafter (Lagrange 1977:49). According to Gerber (1941:121), 279 trains traveled north during the last ten days of August, including: 86 trains for demobilized personnel; 79 trains for people from the area between the Loire and Somme; 44 trains for residents of Alsace and Lorraine; 70 trains for Belgians. The same author quotes statistics for the first ten days of August, when 45,000 vehicles with 184,000 passengers and 18,000 pedestrians and bicyclists crossed into the occupied zone.

Beginning in September 1940, it became much more difficult to cross the demarcation line. As of that month, the repatriation program came to an end at least as far as subsidized and organized movement was concerned. Several repatriation centers continued until December 1940 (Ollier 1970:264), and some repatriation services continued thereafter, including the search for and return of tens of thousands of children lost during the exodus.[21]

The repopulation of Paris deserves special consideration. On June 14 the entering German armies found only some 700,000 inhabitants remaining in the city (Ollier 1970:263). A rapid return, particularly by those who never managed to cross the Loire, swelled the number

quickly, but even on July 7, 1940 the enumeration carried out by the
Germans showed a deficit of some 3 million (Gerber 1941:19).

	1936	July 7, 1940
City of Paris	2,879,746	1,051,506
Suburbs	2,133,221	887,326
Total Paris agglomeration	4,922,967	1,938,832

Massive repatriation was possible only after the restoration of train
service, and by August 10, Paris' population had increased to 2,350,000
(Ollier 1970:264). Soon thereafter the German authorities attempted to
slow down the influx; repatriation from the Atlantic region was suspended and some trains were supposedly send back. From September
1940 onward, it was more difficult to cross the demarcation line, which
was closed altogether for certain categories of population. For the
remainder of the war the population of Paris stayed below the prewar
level, and the 1939 number was reached only in the late 1940s.

Repatriation of Belgian refugees concentrated in southern and western France was handled somewhat differently. France's surrender left
the Belgian government with little choice other than to endorse the
earlier royal decision to capitulate. Consequently, a decision to return
to Belgium was made at the end of June. By that time the government
agencies had located in Suveterre-de-Guyenne, southeast of Bordeaux.
The repatriation plan provided for several motorized columns to leave
on Sunday, June 30 and the following three days, proceeding via
Poitiers-Amboise (crossing the Loire) along Tours-Orléans-Paris-Mons.
In actuality, there were delays and detours, but the convoys finally
arrived in Brussels during July. Ordinary folks were initially advised
to stay put. On July 7 it was announced that Belgians (as well as Dutch,
Luxembourgeois, and Alsatians) with access to autos would be able to
return. At that point cars previously impounded were returned to their
owners; but formalities and repairs took some time, and final permission to return from the free zone materialized only at the beginning of
August (Ollier 1970:284). Repatriation by train took place somewhat
later and accounted for most returns. In August alone, the Red Cross
registered 206 trains. The first train from Marseille departed on August
26, and all repatriation from the free zone was to terminate by mid-
September (Vanwelkenhuyzen and Dumont 1983:290–91).

In the occupied zone the first displaced Belgians appeared at the
Belgian embassy in Paris (under protection of the neutral United

States) shortly after the fall of Paris, and even before the end of hostilities, workers from various plants and agricultural workers, as well as members of CRAB, were among them. Their repatriation started quickly and buses bringing German occupation personnel to Paris were used on their return journey to transport the Belgians. The embassy in Paris continued to serve as transit point and at certain times had to care for 40,000 persons (Vanwelkenhuyzen and Dumont 1983:274). The total number of Belgians repatriated after the end of hostilities was in the range of 1.5 to 2 million (Ollier 1970:182, 275; Vidalenc 1957:150).

As noted earlier, various military and government agencies, both French and German, along with the Red Cross, helped organize the return migration. On the German side, the Nazi party welfare organization, the National Sozialistische Volkswohlfahrt (NSV), immediately set up a French operation to assist the returnees. Its friendly efficiency was appreciated by the repatriates and played up by the German news media (Ollier 1970:263).

Conclusion

The wartime evacuations in four West European countries during the 1939–40 period involved somewhere between 12 and 15 million persons, most of them French (10 to 12 million), but including 2 to 3 million Belgians. An organized evacuation, which affected mostly Paris and the frontier areas of Alsace and Lorraine took place in September 1939; and although some people, particularly Parisians, returned within a month or two, most stayed away until the following summer. In May–June 1940, the German invasion led to a massive exodus affecting most parts of the two countries most seriously afflicted by the Western campaign, Belgium and France. Initially organized and controlled or, in the case of spontaneous outflow, quite orderly, this temporary migration—mostly, but not exclusively, from urban areas—soon degenerated into a chaotic, panicky, uncontrolled affair. Panic arose in part from the activities (some actual, other imagined) of German agents, a Fifth Column, planted behind the lines. Official attempts undertaken in June to stem the flow were unsuccessful. After the end of hostilities, a massive countermovement, at times controlled and regulated, meant the return of most evacuees within the next three months. Consequently, the whole episode lasted about four months for most individuals, but as long as a year for others. Only a relatively small fraction of the evacuees stayed away from their homes for the duration of the war (900,000 according to Ginesy 1948:11).

Apart from the actual movements back and forth of so many people, the 1939 evacuation and the 1940 exodus have had a long-term impact upon French society, as partially expressed in mobility (Ollier 1970). For many persons, this episode was the very first exposure to unfamiliar territory. The mingling of people from different social classes and residential backgrounds may have contributed to the relaxation of class barriers. Forced acquaintance with distant areas may also have influenced later decisions regarding choice of holidays, location of second homes, or places of retirement. In fact, the present-day massive annual holiday migration may, to a certain extent, be the product of l'Exode. On the other hand, the temporary presence of many affluent persons from metropolitan centers could well have affected the expectations and aspirations of rural folks, particulary those who resided in sleepy provincial towns. Post-exodus France was never to be the same again.

USSR, 1941–44

World War II resulted in massive temporary dislocations of residents of the Soviet Union. A conservative estimate is that at least 10 million persons were caught up in such evacuations (including several cousins of the senior author). This was a result of spontaneous flight from zones threatened or affected by hostilities and, to a much greater degree, of deliberate, organized transfers of both people and equipment from areas subsequently occupied by the invading armies.

Surprisingly enough, literature on the subject is quite limited in contrast to the enormous volume of writings on the military aspects of the war. Moreover, in his brief review of studies on evacuation, M. I. Likhomanov complained that evacuating the means of production and other physical resources seems to have attracted more attention than that of people (in Pospelov 1974, vol. 2:181). Nevertheless, some data sources do exist and it is possible to reconstruct the general outlines of this immense movement of population in a country facing the ultimate challenge.

This section is based mainly on secondary published Soviet sources. General comments on evacuations were found in the second volume of the monumental history of the Great Patriotic War (Fokin et al. 1961) and in proceedings of a special session organized in June 1962 by the Institute of History, Soviet Academy of Sciences (Polyakov et al.

1966). Two volumes edited by Pospelov (1974) were also helpful. Services performed by the railways, which carried out the great bulk of the evacuation, were described by Kumanev (1963, 1976) and Klemin (1981). River transport during the war was discussed by Neigoldberg (1965).

The evacuation of Leningrad generated a substantial literature (particularly important is Karasev 1959), which deserves and receives separate treatment in another section of this study, while some publications contain references to other aspects of evacuation (e.g., Kovalchuk 1975). An article by Shtchegolev (1959) deals with the impact of evacuation on rural areas of western Siberia. There are other references in regional histories of various parts of the Soviet Union.

As far as Western authors are concerned, one should particularly mention a careful review of sources and estimates made during the war by Kulischer (1943). The same author later summarized his earlier studies in a major work on European migration (Kulischer 1948). In his monograph on Soviet population, Lorimer (1946) includes a section on evacuation. Useful comments were found in a major joint study edited by Susan Linz (1985). An important work by Erickson contains only limited references to war evacuation (1975). A comprehensive German study by Segbers (1987) was found only after this chapter had been written. Cartographic sources helpful in the present study were maps found in Lorimer and in the atlases edited by Young (1974) and Keegan (1989).

It is apparent that the Soviet authorities tried to keep track of all those movements, so that there is a relatively large volume of published statistics, unfortunately of very unequal quality. Their direct utilization for a general study is not always easy since the data are often fragmentary and repetitious. For example, numbers of people evacuated from certain areas cannot simply be compared to those processed by various evacuation centers. Adding together persons evacuated from Leningrad and passengers ferried by boats along the Volga almost certainly means that some are counted more than once. Often statistics are used as examples of an event taking place at one time or in one place; consequently, they are meaningless out of context. The most valuable would be the result of a 1942 *Census* of evacuees. Unfortunately, only fragmentary data were found, and the quality of the *Census* is not known.

The German invasion began on June 22, 1941 and within the first days it was obvious to Soviet authorities that certain areas would have to be evacuated in order to save resources and work force. The first decree on evacuation, entitled "On Orderly Evacuation and Distribution of Manpower and Valuable Resources," was issued jointly by the Central Committee of the Communist Party and by the government on June 27, 1941 (Polyakov et al. 1966:9). At the highest level, evacuation was coordinated by a number of hastily appointed, frequently changing agencies (see Table 4-8). These included: the Evacuation Council (Soviet po Evakuatsii), which was already in existence on June 24, 1941. Attached to it was: the Administration for Population Evacuation (Upravlenye po Evakuatsii Naselenia), which existed from September 26, 1941 to January 31, 1942; the Committee for Evacuation (Komitet po Evakuatsii), which existed from September 25 to December 19, 1941; and the Committee for Unloading Transit Loads (Komitet po Razgruzke Transitnykh Gruzov), formed on December 25, 1941, which took over the apparatus of the Evacuation Council, which was thereupon abolished. In order to supervise the second wave of evacuation, another Commission on Evacuation (Komisya po Evakuatsii) was formed on June 22, 1942. Executive personnel of all those bodies changed several times, but certain key names appeared in almost all configurations.They included such important persons as L. M. Kaganovich, A. N. Kosygin, N. M. Shvernik, A. I. Mikoyan, and M. Z.

Table 4-8. Official Organization of Evacuation in the Soviet Union, 1941–42

June 24, 1941	Evacuation Council established headed by L. M. Kaganovich, reorganized July 16 and Aug. 16
June 27, 1941	First decree on evacuation by party and government
June 28, 1941	First order on evacuation issued by War Council of the Northern Front
June 30, 1941	State Defense Committee established, headed by J. V. Stalin
Sept. 26, 1941	Administration (Upravlenye) for Population Evacuation established, headed by Vice-Premier of R.S.F.S.R. K. D. Pamfilov (Dissolved Jan. 31, 1942)
Oct. 25, 1941	Committee for Evacuation headed by A. I. Mikoyan (Dissolved Dec. 19, 1941)
Oct. 26, 1941	Plan of Evacuation of Food from N. Caucasus, and Oblasts-Voronezh, Kursk, Orlovsk, Tula, Ryazan, Moscow
Dec. 25, 1941	Dissolution of the Evacuation Council
Dec. 25, 1941	Committee for Unloading Transit Loads. The committee takes over the agencies of the former Evacuation Council
June 22, 1942	Evacuation Commission established, headed by N. M. Shvernik

Source: Polyakov et al. 1966: 6, 10, 11.

Saburov. Representatives of the army and security forces also participated at the highest level (Polyakov et al. 1966:10–11). The institutional
arrangement was not limited to central agencies; a very important role
was played by regional groups and commissions and particularly by
2,112 evacuation points (as of December 1941) (Belonosov in Polyakov
et al. 1966:17).

The evacuation itself was mostly organized in character, sometimes
at a local level (when people were moved only 25 to 30 km away from
the front line), but more frequently covering relatively long distances.
The first central evacuation plan was approved on October 26, 1941
(Polyakov et al. 1966:11). It was followed by many other more or less
specific plans and administrative measures mainly concerned with the
distribution and integration of evacuees (Shtchegolev 1959). A thorough discussion of war management structure is presented by S. R.
Lieberman (1985).

The evacuations began in the early days of war and included two
periods of major movements: July to November, 1941 and mid-May to
October, 1942. In between there was some return of population, but
the major homeward movements began in 1943, only after the German
retreat had begun in earnest. Estimates of the total number of evacuated persons vary a great deal, from 7.5 to 25 million. This has to be
compared with 88 million residents of the areas occupied by the
Germans (Polyakov et al. 1966:6). (See Fig. 4-10 for the extent of the
German advance.) In addition to people, there was a considerable
shipment of machines, equipment, key materials, libraries, archives,
museums, and so on (Polyakov et al. 1966:13). Despite all the many
efforts made to help the persons involved, the scale of disruption and
hardship can hardly be imagined. Total government expenditures on
evacuation, including compensations paid to individuals, were estimated at 3 billion rubles in the second half of 1941, which equaled all
investment in defense industry during 1942 (Fokin et al. 1961, vol. 2:
547). It should be noted that although such war-induced evacuations
were unprecedented, massive forcible transfers of people had been
going on for quite some time in the Soviet Union. Collectivization in
the early 1930s, purges in the mid-1930s, deportations of people from
areas acquired in 1939–40, and exchanges with Nazi Germany in 1939–
40 involved millions of people and undoubtedly provided the Soviet
government agencies with useful experience (Fitzpatrick 1985:132).

Statistics on evacuation streams compiled from various sources are
summarized in Table 4-9. Although the first order on evacuation in the
northern regions was issued by the War Council of the Northern Front

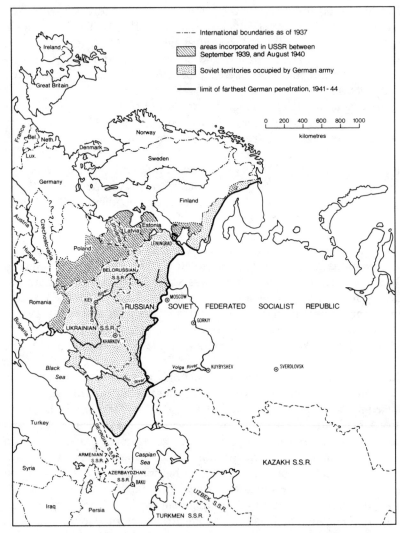

Figure 4-10. USSR: Areas occupied by German forces during World War II (Adapted from Lorimer 1946: Plates XVI and XXII)

Table 4-9. Soviet Areas Evacuated in 1941–42*

Area	Population in1940 (1,000s)	Evacuated Population	Evacuees as Percent of Population
Lithuainian SSR	2,925	200	3.4
Latvian SSR	1,886	200	3.4
Estonian SSR	1,054	200	3.4
Belorussian SSR	9,046	1,500[1]	16.5
Ukrainian SSR	41,340	4,000	9.6
Moldavian SSR	2,468	250	10.1
Karelo-Finnish ASSR	478	} 115	} 19.2
Murmansk City	119		
Leningrad City	3,103	1,500	48.3
Moscow City	4,537	2,000[2]	44.0

*Excluding major portions of the RSFSR.
[1]Not including workers evacuated with their companies.
[2]Including refugees from other areas.
Source: Narodnoe Khoziaystvo SSSR 1972:9, 27.

as early as June 28, 1941 (Kamalov et al. 1966:39), population evacuation was always difficult and never complete. In the extreme north, 115,000 evacuees left Murmansk (mostly for Archangel) and the Karelo-Finnish ASSR (Polyakov et al. 1966:131). Some of these evacuees went initially to Leningrad and subsequently had little choice but to move again.

The Baltic Republics were overrun very quickly by the Germans, and local populations of these areas, only recently incorporated by force into the Soviet Union, were rather reluctant to move east.[22] In fact, many of the inhabitants welcomed the entering Germans as liberators, and there were cases of nationalists attacking retreating Soviet troops. Just before the outbreak of the war, some 100,000 Balts were arrested and most were shipped to Siberia. According to Misiunas and Taagepera (1983:275), the numbers of those deported were estimated at 15,000 from Estonia, 35,000 from Latvia, and 35,000 from Lithuania. In addition, over 100,000 men were forcibly conscripted into the Red Army. The estimates of wartime evacuation from the Baltic states vary. The same authors calculate the flows at 30,000 from Estonia, 40,000 from Latvia, and 20,000 from Lithuania. Differences in the magnitude of evacuation are related in part to the rapidity of the German advance. Lithuania was overrun in three days (June 22–25), the conquest of Latvia followed between June 26 and July 1, but full control of Estonia came only with the fall of Tallinn on August 28 (Misinuas and Taagepera 1983:44, 275). An even higher estimate for the Estonian evacuation is quoted by Segbers (1987:176). Polyakov et al. (1966:13) suggests that 42,500 were evacuated from Lithuania and at least 50,000 from Estonia. In Pospelov (1974:vol. 2, 349) the figures for these republics are somewhat smaller, 20,000 and 40,000 respectively, and the total for the Baltic Republics, by railway only, is given at 120,000. However, according to the data for Leningrad (see Leningrad section, Table 4-15), 148,000 evacuees from the Baltic Republics, who found refuge in Leningrad, were later evacuated from that city. Consequently, the total number of evacuees from the Baltic Republics was likely close to 200,000. Evacuation from Leningrad included 1.5 million from the city proper and at least 147,000 from the surrounding oblasts.[23]

The number of evacuees from Moldavia is given at 250,000, by Polyakov et al. (1966:19) and 300,000 by Segbers (1987:176). For the Ukraine the lower estimate is 3.5 million (Krawchenko 1985:154; Segbers 1987:176) and the higher 4 million (Polyakov et al. 1966:20). The latter included: 400,000 from Kiev and its surrounding area; 300,000 from Odessa between July 9 and October 16, 1941; 73,000 from Dnepropetrovsk, on the Dnieper River (July 20 to mid-August); over 100,000 civilians (and 1,500 barrels of "masandrovsky" wine) from the Crimea (Polyakov et al. 1966:20, 158, 172, 160); 100,000 from Petrozavodsk (August 1 to September 25) with a further 270,000 leaving after its loss via Medvezhegorsk and Povenets (Polyakov et al. 1966:174); and 100,000 from Kharkov in September, when 50,000 went to Kazakhstan, 30,000 to Saratov, and 20,000 to Stalingrad (Kumanev 1963:61). Estimates for Belorussia range from more than 1 million (Polyakov et al. 1966:20) to 1.5 million (Pospelov 1974:vol. 2, 182), with the capital Minsk being affected first.

The western parts of the RFSSR were also affected. The evacuation of Moscow started on June 29, and within the first month 960,000 persons (including persons displaced from other regions) left by train; by mid-November some 2 million persons were evacuated from the capital (Polyakov et al. 1966:133). According to other estimates, 1,614,000 persons left Moscow between June 29 and September 10, and by mid-November the number of evacuees reached 2 million (Kumanev 1963:73).[24] Other areas evacuated included: the oil-producing area of Makhachkala-Baku (actually never occupied by Germans), whence 103,000 left for Krasnovodsk during the second half of 1941 and a further 100,000 in 1942; and 333,000 in Stalingrad, moving across the river between August 23 and mid-December 1942 (Polyakov et al. 1966:164, 185). For most of the evacuations discussed above, the railways were used, but in some areas river transport and airplanes were also of importance. (The special case of Leningrad is discussed elsewhere.) In Upper Volga, 600,000 were transported mainly by boat and barge in Gorki Oblast. The navigation season lasted longer than normal, but, with temperatures dropping in November to −10°C between Rybinsk and Gorki, 51,000 passengers were trapped on barges, most of which never got to their destination that winter. In Lower Volga, where the railway line terminated in Stalingrad, 220,000 were moved. The total number of passengers on inland waterways is given at 2 million from July to November 1941, with an average distance traveled of 78 km (Polyakov et al. 1966:181–82).

Data for selected Ukrainian cities give an idea of the population decline due mainly to evacuation (but also war losses, rather insignificant in the early stages). It appears that in twelve urban centers for which data are available, the population declined by one-half (see Table 4-10). On the other hand, cities in the eastern part of the country experienced a considerable influx of population (see Table 4-11).

The first evacuation transports went to the oblasts of Yaroslavl, Vologda, Ivanovo, and Kirov and to the Volga region. Information provided for some destinations by Pospelov (1974: vol. 2, 184–86) gives an idea of the scale of operations. Oblast Ivanowo (population

Table 4-10. Population of Selected Ukrainian Cities Under German Occupation, 1939–43*

City	Population 1939 (Jan. 17 census)	Population 1943 (Jan. 1, 1943 estimate)	Percentage of 1939 Population
Kiev	846	305(330[1])	36(39[1])
Odessa	604	300[1]	50
Dnepropetrovsk	501	280(152[1])	56(30[1])
Zaporozhe	289	120	42
Mariupol (Zhdanov)	222	178[1]	80
Krivoy Rog	198	125	65
Nikolayev	167	84	50
Dneprodzerzhinsk	148	75	51
Poltava	130	75	58
Kirovgrad	100	63	63
Kherson	97	59	61
Zhitomir	95	42	44
Vinnitsa	93	42	45
Militopol	76	65	86
Total	3,566	1,813	51

*In 1,000s.
[1]Data from various Soviet sources quoted by Kulischer, 1943:90 (for Kiev: October 1942; for Odessa: July 1942; for Dniepropetrovsk and Mariupol: January 1942).
Source: Lorimer 1946:196, based on data from *Deutsche Ukraine Zeitung,* Feb. 2, 1943 (except as otherwise noted).

Table 4-11. Population of Selected Unoccupied Soviet Cities, 1939–41*

City	Population 1939 (Jan. 17 census)	Population 1941 (Fall 1941 estimate)	Percentage Growth
Kazan	401	515	28
Kuybyshev	390	529	36
Syzran	79	126	59
Sverdlovsk	425	544	28
Nizhny Tagil	160	239	49
Omsk	281	400	42
Tashkent	585	660	13

*In 1,000s.
¹The source suggests that the figures are for mid-1941. In actuality, the quoted figures are from the 1939 census.
Source: Fokin et al. 1961:549.

2.6 million in 1939) received 93,000 by mid-1943, coming from Leningrad, Kalinin, Smolensk oblasts, from the Baltic Republics, Ukraine, Belorussia, and Karelia. The Tatar ASSR (2.9 million) received 176,000 by early September 1941, of whom one-half were located in the capital Kazan. Industrial centers in the Urals received 1 million displaced persons. In just the first six months of the war, 200,000 arrived in Chelyabinsk, 150,000 in Omsk. Transit points in Novosibirsk processed 1.5 million. In the Altai region, Barnaul alone received 78,300 persons.

In the spring of 1942, when the first great evacuation had been completed, a special *Census* of displaced persons was conducted. According to published figures (unfortunately without a sufficiently detailed regional breakdown), some 7.4 million people were received in the interior of the country, 80 percent of whom were lodged in various regions of the Russian Republic and the remainder in Central Asia (see Table 4-12).

As mentioned earlier, from December 1941 into the summer of 1942, some people returned into the home areas is they were still free from invasion, but additional German pressure in the summer of 1942 caused a second, much smaller wave of evacuation, which took place from May to October 1942 and included "hundreds of thousands" (Polyakov et al. 1966:28). It was only in the winter of 1942–43 that the final return started.

What then was the total number of evacuees during the two stages? The estimates range quite substantially, and it appears that later calculations tend to favor larger numbers (see Table 4-13). One difficulty is the quality of data and lack of precision in definitions. An unresolved question concerns the difference between stock and flow statistics, well known to any student of migration. The 1942 *Census*

Table 4-12. Evacuees Enumerated in Unoccupied Portions of the Soviet Union, 1942*

Territory		Population (in 1000s)
RSFSR		5,914
incl. Yaroslavl Obl.	500	
Chkalov Obl.	242	
Kuybyshev Obl.	>200	
Kirov Obl.	227	
Novosibirsk Obl.	255	
Tatar ASSR	266	
Kazakh Republic		600
Uzbek Republic		716
Kirghiz Republic		100
Other Central Asian and Caucasus Republics		87
Total		7,417[1]

*Data from special census held in spring in 1942.
[1]This figure does not include students in vocational schools of Red Army conscripts.
Source: Fokin et al. 1961:548.

Table 4-13. Various Estimates of Soviet Evacuation, 1941–42

	Evacuation Total (in millions)	Sources
1941 Evacuation:	7.5–10.0	Vasiliev in Kulischer 1943:91–92
	15.0	Habicht in Kulischer 1943:91–92
	12.5	Rachner in *Reichsarbeitsblatt,* Mar. 5, 1942, as quoted by Kulischer 1943:91
	10.4 (trains only)	Fokin et al. 1961:vol. 2, 548
	7.4 (census, 1942)	Fokin et al. 1961:vol. 2, 548
	17.0	Polyakov et al. 1966:13
Total Evacuation, 1941–42:	12[1]	Kulischer 1948:260
	25	Polyakov et al. 1966:13, 28[2]

[1]Including 1.5 million forcibly transferred and deported from areas incorporated into Soviet Union in 1939–41.
[2]Polyakov quotes as his source *Voyenno-Istoricheski Zhurnal* 1963, No. 2:39.

offers statistics based on the stock (the number of evacuees enumerated at a certain point in time); other statistics are based on flows that can include the same individual more than once.

If the 1942 figures are correct and one can assume that late-1942 evacuation included less than 1 million, then the partly stock-based estimate of evacuees would yield a figure of 8 to 9 million. If major flows are added (Leningrad, Moscow, western and Baltic Republics, and fragmentary figures for western Russian oblasts), then a figure of 14 million is more likely.

Another way to arrive at the likely figure is to construct a general balance sheet of population movements. The prewar population of the occupied territories was estimated at 85 million by Lorimer (1946:194) and 88 million by Polyakov et al. (1966:6). According to Soviet figures, the population remaining there at the time of liberation represented some 63 percent of prewar numbers (see Table 4-14). If the higher figure of population in German-held areas is accepted and negative components are estimated, the balance would suggest an evacuation on the order of 11 million persons.

Prewar population of occupied area	88 million
Natural increase of 1 percent per year	+ 2 million
Population found after liberation, 63 percent	− 57 million
Missing	33 million
of whom war losses, ½ of 20 million	− 10 million
conscription, ½ of 20 million	− 10 million
transfer of ethnic Germans and forced laborers to Germany	− 2 million
Presumed evacuation to the interior	11 million

In either case, the figure of 25 million seems to be a substantial overestimate even if multiple moves are considered. Whatever the

Table 4-14. Population of Soviet Territories at Time of Liberation from German Occupation as Percentage of 1940 Population

Group	Total Liberated Area	Occupied Parts of RSFSR	Ukraine	Belorussia	Moldavia	Karelo-Finnish Republic	Baltic Republics
Total population	63	63	60	62	78	16	77
Urban areas	40	43	38	30	51	15	53
Rural areas	72	69	70	71	82	17	86
Industrial workers	17	17	17	6	15	1	30

Source: Pospelov 1974, vol. 2:177, based on estimates by N. Voznesenskiy 1968, 1971. It was impossible to locate and verify the latter source in spite of a search in Lenin Library in Moscow.

actual total of this great eastward evacuation may have been, it included both urban and rural inhabitants. Although no definitive statistics are available, we are convinced that the participants were predominantly urban. It is difficult to generalize about the selectivity of the evacuees. Officially women, children, and the elderly were given priority, a claim disputed by Segbers (1987:169). It is known that evacuation from various industrial centers included factory and institutional personnel, which would tend to bias the flow toward males. There are reports that when time was still available, tedious bureaucratic procedures remained in place. As a result, obtaining all required clearances could supposedly take up to six days (Segbers 1987:172). Krawchenko (1985:154) argues that "since pull and friends were used to get out ahead of the Germans it was mostly the leading stratum—prominent party and state officials, the labor aristocracy, and the 'higher intelligentsia' that left."

A large concentration of evacuated persons in the unoccupied central and southern regions of the USSR improved the labor force supply in both urban and rural areas. The increase of industrial output needed to offset losses in the western regions was regarded as successful, and Soviet leadership was hoping to retain much of the evacuated population in order to accelerate the long-term eastward shift of both population and productive forces. Lorimer (1946:198) quotes an order issued by the Council of People's Commissars in February 1942 requiring local authorities to make an effort to permanently absorb workers and employees transferred there with their factories and equipment. The contribution of evacuated population to the development of agriculture in western Siberia was emphasized by Shtchegolev (1959).

With the German defeat at Stalingrad in early 1943, the tide of the war was reversed and the front started moving definitely westward. Reconstruction of liberated territories would require returning the evacuated population; on the other hand, a hasty repatriation, apart from the drain on transportation capabilities, would adversely affect production in the east and cancel the positive aspects of west–east redistribution of population. The official Soviet attitude was not uniform. Kulischer quotes articles from *Pravda* (September 7 and 24, 1944) in which workers who left their posts and went home were stigmatized as "deserters from the labour front"; also others (*Pravda*, December 14, 1944) from the "heroic work of reconstruction" (Kulischer 1948:294–95).

Apparently the urge to return was so powerful that, in addition to the organized repatriation, people were flocking back in great numbers and the repeopling of liberated cities proceeded faster than their reconstruction. Kiev's population declined from 850,000 to 330,000 in the early stage of occupation and presumably even further thereafter. By early 1945, "a half million souls were back again in Kiev." The population of Kalinin declined from 225,000 to a small fraction thereof, but by May 1944 it was approaching 170,000. Stalingrad had over 500,000 inhabitants before the war, but only 1,500 when the Germans capitulated in February 1943, yet by December 1944 the population had rebounded to 250,000 (Kulischer 1948:295). Data collected by American correspondents seem to indicate that by July 1944, half of the evacuees had left for home. Nevertheless, some residue of both people and industrial equipment remained in the reception areas, thus contributing to the long-term eastward shift of population. However, in order to calculate the size of this net increment, one has to take into consideration other types of population movements—forcible deportations of peoples who were deemed suspect and were punished by transferring them to the east: Volga Germans, Crimean Tatars, returning POWs, and so on. These moves can hardly be included in our study of evacuations, however.

But whatever the actual magnitude of the war-induced evacuations may have been, and however much or little they may have contributed to the long-term eastward redistribution of people and economic activity in the Soviet Union, there can be little doubt as to the short-term efficacy of these movements. If these temporary shifts had not taken place, the horrendous toll of persons killed, injured, or otherwise mistreated would certainly have been measurably greater.

LENINGRAD, 1941–45

If World War II meant death, destruction, and disruption of normal life on the most massive scale throughout the USSR, the prolonged siege of Leningrad may be the single most outstanding example of the heroism of the Soviet people, given the especially terrible suffering visited upon its residents. It is also a relatively well-documented example of wartime evacuation, one that removed over 1.5 million people from the surrounded city into safer areas. The special circumstances of the Leningrad ordeal oblige us to detach its treatment from the World War II USSR experience at the national level and to examine this extraordinary episode here in some detail.

There is a considerable literature on the siege of Leningrad, and one of the most quoted sources happens to deal in some detail with evacuation. It is a relatively old book by Karasev (1959), and is preceded by an earlier article of his (1951). These sources were extensively used here along with a collection of documents released several years later (Kamalov et al. 1966). Another important data source is the volume by Kovalchuk (1975), which treats the very specific problem of communication across Lake Ladoga. References to the evacuation of Leningrad can also be found in many other sources, including Kumanev's study of railways (1963) and the proceedings of a special session held in Moscow in 1962 (Polyakov et al. 1966). An interesting series of interviews with the survivors and fragments of diaries were published by Adamowicz and Granin (1988).

In Western literature, a monumental study by Salisbury (1969) is probably the most detailed account of the Leningrad ordeal. He provides interesting comments on the Byzantine intrigues during the Stalinist era, which caused both literary fiction and historical research on Leningrad to suffer (pp. 577–82). The so-called "Leningrad Affair," a great Stalinist purge after the fall of one of the most unsavory characters in Stalin's gallery, but a hero of the Leningrad battle, A. A. Zhdanov, and his death in 1948, led to sequestration and possibly destruction of various documents, historical objects, and manuscripts ready for publication. Apparently, in 1949 the Museum of the Defense of Leningrad was closed and the director arrested (he was released from a concentration camp after Stalin's death). Some exhibits reappeared later in a new museum opened in 1959, but others have never been found. Museum archives were seized and Soviet historians were forbidden access to them. Documents collected during the war that were meant to be published have never been published. Even the existence of the Council for the Defense of Leningrad, directed by Zhdanov, was not mentioned until the 1960s. In other words, knowledge of Leningrad's tragedy was affected not only by the lack of documentation, understandable in a war situation, but also by deliberate action of the Soviet leadership in the late 1940s and early 1950s, which led to the destruction of people and sources of information. It should be added, however, that at the present time the Leningrad Historical Museum contains a substantial exhibit dealing with the siege, and a huge monument commemorating the blockade welcomes visitors approaching the city from the south.

The German invasion of the Soviet Union began on June 22, 1941 and the surprisingly swift advance of Hitler's armies prompted massive movements of people, both spontaneous and organized. The first

decision regarding evacuation was taken by the War Council of the
Northern Front on June 28, 1941 (Kamalov et al. 1966:39). Leningrad
(population 3.2 million in 1939) became a destination for refugees
escaping from the Baltic Republics, northern regions, and from the
surrounding area.[25] The first large waves arrived by the end of June,
and on July 8 a special evacuation division was established within the
regional council with evacuation commissions in each city district.
New arrivals were directed to special distribution points at six stations,
and dormitories were set up in forty-two nearby schools, soon to be
augmented by medical facilities, other dormitories, kitchens, and so
on. Some 2,000 Red Cross personnel were involved (Karasev 1959:90).
The influx continued throughout July and most of August. On August
22, checkpoints were established and by August 28 the influx ceased
when the encirclement by the invading troops was complete. (See
Figure 4-11 for Leningrad's transportation situation during the siege.)
One particularly disastrous episode involved evacuation of Tallinn, the
capital of Estonia. After the fall of the city, a huge convoy of 190
ships, including 29 large transports with 23,000 people on board, left
on the night of August 27–28. The convoy was destroyed by mines and
German bombers, with a loss of over 10,000 lives (Salisbury 1969:238).
It is not altogether clear how many people succeeded in reaching

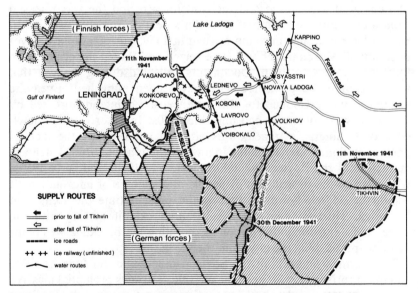

Figure 4-11. Siege of Leningrad, 1941 (Source: Adopted from Keegan 1989:64)

Leningrad during that period, but the total certainly exceeded 300,000, which is the number of non-Leningraders evacuated subsequently from the city (see Table 4-15).[26] Apparently some people were arriving even after August, and 55,000 are said to have entered during the winter of 1941–42 (Salisbury 1969:495). Evacuation of Leningrad began in the second week of the war. The decision to evacuate children was taken on June 29, although some children had been sent away even earlier, mostly to summer camps to the west and southwest of the city in the direction of the future German attack. That very day (June 29) ten trains with over 15,000 children left the city (Karasev 1959:90).

The estimates of total number of children evacuated between June 29 and July 5 vary somewhat. Salisbury (1969:143) reports two figures: 212,000 from one source (of whom 162,000 went to the nearby countryside and the rest to Yaroslavl), while another source suggests a total of 235,000, with 164,000 destined for neighboring villages and camps. Evacuation was prompted by the fear of air raids, but when the German army began its approach, many children (115,000) were returned to Leningrad.[27]

After their return to the city, children were sent off again, this time to more distant areas—Kirov and Sverdlovsk oblasts (Karasev 1959:91). Movements of children, especially in the earlier phase, led to some losses as transports were bombed from the air (Salisbury 1969:143). Evacuation of the adult population followed, even if initially there was a certain reluctance to leave the city. In fact, it was the party personnel who encouraged people not to leave (Salisbury 1969:206).

However, the factories were gradually being removed on orders issued by the State Defense Committee on July 11. By September 1, nearly 100 plants had been evacuated in part or in full. This included the Nevsky Machine-Building Factory (to Sverdlovsk), Kirov Machine Plant (to Barnaul), Russian Diesel Plant (to Gorki), Zhdanov Works (to Tashkent and Urals), part of Kirov (formerly Putilov) Steel Works (to Chelyabinsk). In all, some 60,000 railway cars left the city loaded with equipment, which was to be reassembled elsewhere. Personnel and families went along (Salisbury 1969:207).

By August 11, the total number of evacuees was estimated at 468,000. They were sent to the following areas further east: oblasts Kirov, Vologda, Sverdlovsk, Omsk, and Perm, Udmurt ASSR, Bashkir ASSR, and Kazakh Republic (Karasev 1959:91). On August 10, a decision was taken to evacuate an additional 400,000 women and children below the age of fourteen. In view of the German breakthrough near Pskov, the figure was increased to 700,000, but in reality

Table 4-15. Evacuation From Leningrad, June 29, 1941–April 1, 1943*

Category of Evacuated Population	June 29–Aug. 27, 1941	Aug. 27–Jan. 22, 1942	Jan. 22–Apr. 15, 1942	May 27, 1942–Apr. 1, 1943	Total
Personnel of evacuated enterprises including families	164.3	36.8	351.8	101.4	654.3
Temporarily incapacitated workers, including families	104.7	—	—	55.0	159.7
Women with two or more children	219.7	—	—	102.1	321.8
Students, teachers, artists, writers, and scholars, including families	—	—	37.9	4.9	42.8
Women with one child	—	—	—	35.6	35.6
Children in institutions and their personnel, including families	—	—	12.6	45.5	58.1
Students in vocational school	—	—	32.9	8.4	41.3
Retired persons, invalids, permanently incapacitated workers, including families	—	—	—	29.8	29.8
Disabled veterans of the Patriotic War	—	—	43.1	10.6	53.6
Sick persons, including families	—	—	—	4.0	4.0
Special contingent (prisoners, mentally ill, etc.)	—	—	40.5	6.7	47.2
Leningrad City total	488.7	36.8	518.8	404.0	1,448.2[1]
Leningrad Oblast and former refugees from the Baltic Republics	147.5	67.9	35.4	43.9	294.8[2]
Grand total	636.2	104.7	554.2	447.9	1,743.0

*In 1000s. Data on the Leningrad Urban Evacuation Commission.
[1]Including 414,150 children.
[2]Including 147,300 from Leningrad Oblast and 147,500 from the Baltic Republics.
Source: Kamalov et al. 1966:106 (Document #35).

the first great stage of evacuation was coming to an end. The last evacuation train (282nd since the beginning of the war) left on August 29, and by that date Leningrad was completely encircled and no overland connection remained open (Karasev 1959:92). Evacuation was not without problems. Families were often separated. Sometimes fully loaded trains waited for several days on side tracks with insufficient supplies expecting to leave any time; hence evacuees were unable to get in touch with families (Karasev 1959:92–93).

During the first two months, a number of cultural and scientific institutions and collections were also removed. Hermitage treasures were shipped to Sverdlovsk in two trains (July 1 and 20); a third one never left the city. A collection of the Russian Museum was sent to Gorki and then by barge to Perm. The Philharmonic Orchestra and Pushkin Drama Theatre went to Novosibirsk, Marinskiy Ballet to Perm, Maly Opera to Orenburg, the Musical Conservatory to Tashkent. The Leningrad Public Library managed to ship 360,000 volumes of its collection of 9 million. Voltaire's Library, the Pushkin Archives, Lenfilm Studios, and ninety-two Institutes of the Academy of Sciences all left the city before overland communications were cut (Salisbury 1969:258). Not all transports managed to leave the city. In September 1941 some 2,200 boxcars were left stranded in Leningrad.

By the time the blockade began, 488,700 inhabitants of Leningrad and 147,500 newcomers who sought refuge in the city had left (see Table 4-15). Included were 9,500 persons who went on foot along with cattle (Karasev 1959:94). The number of people remaining in the encircled city exceeded 2.5 million. Apparently, by September 6, some 2,489,400 ration cards had been issued, but in addition there were groups not entitled to individual rations (schools, institutions). The total estimate of 2,544,000 civilians given by Pavlov is quoted approvingly by Karasev 1959:120). In addition, there were 343,000 in the rural zones (as estimated at the end of the blockade).

Since food was in short supply (reserves were estimated to last for about a month) and capitulation was not envisaged, further reduction of nonessential populations was seriously considered. In fact, the Military Council of the Leningrad Front decided on September 4, 1941 to continue evacuation and remove an additional 1.2 million persons (Karasev 1959:93). However, the railway was cut by then and with the fall of Shlisselburg, a port on Lake Ladoga, on September 15, the waterway was also threatened. In October 1941 evacuation by boats was resumed, but it included only 33,500 persons before the ice road was built (Karasev 1959:134). Apparently the small number of available boats and exceptionally bad weather conditions in the fall of 1941 were mainly responsible for the limited success of the first evacuation over water (Adamowicz and Granin, 1988:380). Persons crossing Lake Ladoga could be further evacuated by trains, but the fall of Tikhvin on November 9, 1941 cut this connection. A relief road through the forest was built under enemy fire with great human losses, but three days after the road was completed, on December 9, 1941, Tikhvin was recaptured and the front line was pushed back by the Red Army to reach Volkhov River and beyond by the end of December (see Figure 4-11). The recaptured railway line could not be used without extensive repair work. In addition, the last section of the railway still remained in German hands.

In the latter part of 1941, airplanes were the only means of transportation used to bring food supplies and to remove people and equipment. Apparently some machines of the tank-producing Kirov Works were shipped to Chelyabinsk and Sverdlovsk along with 11,614 workers. In addition, 6,000 workers of the Izhorsk plant and 8,590 wounded military personnel were removed by planes. A separate category of evacuees were researchers of various institutes of the Academy of Sciences and their families (1,100 persons). They were sent by plane along with some of their scientific equipment to Kazan. Transport of military equipment produced in Leningrad continued as well (Karasev 1959:142). The number of persons airlifted during December 1941 is given by Karasev as 35,114 (1959:199). Salisbury gives a higher figure of 50,099 for a longer period, October to December 1941 (1969:382).

The increasing food shortage could not be alleviated by air supply and famine struck the city. One author estimates that starvation caused the death of 632,253 persons (Karasev 1959:185). In addition, there were casualties from air and artillery bombardment and losses during evacuation. However, other estimates give much higher figures of total civilian losses. Salisbury reviews the literature on the subject and suggests "something over 1,000,000 deaths attributable to hunger, and an overall total of deaths, civilian and military, on the order of 1,300,000 to 1,500,000, seems reasonable" (1969:516). However, internal party squabbles and personal intrigues after the war influenced research and published information. "The sacrifice of Leningrad was underrated; the death toll was minimized; the chance of political repercussions was reduced, at least for the time being" (Salisbury 1969:518).

In view of the famine, continuous removal of civilian population was seen as the best solution. The War Council of Leningrad decided on

December 6, 1941 to open an ice road across Lake Ladoga with a capacity of 5,000 persons per day by December 20. In fact, the first attempts to build the ice road date from late November. People were traveling by train to the coast and then crossing over the ice to Kabona (Adamowicz and Granin, 1988:67, 70). Until January 22, most people were trying to get across the frozen lake on their own and losses at that stage were very considerable. Broken vehicles and frozen bodies littered both the ice and the road from Kabona and Syasstroi (Karasev 1959:199). By January 22, 1942, 36,118 persons were evacuated via that route. On that day another decision of the State Defense Committee envisaged evacuation of 500,000 persons. Movement of people accelerated, thanks to better road conditions and the use of buses sent from Moscow. People were moved by train from the Finnish Station in Leningrad to the Borisova Griva Station. From there trucks and buses took them over the 30 km-long ice road across the lake to stations on the other side where they could board the train again at Voibokalo, Novyi Byt, or Volkhovstroi. Special medical services were set up to prevent outbreaks of epidemics. Heating stations were provided on the way at the 7, 11, 20, and 24 km points (Karasev 1959:200). To facilitate the movement, another short railway line was hastily constructed linking the coast with Voibokalo. The decision was taken in January 1942 and the line reached Lavrovo on February 1, Kabona on February 20, and the tip of the penninsula on March 6 (exhibit in the Leningrad Historical Museum). By the time of the spring break-up on April 15, 1942, more than 554,000 people had been evacuated over the ice road (see Table 4-15).

With the change of season, the waterway could be used again and evacuation by boat resumed. According to Karasev (1959:257–58) 338,545 persons were transported from May 27 to July 31, 1942, and on August 7 the War Council decided to evacuate an additional 46,000 by August 15 and thereby complete the mass evacuation of population. During all of 1943, an additional 14,362 were moved. Figures in Table 4-15 are somewhat higher. These higher figures are also quoted by Salisbury (1969:516). The total number of people evacuated reached 1.75 million, including half a million before the blockade started. Only some 500,000 were left in the city when the blockade was lifted by the recapture of Shlisselburg and January 27, 1945 brought the liberation of the city after 882 days of siege.

The presumably complete return of survivors and postwar reconstruction, as well as an influx of immigrants and natural increase, resulted in a rapid regrowth of the city population, which now exceeds

4 million and approaches 5 million for the urban agglomeration. But it is safe to assume that the aftereffects of the siege and the decimation of those who remained could be traced in Leningrad's demography for a good many years after 1945.

GERMANY I AND II, 1939–46

At the beginning of World War II, the aggressive, supremely confident government of Nazi Germany saw no reason to plan any large-scale redistribution of the country's inhabitants in the unlikely event of a major enemy assault. (This attitude contrasted greatly with that of the British during the same period.) Although a partial evacuation of the western frontier zone was planned and carried out in the early days of the war, its principal aim was to facilitate the movements of German troops, and it took place uneventfully. This evacuation is discussed briefly as Germany I. However, the increasing danger and damage to cities caused by intensifying air raids, particularly after 1943, did eventually lead to the evacuation of many city dwellers, indeed an estimated grand total of 10 million persons by the end of the war. We designate this massive event as Germany II.

The data sources for these wartime evacuations are far from perfect, but they are sufficient to provide a composite picture as well as details for selected cities. The most comprehensive collection of documents was published by the West German government well after World War II (FRG, *Betreuung* [1956] and *Dokumente* [1958–64]). An earlier comprehensive study is contained in the U.S. Strategic Bombing Survey (U.S.–SBS) (1947a). Attempts at overall evaluation of the problems of evacuation were made by various German authors (Hampe 1963; Schmidle 1957). Larass (1983) dealt with the specific case of evacuated children. There are a number of books and articles in which the fate of individual cities or regions was analyzed, some of which were consulted for the present study. They refer to Niedersachsen (Malecki 1947), Thüringen (Unrein 1953), Hamburg ("Die Hamburger Evakuierten" 1947), the Ruhr Industrial Region (Steinberg 1978), Baden (Kaiser n.d.), Nordrhein-Westfalen (Lamprecht 1949), Schleswig-Holstein ("Die Evakuierten" 1956) and Kiel (Voigt 1950). The problems of returning evacuees are discussed by Kornrumpf (1951), Fischer (1952), and Koch-Erpach (1951). Finally, various cartographic data are presented by Müller-Miny (1959), who reproduced a most interesting evacuation plan. It should be pointed out that the literature on the subject is more extensive. A comprehensive bibliography appears in Federal Republic of Germany . . . *Dokumente deutscher Kriegschäden,* vol. 5, 1964.

Statistics on evacuation were compiled during the war, but many have been lost. In fact, it seems that the central authorities ordered all records of evacuation destroyed (U.S.–SBS 1947a:179). But, luckily, some data were preserved in archives. Thus we were able to obtain in the Bundesarchiv located in Koblenz a set of data compiled by the Nazi Welfare Agency for the period of September 1943 to January 1945 (Germany, NSDAP 1943, 1943–44). Although the overall plan of evacuation was apparently destroyed during the war, a former employee of the Reichsstelle für Raumordnung, Professor Dr. Isenberg, was able to reconstruct some of its elements using the surviving documentation. These were published and are used in the present report (FRG *Dokumente* 1960, vol. 2, pt. 1:137–79). In addition, useful statistics on population change in German cities were compiled by Meynen (1958).

Last but not least, mention should be made of studies concerned with air raids and their impact. H. Rumpf (1962) has provided general comments, and a series of analytical studies were undertaken more recently by K. Hewitt (n.d., 1983a). A wealth of information is available in the U.S. Strategic Bombing Survey, including area reports (U.S.–SBS 1947b–d) and a final report (U.S.–SBS 1947a). A special publication on Hannover sponsored by the local newspaper (*Tasch* 1983) appeared on the occasion of the fortieth anniversary of the city's most devastating air raid.

Evacuation of the Frontier Zone (Germany I)

The frontier zone, in which defense fortifications against possible French attack were concentrated, received the code name Red Zone (*Rote Zone*). In the event of war, its population was to be evacuated immediately. A contiguous Green Zone (*Grüne Zone*) was to be evacuated in case of actual hostilities. On August 30, 1939, the reponsible civil servants, as well as officers of the Nazi party, received sealed packages with detailed instructions, including a timetable for evacuation, routes to be traveled, and so on.

Growing tension persuaded some inhabitants of the frontier zone to send their families into the Reich interior even before the outbreak of war. The official evacuation began on September 3, 1939 and involved "hundreds of thousands." The areas affected included Saarland (city of Saarbrücken, towns of Saarlouis, Völklinen, Merzig, Mettlach, and a number of villages) and some areas in Baden. Evacuees from Saarland were accommodated in private quarters in both rural and urban localities in Hessen and Thürigen,[28] a distance of some 200 to 400 km; those from Baden went mostly to neighboring areas in the Schwarzwald (Black Forest), a distance of some 20 to 40 km (FRG, *Dokumente*,[29] 1962, vol. 3). Evacuees from Saarland, many of them industrial workers and urban dwellers, were marched to the stations and then transported by train. Although the evacuation itself was carefully prepared and executed in orderly fashion, apparently some families did become separated, and there was a considerable mixing of people of different social backgrounds (FRG, *Dokumente* 1952, vol. 3:521). Farmers traveled on foot for the most part, but bicycles, pushcarts, trucks, and horse-drawn carts were also used, while cattle were driven along the roads on the hoof. Apparently, the day of evacuation was extremely hot, and an afternoon thunderstorm added to the general discomfort. According to the 1940 reports from Baden, farmers suffered considerable losses as a result of their temporary absence, and a special relief fund was established by the Ministry of Food, Agriculture, and Forestry (FRG, *Dokumente* 1962, vol. 3:522).

The military took over the evacuated areas and posted signs warning that looters would be shot. The French did cross the border on September 6, but they occupied only small sections of the borderland on either side of Saarbrücken, not more than 10 km in depth, and withdrew by mid-October 1939 (Maier et al. 1979:271). German civilians, particularly farmers, constantly tried to return, and the authorities had to make special efforts to enforce evacuation orders.

The Germany I evacuation officially terminated on December 19, 1939 but sick and handicapped persons were not allowed to return since another evacuation was anticipated. It is interesting to note the avoidance of publicity. Special orders were given not to organize any reception ceremonies, and press announcements were forbidden (FRG, *Dokumente* 1962, vol. 3:521).

The Red Zone was evacuated once again at the beginning of the French campaign (May 1940) and then again toward the end of the war.

Evacuations Resulting from Air Bombardment and Movement of the Front (Germany II)

Quite early in the war, German cities became targets of air raids and the extent of destruction and loss of life eventually attained alarming dimensions. Although German sources cite May 10–11, 1940[30] as the initiation of air attacks against German cities, and the first air raid against Berlin as taking place on August 26, 1940, massive "area bombing" began in 1942 with an attack against Lübeck on March 28–29. The American 8th Air Fleet joined the British in July 1942 and thereafter the aerial bombardment continued until the end of the war (FRG, *Dokumente* 1958, vol. 1:352). The total quantity of bombs dropped by the Allies on German-controlled territory came to nearly 2 million tons (as compared to 74,000 tons dropped on Britain, including V-1 and V-2 rockets), and in total, 131 cities and towns were hit, some of them several times (e.g., Berlin twenty-nine times; Braunschweig twenty-one times; Ludwigshafen and Mannheim nineteen times, etc.) (FRG, *Dokumente* vol. 1:46).

Losses of housing stock in cities over 20,000 were estimated at 2,842,000 housing units, or 41.2 percent of 1939 units in West Germany and Berlin alone.[31] An overall estimated total for all of Germany comes to about 20 percent (FRG, *Dokumente* 1958, vol. 1:52). Air raids were responsible for an estimated 540,000 civilian deaths within the prewar territory, including 410,000 victims in the present territory of the two German states, and some 130,000 among refugees from the lost territories. In addition, there were some 830,000 injured persons, of whom some 70,000 subsequently died, and these figures should be increased by losses among police and military personnel (24,000) and foreigners and prisoners of war (32,000) (FRG, *Dokument* 1958, vol. 1:60). Figures quoted in recent studies by a Canadian author are similar: 600,000 deaths and 800,000 injuries. In addition, he quotes an estimate of 7.5 million homeless persons (Hewitt 1983a:263).

The evacuation of population from vulnerable or devastated places began fairly early and involved millions of persons. Agencies of the Nazi party rather than government agencies provided most of the supervision. However, allocation of responsibilities changed during the war. Evacuation can be divided into three different categories: evacuation of children; evacuation of population from cities suffering from air raids; and evacuation of civilians from areas invaded by enemy armies during the last stages of the war. Evacuation planning and its implementation were quite different for the three types of movement.

Evacuation of children

This movement is said to have involved some 5 million children ages five to fourteen who were shifted at different times to various places in

Germany or even to other countries. A primary source for the following discussion is the popular account based on interviews with participants in this vast movement recently published by C. Larass (1983). The project was known as *Kinderlandverschickung* (KLV), a term borrowed from earlier activities of charitable or left-wing political organizations who sent underprivileged urban children to rural summer camps. It was this positive connotation that lay behind the choice of such a name (Larass 1983:45). In fact, the first public announcements spoke of intensification of KLV rather than the launching of a new campaign. It appears that the evacuation program was activated following the first air raid against Berlin on August 25, 1940. The initial memo on the subject was circulated on September 27, and the evacuation began on October 3, 1940 when the first trains from Berlin departed for the Sachsen and Sudeten regions (Larass 1983:25–27, 42, 46).

Two party agencies administered the program: Social Services (NSV—*Nationalsozialistische Volkswohlfahrt*) for preschoolers and grades 1 to 4; and Hitler Youth (HJ—*Hitlerjugend*) for older children. Baldur von Schirach, gauleiter of Vienna, assumed responsibility for the program on October 2, 1940. The official name of the agency located in Berlin was State Office of the Führer's Plenipotentiary for Expanded Sending of Children to the Countryside (*Reichsdienststelle des Beauftragten des Führers für die erweiterte Kinderlandverschickung*) (Larass 1983:46).[32]

The entire action was planned in minute detail as set forth in a 256-page booklet of rules and regulations. It covered preparations, transport, bulletins for parents, instructions for teachers and physicians, and so on (Larass 1983:27). From the very beginning, evacuation was voluntary, and initially included mostly underprivileged children, who represented some 70 percent of the total. Eventually, nearly all children left the increasingly uninhabitable urban centers (Larass 1983:33). Only certain categories were excluded (e.g., those with severe asthma or heart conditions); and handicapped children were placed in special camps. Initially, children were assigned to mixed groups set up for evacuation purposes; later whole classes with their teachers went together.

The selected destinations lay in presumably safe areas—east Bayern, Brandenburg, Oberdonau, Sachsen, Thüringen, Silesia, Sudeten, incorporated Polish Wartheland, or even conquered Ostland (Larass 1983:26). Older children found themselves in former youth hostels, inns, hotels, and various other institutions, while the younger ones were billeted with families. On many occasions, close bonds developed with their temporary foster parents, leading sometimes to subsequent adoptions, especially when the natural parents had perished during the evacuation period. Apparently quite a number of today's Catholic Bavarians are of northern Protestant background. The Nazi authorities had hoped that evacuation would contribute to strengthening the hold of the party over youth. That it was by and large unsuccessful in accomplishing this aim was mainly due to the attitude and role of teachers, many of whom were recalled from retirement (Larass 1983:271).

Initially, KLV was limited to selected cities, and the number of persons involved was not too great. It appears that by August 1943, only some 300,000 children had been evacuated (U.S.-SBS 1947a:157). Later the numbers increased considerably and, according to German estimates, 5 million children were ultimately involved, of whom some 500,000 went to foreign countries, including conquered areas in Poland and Czechoslovakia (considered to be parts of Greater Germany) but also Hungary, Bulgaria, parts of Yugoslavia, Latvia, and Denmark. In addition, some 20,000 Belgian and Dutch children were evacuated. Most traveled by trains (apparently more than 20,000 evacuation trains were involved), while tens of thousands journeyed by boat. Children destined for Hungary and Bulgaria often embarked in Vienna and sailed down the Danube. There were also evacuation boats from Hamburg going upstream on the River Elbe/Laabe to Dresden or into Bohemia. Those sent to Bulgaria (boys only) ended up in seaside hotels on the Black Sea coast; evacuees in Hungary were billeted in villages (boys) or camps (girls) (Larass 1983:108, 117).

Very rapid implementation of the program and its massive scale led to many problems apart from family separation and feelings of loneliness. Mixing of social and religious groups, strange food (especially abroad), long travel delays, substandard accommodation, conflicts with natives (especially in occupied territories)—these and other difficulties affected many children. When the reputation of the program began to suffer, the authorities responded with a propaganda blitz. However, films, photos, and stories that exaggerated the attractive aspects of the KLV program led to unreasonable expectations and in turn even greater frustration. In some cases, children who could not cope or were excessively troublesome were either sent back or isolated in special camps; the great majority, however, spent years away from home in regular camps.

The KLV program reached its highest level in the summer and fall of 1944, when air raids were particularly devastating. At that time all

large cities were practically devoid of children, those young evacuees
being cared for in at least 12,000 camps. Most were located in distant
"safe" areas, but some were relatively close to large urban agglomerations, such as the Taunus area near Frankfurt, the Eifel for children
from Köln, Bonn and the Ruhr Industrial Region, and the lake district
around Potsdam for Berliners. Camps of many types varied greatly in
size, some having only twenty to forty youngsters in a pension or villa,
while others were much larger (Larass 1983:158).

Not all areas were wisely selected, particularly toward the end of
the war. Evacuation trains took children to the eastern provinces and
into Bohemia as late as 1944. The number of children in Czech lands
was estimated at 50,000 to 100,000 in January 1945. Early that year
flight from the east began. In some cases there were close calls (e.g.,
evacuation by boat under Soviet fire from Kolberg/Kolobrzeg in Pommern), and lives were lost. However, overall losses of life among
evacuated children were extremely small. On the other hand, boys who
had came of age during the evacuation period and were drafted by the
military or SS experienced many casualties (Larass 1983:168–73).

Apparently, the greatest difficulties developed after capitulation
since the whole program was canceled by the Allies and the former
support system collapsed. The return of millions of children could not
be accomplished overnight. Those who were located relatively close to
home went back on foot, even if that required a long difficult march.
By the winter of 1945–46, most cities had retrieved their children.
However, the return to Berlin continued into summer 1946. The Berlin
authorities wished to delay return even further, until early 1947, but
the Bavarian authorities insisted on earlier departure. Similarly, the
return to Hamburg continued until the fall of 1946 (Larass 1983:254–
58).

Evacuation of civilian population

In the early years of the war, evacuation of civilians was limited in
scope and almost exclusively spontaneous, relying as it did on private
networks for contacts and hospitality. The only exception was the
KLV program. However, with the increasing intensity of aerial bombardment and serious housing losses, the problems of saving lives,
finding substitute accommodations close to the workplace, or, if need
be, moving people some distance away became major challenges to the
German authorities. The ensuing actions were jointly called *Umquar-*

tierungen (organized change of residence) and covered a variety of moves including:

a. Billeting of homeless within the affected community, or in close proximity, in private quarters or public shelters. This was particularly important for critical members of the labor force
b. Evacuation of homeless persons to distant areas deemed safe and having sufficient absorption capacity
c. Precautionary evacuations from endangered cities, involving mostly the older population as well as mothers with small children

In all these categories one could distinguish between spontaneous evacuations (gladly accepted and supported by the authorities) and directed movements. The latter assumed greater importance in later stages of war (Hampe 1963).

The overall responsibility for evacuation rested with the Nazi party's welfare organization, but increasingly both funds and technical support came from the government, particularly the Ministry of Internal Affairs. By April 1943, the minister of interior had issued instructions regarding evacuations, and subsequently an elaborate plan was developed and partially implemented.

As early as 1942, the German authorities began to confront problems arising out of the destruction of cities, as documented by a number of circulars issued by government agencies. By 1943 the problems had greatly intensified, and on the basis of experience gathered as of that date the following principles for evacuation planning were formulated (Hampe 1963:420–21).

A. As much as possible, evacuated individuals were to be accommodated in their own regions *(heimatnahe Gebiete)*. For each urban region, a receiving area should be designated with sufficient capacity to accommodate its evacuees. This capacity can roughly be measured by the number of households in the reception area, which should be equal to the number of households in the urban region in question
B. Members of the labor force were to be transferred not too far from their places of employment, with due regard for their safety but without excessive demands on transportation facilities. Within the evacuating areas, the following zones were proposed:
   1. A *Central Urban Zone* with population density exceeding 200 person per ha. Only essential workers were to remain here

2. A *Peripheral Urban Zone* with densities ranging from 20 to 200 per ha should also be cleared, if possible, of nonactive inhabitants. This zone would also be available for the essential labor force from Zone 1

3. A *Short-Distance Commuting Zone* within which commuting time to the center does not exceed 60 minutes. To be used for housing economically active persons whose families had to leave Zones 1 and 2

4. A *Long-Distance Commuting Zone* in the 60 to 100 minute commuting range to be reserved for people who should be placed in Zone 3 but for whom space is lacking

5. A *Weekend Commuting Zone* within a travel time of 100 to 180 minutes (in exceptional cases up to 240 minutes of travel by train) to be used for family members of those economically active persons left in Zones 1 and 2

6. A *Distant Zone Within Own Region* including areas from which more than a four-hour train trip (including travel to and from station) was required, to be used for accommodating nonactive population without close ties to those left in Zones 1 and 2

C. Separation of families should be avoided
D. Form of housing should match needs. The following forms were to be considered:
   1. Own housing unit
   2. Accommodation in somebody else's apartment but with own kitchen facilities
   3. Subtenancy (without own kitchen)
   4. Accommodation in existing provisional unit that can be further expanded
   5. Accommodation in newly built provisional housing unit
   6. Camps, barracks, etc.
E. Comparison of demand and supply of housing units in receiving area and also an appraisal of transportation capacity in the light of future commuting needs would indicate the necessity for new construction and its location
F. In order to avoid chaos in each urban region, initial receiving centers should be identified. These fully equipped centers, located along principal evacuation routes, were to be used to assemble evacuees who would later be directed to appropriate receiving areas.

At the same time, the following schematic plan was announced in an appendix to a document dated April 15, 1943 (FRG, *Dokumente* 1960, vol 2, pt. 1:127):

Sending Districts	Receiving Districts
Berlin	Brandenburg
	Ostpreussen
	Pommern
Düsseldorf	Thüringen
	Oberdonau
	Mainfranken
	(Moselland)
Essen	Württemberg-Hohenzollern
	Tirol
	Niederdonau
	Steiermark
	Kärnten
	Westfalen-Nord
	Schwaben
	(Moselland)
Hamburg	Schleswig-Holstein
	Bayreuth
	Brandenburg
Köln-Aachen	Baden
	Sachsen
	Niederschlesien
	(Moselland)
Schleswig-Holstein (Kiel)	Schleswig-Holstein
	Franken
Weser-Ems	Weser-Ems
	Sachsen
	Kurhessen
Westfalen-Nord	Westfalen-Nord
	München
Westfalen Süd	Baden
	Sudentenland
	(Moselland)

The overall evacuation plan for all of Germany was ready by the beginning of 1944. Known as the *Reichsumquartierungsplan,* it was prepared by a Center of Regional Planning *(Reichsstelle für Raumord-nung)*. The plan was published after the war (FRG, *Dokumente* 1960, vol. 2, pt. 1:123–79) and is summarized in Hampe (1963:422). It incorporated the principles presented above and specified reception areas for various urban centers. As it turned out, local or not-too-distant accommodations for would-be evacuees could be found for smaller places and even cities in the 150,000 to 900,000 category. The problem arose with the four largest urban agglomerations for which more distant receiving areas had to be found.

The national plan was prepared for a network of forty-two Party Districts *(Gaue)* grouped in seven accommodation regions *(Unterbringungsgaugemeinschaften)*. It provided for the housing of nearly 12 million evacuees, mostly in private households (see Figure 4-12). Nearly 2 million people were to be located in provisional public shelters, of which about one-third were to be newly built, the scale of construction considered realistic under the circumstances (Hampe 1963:422). These regions also contained the two largest urban agglomerations, the Ruhr Industrial Region and Berlin. More detailed data on

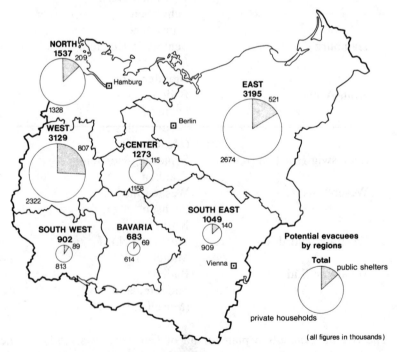

Figure 4-12. Germany: Evacuation plan, 1944

planned evacuations from the four largest urban regions are summarized in Table 4-16. It appears that some 5,736,000 person were to be evacuated, mostly from the west and from Berlin.

In terms of 1939 population figures, evacuees as percent of total population would have ranged from 35 percent in the western region to 44 percent in Berlin, with ca. 40 percent for both Wien and Hamburg. In three cases, the proportion of persons who had to be sent to more distant areas was particularly high. It may be assumed that the percentages of population scheduled for transfer from smaller cities was similar to those for the giant urban agglomerations.[33]

The actual movement of population from threatened cities or those actually destroyed took place progressively during the period 1943–45. The German authorities tried to keep track of evacuee flows as they related to envisaged accommodation capacity in the receiving areas. Table 4-17 and Figures 4-12 and 4-13 summarize a number of reports found in the Bundesarchiv. It appears that the total number registered in receiving areas increased enormously, particularly during 1944. There were fewer than 3 million in September 1943 but almost 9 million by the end of 1944. The latter figure requires some clarification. It includes not only evacuees from air-raided cities but also 2,140,000 people evacuated from areas threatened or occupied by the Allies. The refugees from outside the national territory (both ethnic Germans and foreigners), some 150,000 by the end of 1944, do not enter into this total. Data so adjusted were used in preparing Figure 4-13. Although the authorities encouraged spontaneous migration and were more than happy to see evacuees moving in with their relatives or friends, most of these persons fell into the "organized" category.[34]

Relocation of factories also contributed to the general redistribution of population since personnel usually transferred with the plants. Even though they were not technically classified as evacuees, they must also be included in the total. Thus the total number of evacuees as of the end of 1944 may be estimated at 9,630,000, including: 6,650,000 evacuees from air-raided areas; 2,140,000 from areas threatened or occupied by the enemy (*Räumung*); and 840,000 moved in connection with plant relocations. Apparently the Reich directive of March 6, 1945 gave the much higher figure of 16.5 million, consisting of: 8.5 million civilians in the east and 1.4 million in the west due to enemy occupation of territory; 4.9 million due to "air terror"; and almost 2 million miscellaneous displaced individuals (U.S.–SBS:1947a:165).

The sum of the last two figures (6.9 million) is not much different from the estimate arrived at above (6.65 million). An estimate of

Table 4-16. Planned Evacuation of Major Urban Regions in Germany*

Region	Total Population in 1939	Total Planned Evacuation	In Private Households Neighboring Region[1]	Elsewhere	In Public Shelters
Western Urban Region including Ruhr area	6,750	2,356	959 (West)	670	727
Berlin	4,322	1,905	948 (East)	775	281
Vienna[2]	1,930	800	545 (Southeast)	145	110
Hamburg	1,698	675	334 (North)	249	92

*In 1000s. Evacuation plan as of March 1944.
[1]Accommodation regions are shown in Fig. 15.
[2]Vienna was part of Germany within 1939 boundaries.
Source: FRG, *Dokumente* 1960, vol. 2, pt. 1: 153–66.

Table 4-17. Germany: Number of Evacuees from Endangered Areas in Receiving Regions, 1943–44

Date of Inquiry (Stichtag)	Organized Evacuations	Spontaneous Evacuations	Total
Sept. 9, 1943	1,792,884	977,871	2,770,755
Oct. 18, 1943	1,987,182	1,241,025	3,228,207
Dec. 15, 1943	2,094,964	1,146,290	3,241,254
Jan. 22, 1944	2,157,175	1,180,142	3,337,317
Sept. 9, 1944[1]	4,301,271	1,346,013	5,647,284
Oct. 10, 1944[1]	5,029,124	1,540,566	6,569,690
Nov. 11, 1944[1]	6,044,916	1,724,964	7,769,880
End of 1944[1,4]	7,175,020[2]	1,769,956	8,944,976

[1]Including refugees from areas threatened by invading armies (Räumung).
[2]This number includes 93,276 ethnic-German refugees and 56,494 foreign refugees.
[3]In addition there were 841,105 persons moved with their industrial plants (Betriebsverlagerung + Industrielle Sonderaktion).
[4]Date refer to different dates between Nov. 17, 1944 and Jan. 8, 1945.
Source: Germany, NSDAP.

evacuation totals based on comparing 1939 and 1946 population figures for major cities, and thus quite rough, is given in a postwar German source at 4 to 5 million (FRG, *Dokumente* 1958, vol. 1:104). Territorial distribution as reported in the last available archival report (January 1945) shows a considerable dispersal of evacuees throughout the national territory (see Figure 4-13). The largest numbers, exceeding 300,000 per district, were found in the eastern (Ostpreussen, Pommern, Niederschlesien) and central sections of the country (Brandenburg, Sachsen, Thüringen, Halle-Merseburg, Magdeburg). Similar concentrations were also found in the southwest (Baden, Hessen, and Württemberg) and northwest (Hannover and Westfalen). Among the thirty-seven districts listed, local evacuees dominated in sixteen, those from Ostpreussen in two, and there was no clear dominance in four districts; but in the remaining fifteen, evacuees from the largest cities clearly predominated: from Berlin, four; Köln and Hamburg in three districts each; cities of the Ruhr area, two; Saarland, two; and Wien, one. In all of them, planned movement accounted for most evacuations. Finally, one should point out that at that time the Austrian districts had received relatively fewer evacuees than the others.

The distribution pattern of the evacuated population changed at the beginning of 1945 as both fronts, eastern and western, moved deeper into German territory. Plans for evacuation from the east were first made in September 1944 when four alternatives were considered involving 5 million, 8.4 million, or 10.9 million persons (FRG, *Dokumente* 1960, vol. 2, pt. 1:176). By January 1945, it became obvious that

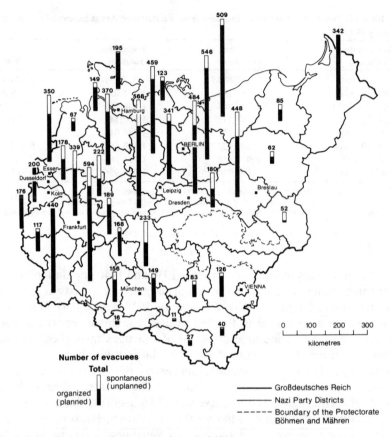

Figure 4-13. Evacuees in Germany by the end of 1944

even though earlier plans were considered far-fetched, massive evacuation of three zones would have to be considered, and the possible number of evacuees could reach 10 million (FRG, *Dokumente* 1960, vol. 2, pt. 1:177). The Reich directive quoted above spoke of 8.35 million, but it seems that in reality this flow was somewhat smaller.

Thus the maximum total number of people evacuated from cities threatened with, or damaged by, air raids can be estimted at 12.5 million including:

Evacuation	6.6 to 6.9 million
Industrial relocation	0.8 million
Evacuation of children	up to 5 million (may be partially included in the general evacuation)

In addition, up to 10 million persons may have been removed from areas occupied by the enemy in the last stages of war.

Estimates of the total number of evacuees by other authors vary a great deal, ranging from 4 million (FRG, *Betreuung* 1956:13) through an intermediate 4 to 5 million (FRG, *Dokumente* 1958, vol. 1:104) up to 10 million (Kornrumpf 1951:39). The task of coming up with a reasonably accurate number is complicated by the fact that a large number of evacuated persons returned even during the war. For example, some 700,000 to 800,000 evacuees left Hamburg after catastrophic air raids in July 1943, but only 400,000 were still absent at the end of the war ("Die Hamburger Evakuierten" 1947:1). Estimates based on flows necessarily differ considerably from those based on residual stock of refugees. In our own estimate of evacuations and industrial relocations, using confidential data found in the Bundesarchiv, the stock concept was used; hence the figures may err on the low side. The number of evacuated children derives from Larass (1983), and is presumably based on flows.

Aftermath of evacuations

Termination of hostilities and the collapse of the German Reich created a new situation. The victorious Allies took political control and proceeded to liquidate the effects of the war. The repatriation of foreign workers and prisoners of war located in Germany and the return of displaced Germans were urgent items on the agenda. At the same time, a massive influx of ethnic Germans expelled from the east, including the former eastern territories of Germany, created new problems. Resettling the evacuated population was particularly difficult in view of the enormous damage to the housing stock. The magnitude of this destruction is apparent in the following estimates derived from an official German publication (FRG, *Dokumente*, 1958; vol. 1:51–55).

Germany within 1937 boundaries:	4 million housing units destroyed or heavily damaged	20% of 1939 housing stock
West Germany: Cities with more than 20,000 (including Berlin)	2.8 million housing units destroyed	41% of 1939 housing stock

All communities	2.2 million housing units	20% of 1943
(excluding Berlin)	destroyed	housing stock
East Germany:	0.6 million housing units	13% of 1939
	destroyed or unusable	housing stock

Data for individual cities indicate different levels of destruction, reaching in extreme cases some two-thirds of total housing units (see Table 4-18).[35] Spontaneous return began immediately and accounted for most evacuees, but even five years after the war had ended, ten out of the eleven largest cities of prewar Germany contained smaller populations than the totals enumerated in 1939 (see Table 4-19). In the aggregate, West German cities over 50,000 had 2.4 million fewer inhabitants in 1946 than in 1939 (Kornrumpf 1951:Table).

As mentioned above, the return of the evacuees began immediately and spontaneously in spite of limited housing capacity in the bomb-battered cities, various administrative difficulties, and the obstacles to travel in a devastated and divided country. Two examples show the scale and speed of these return flows. Cities in the Ruhr Industrial Region increased their population by about 1 million from May 1945 to the end of October 1946 (Steinberg 1978:124). In Thüringen, the number of evacuees declined from 468,000 as of September 20, 1945 to 215,000 by the end of 1945 and further to 114,000 by December 31, 1946 (Unrein 1953:22–23). However, one should also keep in mind that many urban evacuees did not return until 1947. The reasons included lack of proper sanitation, the transfer of persons temporarily housed

Table 4-18 Destruction of Major German Cities

City	Loss of Housing Units (in 1000s)	Percentage Loss of Housing Units (1945/1939)	1946 Population as a Percentage of 1939 Figures
Berlin	556.5[1]	37.0[1]	74
Hamburg	295.7	53.5	83
Munich	82.0	33.0	91
Cologne	176.6	70.0	64
Leipzig	—	25.0	87
Essen	100.0	50.5	79
Dresden	—	60.0	79
Frankfurt/Main	80.6	44.0	77
Dortmund	105.5	65.8	81
Düsseldorf	86.5	50.9	79

[1]West Berlin only.
Source: FRG, *Dokumente* 1958:1, 50–54.

Table 4-19. Population of Major German Cities 1939–50*

City[1]	1939	1946	1950
Berlin[2]	4,322	3,187	3,336
Hamburg	1,698	1,403	1,606
Munich	826	752	831
Cologne	768	491	595
Leipzig	702	608	618
Essen	665	525	605
Dresden	630	468	494
Breslau[3]	621	171	309
Frankfurt/Main	548	424	532
Dortmund	538	436	507
Düsseldorf	536	421	501

*In 1000s.
[1]Included in the table are cities with more than 500,000 in 1939, within 1937 boundaries.
[2]Postwar data calculated for both West and East Berlin.
[3]In 1945 Breslau was transferred to Poland under the name Wroclaw and its German population was expelled.
Source: Meynen 1958:358–59.

in air raid shelters, requisitioning of space by occupation authorities, and a housing shortage intensified by the return of men from POW camps (FRG, *Dokumente* 1958, vol. 1:353).

As late as 1947, the number of wartime evacuees still absent from their home localities was said to be 3.4 million (FRG, *Dokumente* 1958, vol. 1:167). An enumeration carried out in 1951 was not successful (Fischer 1952), but by then the problem of residential evacuees had entered the political agenda of the Federal Republic.

The first attempt to come up with appropriate legislation and an assistance program dates from 1951. Following extensive parliamentary debate, a special law on evacuees came into effect on July 18, 1953. This law and a supplementary measure passed on October 9, 1957 were designed to help those evacuees who wished to return to their original areas (Hampe 1963:429). A working definition of evacuees was announced by the federal minister of interior in 1950. It specified evacuees as (*a*) those persons who left their place of residence prior to May 8, 1945 because of war-related events, either by official order or on their own, and who relocated themselves within the territory of the Federal Republic; and (*b*) persons who had to leave their communities after May 8, 1945 on orders of the military authorities of the three Western occupying powers. Furthermore, war-related causes were defined as follows (FRG, *Dokumente* 1958, vol. 1:110):

- transfer (*Umquartierung*) of inhabitants from frontier zones or occupied areas in order to protect them from hostilities

- transfer of people from areas threatened by air raids
- transfer of persons because of the removal of industrial plants from high-risk areas
- transfer of persons caused by establishment of military facilities
- transfer of persons whose residences were destroyed by bombing raids or other war activities

A second revised bill on evacuees (*Das Bundesevakuiertengesetz*) was enacted on September 26 and went into force on October 13, 1961. It was followed by administrative provisions adopted by various Lander (political jurisdictions) between November 29, 1961 and January 11, 1962. The assistance program scheduled to terminate by the end of 1968 (FRG, *Dokumente* 1964, vol. 4, pt. 1:224–25, 233) provided for free passage, preferential assignment of housing space, and financial help in reintegration.

By the end of 1963, the central register of evacuees contained 187,000 households with 510,000 persons. From this total, 69,000 households (195,000 persons) were eventually removed from the list of various reasons, such as death, refusal to continue, loss of entitlement, and so on. The remaining 117,600 households (316,000 persons) were covered by provision of the law. By the end of 1963, 97,000 households (266,000 persons) had returned while 20,800 households (50,000 persons) still awaited repatriation (FRG, *Dokumente* 1964, vol. 4, pt. 1:176, 232, 514–15). The following figures representing the number of persons still awaiting repatriation show the progress in accomplishing the program's objectives (FRG, *Dokumente* 1964, vol. 4, pt. 1:233): 1957—283,000, of whom 191,000 in the same Land; 1960—116,000, of whom 79,000 in the same Land; 1963—50,000, of whom 36,000 in the same Land. Thus it appears that most applicants were expecting to move within the same Land.

The whole saga of evacuation and return, which involved at least 12 million individuals, had finally came to an end after almost a quarter-century. There is no doubt, however, that the social and psychological impact of this massive involuntary movement of population was to be felt much longer by the affected generations.

JAPAN, 1944–45

The massive aerial bombardment of virtually all of Japan's larger urban centers and many of its lesser ones during the later stages of

World War II produced a huge evacuation of city dwellers. With a total variously estimated as falling between 8.5 and 10 million persons (some 12 to 14 percent of the de facto national population), this exodus may well be the largest in recent history, rivaled or exceeded perhaps only by the eastward transfer of Soviet citizens in 1941–42 or the World War II evacuations of Germans. As is the case with Great Britain, and, to some degree, Germany, but unlike the situation in so many other countries whose cities were devastated during World War II or subsequent conflicts, we are fortunate in having relatively detailed information on this series of events in Japan, in this instance thanks principally to the intensive surveys conducted by the United States Strategic Bombing Survey (U.S.-SBS 1947e–j) in the weeks and months immediately following the end of hostilities, as supplemented by the records kept by various Japanese statistical offices.

The tragic Japanese experience is rather ironic in view of the fact that the regime began hostilities in 1941 without any official policy, plans, or preparations for the relocation of the civilian population in the homeland. Although the government had been considering the problems of defense against attack for some years before Pearl Harbor, there is scant evidence that it seriously considered evacuating large numbers of people from its cities. The worst-case scenario envisioned the occasional token attack, for example, the Doolittle Raid of 1942, against which standard civil defense measures could, and did, suffice. It took all of two years beyond Pearl Harbor before the gradual reversal of Japan's prospects in the Pacific War forced a reappraisal of defense measures. By late 1943, heavy American bombing raids had become a distinct possibility; then, in 1944 they became a reality, and increased in frequency, scope, and destructiveness into the early months of 1945.

On December 21, 1943 the Japanese cabinet formulated the first explicit evacuation program, one in which the largest cities were designated as "strong air-defense cities" (Stanford Research Institute 1953:170). Classified as "evacuation areas" were the four principal industrial districts on Honshu and Kyushu; and the governors of the affected prefectures were to assume responsibility for managing the evacuation of nonessential persons. Although such individuals were strongly urged to remove themselves to safer areas, the decision to leave was voluntary, and, at least initially, precautionary. As it happend, for most evacuees flight from the cities remained voluntary until the very end of the war. Workers in essential industries were, of course, excluded from the nonessential category. Included in it were: the temporarily unemployed; those living on annuities, pensions, rentals, interest, and the like; those whose occupation did not necessitate living in the evacuation area; children in primary schools (second year and below); unweaned children and their mothers; pregnant women requiring the care of a midwife; the aged; the incapacitated; those suffering from serious chronic illness; and a few other minor categories (Stanford Research Institute 1953:171). A rather novel feature of the plan was the effort directed toward increasing Japan's war potential, first by reducing support services for the inhabitants of target areas and, second, by encouraging at least some of the evacuees to contribute toward agricultural and other forms of productivity in the host areas.

Until the regulatory system began to crumble as a consequence of the catastrophic air raids of March 1945, the government maintained reasonably strict supervision of the voluntary exodus and was able to assist the displaced persons in a variety of ways. Potential evacuees went through a screening process by filling out questionnaires detailing relevant personal facts as well as transportation and other needs before they received the mandatory certificates legalizing their move and entitling them to various forms of assistance. These included help in obtaining transportation for persons and baggage, subsidies for moving, and, in some cases, food, temporary shelter, and emergency first aid.

Before the end of the war other categories of evacuees materialized in addition to voluntary evacuees with certificates for changing districts. From March 1945 onward, the tidal wave of humanity leaving the cities became such that many voluntary evacuees were allowed to relocate elsewhere without certificates. Similarly, the growing number of air raid victims—those who lost their homes and possibly also their places of employment and thus were left with few options but onward movement—could be divided into those with, and those without, certificates. A quite special contingent of unfortunates consisted of fire-break refugees. Demolition to create fire-breaks around important factories, communication facilities, and other important buildings, and to clear fire lanes through cities, began in November 1943 (Stanford Research Institute 1953:176). More than half the national total of 1,844,000 persons displaced in the course of this program lost their homes in the period March–June 1945 (U.S.-SBS 1947:169). Aside from receiving advance notice, payment for the demolished structures, and purchase by the city of usable household articles, these fire-break sufferers were treated much the same by the government as were the ordinary voluntary evacuees. Some statistics for Kobe with respect to certain categories of evacuees may reflect the situation for other large cities (U.S.-SBS 1947e:81, 167).

Voluntary evacuees with certificates for changing districts	279,952
Voluntary evacuees without certificates	150,000 (est.)
Air raid victims with certificates	153,958
Air raid victims without certificates	15,000 (est.)
Schoolchildren	76,782
Total	675,692

The final category, that of evacuated schoolchildren, is especially interesting and well documented. Upon instructions from the cabinet in June 1944, many of the schoolchildren enrolled in grades 3 to 6 left the evacuation areas during the period August–September 1944. Although the directive was advisory rather than mandatory, some 53 percent of the pupil population of the major metropolises did relocate to rural localities at this time (see Table 4-20). As was the case with the evacuation in general, the authorities (and the citizenry as well) favored movement in family units. But in those many instances when it was not practical or permissible for the entire family to move or for the child to leave in the company of their relatives, officials dispatched classmates in organized groups, along with their teachers, to the reception areas. In a departure from the patterns developed by other evacuees (but in a manner reminiscent of the German situation), the student groups generally found themselves in small communities quite far from the threatened metropolises. Living quite austerely, these student groups were usually not incorporated into the local school systems but operated as autonomous units. With much of the day spent in growing or foraging for food, only an hour or two of instruction was the rule.

As the bombing campaign intensified in early 1945, another official order appeared on March 16, this time making evacuation compulsory for those schoolchildren in grades 3 to 6 living in certain designated evacuation areas, while those in the remaining target zones were strongly urged to leave. In addition, first- and second-grade pupils were urgently advised to leave in company with family or relatives. This second juvenile exodus took place largely in April 1945, and although it was not as massive as the initial one (411,478 from the major cities as against 796,668 previously), it must have been much

Table 4-20. Japan: Schoolchildren Who Had Been Evacuated from Major Cities, 1944–45*

| | August 1944 | | | | August 1945 | | | |
| | | Evacuees | | | | Evacuees | | |
City	Pupil Population	In Groups	With Guardians	Percent Evacuated	Pupil Population	In Groups	With Guardians	Percent Evacuated
Tokyo	697.3	179.7	195.4	53.8	717.1	203.4	416.8	86.5
Yokohama	124.3	23.2	39.7	50.6	111.2	31.9	61.3	83.8
Kawasaki	38.9	6.4	15.1	55.2	32.1	7.1	20.5	86.0
Yokosuka	25.9	6.8	10.2	65.5	27.8	8.7	10.2	67.9
Nagoya	157.8	32.3	36.5	43.6	105.8	39.4	53.4	87.8
Osaka	328.4	67.9	117.7	56.5	296.5	89.8	178.7	90.6
Kobe	106.2	17.2	34.2	48.3	80.4	26.8	50.0	95.5
Amagasaki	24.8	3.9	10.6	58.7	26.9	7.1	13.1	75.0
Total	1,503.6	337.3	459.3	53.0	1,397.7	414.3	803.9	87.2

*In 1000s. The figures represent population "stock" rather than flow, i.e., they do not necessarily reflect the total number of individuals who were engaged in evacuation before or after August 1944.
Source: U.S. Strategic Bombing Survey 1947e:167.

more frantic. Whereas some 42.3 percent of the first batch of young evacuees had left in groups, the figure was only 18.7 percent for those departing in 1945. In any event, the plan worked well. Altogether, 87.2 percent of the schoolchildren in the larger metropolises (and probably some from lesser cities as well) were sent to safe havens. It is likely that at least 27,000 of them would have perished had they remained in the bomb-battered cities.

As already suggested, the evacuation of Japan's cities began belatedly and haltingly, then accelerated sharply during the final sixteen months of the conflict. The initial hesitation on the part of the city dwellers can be attributed in the main to such universal factors as inertia, ties of family and neighborhood affection, and the absence at first of any plausible danger. In addition, there were mixed signals from a government that, on the one hand, urged nonessential persons to evacuate but, on the other, proclaimed its capability to protect the cities.

Only a trickle of evacuees had departed from Tokyo and other major cities by the end of 1943, and, aside from the removal of many schoolchildren, not much was accomplished until the early B-29 raids on Kyushu in June 1944. Although the month-to-month numbers varied considerably, the volume of out-movement increased markedly during the rest of the year, and by October 31 more than 2 million persons, or some 13.5 percent of their population, had left fourteen of the largest cities (see Table 4-21).

About the time of the first serious B-29 raids on Toyko in late 1944, there was an upsurge of evacuation as the mood of the populace began to change from strong resistance against the notion of leaving to something bordering on panic. In the case of the capital city, there was a curious conjuncture of events that hastened the process, as described by a French journalist stranded there for the duration of the war.

. . . fortunately the intensity of bombing increases gradually and people are getting used to the danger. Nevertheless a massive exodus begins during the early days of December. The city is electrified by the rumor that a massive raid will take place on December 8, the anniversary of Pearl Harbor. Thousands are leaving hastily, laying siege to the stations and taking the trains by assault. On the 7th there are four alarms in Tokyo but the bombs fall further south and hit the town of Shizuoka. This venerable center of green tea culture, which was completely destroyed by a great fire in 1939 and has just been rebuilt, experiences twenty-four hours of tragedy: During the afternoon it is shaken by a violent earth-

Table 4-21. Major Japanese Cities: Estimated Evacuation, 1944–45*

City	Estimated Population, Feb. 1944	Estimated Evacuees as of Oct. 31, 1944	Percent of Population	Estimated Evacuees and Refugees as of Aug. 15, 1945	Percent of Population
Osaka	2,842	384	13.5	1,809	63.7
Tokyo	6,569	1,040	15.8	4,139	63.0
Nagoya	1,348	144	10.7	848	62.9
Kobe	918	152	16.6	558	60.8
Kawasaki	380	50	13.2	230	60.5
Yokohama	1,033	153	14.8	433	41.9
Amagasaki	270	42	15.5	70	25.9
Moji	135	11	8.1	35	25.9
Yawata	252	37	14.7	52	20.6
Yokosuka	298	32	10.7	58	19.5
Wakamatsu	87	7	8.0	17	19.5
Kokura	184	25	13.6	34	18.5
Tohata	82	13	15.9	12	14.6
Kyoto	1,090	—	—	46	4.2
Total	15,488	2,090	13.5	8,341	53.9

*In 1,000s.
Source: Stanford Research Institute 1953:180; U.S. Strategic Bombing Survey 1947j:171.

quake; two hours later American superfortresses drop incendiary bombs; and at midnight another earthquake. But in Tokyo the 7th and 8th pass uneventfully. (Guillain 1947:201)

After the first great fire raid on Tokyo in March 1945, the volume and rate of urban flight reached unprecedented levels.

Hundreds of thousands began a desperate flight from that city, and the urban area raids on Nagoya, Osaka, and Kobe which followed spread the contagion to those places as well. Up to this time only about 3 percent of all evacuees had been bombed out, but during March about 2 million people lost their homes and mass flights of the bombed-out began. Even those who left because of fear of bombing rather than actual disaster now knew, by experience, what they feared so greatly. Although bombing was intermittent during the spring of 1945, evacuees continued to leave, and the government had to adopt emergency measures to assist a migration which it could not control. Emergency rations were issued even to those who had no certificates proving that their homes had burned. People were urged to leave if they had any place to go. The government no longer made any attempt at all to select refuge areas. New organizations were set up—at least on paper—to assist evacuees. Work on fire lanes was speeded up, even in smaller cities, and this added to the number of homeless. (U.S.-SBS 1947i:74)

During the summer months of 1945, it was the smaller cities and towns that began to provide many of the evacuees since they too had finally become bombing targets. By the time of surrender, then, there was no city that had not lost some of its inhabitants through flight.

How many Japanese had evacuated their city homes by the end of the war? We can never know for certain. The official total of 8.5 million, as provided by Japan's Home Affairs Ministry is almost certainly an underestimate. The 8,341,000 evacuees indicated in Table 4-21 include only those from the larger cities. If we were to add the significant volume of persons leaving smaller urban places and if we also classify as evacuees the considerable number of individuals involved in intra-urban shifts, a total exceeding 10 million is not unreasonable (Havens 1978:154). Furthermore, quite apart from 900,000 civilians killed (and some 1,300,000 injured) by the bombing campaign (U.S.-SBS 1947i:194), such a total does not include the very special cases of Hiroshima and Nagasaki. Leighton (1949:22) suggests that 90,000 of Hiroshima's inhabitants had been evacuated prior to August 1945. Because of the total breakdown of record-keeping and most other governmental systems on August 6, one can only speculate as to how many survivors of the atomic bomb sought refuge elsewhere, but the number must have been significant. The record is marginally better for Nagasaki, which had suffered only moderate bombing damage before the catastrophe of August 9. Available data relating to evacuation and welfare up to the cessation of hostilities show 14,900 voluntary evacuees, 10,292 fire-break evacuees, 47,355 dead and wounded, and 214,900 air raid sufferers (Stanford Research Institute 1953:182). Just how many of the persons in the last category became evacuees is not at all clear.

What is clear from Table 4-21 is the enormous attrition of Japan's metropolitan population in the months leading up to surrender. Quite obviously the evacuation rate was correlated positively with the severity of destruction through bombing and fire, and the latter, in turn, was a function of city size and industrial significance. Five of the major cities temporarily lost upwards of 60 percent of their citizens. In fact, Kyoto was the single large population center to experience only a minor outflow of inhabitants. Given its status as an important cultural and historical center, with only minimal military significance, Kyoto suffered only two minor raids in 1945 (U.S.-SBS 1947f:51).

Those urban residents whose homes were destroyed or badly damaged had two choices at their disposal: to remove themselves some
distance from the target area or to find usable quarters somewhere else
within the city. A surprising number adopted the latter strategy. Once
again, we call upon Robert Guillain's eyewitness account.

> Despite all the departures, population density has not been reduced, just
> the opposite. Living space vacated by departing residents is immediately
> occupied by twice as many persons: relatives or friends who are unable
> or unwilling to leave Tokyo, or simply refugees from destroyed areas who
> settle in two or three families per floor and quickly create confusion.
> Those who leave are mostly useless persons whom the authorities should
> have evacuated long ago. But the evacuation orders arrived too late and
> in the prevailing negligence and chaos they were not implemented.
> (Guillain 1947:219).

A paradoxical situation appeared in Japan (as it did also in Germany)
in which there was an increase in population density within the
relatively untouched neighborhoods of bombed cities. This came about
as air raid victims moved themselves and their remaining belongings
into vacant residential or nonresidential buildings, doubled up with
relatives, friends, or others, or contrived makeshift shelter. Furthermore, according to the statistical analyses performed by Iklé (1958:59,
61–63), the total population of Japan's urban places began to decline
only when housing destruction exceeded 10 percent. Apparently the
elasticity of the housing supply, or at least the temporary supply, was
such as to make local reaccommodation as attractive an option as
flight.

Another of Iklé's interesting findings is that there was a greater
tendency for Japanese city dwellers to evacuate rather than to shift
residence within their partially destroyed cities, as compared to the
German situation (Iklé 1958:61–63). To some degree this may be an
artifact of differences in official definitions and statistical systems, but
it may also reflect the fact that massive urbanization was a relatively
late phenomenon in Japan, so that many urbanites retained kinship
and other social connections with the countryside. Consequently, the
opportunities for refuge in a rather familiar environment may have
been relatively abundant for the residents of Japanese cities.

Those who did flee were not a random sample of the urban population. We have already seen that a great majority of the schoolchildren
were evacuated with their families or with their classmates in response

to varying degrees of persuasion and compulsion. Athough there was a strong propensity for entire families to evacuate—and indeed a small majority of the evacuees left in family groups—many individuals or fractions of families were relocated, and this selected population did not accord particularly well with guidelines established by government edict. More of the elderly were left behind than might have been anticipated, so that the evacuating population was skewed toward the younger age groups, who, of course, are inherently more mobile.

> Women, even with all their family duties, seem to have been quite mobile . . . for a greater proportion of females was found among evacuees than among city people who did not leave. Family duties may be performed anywhere; men are geographically tied to jobs. (U.S.–SBS 1947i:75)

Other differentials appeared.

> The evacuee group had a somewhat higher educational status, due largely to youth, but in at least one economic aspect it appears to be below average; one-third fewer evacuees than urban people belonged to families which owned land or their homes. Another outstanding fact was that, despite government directives to the contrary, the proportion of war industry employees was greater among evacuees (37 percent) than among unevacuated citydwellers (26 percent). Furthermore, only four percent of evacuee war industry employees had moved with their factories. (Stanford Research Institute 1953:184)

The explanation for this rather surprising fact may be that some of these officially essential workers no longer had factories in which to work, others may have been draftees from supposedly nonessential work who were dissatisfied with their new assignments and were eager to move; but the most compelling reason may have been the realistic perception that their homes and plants were targets of choice, even if the factories were relatively intact (U.S.–SBS 1947i:75).

The individual family members who were left behind were predominantly middle-aged, married men, reasonably well educated who had sent their families away. The general conclusion concerning the selection process separating evacuees from stayers was that the former tended to have less stable roots in the community and were less fixed by property or other interests.

> The implication is clear that adult evacuees will tend to be the people who can most easily evacuate during unplanned wholesale evacuation,

but that they will not necessarily be those who should evacuate from the standpoint of national interest, war production, and the defense of cities. (Stanford Research Institute 1953:185)

Moving large masses of people out from large cities and doing so expeditiously was no simple task. Fortunately for the Japanese, two factors operated in their favor. An excellent system of railroads and highways radiated outward from the major metropolises; and the Americans had not made any methodical effort to destroy or disrupt the system. Another saving grace, one shared with Great Britain, is the simple territorial compactness of the Japanese archipelago. Distances from evacuation site to destination were generally on the order of scores of kilometers not the hundreds or thousands encountered by the Soviets in World War II or the victims of certain other disasters.

During the earlier phases of evacuation in 1944, the official agency set up to control the process did manage the emergency rather effectively. The evacuees had chosen, or were assigned to, specific destinations; and those traveling more than twenty-five to thirty miles were allocated to trains, often special trains reserved for evacuees. Despite the shortage of labor and fuel, difficulties in finding packing materials and in handling huge mounds of baggage, and long delays in the congested terminals, the crowded trains did carry out their mission of transferring some 2 million persons to virtually every portion of the country. The travel office also established priorities for the use of trucks and carts.

With the enormous upsurge of evacuees in 1945, especially after the fire-bombing of Tokyo in March, transportation problems greatly intensified to the point of crisis. The number of persons swamping the railroad stations was such that averting total chaos—which was barely achieved—was a heroic accomplishment. Because of the delays and congestion at the depots, many persons resorted to other modes of transportation. Where available, trolleys were used to nearby towns and villages. Evacuees used trucks, buses, oxcarts, and other highway vehicles to the limit, but a great many simply traveled on foot. Evidently there was little use of water transport because most harbors had been heavily damaged, and voyages were not especially safe. In the extraordinary cases of Hiroshima and Nagasaki, where, it must be assumed, no other means of travel were available after the atomic assault, virtually all evacuees must have been pedestrians.

Our knowledge of the destinations for the evacuees is much vaguer than that concerning their sources. Initially, the government authorities did attempt to supervise and control the exodus; but, eventually, the sheer volume and urgency of movement was such that it was every individual or family for itself with no official attempt to channel the flow. The result was that the entire rural hinterland of the Home Islands became a host area, and there was no district that did not receive some evacuees. The flow was guided by the traditional ties of family and friendship and the vagaries of transportation. Indeed the strength of the social bond proved to be indispensable, since approximately 80 percent of the evacuees found shelter among friends or relatives in the countryside.

Although the evacuees spread to every corner of Japan, for the most part they did concentrate in the areas relatively close to the places evacuated (Stanford Research Institute 1953:187). In part, of course, this is simply the result of the distance-decay effect, that is, travelers selecting the closest available destination; but it may also reflect the fact that such nearby sites had previously been the dominant sources of migrants to the cities in question. The fact that proximity was a major consideration appears when we map the data available for a single case, that of the evacuees from Kobe (see Figure 4-14). (There are two relevant maps produced by Ogasawara [1948: Figures 1 and 2] portraying change in final population over the period 1937–46 by small districts, but it is difficult to relate the map patterns to flows of evacuees.) It also materializes in the information available for the evacuees moving into the rural portions of Kyoto Prefecture (U.S.–SBS 1947f:50). Exactly half of the 186,000 individuals in question arrived from nearby localities: Kyoto City (29,000), Maizuru City (7,000), Osaka Prefecture (45,000), and Hyogo Prefecture (12,000). The smaller group of fire-break refugees from Kyoto City also confirms the principle. Of the total 69,320, more than 52,600 relocated elsewhere within the city, and 4,389 shifted to the rural tracts of Kyoto Prefecture (U.S.–SBS 1947f:50). Some of the evacuations by manufacturing employees were local and less than complete (as also occurred in Germany). It is reported that

the larger part of the workers who left the city continued to work in Nagoya's factories, communting from their new quarters outside the city . . . the number of industrial workers residing in Nagoya fell 60 percent between December 1944 and June 1945. . . . In the same period, the number of industrial workers actually working in an 80 percent sample of industry in Nagoya and its environs fell from 264,379 to 207,595, a decline of only 22 percent. (U.S.–SBS 1947f:14)

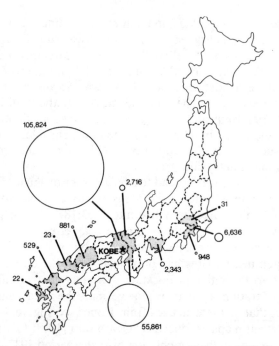

Figure 4-14. Destinations of evacuees from Kobe, 1944–45 (Source: U.S. Strategic Bombing Survey 1947e:81–82)

The one belated governmental effort to direct the stream of evacuees to a particular destination was a conspicuous failure (Stanford Research Institute 1953:179–80). In an attempt to bolster food production, the Agricultural, Commerce, and Home Ministries promulgated a plan on May 31, 1945 whereby 50,000 families, or 200,000 evacuees, would have been resettled during the approaching summer on 1,250,000 acres of then uncultivated farmland in the northern island of Hokkaido. Despite the gift of 25 to 35 acres to each family, generous subsidies, and other forms of aid, only 17,569 persons (7,832 of them from Tokyo) actually went to Hokkaido under the program. The reason for the lackadaisical response was discouraging reports about the hardships suffered by earlier pioneers in an unfamiliar habitat in addition to the normal reluctance to relocate far from home.

Obviously it was impossible to shift such a substantial fraction of Japan's urban population to the countryside without great strain upon housing facilities.

Inns, abandoned business quarters, schools, and temples were made available to evacuees in very many places. Sometimes new houses, or at least barracks, were erected. This, however, was much easier to do in the case of people who came in groups, such as students, than when individual families or part thereof came flooding into the countryside. In some cases vacant homes were found: evacuees from Tokyo to Yamagata, for instance, sometimes occupied quarters vacated by evacuees from Yamagata. There were many more cases, however, of rooms vacated by the departure of a war worker or a soldier, and into such cramped quarters millions of evacuees had to move. (U.S.–SBS 1947i:230)

Of the approximately 20 percent of evacuees who were unable to take refuge with kinfolk or friends, many were obliged to squeeze into the homes of strangers. In addition to the difficulties of providing the bare necessities of life for these and other evacuees in a country already suffering from wartime shortages of food, fuel, clothing, and other items, and the inevitable problems of morale, some social and cultural friction undoubtedly developed between hosts and guests, as happened in parallel settings in Great Britain, Germany, and elsewhere during World War II (Havens 1978:171). Its extent, however, is difficult to gauge (U.S.–SBS 1947i:226–29).

The postwar return of the evacuees to their stricken cities clearly occurred at a more leisurely pace than the out-movement. The prime deterrent to a rapid influx was the enormous devastation. Given the severe shortage of urban housing and employment, the shattered utility systems, and inadequacies of other basic services, the repopulation of the major cities took not months but years. Okazaki's (1949:37) statement that "those who took refuge in the country, have returned to their original places of residence in the urban districts after the termination of the war" by 1949 is belied by the available statistics. In Table 4-22 (which excludes the male population, many of whom were abroad and/or in the military), it appears that, as of late April 1946, the major metropolitan and industrial prefectures had rebounded only modestly from their demographic hemorrhaging in 1944–45, and that the more lightly urbanized prefectures were still crowded with evacuees. In still another tabulation covering the period 1940–50 (Taeuber 1958: 353), we find that in 1945 the population of the six largest cities had fallen to 44.2 percent of its 1940 level in 1945 and had risen to no more than 62.8 and 77.9 percent of that value, respectively, in 1947 and 1950. We can assume complete recovery only by the early 1950s. The return or redistribution of the schoolchildren previously evacuated in groups may have been more rapid than that of other groups of evacuees. But because of the lack of adequate housing, the majority of the pupils did

Table 4-22. Japan: Female Population of the Prefectures, 1944–46

	Numbers (in 1,000s)			Ratio to 1944 as 100	
Area	Feb. 22, 1944	Nov. 1, 1945	Apr. 26, 1946	Nov. 1, 1945	Apr. 26, 1946
All Japan	38,144	38,104	38,209	100	100
Metropolitan[1]	6,086	3,147	3,597	52	59
Industrial[2]	6,981	6,124	6,352	89	91
Intermediate[3]	11,281	12,791	12,537	113	111
Agricultural[4]	12,119	14,172	13,948	117	115
Hokkaido	1,648	1,780	1,775	108	108

[1]Tokyo, Osaka.
[2]Kanagawa, Aichi, Kyoto, Hyogo, Fukuoka.
[3]Gumma, Toyama, Ishikawa, Fukui, Nagano, Gifu, Shizuoka, Mie, Nara, Wakayama, Okayama, Hiroshima, Yamaguchi, Tokushima, Kagawa, Ehime, Kochi, Saga, Nagasaki.
[4]Aomori, Iwate, Miyagi, Akita, Yamagata, Fukushima, Ibaraki, Tochigi, Saitama, Chiba, Niigata, Yamanashi, Shiga, Tottori, Shimane, Kumamoto, Oita, Miyazaki, Kagoshima.
Source: Taeuber 1958:341–42.

not return until the end of the school term in March 1946 (U.S.–SBS 1947j:166–67).

How effective was the massive Japanese evacuation of 1944–45? In terms of enhancing the nation's war-making potential, the answer is not at all clear. But, in terms of averting death and injury to perhaps hundreds of thousands of vulnerable individuals, there is little question that it was a success. It is also demonstrable that many of the 900,000 killed and 1.3 million injured would have been spared had the exodus been carried out in 1943 or by mid-1944 at the latest. As it was, however, the social and economic costs of the vast redistribution of urban residents that did come to pass were extremely great; and it is not at all clear how long the evacuation could have been sustained in full force. The feasibility of shifting some 10 million persons in the 1940s, when somewhere between 40 and 50 percent of the population might be considered urban and when the human ties between town and country were still strong was a far different proposition from replicating the experience today, when at least 76 percent of the Japanese are city dwellers, and the gulf is ever widening between the growing urban sector and a rural world whose population is static or declining. Thus the lessons for present day Japan remain obscure.

NOTES

1. An eyewitness account indicates quite vividly how much this self-propelled exodus differed from the simultaneous mass herding of mothers and

children. [Something over two million people (almost certainly an overestimate) hurried out of London, under their own steam or in their own motorcars, as soon as war broke out. Many of them stayed away, and *The Times* was to write, in early 1941, of country hotels "filled with well-to-do refugees, who too often have fled from nothing. They sit and read and knit and eat and drink. . . ." A high proportion had already reserved accommodation for themselves in safe areas; others just locked up their London flats and drove off. This author remembers a constant stream of private cars and London taxis driving up to his mother's front door in the Thames Valley in September of '39, filled with men and women of all ages and in various stages of hunger, exhaustion and fear, offering absurd sums for accommodation in her already overcrowded house, and even for food. The horde of satin-clad, pin-striped refugees poured through for two or three days, eating everything that was for sale, downing all the spirits in the pubs, and then vanished. This was to happen again, though on a smaller scale, when the bombing actually started a year later. It was undoubtedly an excellent thing that London was rid of these people when it faced the bombs. They would only have been in the way, and they presumably spent a pleasant, if boring, war in their country hotels. (Fitz Gibbon 1975:26)]

2. The German authorities introduced a legal classification of Jewish and Aryan (e.g., Polish gentile) population, and some statistics were kept on this basis. The researcher is faced with an awkward terminological problem here. Polish Jews represented part of the Polish population of the city, and the exclusive use of the term Polish in relation to the "Aryan" part would obviously be inappropriate. On the other hand, physical and legal separation between the two communities became very rigorous, and it would make no sense to try and lump them together. The use of the term "Aryan" has obvious unacceptable connotations.

3. Landau (1962, vol. 1:30) quotes the example of an acquaintance of his who went to Kowel and back on foot, a distance of 700 km. He returned by September 30.

4. Sakowska quotes estimates ranging between 275,000 and 310,000 (1975:299–300). According to Gilbert's atlas, some 260,000 were shipped during four major "actions"(1975:108–17).

5. An even higher maximum of 520,000 in mid-1941 is quoted by Ratyńska (1982:362) on the basis of the Polish underground sources.

6. Szarota (1988:73) quotes several estimates from the end of 1943 based on either underground or German sources. The number of Poles was variously given as 960,000, 975,000, and 921,000. He dismisses as excessive an estimate of 1.1 million by the Polish Welfare Committee.

7. According to information from German officers, troops were ordered initially to kill all Poles, after August 7 only men, then a few days later only armed men (Madajczyk 1974, vol. 1, pt. 1:321). However, massacres continued throughout until the end of the fighting.

8. The front line stabilized along the Vistula river during the summer of 1944. This left only part of the General Government as a possible reception area.

9. According to the same source, earlier evacuations included 15,000 on September 7; 30,000 on September 8; 5,000 from Mokotów after September; and 15,000 from Żoliborz after September 30.

10. These included the General Instruction of 1918, Law of 1927, Instruction of 1930, Circular of the Ministry of Interior of 1931, and General Instructions of 1935, 10 January 1938, and July 1938 (Ollier 1970:29).

11. One should keep in mind that an unrelated, but equally unnerving, situation prevailed along France's southern border. The last stages of the Spanish civil war caused an influx of an estimated 200,000 Republican refugees (Kulischer 1948:249). Basques had been arriving in small numbers even earlier to find refuge among co-ethnics along the Atlantic coast, but the great wave of Spanish refugees reached France after the fall of Barcelona on January 26, 1939 (Laurens 1980:46).

12. In some areas evacuation began even earlier. Vidalenc (1957:36) quotes an example of the Wissembourg region in Alsace where the transfers started on August 28, 1939.

13. Padley and Cole (1940:289) mention more than half a million evacuees, including 181,000 from Strasbourg.

14. These figures are given by Vanwelkenhuyzen and Dumont (1983:182). According to a contemporary German source, there were 70,000 Luxembourgeois and very few Dutch (Gerber 1941:14).

15. According to Gerber (1941:14), the number of Belgians entering France was close to 3 million or ca. one-third of the total. Other estimates quoted by Vidalenc (1957:150) are: an estimate by the Belgian Red Cross—1.5 million; by the Belgian Embassy in France—2.2 million (both refer to the number of Belgians repatriated after the war); and 2 to 3 million mentioned by M. L. Piérard in an unknown article. Ollier (1970:260) speaks about 1.5 to 2 million Belgian and Dutch evacuees.

16. The number of returnees is given at 1.5 million by Gerber (1941:15), but French sources mention only a quite limited return flow (Vidalenc 1957:160).

17. From Gare d'Austerlitz, 238 special trains left between June 8 and 12; from Gare de Lyon, 12 additional trains on June 11 alone (Ollier 1970:137).

18. There are known cases where evacuated people had to walk 40 or even 100 km before they were able to board the train (Meynier 1950:47).

19. Apparently exposure to newsreels reporting the devastation suffered by Polish towns during the 1939 campaign heightened the apprehension of the French population and helped trigger panic behavior.

20. Apparently, well-placed bribes could reduce waiting time for such permits from three weeks to two hours (Ollier 1970:261).

21. During 1940–42, the Red Cross repatriated 90,000 children (Ollier 1970:270).

22. The territorial expansion enjoyed by the Soviet Union between 1939 and 1941, when the leadership acted in collusion with Nazi Germany, led to acquiring some 22 million people who were offered Soviet citizenship (Lorimer 1946:188). Since this expansion met with hostility on the part of most of these new residents, strong security measures were undertaken to thwart potential or actual resistance. Massive deportations of at least 1 million people took place in 1940–41. Whether deportees are included in Soviet statistics on evacuations is unclear. Kulischer (1948:302) does include them in his estimations.

23. The evacuation of civilians undertaken by the German authorities also deserves mention. According to Kulischer (1948:269), some 65,000 Ingrians (Ingermanländers), people of Ugro-Finnic stock inhabiting the area around Leningrad, were evacuated, first to Estonia and subsequently to Finland. Their movement began in the spring of 1943, when food shortages had become appalling, and by May 1944, 65,000 had arrived in Finland where they were employed in agriculture. Some 46,000 to 47,000 of these persons applied for return.

24. Kumanev (1963:73) quotes another source that contains similar estimates. Samsonov (1958:147) argues that of 4.5 million Muscovites only 2.5 million were left in November 1941.

25. Many evacuees from the Baltic Republics were Russian administrators and security personnel with families. The three republics had been annexed by force by the Soviet Union in 1940, and among the local population there was considerable hostility toward the new regime. Mass arrests (said to amount to 100,000) and deportations of real and suspected enemies carried out in mid-June 1941 did nothing to reduce the tensions. Not surprisingly, during the first stages of the war the nationalists attacked retreating Soviet units and the German troops were welcomed as liberators (Salisbury 1969:150ff.).

26. Salisbury claims that the outflow of 467,000 prior to August 11 was largely nullified by the influx from the Baltic states (1969:206).

27. It is unclear if the entry in Table 4-15 of 220,000 women with children being evacuated from June 29 to August 27 refers to the initial evacuation of children or only to the final net outflow at that time.

28. By September 6, 1939, some 47,168 persons evacuated from Saarland were already in Thüringen (Unrein 1953:21).

29. According to other sources, evacuation began August 26, 1939 (FRG, *Dokumente* 1958, vol. 1:352).

30. According to a report by the German Army's High Command, the first air raids hit Freiburg on May 10, 1940 and three settlements in the Ruhr Region on May 10–11. Further investigation has shown that Freiburg was, in fact, bombarded by German aircraft, whose pilots mistook it for a French town on the other side of the Rhine (FRG, *Dokumente* 1958, vol. 1:23).

31. Estimates of losses vary considerably. They may be calculated for Germany within 1939 boundaries, for postwar territory, or for FRG alone.

Sometimes all settlements are considered, at other times only those with more than 20,000, or else selected large cities; sometimes only losses caused by air raids are calculated; on other occasions total losses, including those caused by fighting on the ground. Another reason for disparities is inclusion of partially destroyed housing units in the totals.

32. A tragic coincidence of dates and events can be seen from the following. The British ship "Empress of Britain" was sunk on October 1, 1940 with substantial losses among British children being evacuated to Canada. During the meeting between Hitler and von Schirach on October 2, two topics were discussed: deportation of the remaining 60,000 Jews from Wien to General Government and evacuation of children (Larass 1983:27, 42).

33. Estimates for sixteen cities (not including Berlin, Hamburg, and Vienna) made by the U.S. Bombing Survey and quoted by Senese (1988:12) range from 2 to 79 percent, with an average of 41 percent.

34. It should be noted that the term *planmässig,* which is translated here as "organized," refers to movements flowing into the designated receiving areas. These were either supervised or (sometimes) spontaneous. Flows going into nondesignated areas were almost always spontaneous.

35. If we use amount of built-up area devastated as the criterion, the level of destruction was even greater. Data for fifty-three cities over 100,000 are given by Hewitt (1983a:266).

Chapter 5

Evacuations Related to Industrial Accidents

It is logical to assign the treatment of major industrial disasters and their associated evacuations to the closing group of case studies for the simple reason that this is where they belong chronologically. We are aware, of course, of a long sequence of tragedies in shops, mines, and factories—the great majority of them unrecorded or poorly documented—that dates back to the earliest history of humankind and resulted in death or injury to those on the premises and, occasionally, to nearby residents and passersby. But to the best of our knowledge, it is only during the present century that evacuation from the vicinity of an industrial disaster site has materialized on any appreciable scale.

The reasons for the belatedness of such developments are self-evident. It is only in recent times that we have had large industrial plants located in populous areas and producing or handling large quantities of toxic chemicals, potentially explosive fuels, and radioactive materials—or trains, trucks, pipelines, and ships conveying them in bulk through congested zones. Is it surprising, then, that the inevitable has occurred with some frequency because of mechanical failure, human error, or some combination thereof? In fact, small-scale evacuations caused by train derailments, accidental releases of noxious substances by factories, pipeline ruptures, or ships carrying dangerous cargos running aground or otherwise imperilling local populations have become almost routine news items, and not just in the advanced urban industrial countries. People no longer object to evacuation but rather to failure by the authorities to act in timely fashion, whether by reason of negligence or political factors, to remove inhabitants temporarily from areas exposed to danger.

197

We have confined ourselves here to four exceptionally interesting events. Only one of them, the Mississauga evacuation of November 1979, is of less than international import; but we are justified in including it because the incident so admirably typifies the effective management of a large emergency evacuation in a major metropolitan area and because of the excellence of documentation. The other three cases—Three Mile Island, Bhopal, and Chernobyl—have been truly extraordinary in their impact worldwide upon perceptions of, and attitudes toward, both nuclear and non-nuclear industrial accidents. This trio of catastrophes is without historical precedent in terms of their character and the scale of resulting psychic distress, in addition to the large number of person temporarily or permanently dislocated. We must also point out that in two of the four cases—Three Mile Island and Chernobyl—the site of the mishap may not have been in densely occupied metropolitan territory but that urban populations were nonetheless very much involved: the Greater Harrisburg area in one instance and Kiev and other Ukrainian cities in the other.

THREE MILE ISLAND, 1979

The series of events that began during the early hours of Wednesday, March 28, 1979 in and near the nuclear power plant at Three Mile Island, a few miles southeast of Harrisburg, Pennsylvania, and well within the greater Harrisburg metropolitan area, is of extraordinary theoretical and practical interest for students of evacuation behavior. Because of the unprecedented nature of the industrial accident, its proximity to some of the most densely inhabited sections of the United States, and thus the potential for inflicting death or injury on great numbers of victims, TMI created instant headlines around the world and attracted a large corps of journalists and other observers. Governmental authorities, scientists, and academicians promptly set up systems to collect data measuring the human response to the event, as well as its several other aspects. The result has been an imposingly large literature, very likely the largest of its genre, and one that is still growing steadily. Among its other attributes, this body of work provides us with the most detailed account to date for any evacuation of an urbanized locality of the numbers and characteristics of evacuees and stayers and the spatial and temporal patterns of the outward movement and eventual return: a richly documented record of an unplanned experiment in public response to an unusual disaster.

Table 5-1. Selected Evacuations Caused by Industrial Accidents

	Three Mile Island	Mississauga	Bhopal I	Bhopal II	Chernobyl
Date	Mar. 29, 1979	Nov. 10, 1979	Dec. 2–3, 1984	Dec. 16–17, 1984	Apr. 26, 1986
Nature of disaster	Nuclear power plant accident and threat of major release of radioactive material	Release of lethal chemicals caused by railroad accident	Large accidental release of lethal chemical	Deactivation of remaining chemicals perceived as potential disaster	Major accidental release of radioactive material
Urban population at risk (in 1,000s)	375	225	1,000–1,200	1,000–1,200	2,200+
Number evacuated (in 1,000s)	144–150	220	70–500	100–300	445–500
Percent of population at risk	38–40	98	6–50	8–30	20–23

Goldhaber and Lehman (1982:4–5) have provided a capsule account of the accident that will suffice for our purposes:

> The accident . . . began . . . as a result of a series of unlikely events. In attempting to clear a minor plumbing problem in the plant's secondary cooling system, workmen accidentally shut off the flow of water to the primary coolant loop around the nuclear core. An emergency back-up system came on but a relief valve which opened to let off pressure failed to close again, and the primary coolant water boiled away from the nuclear core. Because of a poorly placed meter in the control room, plant operators did not notice for several hours the dangerous over-heating of the core. As a result, thousands of gallons of radioactive water spilled within the plant buildings. Within the next few days an estimated 2.5–10 million curies of radioactivity escaped into the atmosphere in the form of xenon, cesium and some iodine gases. Chemical reactions in the nuclear core produced potentially explosive hydrogen gas, which was to become a major source of concern for plant safety.
>
>   In the first couple of days after the accident no one was certain how badly the plant was damaged or how much radiation had escaped into the environment. The plant operators quickly assured the public and government officials that the accident was minor and that there was no danger to health or property. The severity of the accident, however, soon became apparent. State and federal authorities moved into major decision-making roles, but were unable to fully assess the condition of the plant or to determine the amount of radiation already released. There was a mounting sense of apprehension and uncertainty.

It was indeed an unprecedented situation and one that generated considerable confusion. There had never been a similar industrial accident; it was impossible then to ascertain the precise nature of the mishap or its extent, or the possibilities for a catastrophic release of radioactivity into the atmosphere. Indeed even now, several years later, while salvage and repair work on the damaged reactor unit is far from complete, engineers are still unable to reconstruct in detail the entire sequence of the accident or to observe its final products within the core. What is certain is that no deaths or injuries resulted directly from the accident, nor from the subsequent evacuation, for that matter. Whether the release of radioactive gases has had any delayed effect on disease and mortality patterns within the adjacent areas is still a matter of controversy, in part because of imperfect monitoring of discharges during and after the accident. Thus the substantial out-movement of local residents was the result of apprehension, of what *might* have happened, rather than a full-fledged disaster. Because of the absence of an adequate, centralized source of information and the confused series of bulletins and directives from federal, state, and local authorities, plant officials, and the news media, not to mention the shifting direction of the winds, temporary absence from the scene was clearly the most prudent policy.

How well prepared were the local residents for any such exodus? In terms of formal planning, hardly at all.

> Until the accident at Three Mile Island, emergency-response and evacuation planning received surprisingly little attention from either the Nuclear Regulatory Commission or government officials. Prior to the TMI accident, NRC had required nuclear plant operators to develop emergency plans only for the facility itself and the surrounding low-population zone. The zone around TMI extended only 2.2 miles from the facility. At the time of the accident, no evacuation plans existed for the local jurisdictions in the area. Although the three closest counties had five-mile emergency-response plans on file, only one plan incorporated a fully developed course of action. Two emergency plans were developed for the state at the time of the accident, but neither one had been approved by NRC. (Ziegler, Brunn, and Johnson 1981:15)

As matters did develop, many residents managed to vacate the area spontaneously with little or no official direction in a more or less rational response to nonbinding advisories and incomplete information about the nature of the accident and the prospects for even greater difficulties. Some persons decided to leave their homes a matter of only several hours after the accident once they had learned or guessed something about its severity. With the recognition of radioactive releases from the plant by the morning of Friday, March 30, both the Nuclear Regulatory Commission (NRC) and the Pennsylvania Emergency Management Agency (PEMA) had begun to consider evacuation measures for residents living within a five- to ten-mile radius from the plant. Without waiting for official instructions, local primary and secondary schools and colleges suspended classes for several days; and householders were urged to remain indoors with windows closed. That same morning Governor Thornburgh issued the most definitive statement regarding evacuation that was to materialize during the entire episode.

> My advisory that pregnant women and pre-school children stay out of the area within five miles of the plant will remain in effect for at least another

night. Evacuation of a broader nature continues to be unnecessary at this time. A decision regarding school closings and leave policy for state employees will be made and announced as soon as possible Sunday.

Local officials began planning for the possible evacuation of prisons and detention homes, and were soon advised by the state to consider plans for evacuating the area within twenty miles of the plant.

As is turned out, only three types of official public announcements relevant to public evacuation were carried by the local media: newspapers which printed details of evacuation plans and routes along with recommendations for personal evacuation preparations; a radio broadcast on Friday morning, March 30, by the Dauphin County emergency preparedness director regarding a possible forthcoming evacuation notice; and Governor Thornburgh's Friday morning advisory to pregnant women and preschool children to leave within a 5-mile radius carried by all media. (Dynes et al. 1979:143)

Thanks to the several surveys initiated within weeks or months after the event by government and academic personnel, we can reconstruct with a fair degree of precision the number of evacuees, their residential location and social characteristics, the nature and location of destinations, and the timing of their outward and return movements, as well as the attributes of the stayers. An estimated 144,000 persons, or 39 percent of the population, living within the fifteen-mile zone centered on the plant evacuated their homes (Ziegler, Brunn, and Johnson 1981:3). A smaller, but still significant, proportion of those residing beyond the fifteen-mile line, some as far distant as forty miles, opted for evacuation, so that a grand total of 150,000 is not unreasonable. It is worth noting that many more individuals gave serious thought to moving temporarily, and not only those within close proximity of TMI. One of the authors vividly recalls the level of anxiety among some residents of State College, Pennsylvania some ninety miles northwest of the plant. One study (Barnes et al. 1979) estimates that 33 percent of those living within a twenty-miles radius of the plant made preparation to leave, but did not do so, while another survey (Brunn, Johnson, and Ziegler 1979) indicates that two-thirds of those who did not leave considered evacuation.

The most striking attribute of the Three Mile Island experience, especially as compared with other evacuations of a non-nuclear character, is that both the number of evacuees and their territorial range far exceeded—by at least an order of magnitude—the values that would have been projected on the basis of prior experience or the official advisories (Indell and Perry 1982:423; Ziegler and Johnson 1984:208). The term "evacuation shadow," evidently coined by Ziegler and Johnson, would seem to be an apt description of the phenomenon. Stated in other words, people evacuated spontaneously in far greater numbers and over a much broader area—given the uncertainties of an unfamiliar hazard, one that could not be seen, heard, smelled, felt or otherwise sensed—than one would have anticipated from the general reluctance displayed in other crises (Goldhaber and Lehman 1982:17).

What were the characteristics of the persons who did evacuate and of those who did not? The largest and probably most detailed set of data available was collected three months after the event by means of a special *Census* conducted by personnel from the Pennsylvania Department of Health, the National Centers for Disease Control, and the U.S. Bureau of the Census. In all, nearly 36,000 persons residing within five miles of the plant (rather more than 95 percent of the population within that zone) were registered. Table 5–2 summarizes the results for residents of single-family homes and apartment houses living in the area at the time of the accident. It is obvious that both the decision to stay or leave, and the timing of the latter, varied significantly with the demographic attributes of the population at risk. The Goldhaber-Lehman report confirms the general findings of other studies (e.g., Dynes et al. 1979:152; Flynn 1982:50; Ziegler and Johnson 1984:208), namely

> that women were more prone to evacuate than men. Younger persons were more likely to evacuate than older persons. Families with small children, higher than average income were the most likely to evacuate. The presence of a pregnant woman in the family contributed significantly to the decision to leave the area. (Goldhaber and Lehman 1982:7–8)

When the time dimension, that is, duration of absence, is included,

> The characteristics of the moderate evacuation group [those who evacuated for periods of 1 to 5 days] most resemble that [sic] of the general population while the characteristics of the two extreme groups [stayers and evacuees of more than 5 days] contrast sharply. The non-evacuees were older than the general population, less educated, and included a greater proportion of single persons living alone. The lengthy evacuators were younger, more educated, more likely to be female, more likely to be white collar workers and included a greater proportion of persons living in married households. By far the major distinction between the evacua-

Table 5-2. Three Mile Island: Persons 17 and Over in Each of the Four Evacuation Groups, by Demographic Characteristics, 1979*

				Evacuation Group	
Demographic Characteristics	All Groups N=23,900	Did Not Evacuate N=10,130	Evacuated 1–2 Days N=2,122	Evacuated 3–5 Days N=4,461	Evacuated 6 or More Days N=7,187
Median age (years)	37	45	38	37	31
Mean household size (persons)	3.3	3.1	3.3	3.5	3.5
Mean distance from TMI (miles)	3.6	3.6	3.6	3.5	3.5
Male	48.8%	54.3%	53.1%	48.1%	40.2%
Education:					
Less than high school	29.9%	35.9%	28.8%	26.5%	23.7%
High school graduate	50.1	47.4	52.3	52.4	51.8
Some college	9.7	8.5	10.4	9.4	11.3
College graduate	9.1	6.6	8.0	11.1	11.7
No answer	1.2	1.5	0.5	0.5	1.5
White-collar worker	42.7	37.3	42.3	47.2	47.7
Person living in married household	73.8	68.4	74.0	77.0	79.5
Person living alone	8.9	11.3	7.3	6.9	7.1
Pregnant woman	1.8	0.3	0.3	0.6	5.1
Pregnancy in household	4.1	1.6	2.0	2.7	9.1
Preschooler in household	20.3	6.5	15.1	14.7	45.0
Child age 6–16 in household	35.5	29.3	39.8	40.0	40.2
TMI worker in household	4.0	4.6	3.1	4.2	3.2

*Excludes persons living in institutional dwellings and persons moving into the area after the TMI accident.
Source: Goldhaber and Lehman 1982, based on TMI Population Registry.

tion groups was the presence of preschoolers and pregnant women in the household. (Goldhaber and Lehman 1982:15)

The Ziegler-Brunn-Johnson survey disclosed another striking fact: "that while the majority of evacuees left in complete family units, the proportion of partial families fleeing the disaster was larger than would be expected from the conclusions of natural-hazard research" (Ziegler, Brunn, and Johnson 1981:4–5). The investigators attribute this pattern to the degree of uncertainty surrounding the accident and the general inability to assess the magnitude of the malfunction at the plant.

In another respect, however, the TMI evacuation did not differ from the "normal" emergency evacuations experienced by Americans. Nearly all families and individuals left their residences in private automobiles, and did so in orderly fashion. Whatever the psychology prompting the movement, the actual exodus was not panicky, and there does not seem to have been any unusual traffic congestion or injuries or deaths resulting from the temporary displacement of approximately 150,000 persons.

In still another respect, the behavior of persons living within forty miles or so of the TMI plant does conform with expectations, for we have here an almost classic instance of the distance-decay effect. This fact is most clearly demonstrated by mapping the results of the Flynn (1979) telephone survey (see Figure 5-1), which indicates a steady drop-off in percentage of resident population evacuating in every five-mile ring as one moves outward from the plant site, but with an especially sharp decline beyond the fifteen-mile line. Other studies corroborate this finding (see Table 5-3). Thus Ziegler, Brunn, and Johnson (1981:7) have documented a rather modest initial decrease in percentage of responding households from which some members evacuated, with values sloping from 55 percent in the one- to three-mile distance to 47 percent in the ten- to twelve-mile ring; but the figure drops abruptly to 13 percent at the thirteen- to fifteen-mile distance and to only 9 percent beyond fifteen miles, so that the twelve-mile distance seems to represent a genuine discontinuity.

Figure 5-1 suggests that compass direction from TMI *may* have played a role in the decision to stay or leave. Leaving aside the question of statistical significance raised by the relatively small number of respondents in the various quadrants, residents located more than fifteen miles from the plant site and in other than a westerly direction thereof (normally the windward direction) seem to have been more willing to evacuate than those to the west of TMI.

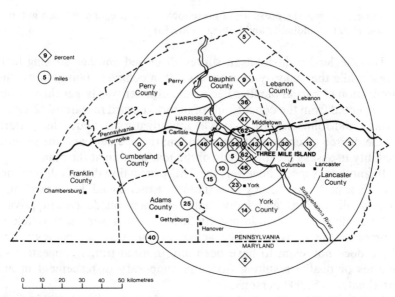

Figure 5-1. Persons evacuating by direction and distance from Three Mile Island (Source: Flynn 1982:53)

Table 5-3. Three Mile Island: Population Evacuating by Distance from TMI Plant*

| Survey | Distance from TMI | | | |
	0–5 Miles	5–10 Miles	10–15 Miles	Total
Flynn	60	44	32	39
Pennsylvania Dept. of Health	60			
Smith	50			
Kraybill				42
Barnes et al.	33			
	(0–10 miles)			
Dohrenwend, Goldsteen, et al.				52
Brunn, Johnson, and Ziegler	55	54	28	

*In percent.
Source: Flynn 1982:52.

More surprising than the configuration of the evacuation field are the distances traveled by the evacuees to their temporary destinations. The various studies indicate a median distance in the 85- to 100-mile range (Dynes et al. 1979:151; Ziegler, Brunn, and Johnson 1981:7).

> In comparison with the list of evacuations compiled by Hans and Sell, the median flight of evacuation from Three Mile Island is the longest on record. The longest median distance given in that study was eighty miles in response to Hurricane Carla in 1961. (Ziegler, Brunn, and Johnson 1981:7–8)

Goldhaber and Lehman (1982:15) discovered a positive correlation between duration of the evacuation and distance traveled. Thus those who left their homes for periods upwards of three days tended to travel farther than those who absented themselves for only one or two days.

An unexpected peculiarity of the survey findings was the appearance of a strong positive relationship between distance of home from TMI and distance traveled, since, a priori, just the opposite situations would have been anticipated (Flynn and Chalmers 1980:17). There is no obvious explanation for the fact that persons living closer to TMI tended to move shorter distances than those living farther away. However, the speculations advanced by Ziegler, Brunn, and Johnson may have some merit:

> First, persons living closest to the plant were likely to be the most concerned about the safety of their homes and property. They were therefore inclined to remain as close as possible to home. Second, only in the closest distance zones were residents with high personal evacuation thresholds sufficiently motivated to abandon their homes. If these evacuees lived a few miles further from TMI, they probably would not have evacuated at all. Third, residents who live far from the disabled reactor would be expected to shun evacuation sites in the closest zones because they would offer little or no improvement over the conditions of the home site. It can be hypothesized that evacuees originating at great distances from Three Mile Island would include the segment of the populations with low personal evacuation thresholds that would consequently be likely to seek more distant destinations. Fourth, because evacuation units residing more than fifteen miles away were predominantly women and children, many constraints on evacuation might have lessened. (Ziegler, Brunn, and Johnson 1981:10–11)

In any event the conclusion is inescapble that, in the light of other evacuations in response to "normal" disasters, the response to TMI was much greater than could have been predicted whether measured in numbers of persons displaced, magnitude of the evacuation field, or distance traveled. The terms "over-response" and "evacuation shadow" seem quite appropriate. In another departure from historic patterns, there seems to have been little or no convergence toward the scene of the disaster (at least during the critical period) on the part of the idly curious, although considerable numbers of journalists, technicians, academics, and government officials did flock to TMI and the vicinity.

The location and identity of the evacuees' destinations is a matter of some interest. As already noted, evacuees tended to travel considerable distances. Nevertheless, 72 percent remained within Pennsylvania, while significant percentages—6.6, 5.8, and 3.8, respectively—journeyed to the nearby states of New Jersey, Maryland, and Virginia. Some individuals went as far as California, Oklahoma, and Florida, while, in all, some twenty-one states received evacuees (Flynn and Chalmers 1980:18). The vast majority (estimates range from 74 to 90 percent) found shelter with relatives (ca. 67 percent) or friends (ca. 15 percent), and 8 percent went to hotels or motels (Flynn 1982:54; Goldhaber and Lehman 1982:6; Hu and Slaysman 1981:29). Cutter and Barnes (1982a:117) claim, quite plausibly, that 20 percent of the evacuees simply went to their own vacation cabins or second homes. Surprisingly few persons took advantage of the official evacuation center at Hershey, Pennsylvania.

> The maximum number of people who stayed at Hershey during one day was about 180, but as many as 800 may have stayed there for a short time. On at least one occasion, there were more reporters than evacuees at the center. (Flynn 1982:54)

Analysis of the data discloses a strong directional bias in the dispersion of evacuees.

> Although only one of every ten evacuation units [families or portions thereof] chose destinations in the quadrant southeast of TMI, almost half chose destinations in the quadrant northwest of the crippled reactor. The directional bias was the consequence of several interrelated factors. The most important considerations seem to have been a preference for a site upwind from the plant, a psychological attraction to the mountains in time of danger, and a reluctance to select a destination in the more densely populated metropolitan areas to the east. (Ziegler, Brunn, and Johnson 1981:9)

Several students of the event have examined its temporal questions, that is, the departure dates for the evacuees and the duration of their displacement. All agree that a majority of families and individuals (ca. 54 percent) left on Friday, March 30 because of a combination of factors (Dynes et al. 1979:147–48; Ziegler, Brunn, and Johnson 1981:12).

> First, the governor's sheltering and evacuation directives were issued on Friday when serious consideration of a full evacuation first became public. Second, two major constraints on evacuation were lifted because Friday is the end of both the work week and the school week. (Ziegler, Brunn, and Johnson 1981:12)

The length of stay away from home ranged from one to sixteen days, but intermediate values were much more frequent. The modal number of days absent may well have been five, with a return on Wednesday, April 4 (Dynes et al. 1979:151); but in the survey reported by Goldhaber and Lehman (1982: Table 1), 2,122 (15.4 percent) of the evacuees remained away from home one or two days, 4,461 (32.4 percent) three to five, and the remaining 7,187 (52.5 percent) six or more days. Evacuees living near the plant were, for obvious reasons, more likely to leave earlier than those residing in outlying communities (Ziegler, Brunn, and Johnson 1981:12). As already noted, Wednesday, April 4 was the median date for a return movement that was as orderly as the earlier dispersal. "However, the governor's advisory to pregnant women and preschool children was not lifted until 9 April, and schools located within 5 miles of TMI did not open until 11 April" (Flynn 1982:54).

Various investigators have produced estimates of the economic costs of the TMI evacuation, and they have been ably synopsized in Hu and Slaysman (1981). There is near-agreement on the cost per household, with values ranging between $202 and $212 (Hu and Slaysman 1981:31). The overall economic impact of the event can be summarized as follows.

> The Governor's report on the impact of the TMI accident . . . indicated a monetary loss of $7.7 million in the value of production in manufacturing industries, $74.2 million in business sales in nonmanufacturing industries, and about $.25 to $.50 million in the agricultural sector, for a total monetary loss of about $82 million incurred by industry. Our study shows that households incurred about $6 to $10 million loss, or about 7 to 12

percent of the industry and business loss estimated by the Governor's report. (Hu and Slaysman 1981:37)

The long-term effects of the TMI accident have been of concern to many parties. Setting aside its impact on national energy policy and related issues, what is the local legacy in demographic, social, and economic terms? The answer, at least to date, seems to be surprisingly little that can be quantified, apart from greater attention to planning for future emergency evacuations. From all accounts, the evacuation appears to have been a temporary affair with all residents returning within a matter of days or weeks. A telephone survey conducted during October–November 1980 involving 768 households within five miles of the plant was unable to detect any statistically significant change in the demographic makeup or mobility behavior of the pre-accident population (Flynn 1982:59; Goldhaber, Houts, and DiSabella 1983). Furthermore, the demographic characteristics of new people moving into the area were not different from those who had moved out during the previous nineteen-month period (at a normal rate).

Although the news media periodically report complaints among some local residents over lingering psychological stress and other possible medical difficulties, the reported data fail to substantiate these concerns, with one interesting possible exception. For the past several years, a controversy has raged as to whether the atmospheric release of radioactive substances during and after the accident resulted in a significant increase in local infant mortality rates and the incidence of certain forms of cancer (e.g., Tokuhata and Digon 1985). The question remains unresolved, and, in the case of cancer, definitive answers may come many years in the future. On the other hand, three data sets that could tell us about the effects of resident's stress level on number of physician visits—household survey data, physician survey data, and Pennsylvania Blue Shield physicians' claim data—all suggest increases no greater than 1 to 2 percent, values that are too slight to be statistically significant (Hu and Slaysman 1981:v). Interesting though such questions may be, they are at best peripheral to this investigation, since they are not directly linked to the evacuation experience. In similar fashion, a postaccident study of real estate data was unable to find any measurable impact of the TMI episode on residential values or sales (Gamble and Downing 1981).

What general conclusions can we derive from the case of the Three Mile Island accident and its associated evacuation? In the light of the many subsequent surveys and analyses carried out over the past several years, the initial reaction of some veteran students of disasters and evacuation behavior, namely that "this evacuation was more nearly like, rather than uniquely different, from those found in other types of emergencies" (Dynes et al. 1979:156), does not seem well founded. Some parallels to earlier American experience did materialize, of course, for example, the lack of outright panic, the reluctance to leave at the first hint of possible danger, the predominance of family units among the evacuees, and the tendency to seek temporary housing with friends or relatives. But taking all the evidence into account, and, most especially, the geographic dimensions of the event, much greater credence can be given to the conclusions reached by Ziegler and Johnson (1984).

> The behavioral response to nuclear accidents appears to be quite different from responses to other emergencies, particularly in terms of the evacuation process. Spontaneous evacuation and its geographic manifestation, the evacuation shadow phenomenon, seem to place nuclear power accidents in a class by themselves. We are unable to cite any other class of accidents or disasters which has precipitated such extreme evacuation behavior, particularly in its geographic dimensions . . . the results of the Shoreham evacuation survey seem to support our hypothesis that human behaviors during nuclear emergencies cannot be predicted on the basis of what we know about other emergencies. (Ziegler and Johnson 1984:213–14)

And as detailed information concerning the Chernobyl disaster of April–May 1986 gradually emerges, it would seem to strengthen the Ziegler-Johnson thesis.

MISSISSAUGA, 1979

The evacuation of Mississauga in November 1979 has been hailed as a prime example of a successful response to an emergency. Nearly all inhabitants of this industrial city located between Toronto and Hamilton were evacuated promptly following an industrial accident. Evacuation lasted about one week and involved over 200,000 persons.

Fortunately, immediately after the accident a thorough study was undertaken by the Institute for Environmental Studies, University of Toronto, commissioned by the Office of Solicitor General of the Province of Ontario. The detailed report resulting from this study contains a wealth of information (Burton et al. 1981) and has been used as a principal source for this discussion. A brief study based on a separate survey was published by Liverman and Wilson (1981), while another report for the government of Ontario was produced by Harvey et al. (1980). Other reports by public agencies were published by the Canadian Red Cross Society (1980), Emergency Planning Canada (1979), and the Canadian Police College (Scanlon 1980). A report based on a special inquiry was published under the name of Justice Samuel Grange (1981). The case has found its way into the general literature on the subject (Lagadec 1982:126–36). And of course there was sub-stantial press coverage at the time in publications such as the *Globe and Mail,* Toronto *Star,* and *Maclean's.*

The accident was caused by the derailment of a freight train and a subsequent fire causing the release of toxic gas. It occurred as a train consisting of 106 cars, including 38 carrying hazardous materials, was crossing the city on its way from Sarnia (a major center of chemical industry) to Toronto. Apparently, an axle bearing burnt through in one of the cars, and three minutes later several cars derailed and the resulting crashes and collisions caused several explosions and a fire. Chlorine leakage was the principal reason for evacuating Mississauga. One of the tanker cars contained ninety tons of liquid chlorine, a chemical that forms a toxic gas when it vaporizes into the atmosphere. This gas, notorious for its military use in World War I, can cause fatal lung damage at concentrations exceeding three parts per million.

The emergency response was immediate and the first evacuation orders were issued less than two hours after the accident. Most of the evacuation was completed within twenty-four hours. The return of evacuees occurred in two stages when the danger of chlorine explosion was over (see Figure 5-2).

Emergency and Organizational Response

The derailment and explosion took place on Saturday, November 10, 1979 at 11:54 P.M. (see Figure 5-2). Fortunately, the burning section of the train was located in an industrial area of the city, but residential neighborhoods were not far away. Police and fire teams were on the scene within minutes, and the first police command post was estab-lished at 12:19 A.M. Sunday morning. The strong probability that the car with toxic chlorine was in the burning section was established at 1:38 A.M. and confirmed at 3:21 A.M. In the meantime, the first

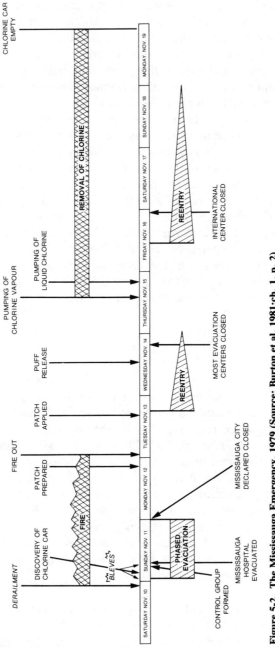

Figure 5-2. The Mississauga Emergency, 1979 (Source: Burton et al. 1981:ch. 1, p. 2)

evacuation had begun. The fire was extinguished after some fifty hours on Tuesday, November 13 at 3:47 A.M. The car containing chlorine was damaged early during the fire, and most of the chlorine was sucked up by the heat and escaped high into the air. Later a patch was applied to seal the rupture and the remaining chlorine, both vapor and liquid, was slowly drained by a chemical emergency crew who completed the task Friday night. At that point the danger had subsided.

The city of Mississauga is located in the regional municipality of Peel, which is a dynamic urban-industrial area with a dense network of communications and transport facilities. Hazardous events, some connected with transportation, had occurred during the previous decade: two air crashes near the Toronto International Airport at Malton; natural gas explosions; and an oil refinery fire resulting in evacuation of some 1,000 persons. As a result, various agencies involved in rescue operations—police, fire department, and ambulance services—did have considerable experience. The Peel Regional Police Disaster Plan was developed as a result of the 1969 gas explosion, and it was this plan that was put into effect to deal with the 1979 Mississauga disaster. Overall command during the emergency remained in the hands of the police chief.

Evacuation

The danger of chlorine leakage or explosion was perceived very early, and the first evacuation order was issued on Sunday at 1:47 A.M. According to police records, 213,000 persons were evacuated from sixteen zones (see Figure 5-3 and Table 5-4). The Mississauga Municipal Planning Department puts the total population of the evacuated area at 226,000, and this figure is used in the official report (Burton et al. 1981:5–7). Evacuation proceeded in stages, and there was usually a certain delay between evacuation order and actual departure. Nevertheless, 50 percent of the households left within thirty minutes and 80 percent within one hour (Burton et al. 1981:5–6). Analysts emphasize that speedy and successful evacuation was facilitated by a number of factors (Liverman and Wilson 1981:373).

a. The highly visible and audible nature of the disaster
b. Most families were together on Sunday night; only in some cases did looking for a missing family member delay departure

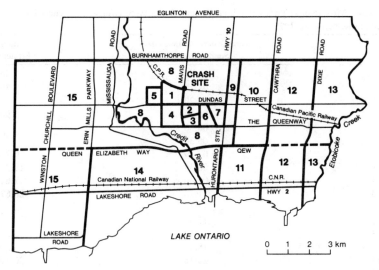

Figure 5-3. Mississauga, 1979: The evacuation zones (Source: Burton et al., 1981:ch. 2, p. 25)

c. A general perception that absences would be very short, much shorter than they turned out to be in actuality
d. The vast majority of residents owned cars; many could afford hotels; some owned second houses
e. Most people had friends and relatives with whom they could stay
f. Mississauga has an excellent road network
g. Looting was very unlikely

Information delivered to the door and via radio and television was the dominant source of evacuation instructions; TV, radio, and police requests were the most frequent evacuation stimuli (Liverman and Wilson 1981:386).

Most people left by private vehicles. In fact, some 88 percent used their own cars; 9 percent went in friends'/neighbors' cars; 2 percent used taxis or public transportation. Had the evacuation been declared for the whole area at once, one could anticipate some 76,000 vehicles on the road within the first hour. Since evacuation was staggered, the maximum flow reached a tolerable 9,000 vehicles between 10 and 11 on Sunday morning (Burton et al. 1981:5–10).

The distance and direction of travel appeared to be influenced by (Burton et al. 1981:5–13):

Table 5-4. Mississauga: Times at Which Various Zones Were Officially Evacuated and Populations Involved, 1979

Zone	Time Ordered to Evacuate, Sunday, Nov. 11	Population Estimates
1	01:47	3,500
2	04:15	350
3	06:20	575
4	06:30	900
5	06:30	
6	06:30	4,400
7	07:29	6,200
8	08:30	19,315
9	09:40	7,618
10	11:10	28,672
11	13:10	
12	17:00	17,430
13	17:10	58,280
14	18:45	38,390
15	20:16	26,210
16	23:30	1,500
Total		213,000[1]

[1]These population estimates (from Peel Regional Police) add up to 213,000 whereas Burton et al. (1981) uses a figure of 226,000 for the population of the evacuated area, based on data from the Mississauga Municipal Planning Department. The exact population is difficult to determine because of the number of new housing developments and the length of time elapsed since the previous census in 1971.
Source: Burton et al. 1981:5–7.

a. The expectation of returning within twenty-four hours
b. The nearness of major urban centers—Toronto and Hamilton
c. The spatial pattern of social networks
d. The decision to go to a private home or hotel, or to an evacuation center

On the other hand, distance and direction did not appear to have been influenced by:

a. The time of evacuation
b. The phasing of the evacuation zones in relation to desired travel directions
c. The size and socioeconomic characteristics of a household

Most people went to private homes, no fewer than 87 percent in the first move, and a clear majority of the evacuees in the second and third exodus (Burton et al. 1981:5–20).

According to estimates based on the surveys, some 14,000 persons went through official evacuation centers. Over one-third (38 percent) of them stayed there for less than twenty-four hours, then moved on to hotels or private homes. Those who stayed longer (8,700 persons), some for a seven-day period, tended to be: in lower-income categories; members of larger families; the old; single persons; non-English speakers; and persons with pets. On the whole, evacuees were quiet and cooperative. Some young people (particularly those who were not really evacuees but "free-loaders") tended to cause difficulties. In two centers there were reports of vandalism and fights between youths (Burton et al. 1981:5–30).

There was clearly a distance-decay function at work. Twenty-five percent of evacuees remained within the 5 km zone, 60 percent within 10 km, and 95 percent within 100 km. Over one-quarter chose to move initially to other parts of Mississauga, but as additional zones were evacuated these people had to move again. In fact, 29 percent of evacuees moved twice and 7 percent three times. Surveys indicate that Toronto on the north and several towns to the south and west attracted most evacuees. The time of absence varied between one and eight days, with 32 percent staying away three days and another 19 percent two days.

Return of Evacuees

A fairly high proportion of evacuees (19 percent of the sample surveyed, which implies 14,500 persons) attempted to reenter the evacuation zone before the area was officially reopened. Apparently the police, who toward the end of the week escorted many people home, perceived such attempts at reentry as a major problem. Most attempts were made on the third and sixth days (over 3,000 each). The most common causes identified in the interviews were to look after pets and get some clothes (28 percent each). Most people who succeeded in getting back, whether with police escort or without it, were in the house for a very short time, but some remained home for the rest of the evacuation period. Although police did turn many people back, Burton et al. estimate that between 1,000 and 4,000 people were going in and out of evacuated zones each day after Monday, November 12 (Burton et al. 1981:5–41).

As the situation improved, restrictions were removed and people were permitted to return (see Figure 5-4). The first major wave of

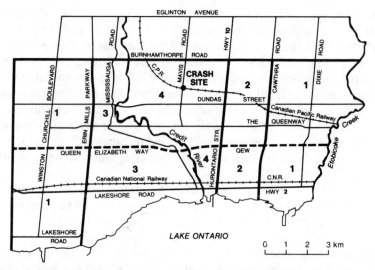

Figure 5-4. Mississauga evacuation, 1979: The reentry zones (Source: Burton et al. 1981:ch 2, p. 45)

returnees was allowed back on Tuesday, November 13 (Burton et al. 1981:2–49, 5–25). The announcement was made in the afternoon and the actual return of some 144,500 people into the outer zones extended into the following day (see Zones 1 and 2 in Figure 5-4). There was some traffic congestion on the roads aggravated by confusion as some people tried to return prematurely into the areas still closed. The number of vehicles that had to be turned back was estimated at 18,000. The problems were partly caused by lack of coordination between media announcements and police orders regarding timing of return and the areas to which the return was allowed.

Problems with the chlorine tank car (a leaking patch and a sudden release of a large puff of water vapor or chlorine mixed with water vapor on Wednesday noon) delayed reentry. However, the second major reentry was scheduled after the danger of chlorine leakage was no longer perceived to be serious. This second return occurred in several stages on Friday and Saturday. At 2:55 P.M. Friday, Zone 3 was reopened and 37,000 to 40,000 were allowed back. At 7:40 P.M. the remaining area (Zone 4, with 30,000 to 35,000 inhabitants) was declared safe for return. The next return started on Friday evening and extended into Saturday; by then the whole episode of evacuation was finally over. Timing of return was somewhat different for those using evacuation centers, who tended to return rather later than did most evacuees (see Table 5-5). The return of evacuees was nearly complete after six days.

Persons Who Stayed Behind

In spite of the danger and official evacuation advisories, some people chose to stay behind. It appears that at least 1,200 families decided not to evacuate. Surveys and interviews suggest that these were mostly persons in their fifties and sixties, highly educated, in professional/ managerial and sales occupations, and with relatively high incomes. They lived mostly very close to the boundaries of the evacuation zones, but some were only two to three km from the place of the accident. Apparently the decision to stay was always made collectively. In some cases, however, the families split up, with some members evacuating and others staying behind.

The factors contributing to the decision of some families not to evacuate included:

a. Their belief that there was no real danger to them
b. The belief that should the situation change, they would be prepared to leave on short notice
c. The need to stay to look after a large number of plants or animals
d. Attitudes about the rights of individuals versus those of authorities
e. They were not approached directly by the police
f. They had no friends/relatives to stay with

Table 5-5. Mississauga: Days on Which Evacuees Returned to Their Homes, 1979

Returned on:	All Evacuees (N = 545)	Those Using Evacuation Centers (N = 175)
Monday, Nov. 12	0.4%	1.6%
Tuesday, Nov. 13	37.0	27.0
Wednesday, Nov. 14	13.0	5.0
Thursday, Nov. 15	3.0	3.0
Friday, Nov. 16	33.0	47.0
Saturday, Nov. 17	11.0	13.0
Later than Nov. 17	2.0	3.0
Total	99.4%	99.6%

Source: Burton et al. 1981:5–25.

g. Previous experience with war emergencies and the London smog of 1952, which made them downplay the danger in Mississauga. Some persons in this category had unpleasant memories of wartime evacuations. It is interesting to note that of fourteen non-evacuating families interviewed, in ten at least one adult had been in Europe during World War II (Burton et al. 1981:5–35).

Behavior of Inhabitants on Perimeter of Evacuation Zone

The northern zone of Mississauga, north of Burnhamthorpe Road, was not officially evacuated. Nevertheless, some inhabitants of this area located 4 to 8 km from the accident did leave on Sunday (and some even on Monday). Most expected to be away for the day but were prevented from returning by police roadblocks since access roads were closed to traffic. Most returned home on Tuesday and Wednesday.

The survey carried out among the population of this area suggests that 59 percent of households evacuated completely, 4 percent sent away some family members (mainly mothers and children) and the remaining populations stayed home (Burton et al. 1981:5–43, 5–44). The reasons for evacuating or remaining are presented in Table 5-6.

Problems and Consequences

The accident and the evacuation did not cause any deaths or injuries, but minor health problems and heightened anxiety were reported by some inhabitants of the area. Temporary lack of access to medical attention and medication may have exacerbated existing health problems. It appears that the breakdown in contact between doctors and their regular patients was one of the problems of the evacuation. An ad hoc clearing service established by one physician was insufficient and not adequately publicized. Emergency health services did operate, but they were not a completely adequate response to the problem (Burton et al. 1981:6–12).

Special problems were presented by the evacuation of institutions—three hospitals and nursing homes—and of the elderly living at home, but the overall evaluation of this type of movement indicated that the elderly did not suffer any particular hardships (Burton et al. 1981:6–20). Non-English speakers (mainly Italians and Portuese) usually

Table 5-6. Mississauga: Reasons Given by Perimeter People North of Burnhamthorpe Road Who Did and Did Not Evacuate, 1979

	Percent
Did Evacuate Because:	
Worried in case of danger	34
Believed they were told to go	14
Because near evacuation zone	11
Saw others go	9
Concern about pregnancy/children	8
Concern about health	6
Other reasons	18
N = 126	100
Did Not Evacuate Because:	
Not asked to evacuate	53
Not at risk	14
News reassuring	10
Have no children	3
Housing evacuees	3
Nowhere to go	2
Other reasons	17
N = 74	100

Source:Burton et al. 1981:5–44.

had someone in the household who could serve as an interpreter and there was no major communication problem (Burton et al. 1981:6–20).

Persons who used facilities provided by evacuation centers were later interviewed about their experiences. Sleeping and recreation were two facilities that scored low (over 50 percent said these facilities were inadequate), while food and health care were on the whole satisfactory. People who stayed longer tended to be more satisfied, partly because the facilities improved and partly because the short-term stayers tended to be more impatient. Age was another important variable. It appears that the experience seems to have suited young people best, with unlimited access to fast food like hamburgers, organized films and games, and plenty of companionship. For older people, the noise, lack of privacy, boredom during the day, and difficulty in sleeping during the night stand out in their memories (Burton et al. 1981:6–32). As a result, 25 percent of the older people (8 percent of all evacuees) said that next time they would go to a hotel rather than the evacuation center.[1]

About half of all homes in Mississauga have at least one pet, and the problem of animal care was quite serious (Burton et al. 1981:6–35).

Most dog owners (88 percent) took their pets along, but only 55 percent of cats were evacuated. It was estimated that some 2,000 dogs, 5,000 cats, and 8,000 fish, rodents, and birds were left behind. Most had enough food and water for one day, but by Tuesday the owners became quite anxious and either tried to reenter the area or phone the Ontario Humane Society for help. On Tuesday afternoon, an Emergency Animal Care Program was set up and visits to care for pets were organized. Owners were asked to give the keys (sometimes the only keys) and permission to enter, and volunteers visited homes accompanied by police. This service lasted until Friday night. Owners who took their pets with them went to evacuation centers (hence complaints about the presence of animals there), and if they went to hotels that did not accept animals, arrangements were made to place them in private kennels. In the final analysis, very few pets (mostly birds and rodents) were lost.

Not surprisingly, the experience has increased the awareness of Mississauga residents of various risks and increased their perception of the probability of an accident. Short-term and long-term social costs and benefits as reported by the evacuees interviewed after the event are presented in Table 5-7. It appears that the experience has not been totally negative and that there were certain benefits perceived as well.

BHOPAL, INDIA, 1984 (BHOPAL I AND II)

Bhopal I

During the night of December 2–3, 1984, the accidental release of a huge cloud of methyl isocyanate (MIC), an extremely lethal substance, from the Union Carbide plant in Bhopal, India resulted in the most catastrophic industrial accident of recorded history, and also initiated the first of two large spontaneous evacuations of the city.

Any discussion of these evacuations must be prefaced by a few words concerning the data situation. Although the Republic of India may pride itself on the relative sophistication of its administrative apparatus and the general quality of its statistical record-keeping, especially as compared with most other Third World countries, the emergency situation in Bhopal was such that no reliable enumerations, or even estimates, have been forthcoming from official or unofficial sources, concerning evacuees. With respect to deaths and injuries, such figures as we do have range quite widely between improbable

Table 5-7. Short- and Long-Term Social Costs and Benefits Reported by 1979 Mississauga Evacuees

	Social Costs, % Evacuees Reporting		Social Benefits, % Evacuees Reporting	
Short Term (one month):	Inconvenience	28	None	56
	None	18	Met people	11
	Concern about losing income	16	Good learning experience	8
	Worry	14	Expected financial compensation	6
	Children missing school	9	Demonstrated good response	5
	Concern about home and people	9	Appreciate life	4
	Frustration	5		
Long term (one year):	None	30	None	30
	Permanent effects	12	More aware	12
	More nervous	11	Greater confidence in government	9
			Appreciate life	8
			More prepared for emergencies	2

Note: Some evacuees mentioned more than one cost or benefit.
Source:Burton et al. 1981:9–6.

extremes, and all must be treated with great caution. The fact that many journalists covered the story for some weeks has only slightly alleviated the plight of the analyst seeking material on disaster-induced mobility. The Bhopal story continues to attract worldwide attention—and will probably continue to do so for some years to come—but the substantial literature that has been accumulating on the tragedy is centered on complex technological, medical, legal, financial, and political issues to the virtual exclusion of demographic topics.

Considerable uncertainty surrounds the most elementary of facts: the size of the population at risk. The city of Bhopal, the capital of Madhya Pradesh, the most centrally located of India's states, has been a sizable place for many generations; but its rate of growth accelerated dramatically with the construction of the large Union Carbide facility in 1969, which eventually produced a large share of the pesticides purchased by Indian cultivators. As a result, 895,815 inhabitants were counted in the *Census* of 1981 as against an estimated population of 250,000 in 1969 (Bowonder, Kasperson, and Kasperson 1985:7). The influx of migrants continued during the subsequent three years, and in December 1984 Bhopal probably contained a population ranging between 1 and 1.2 million.

Quite apart from its general stimulation of Bhopal's growth, the
Union Carbide plant, with its north-central site well within the limits
of the municipality, generated a large, crowded squatter settlement
immediately south of its gates, an area with at least 20,000 occupants
(see Figure 5-5). As it turned out, this was the portion of the city most
drastically affected by the accident. The precise sequence of events
that led to the catastrophe is not entirely clear, as is also the case for
the physics or chemistry of the event, none of which is directly relevant
to this discussion. There is little doubt, however, concerning the
immediate results. Alfred de Grazia has briefly summarized the situation:

> The cloud, called appropriately by some Indian newspapers "the killer
> cloud," emerged in full hissing fury close to 1:00 a.m. from a venting
> tower, after passing through an apparatus designed to render harmless
> the poisonous gas of methylisocyanate (MIC). The gas ascended the vent
> pipe in a long-drawn-out explosion lasting nearly two hours. It was
> initially propelled from the extremely high pressure of the tank that had

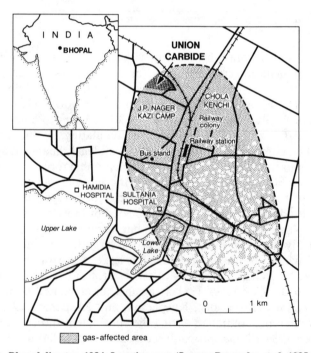

Figure 5-5. Bhopal disaster, 1984: Location map (Source: Bowonder et al. 1985:9)

held it in liquid form and emerged from the pipe into the atmosphere. Then, directed by the wind, it streamed out, not losing its internal turbulence until expanded and cooled. . . . The air temperature was in the mid-fifties Fahrenheit, a cool night for Bhopal. A fairly stiff breeze was blowing from the countryside down upon the eastern sectors of the city. Both conditions—the temperature and the wind—were misfortunes: The chilled air forced the hot and heavy poisoned moisture of the release to carry along close to the ground, preventing it from rising and dissipating.

The wind blew the gas through the most densely settled sectors of the city. About twenty-five square miles of territory were covered by lethal vapors during the prolonged venting. (de Grazia 1985:11–12)

The affected areas, which extended from the north-central to the southeastern sections of the city, included not only some of the most congested slum colonies but also much of the downtown area, the railroad and bus stations, hospitals, and some well-to-do neighborhoods. De Grazia (1985:68) and Bowonder, Kasperson, and Kasperson (1985:9) have produced maps depicting the zone of serious gassing as reconstruced from various eyewitness accounts. Unfortunately, many of the evacuees fled in the same generally southeastward direction taken by the lethal cloud of gas, thus greatly reducing their chance for survival.

Neither the plant management nor governmental authorities had prepared plans for a major disaster involving Bhopal, nor were there any provisions for mass evacuation, and the result was predictably calamitous. The Union Carbide officials did not sound any general alarm until some hours after the accident, while public officials were equally sluggish in reacting to the emergency. Indeed it was reported that some key personnel in charge of public safety had simply departed hastily with their families rather than report to their stations. It was not until late in the morning, long after many residents had died or been seriously injured or fled, that any form of organized response took shape.

When daylight arrived on December 3, the scene was horrendous in the extreme, as attested by many a journalistic account. We will never know even the approximate total number of fatalities, largely because of the hasty mass burials and cremations and the fact that many of the fatally stricken died after fleeing the city. The estimates vary from a low of 1,400 to a high of 10,000 (Bowonder, Kasperson, and Kasperson 1985:12). To this total, whatever it might be, one might add a considerable number of livestock killed or injured and damaged to the local vegetation. Within the human population, at least 200,000 persons received medical attention, about 60,000 of whom displayed serious symptoms from exposure to MIC, while as many as 17,000 persons may have been permanently disabled.

As soon as the persons in the affected districts—most of them asleep, of course—detected the noxious fumes, they began fleeing for their lives if they were physically capable of doing so, without waiting for official announcements or directives. If ever there has been a panic movement, this was it. "Havoc, chaos, madness in the mass: such words could be used for once literally" (de Grazia 1985:13). Foot travel was the obvious expedient for nearly everyone during the first minutes and hours of the emergency, but shortly thereafter every available mode of transportation—automotive, bicycle, animal power, bus, train, and airplane—was called into service by a great wave of dispersing city dwellers, all in addition to the massive columns of pedestrians.

Even less certain than the body count was the size of this exodus, which for the purposes of this discussion, we can term Bhopal I. There were no facilities for counting, or even roughly estimating, the volume of evacuees; and no one seemed much interested in making the attempt while the exodus was in progress. A quite conservative guess puts the figure at between 70,000 and 100,000 (Bowonder, Kasperson, and Kasperson 1985:11). An obviously suspect early report from the local police, who had placed a cordon around the city to prevent trains, planes, and other vehicles from entering, stated that "as many as 20,000 people had fled the city and that there were several injuries from traffic accidents in the panic" (Philadelphia *Inquirer*, Dec. 4, 1984:1A). More realistic are the statements that "more than a quarter of the total eight lakh [800,000] population in the city had fled in panic" (*The Hindu*, Dec. 17, 1984:1) or that "Of Bhopal's population of 1 million (unofficial figure is 1.2 million) over 500,000 had fled in one night" (*The Week* [Kerala State], Dec. 12–16, 1984:14). The official estimate—or underestimate—is 85,000, but "No one knows how they arrived at that figure. Journalists who scoured the 'old city' (which has a population of 300,000) found it virtually deserted after the accident and so conclude that perhaps that many got up and left" (Weisman 1985). "At least 13 neighborhoods within a 2½ mile radius of the plant were empty" (Philadelphia *Inquirer*, Dec. 14, 1984:18A). It was an unprecedented situation attended by great uncertainty and confusion. The outward flight of Bhopal residents continued for some days after the deadly morning of December 3, even as the influx into the hospitals abated.

The rate of exodus in the last one week has been fluctuating like a fever chart, depending on the day to day intensity of scare wave caused by varied rumors pertaining to the persistence of air pollution, possible after effects of the gas spread and apprehension about fresh leakage. (*Times of India*, Dec. 13, 1984)

The havoc caused by the poisonous gas leakage in the city last week is so much on the mind of people that despite the State Government's assurance that the atmosphere is clear and the air and water in the city are "absolutely safe" people have started sending their family members, especially women, children and old people outside Bhopal. (*Indian Express*, Dec. 12, 1984)

A quick check at the railway station and the main bus stand in the city revealed that the traffic to out-station had increased by at least 60% from Wednesday last [December 3], as compared to normal traffic. (*Indian Express*, Dec. 12, 1984)

The depopulation of Bhopal was not limited to those sections of the city to which the MIC fumes had drifted.

People fled from the new Bhopal area which had been quite unaffected by the disaster and what is particularly to be noted is that the poor folks of jhuggi jhopdis [shanty-towns] made a desperate run for life rightly believing that in the wake of a sudden calamity they would be the worst affected for lack of transport, whereas the rich can make a dash in their cars and scooters. Having no intention to wait until the last minute, jhuggis as far off from the affected area as those of Arjun Nagar, 74 Bungalows, Arera Colony, Janatha Quarters and Christian Church, as well as those nearer by like those of the Station Bajariya and Chola Road, became deserted. (*Nai Duniya*, Dec. 12, 1984)

Details concerning the destinations of evacuees during Bhopal I are extremely sketchy. What is self-evident is that the nearby towns and villages must have been crowded to capacity. "Indore, two hours away, Dewas, Hosangabad, Obaidullanagar and other small towns were suddenly inundated with gasping and mostly dying people" (*The Week* [Kerala State], Dec. 12–15, 1984:14–16). A sampling of the Indian press affords some glimmer of the situation:

About 10,000 men, women and children reached Sehore [some 35 km from Bhopal] between 2:00 a.m. and 4:00 a.m. People came in trucks, cars, cycles and on foot. They flocked to the district hospital where they were given primary treatment by the doctors. (*Nai Duniya*, Dec. 12, 1984)

Hundreds of people who had dashed to Ujjain and Indore [both 165 km distant] have also been hospitalized there. (*Free Press Journal*, Dec. 12, 1984)

Many trekked more than 200 km to Hoshangbad and Indore. (*Hindustan Times*, Dec. 5, 1984)

It is reasonable to assume that many of the Bhopal residents who left their homes during the days following the initial panic found refuge among kinfolk and friends in the villages from which they had previously migrated. One may also guess that there was a positive correlation between socioeconomic standing and distance traversed. We have no information at all concerning the impact of this sudden influx on the reception areas.

The countermovement into the metropolis during both Bhopal I and Bhopal II or thereafter was somewhat unusual, and certainly far smaller than the exodus. It is obvious that few or none of the idly curious came flocking in. Instead there was the rapid arrival of government officials, members of the armed forces (ca. 2,000), relief workers and medical personnel from other Indian localities, a battalion of journalists from virtually everywhere, and a veritable horde of attorneys.

Bhopal II

It is likely, even in the absence of any direct evidence, that a fair number of evacuees had begun to trickle back to Bhopal a few days after the immediate danger had dissipated. But any such trend was abruptly aborted by the announcement that was to generate Bhopal II.

For a variety of technical reasons, Union Carbide engineers and officials deemed it expedient to neutralize chemically the remaining stock of MIC rather promptly; and, consequently, they would have to reactivate the plant for a few days, beginning December 16, for what came to be called "Operation Faith." During the short period leading up to the announced date, government and company officials went to extraordinary lengths to reassure the populace that the processing of the remaining chemicals in the Bhopal plant would be so closely supervised and controlled that the possibility of an accident would be nil. Maximum publicity surrounded the precautionary measures, some of them actually much more for show than any physical effect. The government set up temporary facilities for some 50,000 to 100,000 individuals in nine, or according to some reports, twelve camps within the southern outskirts of the city at the side farthest from the plant, and offered free transportation to these sites for any individuals who remained apprehensive. But all this effort was to no avail: the announcement of the decision to restart the plant meant instant terror and precipitated a second exodus almost as panicky as the first and possibly as large.

> Spurning official refugee camps on the city's outskirts, residents were taking any form of transportation today to leave the area. Police said that 4,000 private vehicles left the central Indian city and that ticket lines at the main railway stations stretched into the street. For the second consecutive day, passengers clambered onto the roofs of buses and trains and hung from windows in an effort to leave. (Kalbog 1984:1)

According to press reports, all airplane space was promptly booked to capacity; both regular and special trains were packed to overflowing with some 18,000 persons leaving daily; a single bus depot (Hamidia Road) sold 60,000 tickets, while many passengers boarded vehicles without tickets; others jammed onto bicycles, rickshaws, horse carts, or taxis to leave the city behind during Bhopal II. Partially replacing the evacuees were some 2,000 paramilitary troops and special armed police, along with 300 or 400 journalists, to guard deserted homes and shops and to cover the event.

Once again, we have only impressionistic estimates of the volume of this massive evacuation. Possibly as many as half the residents still remaining after Bhopal I may have taken flight, almost certainly at least one-quarter of the population. The most conservative guess would put the figure at 100,000 on top of the previous evacuation. One reporter quotes an official as saying that 200,000 persons had left (Worcester *Evening Gazette*, Dec. 17, 1984:2), while still another source (Zahreli 1985:2) sets the number at 300,000. Whatever the size of this great spontaneous exodus, Bhopal II may have been more selective in character than its predecessor, for "some men were sending their wives and children away but staying behind themselves" (Fineman 1984:2A). No information is available as to the destinations of those who did not seek shelter in the official camps; one can only speculate that the geographical pattern may have resembled that for Bhopal I, with many or most persons descending on relatives and friends at some remove from the metropolis.

What is certain is that the emergency facilities on the metropolitan periphery were woefully underutilized. In the absence of an official report, one must again rely on journalistic accounts that offer estimates wildly at variance one with another: total camp populations ranging from 2,000 to 15,000 depending upon which source one chooses to believe. A plausible guess is that no more than 10 percent of the space in the camps was occupied at any time. Moreover, at least 1,000 of the temporary residents of the camps decided to leave and move further on (Worcester *Evening Gazette*, Dec. 17, 1984:2). In any event, "Bhopal . . . looked almost barren when top scientists started the factory to convert MIC into the insecticide Sevin," and most of the houses and shops were closed and the remaining residents kept indoors (*The Hindu*, Dec. 17, 1984:1).

Details concerning the return of the evacuees are as vague and varied as those relating to the exodus. The conversion of MIC to a relatively innocuous substance was essentially completed by the evening of December 17. If we can believe Madhya Pradesh's chief minister, some of the residents of the neighborhoods near the Union Carbide plant had begun returning as early as December 16 (*Times of India*, Dec. 17, 1984). More credible is the report that a few thousand of the absentees had returned to the city by nightfall December 17 (Philadelphia *Inquirer*, Dec. 18, 1984). A December 18 dispatch claims that about 3,500 persons who had taken refuge in government camps had returned home by that morning (*National Herald*, Dec. 19, 1984). By the following day, as many as half of the camp residents may have found their way back to their regular residences (Rana 1984:13A). According to a government spokesman, about half of all the evacuees had returned to Bhopal as of December 21 (Reinhold 1984:4). More conservative is the statement that "After a week or so people started trickling back" (Zahreli 1985:3).

When did all the evacuees finally return? Or are some individuals still hanging back fearful of the prospects of residing in Bhopal? Alfred de Grazia suggests such a possibility.

> When Bhopal voted, along with several other parts of India, in a special delayed election, six weeks after the disaster, participation was at least 25% below normal, 40% as contrasted with an average of 65% in all other areas voting. Where had this 100,000 people or so of voting age gone? Perhaps there were still refugees. If so, add another 100,000 for the young, making 200,000 semi-permanent refugees. (de Grazia 1985:37)

Although such electoral data are instructive, we must treat them with caution. Voter turnout in Bhopal as of January 1985 would have been reduced not only by the absence of the remaining evacuees but also by the substantial number of persons still hospitalized or otherwise incapacitated as a result of the accident.

The timing of the return of the Bhopal I and II evacuees is only part of the larger question of the long-term demographic impact of the disaster. Complicating the search for answers is the effect of the long-term shutdown of the Union Carbide plant, previously a major generator of employment in Bhopal, not only directly but also indirectly through the multiplier effect. More data and more time are needed before we can extract the full theoretical implications of Bhopal I and II for the study of emergency evacuations, but they are obviously great.

CHERNOBYL, 1986

An accident in the Soviet nuclear plant near Chernobyl, USSR in the early hours of April 26, 1986 and its worldwide consequences generated considerable news coverage in both the Soviet Union and abroad as well as an analytical literature on the subject that is still growing. This report is based largely on: Shabad's excellent account (1986); two books by Canadian authors (Marples 1986a; Silver 1987); a special issue of the *Problems of Communism* devoted to the Chernobyl disaster (Jones and Woodbury 1986; Kramer 1986; Marples 1986b; Thornton 1986); a study by Ramberg (1986–87); and a more recent book by Hamman and Parrott (1987). The U.S. Nuclear Regulatory Commission (NRC) Report (U.S.-NRC 1987) was not available to the authors at the time of preparing this chapter.

The informational media devoted much attention to the Chernobyl tragedy both during and after the accident. Reports on Soviet media coverage can be found in the *Current Digest of the Soviet Press* (CDSP), and for Western coverage the Canadian *Globe and Mail* (GM) was scanned for the period of April 29 to July 4, 1986. Evacuation of population was discussed in all these sources, although technical and political aspects usually predominated. The first anniversary of the disaster provided an opportunity to look back at the events and their aftermath. At the April 1987 Association of American Geographers conference held in Portland, Oregon, a special session, "Chernobyl—One Year Later," in which William A. Dando and Ted Shabad participated, was organized by Philip P. Micklin. At that time new sources were identified and participants were briefed on recent developments.

Research into the accident is still going on and major projects currently underway will likely provide further insights into the accident. Whether or not more will be learned about the evacuation itself remains to be seen.

Background Information

The nuclear power station in question is located in a rural area of the Ukrainian Republic, some 110 km north of its capital, Kiev (population over 2 million). The selection of its site was influenced by the low density of population in this area on the eastern margins of the Pripyat Marshes and the availability of water from the Pripyat River. The river itself was dammed below and a vast reservoir extended for some 100 km from the town of Chernobyl almost to Kiev (see Figure 5-6). The station was built near the old agricultural town of Chernobyl, with some 15,000 inhabitants. Its construction started in the early 1970s and the first of its four (ultimately six) generators with 1,000 MW capacity each began yielding commercial power in 1977 (Shabad 1986). The Chernobyl reactors were known by the Russian initials RBMK, one of the two basic types used in the USSR. The graphite-type water-cooled reactors are relatively easy to build but difficult to maintain (Hamman and Parrott 1987:88). Their great advantage is on-line refueling, which means that the time between shut-downs is relatively long since the reactor does not have to be shut down for refueling.

Construction of the power plant was accompanied by the emergence of a new town, Pripyat, built in the 1970s at the Yanov rail stations. Initially a "workers' settlement," it was soon upgraded in the official urban hierarchy, and by 1986 it had some 35,000 inhabitants, twice as many as the old Chernobyl. Its basic function was to provide housing and services for people employed at the power station.

Apart from the two towns, the remaining settlements were all agricultural villages. Their economy was based mostly on rye, flax, and cattle production, thus differing from the much more intensive agricultural economy of the southern Ukraine. It is worth noting that some 40 percent of the farm animals were apparently privately owned (Shabad 1986:508).

Nuclear Accident

The tragic accident resulted from an unauthorized (but not unusual) experiment in Reactor No. 4 at the power plant. Apparently the

Figure 5-6. Geographic setting for Chernobyl (Adapted from Shabad 1986:506)

Chernobyl power station was plagued by some problems before (Marples 1986), and a series of errors were committed during the experiment itself, conducted during the night of April 25–26, 1986 (see Table 5-8). Shortly after midnight, a powerful steam explosion was followed a few seconds later by a hydrogen explosion (hydrogen having been produced by the reaction of steam with the zirconium cladding of the tubes containing the nuclear fuel); and some thirty fires in and around the plant released a substantial amount of radioactive material, which affected not only the local area but was carried out by the winds to neighboring countries and, indeed, around the globe (Gould 1988). Part of the reactor core was emitted as a result of the explosion, and among the radioactive material released the most dangerous items were 80 million curies of iodine-131 and 6 million curies of caesium-137 (com-

Table 5-8. Chernobyl Disaster, 1986: Chronology of Events

Date	Accident and Related Events	Evacuation
Apr. 25, 1986	Decision to conduct experiment in the power plant; experiment begins and is interrupted.	
Apr. 26: 1:00 a.m.	Resumption of the experiment in Generator No. 4.	
1:23 a.m.	Massive steam explosion followed a few seconds later by a hydrogen explosion in which part of the radioactive reactor core is ejected. Some thirty fires in and around the plant extinguished soon after, except graphite fire in core of the reactor which continues long after.	
ca. 3:00 a.m.	Local security forces under Maj. Gen. G. Berdov seal off area.	
8:00 a.m.	Doctors and technicians arrive from Moscow.	
Evening		Mobilization of buses in Kiev.
Apr. 27		After midnight, 1,216 buses and 300 trucks leave for Chernobyl zone and by 2 p.m. enter the 10 km zone. Evacuation of Pripyat from 2 p.m. to 4:20 p.m.
Apr. 28	Swedish authorities detect abnormal level of radioactivity, demand explanations from Moscow. Accident announced for the first time on Soviet TV evening news.	

Apr. 29	Moscow requests help from Sweden and West Germany in fighting reactor fires. Polish government announces various preventive measures.
May 1	100 British students leave Kiev and Moscow. Finnish chartered plane removes 200 from Kiev area.
May 2	Exclusion zone expanded to 30 km.
May 6	*Pravda* reports of cases of panic; 49,000 removed by this date.
May 8	Wind changes direction, radiation rises. Panic in Kiev. Spontaneous evacuation of many people; extra long-distance trains made available.
May 9	92,000 residents have left exclusion zone by this date.
May 10	Civic authorities in Kiev announce mass exodus of children from Kiev to begin May 15 (ten days earlier than normal vacations).
May 13	Radioactive emissions cease.
May 14	Gorbachev's televised speech.
May 19	Belorussian *Izvestia* reports evacuation of 26,000 from contaminated zone.
June 5	60,000 children evacuated from danger zone in Belorussia.
Aug. 21	Massive report on accident published in USSR.
Aug. 25–29	IAEA meeting in Vienna; Soviet report made available.

pared to 15 curies of iodine-131 released in the Three Mile Island accident) (Thornton 1986:5). The release of radiation diminished as a result of action undertaken by the authorities—bombardment from the air with sand, boron, and lead pellets—but between May 2 and May 6 another rapid rise in the release of fission product occurred. A final decline of radioactivity was recorded after May 6. In the meantime, deadly clouds spread around much of Europe with nearby countries such as Poland and Sweden most seriously affected. The effects were very uneven and two neighboring areas could receive vastly different amounts of fallout depending mainly on rain patterns.

Two people were killed in the explosion, but the total death toll was higher due to the radiation exposure of a number of people who participated in rescue operations, particularly firefighters who responded immediately to the emergency. The total death toll was estimated at thirty-one, but the long-term effects are likely to include many cases of cancer and the resulting deaths. Estimates of such fatalities vary from a few thousand to about 1 million (Hamman and Parrott 1987:167).

The reaction of the Soviet authorities was swift even if public disclosure was slow and not always accurate. Major-General G. V. Berdov, a Ukrainian deputy minister of interior, arrived in Pripyat at dawn; advance teams from Moscow, including physicians and highly placed atomic physicists, also arrived the morning of April 26. They were followed by a government commission that remained in Chernobyl during the emergency (even if individuals rotated, apparently for health reasons). The commission was responsible for the decision to evacuate the population.

The accident was first revealed by Swedish authorities, alarmed by an unusually high level of radioactivity. The Soviet sources were slow in acknowledging and explaining the accident, and in fact May Day parades were held in various cities, including Kiev, as if nothing had happened; but gradually information was made available to the public, and eventually press coverage became quite extensive. Subsequently, a report submitted by the Soviets to the International Atomic Energy Agency (IAEA) in August 1986 contained a relatively full disclosure and discussion of the accident and its consequences.

Evacuation

Evacuation of the affected population was organized quickly and efficiently using mainly public buses and trucks brought from nearby

Kiev. On the Ukrainian side, 90,000 residents were transported between April 27 and May 6, of whom 23,000 were moved to the town of Polesskoye and the remainder to farmsteads in the area. On the Belorussian side, the evacuation continued longer because some hotspots of radiation were discovered even later. Some 18,000 were evacuated, and, in addition, the town of Bragin with 7,000 inhabitants, was decontaminated without evacuating its population (Marples 1986b:21).

According to other sources, the evacuation from the Ukrainian part of the contaminated zone (the area within 30 km of the plant) totaled 92,000, including 35,000 from the town of Pripyat, 15,000 from Chernobyl, and 40,000 from rural areas. The number of persons evacuated from the Belorussian side was given at 26,000. The total was later raised to 135,000 (Shabad 1986:511), and this is the figure officially maintained. In addition, 86,000 farm animals were shipped out by truck (Hamman and Parrott 1987:171).

A convoy of 300 trucks and 1,216 buses left Kiev shortly after midnight, and on April 27 at 2:00 A.M. entered the 10 km zone, which was the first to be evacuated. According to Soviet sources, quoted by Shabad, the decision to evacuate Pripyat was taken on the evening of April 26, and immediately members of the Komsomol visited apartments in order to list residents and advise them about evacuation. Some people were reluctant to go but eventually complete evacuation was rapidly implemented. Some 35,000 people were removed during a two-hour and forty-five-minute period (or, according to other sources, four hours) (Shabad 1986:511). Ten thousand children were taken directly to summer camps in the Ukraine and other republics; 25,000 adults were directed west to the region of Poleskoye, whose population doubled when the evacuees arrived during the night of April 27–28, and were initially billeted with rural families. Apparently some specialized workers and their families were resettled again, radio workers to Vilnius, power plant workers to other nuclear power stations, and so on. It is important to realize that at the time of removal, virtually all the evacuees believed that their absence from home would be temporary; and it is this belief, which proved to be unfounded for the great majority, that leads us to classify these persons as evacuees rather than migrants or refugees.

Initially people traveled light, expecting to return soon. When it was obvious that the evacuation would continue, residents were permitted to return for brief supervised visits to retrieve some of their belongings, and a special team of drivers was used to recover several hundred private cars, which were not used in the initial evacuation on the advice of authorities concerned about traffic jams.

While Pripyat was evacuated quickly and with hardly any warning time, the evacuation from other areas proceeded in more organized, less hurried fashion. The exclusion zone was initially limited to 10 km, but on May 2 it was expanded to 30 km after a visit by two senior Politburo members, Premier N. Ryzhkov and propaganda chief Y. Ligachov. At that point the town of Chernobyl and many villages, with a total population of 92,000 on the Ukrainian side and 26,000 on the Belorussian side, were evacuated (Hamman and Parrott 1987:174). The people of Chernobyl were mainly sent south to Borodyanka Rayon which, during a three-day period, received 19,000 persons (of whom 4,500 went to the central town) and 17,000 head of livestock. Sixteen villages accommodated the evacuees.

In addition to the evacuation of the exclusion zone, other areas were also affected, even if only on a temporary basis. In Kiev, the initial calm was shattered on May 8 when Ukrainian Health Minister A. Ramanenko announced on television that the wind had changed and was now blowing toward the city. Although there was no reason for excessive concern, he indicated that children under ten would be sent to their summer camps earlier. Panic resulted and a large number of people fled the city. By mid-May some 250,000 children left Kiev; many pregnant women and mothers had also left. Another area from which 60,000 children were sent away was the Gomel region (Hamman and Parrott 1987:176).

As one would expect, there were a number of problems caused by the evacuation. First, there was a reluctance to move, particularly at the very beginning. Residents of Pripyat sent a delegation to Major-General Berdov to protest the evacuation order. Some rural inhabitants tried to hide rather than go (Hamman and Parrott 1987:173–74). Second, many families became separated, and even weeks later people were searching for relatives. Some people escaped the area altogether, and there were stories of some individuals (including party members) disappearing. Third, some evacuees were inconvenienced by a shortage of basic necessities (Hamman and Parrott 1987:173). Fourth, people were led to believe mistakenly that they were being evacuated for a short time and did not take their belongings with them. When the radiation level declined, some 14,000 were permitted to return, and if the objects left behind were not radioactive, they could remove them. Fifth, there were cases of looting, including the smuggling and subsequent sale of untested, possibly radioactive articles stolen from apartments, stores, and warehouses within the exclusion zone. The suspects were drivers and/or members of rescue teams (*Current Digest of the Soviet Press* 38, no. 46 [1986]:15). Finally, some animals were left behind and Soviet reports mentioned abandoned dogs and foxes devouring untended chickens (Hamman and Parrott 1987:177).

Rehabilitation and Housing

From the first days onward, steps were taken to minimize the risks of exposure to radiation. Roads used for evacuation and their shoulders were frequently washed to keep dust down or covered with thin plastic film. Buses and trucks were decontaminated before returning to normal service. Evacuees and also residents of surrounding areas were checked for radiation disease. Evacuation of the town of Bragin (6,000 to 7,000), situated outside of the exclusion zone, was considered, but eventually only thorough decontamination was carried out. The population of two small villages within the 30 km zone was permitted to return after decontamination, but most evacuees were to be kept away indefinitely.

When it became clear that immediate return was unlikely, alternative permanent housing had to be provided. As early as June the evacuees were promised new housing before winter. Construction crews were ordered to build houses for the victims. A team from Moscow and another from Baku were busy building new houses east of Kiev; in Makarov Rayon (west of Kiev) 2,000 homes were to be built in sixteen villages; in Boradyanka Rayon 7,000 new homes were planned (Shabad 1986:513). In the Belorussian Republic the initial plan was to build new homes for evacuees in the northern parts of neighboring rayons—Bragin, Khoyniki, and Narovlya—but finally a decision was made to move them to the more distant northern rayons of Gomel district, which happened to have a shortage of workers (Shabad 1986:515). Four thousand new houses were to be opened for occupancy by October 1 (*Current Digest of the Soviet Press* 38, no. 34 [1986]:14).

Maintenance and repair workers at the power plant, which was temporarily shut down, were initially housed in a children's summer camp 17 km southwest of Chernobyl. From there they were ferried by buses, and from Kopachi by armored personnel carriers to the plant. As the number of personnel increased, the demand exceeded the camp's capacity and accommodation for 2,000 persons was provided in river cruise ships moored near Zeleny Mys. In July, *Pravda* reported that a permanent settlement for 10,000 people was to be built in Zeleny Mys as a replacement for the abandoned Pripyat. Residents of Pripyat, initially evacuated to rural areas of Polesskoye Rayon, were to be allocated city apartments in Kiev (7,500) and Chernigov (500). Station workers on a tour of duty would be housed on a temporary basis in Zeleny Mys but reside permanently in their city apartments (Shabad 1986:519). In addition, another new town, Slavutych, was to be built east of the exclusion zone (Shabad, personal communication).

In all, fifty-two new villages were built for the evacuees. To replace 11,655 rural homes left in the exclusion zone (one-third of which were in poor repair), 7,000 new brick houses were built by October 1986 and another 5,000 were to be finished by June 1, 1987 (*Current Digest of the Soviet Press* 38, no. 43 [1986]:16).

The power station was eventually restarted (except for entombed Reactor No. 4), but the area within 30 km of the plant remains without permanent residents. This is a case, then, when what was initially perceived by the residents involved and, presumably, the authorities as well to be a temporary evacuation has developed into a permanent transfer for the great majority of the population.

According to recent press reports, population movements within and beyond the original exclusion zone have continued. Some 1,100 elderly persons defied the authorities and, disregarding warnings, returned to their homes. On the other hand, there were further evacuations and removals of population, both spontaneous and organized, from areas adjoining the exclusion zone. By late 1989, some 15,000 persons (including troops) were working in the zone, commuting daily from exterior points (*Globe and Mail*, Oct. 16, 1989). Apparently the contaminated area was much larger than originally thought. According to Soviet sources reported by Reuter, more than 200,000 individuals still live in areas where recorded radiation levels exceed five curies. Of these, 14,000 were to be moved during 1990 (*Globe and Mail*, April 24, 1990).

It appears that concern over the human consequences of the disaster continues, and further measures, including resettlement of people from an area much larger than the original exclusion zone and possibly closure of the power plant, can be expected.

NOTE

1. There are some discrepancies in figures as reported by Burton et al. on numbers of returnees (1981:2–50 and 5–26).

Chapter 6

Comparative Analysis

In this section we examine and briefly discuss all those variables we have been able to tabulate in some quantitative or methodical manner for the twenty-seven emergency evacuations treated in this study. There are thirteen such items in all, but since two pairs of them are rather closely related, eleven tables have sufficed to display our data.

It should be noted at the outset that in only the first table of the set (but partially in Table 6-7) was it feasible to use hard numbers. Elsewhere we have resorted to rank-ordering events on some continuum or classifying them within a series of categories. Such stratagems are necessary because, as noted in the introductory chapter, statistical data with any degree of reliability or completeness are seldom available for this class of unusual events. And so, once again, apologizing for the unavoidable approximations and occasion guesswork, let us proceed to our best reconstruction of the facts.

MAGNITUDE OF EVACUATIONS (TABLE 6-1)

The most obvious feature of Table 6-1 is the enormous range of values in both number of city dwellers at risk and the estimated number of evacuees. Although the former quantity is perhaps the least questionable statistic appearing in our series of tables, it is still subject to a certain amount of uncertainty. Rarely did disaster strike during or near a census year; some of the communities in question, such as El Asnam, Managua, and Bhopal, were growing at a rapid rate; the territorial bounding of urban populations is not easy to determine; and in several cases we are dealing with groups of cities rather than a single place. In any event, the numbers run from the vicinity of 50,000 to the tens of

241

Table 6-1. Magnitude of Evacuations

Event	Urban Population at Risk (in 1,000s)	Estimated Evacuated Population[1] (in 1,000s)	Approximate Percent Evacuated
Anchorage	49	1.5–2.1	3–4
El Asnam	80	52	65
Belize	40	<10 (+10 redistributed in city)	<25
Bhopal I	1,000–1,200	70–500	6–50
Bhopal II	1,000–1,200	100–300	10–30
Chernobyl (+ Kiev[2])	120 (2,200+)	445–500	18–21
Darwin	45–47	34.5–36.5	73–81
France I	12,600[3]	1,000–1,250	8–10
France II	17,600[3]	10,000–12,000	57–68
Germany I	n.a.	n.a.[4]	—
Germany II	38,000[3]	10,000–12,500	26–33
Gulf Coast Hurricanes	(variable)	2,576–2,776	—
Japan	15,500	8,500–10,000	55–65
Leningrad	3,000	1,750	58
Managua	400	200–300	50–75
Mississauga	225	220	98
Ohio River Flood	1,179	294–421+	25–36
Skopje	170	100–150	59–88
La Soufrière	75[3]	38–72	51–96
Three Mile Island	375[3]	144–150	38–40
United Kingdom I	13,000	2,000	15
United Kingdom IIa	13,000	1,500–1,750	12–14
United Kingdom IIb	13,000	1,250	10
USSR	82,000–85,000[3]	10,000–23,000	12–28
Warsaw I	1,300	100–200	8–16
Warsaw II	1,000	800	80
Winnipeg	330	65–107	20–32
Total	174,688–178,090	49,499–69,547	28–40

[1]Including individuals involved in two or more evacuations.
[2]The Chernobyl case involves an exclusion zone, both urban and rural, around the power plant plus the nearby city of Kiev, whose population is shown in parentheses.
[3]Including an undetermined number of rural inhabitants.
[4]No usable estimate available, but number of persons evacuated amounted to "hundreds of thousands."

millions, while the continuum is equally broad for the estimated volume of the evacuation.

Taking the twenty-seven events in their totality, the sheer volume of these evacuations is impressive. Even allowing for some double-counting, especially in the Bhopal, Great Britain, and Warsaw cases, the grand total of somewhere between 49 and 70 million is a significant fraction of world population during the fifty-year period in question—somewhere in the neighborhood of 2 percent. And, of course, this study has ignored that large universe of evacuations for which documentation is inaccessible.

But more interesting than absolute numbers is evacuated population as a percentage of persons at risk. Here again the range of values is considerable. At the low end we have Anchorage, where only 3 to 4 percent of the inhabitants seem to have chosen the evacuation option. At the other extreme, virtually everyone left Mississauga, or at least the officially designated evacuation zones, during its brief crisis. The same statement applies to Chernobyl, and to Warsaw as well during the forced evacuation of 1944, while the great majority of the residents of Darwin, Skopje, and the flanks of La Soufrière were also obliged to leave their homes.

What were the determinants of these varied levels of temporary depopulation? It is plausible that the most crucial factor was the perception of the severity of the disaster, whether actual or prospective, and thus the possible threat to personal safety and well-being on the part of the official decision makers and/or the general public. Where the authorities maintained control of the situation, they were able to manage both the timing and extent of the exodus with a certain degree of effectiveness as they acted on the basis of these perceptions. Clearly such was the case for Darwin, the British cities, Leningrad (and, in a rather less methodical fashion, other western Soviet cities), many of the cities afflicted by the Ohio River Flood and the various Gulf Coast hurricanes, La Soufrière, France I, Germany I, Chernobyl (proper), Winnipeg, and Mississauga. When matters were left almost entirely up to individual and family decisions, as in Anchorage, Bhopal, France II, Three Mile Island, United Kingdom I, and Kiev, we can infer that the rates of departure give us clues as to how ordinary citizens calculated the urgency of the situation. In still other instances we find a mixture of official and private decisions. Such would seem to have been the pattern in the evacuation of German and Japanese and probably many of the Soviet cities as well.

Motivations other than the perception of impending physical danger or intolerable living conditions obviously also came into play. There was little choice available to those persons in El Asnam, Belize, Managua, Skopje, the flooded portions of Ohio River cities, or bombed-out districts of German and Japanese cities who could not find shelter or the other necessities of life nearby. With or without governmental aid and supervision, flight was the only alternative. And, of course, strong official coercion, as in Warsaw II, Darwin, and Chernobyl, left little scope for individual initiative.

The logistics of moving from a distressed area to relative safety and comfort may also have affected the extent of evacuation. Thus it is plausible that many more residents of Anchorage might have left their crippled city if potential destinations had not been so distant and costly to reach. Similarly, the formidable difficulties of travel may have dissuaded many Soviet urbanities from taking the trek eastward, however horrendous the prospect of German rule. Recollections of the Stalinist atrocities in the years preceding the invasion may have made some potential evacuees reluctant to depart.

Quite difficult to gauge but plainly relevant both to incidence of evacuation and patterns of return is the strength of social and emotional attachment to one's familiar surroundings. This may have been a negligible factor for the predominantly transient inhabitants of Darwin or Anchorage, but it certainly frustrated the best-laid plans of those administering United Kingdom IIa and IIb. As we have learned, fewer persons left the British cities than had been anticipated, and most of those who did evacuate made the return trip prematurely. The same sort of obstinacy or inertia was also evident among many German and Japanese city folk—and quite conceivably their Soviet counterparts as well—who balked at the notion of relocation.

PLANNING AND CONTROL OF EVACUATIONS (TABLE 6-2)

Although there is an obvious correlation between, on the one hand, the degree to which governmental agencies had anticipated disasters and had made contingency plans, including population evacuation, and, on the other, the extent of administrative control and coercion, the two variables do not fully coincide. Thus, in the case of the Darwin disaster, little or no forethought seems to have been given to the eventuality of a destructive tropical storm or how to handle its human consequences; but, when the unexpected happened, an evacuation

Table 6-2. Planning and Control of Evacuations

Preparation and Planning	Degree of Administrative Control and Coercion
No Prior or Subsequent Plan: Anchorage Belize Bhopal I France II Managua United Kingdom I Warsaw I	*Totally Spontaneous; No Effective Control:* Bhopal I France II Managua United Kingdom I Warsaw I
Plan Improvised During or Just After Disaster: El Asnam Bhopal II Darwin Germany II Japan Leningrad Ohio River Flood Skopje USSR Warsaw II Winnipeg	*Mostly Spontaneous; Some Control:* Anchorage Belize Bhopal II Three Mile Island *Spontaneity and Control in Rough Balance:* El Asnam Germany II Gulf Coast Hurricanes Japan Ohio River Flood Skopje Winnipeg
Inadequate Advance Plan: Chernobyl (?) Three Mile Island	*Predominantly to Totally Controlled:* Chernobyl[1] Darwin France I
Satisfactory Plan Prepared in Advance or Adequately Revised During Event: France I Germany I Gulf Coast Hurricanes Mississauga La Soufrière United Kingdom IIa United Kingdom IIb	Germany I Leningrad Mississauga La Soufrière United Kingdom IIa United Kingdom IIb USSR Warsaw II Winnipeg

[1]Degree of control of evacuation from exclusion area around Chernobyl was much greater than that for Kiev.

program was improvised on the spot and carried out most effectively under martial law. A quite contrary experience developed in the Three Mile Island incident. Plans did exist on paper for evacuating the local inhabitants in the remote eventuality of a major accident; but neither the plant managers nor the state and local authorities could bring themselves to implement them when the moment of truth arrived, and a bewildered citizenry was largely left to fend for themselves.

Table 6-2 suggests at least two generalizations. First it would appear that adequate preparation and planning for emergency evacuations is much more likely to be found among the relatively "advanced" countries than in the Third World communities. It was there that we also encounter the highest level of administrative control of the actual evacuations. The obvious explanation is the greater supply of financial and administrative resources in the former. The one apparent exception, namely La Soufrière, simply confirms the rule, since for all practical purposes the management of the near-disaster in Guadeloupe was conducted by authorities working out of Paris in collaboration with experts from other advanced countries.

Another inference to be drawn from the table is that only one country, Great Britain, made any detailed plans in advance for the relocation of civilian populations endangered by intensive bombing. (France I and Germany I are not valid exceptions because the plans in question were limited to small fractions of the national territory or population.) As matters eventually developed, the British authorities did act, with exemplary thoroughness, but prematurely. Indeed it may be argued they overreacted in light of the fact that, great though the havoc wrought by the German bombing campaign may have been, it was not great enough to justify mass evacuations. Hence the mediocre results of the well-organized government program.

Ironically, in those countries, namely Germany, the Soviet Union, Japan, France, and the Low Countries, where large-scale dispersion of urban populations might have made good sense in the face of saturation air raids or advancing armies, there was scarcely any advance planning, and what planning and organization did come to pass belatedly was only partially effective. In many cases, ordinary persons made their own decisions and acted upon them as best they could.

WARNING AND PANIC AS FACTORS IN EVACUATION BEHAVIOR (TABLE 6-3)

In Table 6-3 we have again conjoined two related variables: adequacy of warning of imminent disaster and the degree of panic associated

Table 6-3. **Warning and Panic as Factors in Evacuation Behavior**

Adequacy of Warning	Degree of Panic[1]
Accurate Warning or Forecast:	*No Panic:*
Belize	Anchorage
Bhopal II	Darwin
Darwin	France I
France I	Germany I
Germany I	Gulf Coast Hurricanes
Germany II	Mississauga
Gulf Coast Hurricanes	Ohio River Flood
Japan	United Kingdom IIa
United Kingdom I	United Kingdom IIb
United Kingdom IIa	Warsaw II
United Kingdom IIb	Winnipeg
Winnipeg	
	Limited Panic:
Vague, Inadequate, or Short-Term	El Asnam
Warning or Forecast:	Chernobyl (Kiev)
France II	Germany II
Leningrad	Japan
Ohio River Flood	Leningrad
La Soufrière	La Soufrière
USSR	Three Mile Island
Warsaw I	United Kingdom I
Warsaw II	USSR
No Warning At All:	*Considerable Panic:*
Anchorage	Bhopal I
El Asnam	Bhopal II
Bhopal I	France II
Chernobyl (Kiev[2])	Warsaw I
Managua	
Mississauga	*No Information (But Some Panic Likely):*
Skopje	Belize
Three Mile Island	Managua
	Skopje

[1]Discounting whatever anxiety or shock may have been present.
[2]Disaster at Chernobyl occurred without warning, but inhabitants of Kiev profited from a short-term warning.

with the resulting evacuation. Contrary to the assertions of a number
of American authors, for example, Perry (1985:97–99), panic can and
does occur during some evacuations. It is quite reasonable to assume
that accurate warnings or forecasts of impending disasters would
minimize or even eliminate any possibility of panic behavior on the
part of the impacted population, especially if they were disseminated
well ahead of the event. And panic, of course, would compromise the
effectiveness of any evacuation.

But, as often happens, reality does not necessarily follow the dictates of logic. In those eight events we have tabulated where warnings
were not forthcoming, we have noted "considerable panic" in only a
single case, that of Bhopal I, while in two other instances, those of
Anchorage and Mississauga, we encounter no record of any panic at
all. In the remaining five events, panic seems to have occurred, but
was limited in degree or number of persons involved. On the other
hand, where residents were adequately forewarned, evacuation was
often a relatively orderly process. In seven of the twelve cases we have
listed, no panic developed, while it was limited in scope in four other
cases. The one event that totally confounds expectations, Bhopal II, is
a curious exception in that the timing, location, and precise nature of
what proved to be a nondisaster were widely publicized, but the
assurances of no danger met with disbelief, and instead the soothing
announcements generated extreme panic. In retrospect, perhaps it
would have been prudent to have refrained from issuing any sort of
notice.

In general, however, even when the warnings were belated or otherwise inadequate, they may have served a useful purpose. Among the
seven events falling into the intermediate category, four managed to
do without panic. The two great exceptions—Warsaw I and France
II—illustrate the futility of panic. Leaving aside those who were
politically or "racially" vulnerable, the residents of Warsaw and the
cities of the Low Countries and northern France would have been well-
advised to remain at home.

It scarcely needs saying that the nature of the disaster is the principal
determinant of its predictability. Meteorologists have augmented their
skills in short-term forecasting quite significantly in recent years, and
now are usually able to plot the future careers of major storms with
some confidence. And as these skills have been sharpened, the populations at risk have become increasingly responsive, especially after
some earlier, tragic failures to pay attention. There have been parallel
advances in flood warning techniques. Perhaps the greatest obstacle to

accepting potentially disastrous weather advisories is the absence of local experience, as was so vividly documented in the case of Darwin. But persons residing in regions visited by frequent hurricanes, such as the Gulf Coast, or flood-prone valleys, such as those of the Red River, Ohio, and Mississippi, have learned to take official warnings seriously.

The science or art of predicting volcanic eruptions has made significant progress in recent years, though clearly much remains to be learned. When warnings are issued in areas with powerful memories of past tragedies, as in the Lesser Antilles and southern Italy, most residents are inclined to accept them at face value. The crucial variable is the resourcefulness or responsiveness of the administrative and emergency services, a fact illustrated by the totally dissimilar cases of La Soufrière and Nevado del Ruiz in Colombia. Seismologists have just begun venturing some tentative efforts at forecasting destructive earthquakes, but, whatever success they may have in the future, they are not yet prepared to offer specific warnings for particular times and places.

It is difficult to generalize about the predictability of military disasters insofar as they involve civilians, but in all eleven of the relevant case studies considered here any intelligent public official could have anticipated great hazards for urban populations (whether it would have been politically expedient to admit such dangers is another question). And indeed, in most instances, except perhaps in Poland and the Soviet Union, there was some degree of apprehension and preparedness. The one class of disasters that remains totally unpredictable to date includes those of an industrial character, as was so vividly illustrated by the accidents at Three Mile Island, Bhopal, and Chernobyl. And in the three cases cited the unfamiliarity of the lethal agent made the factor of surprise all the more painful.

As already suggested, there would seem to be some sort of relationship between a community's familiarity with a specific type of disaster and the degree to which it overreacts or panics upon being confronted with such a disaster. In order to explore these interrelationships, we have constructed Figure 6-1, in which we have plotted each of our twenty-seven events as realistically as possible within a two-dimensional matrix, one that is qualitative or ordinal in character rather than quantitative. The *x*-axis represents degree of familiarity with the type of disaster in question from least to most, while the various evacuations are arrayed along the *y*-axis in terms of panic, again from least to most.

One would logically anticipate a positive correlation between the panic and unfamiliarity factors, and, in quite general terms, that is

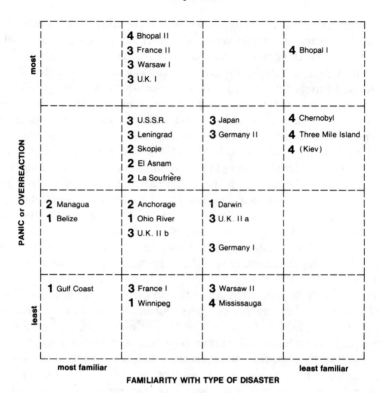

Figure 6-1. Approximate relationship between level of familiarity with disaster and reaction thereto

indeed what we do discover. Most of the events tend to cluster along or near the diagonal running from least panic/greatest familiarity to most panic/least familiarity. But it is the six outliers occupying a pair of cells in the upper and lower rows of the diagram that give one pause. It is evident that vivid recollections of the hardships and perils of World War I increased, rather than alleviated, anxiety among the participants in United Kingdom I, Warsaw I, and France II. Similarly, the horrors of the mishap at the Union Carbide plant just a few days earlier generated an extraordinary level of terror among the nearby residents and thus Bhopal II. In these exceptional cases, familiarity does not breed complacency. In the other exceptions—Warsaw II and Mississauga, when urban populations encountered situations rather novel to them—tight administrative management and control may help account for the minimal amount of panic. Or is it being cynical to suggest that the authorities consider it to their best interests to ignore or underreport the incidence of panic?

In examining our twenty-seven events as arrayed in terms of degree of panic, we can extract one general finding. In every case where panic was not observed the disaster had occurred in an advanced community, as measured in socioeconomic terms. In contrast, we have reports of some level of panic in all those evacuations taking place in the Third World localities we have studied, or have reason to assume that such was the case. The unavoidable explanation is a superior supply of information and, more to the point perhaps, a relatively adequate emergency management system. But we cannot ignore the two glaring exceptions to the rule: the panic flight of so many persons in Warsaw I and France II. The moral may be that under certain extraordinary circumstances all of us are susceptible to panic.

DISTANCES TRAVELED BY EVACUEES (TABLE 6-4)

In compiling Table 6-4 we have been handicapped by the paucity of usable statistics on numbers of evacuees by destination. Consequently, we have resorted to four rather general categories (from "none" to "most") for five distance bands centered on the urban areas in question. (The innermost band includes points within the outer metropolitan area, that is, within a few kilometers of the municipal boundary.) In only four instances—those of United Kingdom IIa and IIb, Three Mile Island, and Mississauga—do we have anything approaching adequate data. For the other events we rely upon fragmentary information

Table 6-4. Distances Traveled by Evacuees

Event	X: No data. 0: None. 1: Few or some. 2: Many. 3: Most.				
	Redistributed Within Nearby Areas	<50 km	50–150 km	100s of km	1,000s of km
Anchorage	2	?	0	1	3
El Asnam	3	1	1	1	0
Belize	3	2	1	1	1
Bhopal I	0?	2	3?	1	0
Bhopal II	1	1	2	3	?
Chernobyl (Kiev)	0	1	2	2	1
Darwin	2	0	0	1	3
France I	0	0	1	2	0
France II	0	1	1	3	0
Germany I	0	1	2	2	0
Germany II	2	2	2	1	0
Gulf Coast Hurricanes	2	2	2	1	0
Japan	2	2	2	1	0
Leningrad	0	0	1	3	2
Managua	2	2	2	X	0
Mississauga	2	3	2	X	0
Ohio River Flood	2	2	2	1	0
Skopje	3	1	1	1	0
La Soufrière	0	3	1	0	0
Three Mile Island	0	1	3	1	0
United Kingdom I	0	0	1	3	1
United Kingdom IIa	0	1	3	1	0
United Kingdom IIb	0	1	3	2	0
USSR	0	1	1	3	2
Warsaw I	2	2	1	1	0
Warsaw II	2	2	2	2	0
Winnipeg	2	2	1	1	0

and conjecture. The tabulation is further complicated by the problem of how to distinguish evacuees who relocated elsewhere within the metropolitan area from those who ventured beyond, but only to adjacent places.

The routes and distances traveled by the evacuees do not lend themselves to any meaningful generalization apart from the insights into the validity of the gravity model as indicated in Table 6-5. The reason for this situation is the tendency for each emergency evacuation to generate its own quite specific, perhaps even unique, pattern. So much depends on the location of the disaster, available means of transportation, the accessibility of safe havens, and other local circumstances. All we can confidently say is that there is the widest possible disparity among the spatial arrays of evacuees. At one extreme we observe the Darwinians and those residents of Anchorage who abandoned their cities temporarily or never to return, then found themselves many hundreds or even thousands of kilometers from their predisaster homes. In the cases of El Asnam, Skopje, Winnipeg, La Soufrière, and Belize, the picture is totally different: relocation for the duration at the nearest feasible site. And between these opposing patterns there is a variety of intermediate variants.

DISTANCE-DECAY EFFECT IN EVACUATION JOURNEYS (TABLE 6-5)

The distance-decay principle, which becomes the gravity model when spelled out in mathematical terms, is one of the most widely accepted formulations in migration theory and for a variety of relevant phenomena in human geography involving the movement of material and nonmaterial objects. Does the basic notion that the friction of distance is the dominant factor in determining the spatial disposition of items dispersed from a central locus apply to evacuees fleeing disasters in urban places? In assessing the evidence, we must honor a special proviso, what we might call the "doughnut effect." That is to say, we frequently observe a zone surrounding the disaster site that is perceived to be hazardous and, as a consequence, is shunned by evacuees; but just beyond the edge of this zone there may be a maximum accumulation of evacuees whose numbers tend to diminish as one moves outward.

In ten of our twenty-seven studies the available data strongly confirm the existence of a distance-decay effect. In fact, the Three Mile Island

Table 6-5. Distance-Decay Effect in Evacuation Journeys*

Strongly to Totally Dominant	Observable But Limited	Absent or Inverse Effect
El Asnam	Bhopal I	Anchorage
Belize	Bhopal II	France I
Gulf Coast Hurricanes	Germany II	Darwin
Managua	Japan	France II
Mississauga	Leningrad	Germany I
Skopje	Ohio River Flood	United Kingdom I
Warsaw I	United Kingdom IIa	
Winnipeg	United Kingdom IIb	
	USSR	
	Warsaw II[1]	

*Allowing for "Doughnut Effect."
[1]No effect observable among those shipped to labor and concentration camps, but distance-decay obvious for residual population.

pattern is a classic example, and the spatial disposition of evacuees from Mississauga, Managua, and the various Gulf Coast hurricanes also definitely matches expectations. In eleven other instances there are indications of an inverse correlation with distance, but much less clear-cut than in the initial examples. What is most thought-provoking are the six events that defy the formula. As best we can determine from the available information, evacuees generated by Anchorage, Darwin, France I, France II, Germany I, and United Kingdom I tended, either of their own volition or because of administrative dictates, to maximize the distances from their starting points. Although the motivations are quite different, much the same inversion of the distance-decay effect, that is, a positive rather than negative correlation with distance traveled, tends to prevail for touristic journeys and for much retirement migration. In any case, the implications for general mobility theory may be significant.

MODE OF TRANSPORT USED BY EVACUEES (TABLE 6-6)

The variety of relevant circumstances is so great that few meaningful generalizations can be offered as to the physical means used to leave our imperiled cities. Thus, in terms of absolute uniqueness, it is improbable that any evacuation, past or future, can match the combination of rail, air, ship, and truck traffic over an ice highway experienced by Leningraders. Despite these reservations, however, we can

Table 6-6. Mode of Transport Used by Evacuees

X: No data. 0: None. 1: Used by some. 2: Used by many.
3: Used by most. 4: Used by nearly all.

Event	By Foot	Animal-drawn Vehicle	Ship or Boat	Rail	Private Auto or Bicycle	Bus or Other Public Transport	Air
Anchorage	0	0	X	0	2	X	3
El Asnam	2	X	0	X	1?	1?	0?
Belize	X	X	1	0	2	2	1?
Bhopal I	2	2	0	1	1	1	0
Bhopal II	2	2	0	2	1	2	1?
Chernobyl (Kiev)[1]	0	1?	0	2	1?	3	1?
Darwin	0	0	0	0	2	X	3
France I	0	0	0	3	1	1	0
France II	2	2	0	2	2	2	0
Germany I	0	0	0	3	0	1	0
Germany II	1	0	0	3	1	2	0
Gulf Coast Hurricanes	1	X	0	1	3	1	X
Japan	1	X	0	2	2	2	X
Leningrad	0	1	2	3	0	2	2
Managua	2	1	0	X	1	3?	X
Mississauga	0	0	0	0	4	1	0
Ohio River Flood	2	X	1	2	2	2	0
Skopje	2	1	0	2	1	2	1?
La Soufrière	1?	1	1	0	1	2	1
Three Mile Island	0	0	0	0	4	1	X
United Kingdom I	0	0	2	2	3	1	0?
United Kingdom IIa	0	0	1	4	X	1	0
United Kingdom IIb	0	0	1	4	X	1	1
USSR	1	1	2	3	0	1	1
Warsaw I	2	2	0	2	1	1	0
Warsaw II	1	1	0	3	0	0	0
Winnipeg	0	0	0	2	2	2	0

[1]Rail, and possibly air and water, transport were used in the partial evacuation of Kiev.

say, as is the case with distance traveled by evacuees, that the mode of transportation used by them is determined, to a significant degree, by the location of the cities in question. Thus whether or not the actual or anticipated disasters were at sites on or near available rail lines or highways and the distances to likely destinations have certainly been material factors. But two other variables may be equally important, or even more so: the geographical configuration as well as the traffic capabilities of the transportation system, and the level of affluence of the population at risk, that is, the extent to which they are capable of patronizing the available facilities.

Thus at one extreme we have the examples of Three Mile Island and Mississauga, where nearly all the affected households had access to one or more private automotive vehicles within an area containing a dense network of highways and where, given the abundance of temporary shelter within a reasonable distance, the availability of air and rail (and much more questionably, water) transport did not much matter. Similarly, the excellence of the railroad system explains its crucial role in carrying the evacuees involved in United Kingdom IIa and IIb and also in France I, Germany I, and Japan. The dominant role of air transport in the Anchorage and Darwin events also bespeaks the relative prosperity of the populations (and governments) in question. (It was also important in the Leningrad evacuation, especially for key personnel, but in this instance it was a matter of desperation.) On the other hand, even where relatively advanced transportation systems are at hand, they can become overloaded during extreme emergencies. This eventuality was most dramatically illustrated in the case of France II when many panic-stricken travelers were compelled to become pedestrians or cyclists or to use horse-drawn carts for lack of better alternatives along highways jammed to capacity. Parallel instances of saturated rail and other public transport facilities also materialized in the Warsaw I, USSR, and Bhopal II events. The date of the event is also a significant factor in the choice of transportation mode. Thus the railroads were much more important for evacuees in the 1930s and 1940s than in the 1980s, when ready access to automobiles and aircraft had become available to much of the world's population.

As might be expected, evacuees escaping disasters in the less-developed regions of the world have tended to use relatively simple modes of transport. The classic case may well have been Bhopal I, given its combination of extreme urgency and the minimal financial resources of so many of the evacuees, so that foot travel and animal-drawn vehicles apparently accounted for the great majority of movements. But there, as in El Asnam, Managua, and La Soufrière, the rigors of travel were mitigated greatly by the fact that destinations were reasonably close by within densely populated regions.

One generalization that seems to hold for most cases regardless of level of socioeconomic development is the relative unimportance of water transport, even though the great majority of the cities studied are located on or near navigable oceans, lakes, or streams. The most important exceptions are those evacuees in United Kingdom I who boarded ocean steamers to foreign destinations and the significant numbers of persons leaving Leningrad and other Soviet cities who did avail themselves of lake and river facilities.

TYPES OF DESTINATIONS REACHED BY EVACUEES
(TABLE 6-7)

The data problems for this particular topic are among our more serious ones. The only events for which we have a reasonably complete and accurate account of the categories of temporary shelter occupied by the evacuees are the Ohio River Flood, La Soufrière, Three Mile Island, and United Kingdom IIa and IIb. For the remaining cases we must rely largely on logical inference and speculation.

But two usable generalizations do emerge from this flawed data set. First, two types of places account for the great majority of these emergency residences: official shelters and billets operated or designated by governmental agencies; and the homes of friends and relatives. The only apparent exceptions are La Soufrière and United Kingdom I, in both of which commercial facilities appear to have housed a plurality or majority of the sojourners. A second observation is that the firmer the control of the exodus by the authorities the more likely were evacuees to find themselves in official shelters and billets. That was undoubtedly true for Chernobyl, Germany I, the Ohio River Flood, Skopje, Leningrad, the USSR and United Kingdom IIa and IIb.

We can also conclude that a pattern of dense nearby settlement, a zone where evacuees had maintained ties with kinfolk and former neighbors, would have furnished optimum conditions for temporary accommodations. The ideal example is to be found in the Managua event, but it seems safe to speculate that this situation may also be discernible in the cases of Japan, Bhopal I and II, and La Soufrière. This phenomenon is not limited to less developed or developing communities. We find friends and relatives receiving a surprisingly large share of the persons fleeing Anchorage, Darwin, Mississauga, and Three Mile Island. In the latter two instances, of course, we are dealing with shifts within rather substantial metropolitan areas where the existence of an ongoing social network must be assumed, even given the supposed anomie of the post-industrial world, along with the availability of vacation cottages belonging to the evacuees or their friends and kin.

EXTENT OF EVACUEE RETURN (TABLE 6-8)

In the normal course of events, all or nearly all persons evacuated from their urban residences because of emergency situations do man-

Table 6-7. Types of Destinations Reached by Evacuees

X: No data. 0: None. 1: Some (1–15%). 2: Many (16–49%).
3: Most (50–89%). 4: Nearly All (90–99%). 5: All.

Event	Official Shelters and Billets	Commercial Facilities	Relatives	Friends	Own Property	Other
Anchorage	0	1	——4——		X	
El Asnam	3	0	1	1	0	1[a,b]
Belize	2	X	1	1	X	
Bhopal I	0	0	2	2	0	2[b]
Bhopal II	1	X	3	3	0	X
Chernobyl (Kiev[1])	3	0	1	1	0	2[c]
Darwin	0	1	— 3(61%)—		0	1[a]
France I	3	0	1	1	0	
France II	1	2	1	1	1	2[b]
Germany I	4	0	0	0	0	
Germany II	2	1	1	1	1	
Gulf Coast Hurricanes	2(33%)	2	——2——		1	
Japan	2	1	——3——		X	
Leningrad	4	0	0	0	0	1[a,b,c]
Managua	1	0	— 3(80%)—		0	
Mississauga	1	1	— 3(85%)—		1	1
Ohio River Flood	2(47%)	2(20%)	— 2(31%)—		1	
Skopje	3	0	1	1	1	1[a,b]
La Soufrière	2(28%)	2(37%)	— 2(31%)—		1(4%)	
Three Mile Island	0(<1%)	1–2(9–25%)	——3(74–90%)——			
United Kingdom I	0	3	1	1	2(?)	1[d]
United Kingdom IIa	5	0	0	0	0	
United Kingdom IIb	4	1	1	1	1	
USSR	4	0	0	0	0	
Warsaw I	0	1	——2——		0	2[b]
Warsaw II	3	0	1	1	0	1[a]
Winnipeg	2	1	1	1	1	1[e]

[1]Summer camps were used to accommodate most children evacuated from Kiev.
[a]Hospitals. [b]Improvised quarters. [c]Summer camps. [d]Overseas foster parents. [e]Second homes loaned by owners.

Table 6-8. Extent of Evacuee Return

Event	Total	Nearly Complete	Partial
Anchorage		X[1]	
El Asnam	X		
Belize		X[2]	
Bhopal I			X
Bhopal II		X?	
Chernobyl (Kiev[1])	(X)[3]		
Darwin		X[1]	
France I		X	
France II		X	
Germany I		X	
Germany II		X	
Gulf Coast Hurricanes	X		
Japan	X		
Leningrad		X	
Managua		X[1]	
Mississauga	X		
Ohio River Flood	X		
Skopje	X		
La Soufrière	X		
Three Mile Island	X		
United Kingdom I	X		
United Kingdom IIa	X		
United Kingdom IIb	X		
USSR			X[1]
Warsaw I		X	
Warsaw II			X[4]
Winnipeg	X		

[1]Acceleration of normal migration.
[2]Out-migration to new settlements occasioned by disaster.
[3]Total return to Kiev and other localities beyond contaminated zone, which remains depopulated.
[4]Many evacuees eventually became permanent internal or international migrants.

age to return. Unfortunately, we have so little reliable data on the timing of this countermovement that we are unable to hazard any sort of tabulation for the topic. All that can be safely said is that the period in question may range from only a day or two up to several years.

What we have been able to do is to construct a rather schematic diagram (see Figure 6-2) in which our twenty-seven events have been cross-tabulated in terms of the timing of evacuation (long before; shortly before; simultaneous with the disaster; or immediately after it) and the approximate duration of the evacuation (days; weeks; months; years). This graphic display suggests only a few generalities. First, just a few evacuations occurred in advance of the anticipated disasters, while the great majority were concurrent with the event or took place shortly (within hours or days) afterward. The modal duration of our evacuations was on the order of a few weeks, and most of those in the "weeks" category were simultaneous with the disaster. A noteworthy negative finding is that, except for some war-related events, the nature of the disaster has little to do with the duration of the evacuation. It also appears that the only evacuations materializing well before a disaster were war-related.

The only meaningful exceptions to the rule noted above, at least within the group of events studied here, namely that evacuations have a certain duration, are the Soviet evacuations, Warsaw II, and Chernobyl. In the first two instances, political circumstances inhibited repatriation or hastened trends in population redistribution that would have materialized in any case. As for Chernobyl, the radiological conditions near the disaster site obviously preclude any restoration of the former residents for an indefinite period—in contrast to the prompt return of those who fled Kiev and other outlying Ukrainian localities.

The partial return of those displaced by Bhopal I is not really relevant because any decision to return could have been aborted by Bhopal II just a short time after the initial disaster. In similar fashion, many of the persons caught up in France I and Germany I were overtaken by subsequent developments. In some cases where the return has been classified as "nearly complete" we can assume that, again, most of those who did not make the return journey were simply carrying out migrations that would normally have occurred somewhat later. At least such is a reasonable supposition for Anchorage, Darwin, Leningrad, and Managua. In the cases of France II, Germany II, and Warsaw I, political and military complications rendered a complete return difficult or impossible. The Belize situation is exceptional to the degree that an appreciable fraction of the original population was

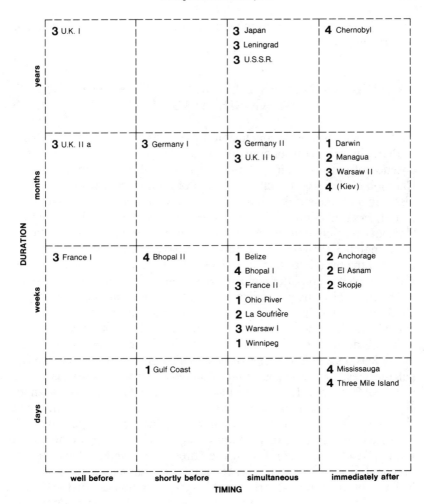

Figure 6-2. Duration and timing of evacuation

shifted inland to the new national capital (and a few lesser settlements) by administrative fiat.

PARTICIPATION IN EVACUATION BY SELECTED SOCIAL CATEGORIES (TABLE 6-9)

The most sweeping conclusion to be drawn from the available evidence is the great amount of variation from case to case and the absence of close similarity between any pair of events. In one event, Chernobyl, there was total evacuation of all residents within a stated distance from the stricken power plant. In two other instances—France II and, in all likelihood, Bhopal I—we can assume that all population elements participated in the exodus in nearly equal measure. But in the remaining episodes there appear to have been appreciable differences in the proclivity to stay or leave in terms of gender, age, marital status, physical condition, and socioeconomic or occupational status.

The most obvious generalization to be drawn from Table 6-9 is that children and females (and most especially mothers) were the principal candidates for evacuation, and logically so since these groups are normally deemed by society most physically helpless and vulnerable, or the least essential in terms of maintaining or restoring basic municipal services, or sustaining military activity and war industries in the war-related events. In the case of the wartime evacuation of German, Japanese, French, and British cities, the percentage of women and children within the stream of evacuees may have been especially high because of the absence of so many younger males serving in the armed forces (Hewitt 1987:466). During the Three Mile Island unpleasantness, pregnant women were probably the least reluctant among the evacuees because of the potential threat to the unborn. In no case that we know of were special efforts made to retain women and children within the afflicted area. We can also detect a general tendency for entire families to evacuate as a unit. Another category of residents particularly likely to be evacuated was the incapacitated, those who were ill or injured before or during the disaster, and perhaps already hospitalized as well as other institutionalized individuals. This phenomenon is well documented for United Kingdom IIa and IIb, Darwin, La Soufrière, and Winnipeg.

Another interesting inference to be distilled from our data is that, ceteris paribus, the elderly (the institutionalized excepted) are less likely to evacuate then younger age cohorts—just as they tended to be

Table 6-9. Participation in Evacuation by Selected Social Categories

+: Overrepresented.   −: Underrepresented.

Event	Families	Single Persons	Women/ Mothers	Children	Elderly	The Ill or Injured	Well-to-do Elite	Non-essential Workers
Anchorage	+		+	+				+
El Asnam		+		+				
Belize						+	+?	
Bhopal I	+							
Bhopal II			+	+				
Chernobyl (Kiev)[1]			(+)	(+)			(+)	
Darwin	+		+	+	+	+		+
France I	+		+	+			+	
France II[2]								
Germany I				+				
Germany II	+		+	+				?
Gulf Coast Hurricanes	+		+	+	−			
Japan			+	+	−			
Leningrad			+	+			+	−/+[3]
Managua	+					+?	+	

continued

Table 6-9. Participation in Evacuation by Selected Social Categories

+: Overrepresented.   −: Underrepresented.

Event	Families	Single Persons	Women/ Mothers	Children	Elderly	The Ill or Injured	Well-to-do Elite	Non-essential Workers
Mississauga[4]	+		+	+	−		−	−
Ohio River Flood			+	+				+
Skopje			+	+				+
La Soufrière			+	+	−	+		
Three Mile Island		+	+	+			+	
United Kingdom I			+	+		+		
United Kingdom IIa			+	+	−	+		+
United Kingdom IIb			+	+	−	+		+
USSR	+						+	−
Warsaw I		+					+	−
Warsaw II[2]								
Winnipeg	+		+	+	+	+		

[1]Symbols refer to Kiev and other cities in the general zone. Total evacuation of population from exclusion zone surrounding Chernobyl power plant.
[2]Total population affected in equal measure.
[3]Underrepresented in earlier stages of Leningrad evacuation. Overrepresented in later phases.
[4]Symbols apply to peripheral zone; central zone was totally evacuated.

relatively less mobile in terms of routine mobility or migration. Part of the explanation is, of course, a stronger attachment to place among many long-term residents and a smaller investment in the future among the elderly. Our two exceptions are found in Darwin and Winnipeg, events during which the authorities felt obliged to remove the nonessential and/or relatively vulnerable.

The one category of individuals that displays the greatest inconsistency in terms of participating in evacuations is clearly that of nonessential workers. During the emergencies experienced by Anchorage, Darwin, the flooded Ohio River communities, Leningrad, and Skopje, when the necessities of life were in short supply, there was every reason to allow such members of the labor force to leave, or even to insist on their departure. The same logic was applicable in United Kingdom IIa and IIb. But the priorities were reversed during the Soviet evacuations, when the eastward removal of essential workers was crucial for the war effort; and somewhat comparable conditions prevailed during Warsaw I. There is no ready explanation for the rather anomalous, reasonably well-documented underrepresentation of nonessential workers during the Japanese evacuation.

One final generalization has to do with the greater propensity for the well-to-do to evacuate as compared to less fortunate members of the community. This differential may result as much from superior access to information as from their greater financial resources and thus mobility. In the contrary case, that of Mississauga, those persons in peripheral zone who were better informed may have evaluated the risks of remaining in place as being less than the rigors of evacuation.

CONVERGENT BEHAVIOR (TABLE 6-10)

One of the demographer's time-honored axioms is that virtually every population movement generates a reverse flow. As we have already seen, the great majority of evacuees do return to their domiciles as expeditiously as possible. But there is also another group of inbound persons, certain nonresidents, who frequently converge upon the scene of those disasters severe enough to induce evacuation. In the case of major floods, storms, earthquakes, and industrial accidents the rapid arrival of medical personnel, temporary administrators, and other individuals trained to handle emergency situations has become almost routine; and such is indeed the story in at least twelve of the events covered here. In those instances where the capabilities of the

Table 6-10. Disasters and Convergent Behavior by Type of Person

Emergency Personnel	Military Personnel	Construction workers	Idly Curious	Others[1]	None
Anchorage	Bhopal I	Anchorage	Gulf Coast Hurricanes	Anchorage	France I
El Asnam	Leningrad	Darwin	TMI	Bhopal I	France II
Belize	Warsaw I[2]	Skopje		Bhopal II	Germany I
Bhopal I				Darwin	Germany II
Chernobyl				Skopje	Japan
Darwin				La Soufrière	(Kiev)
Gulf Coast Hurricanes				TMI	United Kingdom I
Managua				Winnipeg	United Kingdom IIa
Mississauga					United Kingdom IIb
Ohio River Flood					USSR
Skopje					Warsaw II
La Soufrière					
TMI					

[1]Scientists, journalist, lawyers, etc.
[2]Military units entering the city in preparation for defense and evacuees from other places entering city.

local work force are insufficient, as happened in Anchorage, Darwin, and Skopje, we also witness an influx of construction workers who may be employed for some weeks or months before departing. In at least three other cases, those of Leningrad, Warsaw I, and Bhopal, military personnel were shipped in from elsewhere for reasons of military strategy and/or internal policing. But, for obvious reasons, in the other evacuations occasioned by military events the in-movement of outsiders was either unnecessary or impossible. A complicating factor in the Warsaw I and Leningrad cases, and perhaps in France II and the USSR episodes as well, was the influx of persons from areas overrun by the invading German troops.

When the disaster was exceptionally important journalistically or scientifically, we find significant numbers of journalists, scientists, and occasionally attorneys converging upon the scene. Three Mile Island and the Bhopal events may best exemplify such a situation. And, finally, many nonmilitary disasters have the potential to pull in the idly curious, the rubberneckers, if the site is accessible to large numbers of people living not too far away. And this seems to have happened in some cases, usually after the immediate crisis has passed, despite efforts by the authorities to discourage such ghoulish tourism, in some of the places afflicted by hurricanes along the Gulf Coast. Three Mile Island continues to attract the curious.

PRESENCE OR ABSENCE OF LOOTING (TABLE 6-11)

Contrary to various statements appearing in the American literature, looting can and does occur during or after the emergency evacuation

Table 6-11. Disasters: Presence or Absence of Looting

Much	Some	None	No Information But Likely	Little or No Information But Unlikely
Belize	Chernobyl	Anchorage	El Asnam	France I
Managua	Darwin	Germany I	Bhopal I	Germany II
Warsaw I		Gulf Coast Hurricanes	Bhopal II	Japan
		Mississauga	France II	Ohio River Flood
		La Soufrière	Leningrad	Warsaw II
		Three Mile Island	Skopje	
		United Kingdom I	USSR	
		United Kingdom IIa		
		United Kingdom IIb		
		Winnipeg		

of cities. But, by the nature of the phenomenon, its absence is seldom noted in published accounts, while occurrences are not always documented.

In the ten cases where all the evidence suggests no looting, we are dealing with First World communities or, in La Soufrière's case, with a carefully policed situation managed, at some distance, by a European administration. But the correlation with socioeconomic status is far from perfect. Serious looting accompanied Warsaw I, along with milder outbreaks in Chernobyl and Darwin; and we have reason to suspect such lawlessness for France II, Leningrad, the USSR, and Skopje given the temporary breakdown of public order and a degree of near-chaos. On the other hand, the stresses of wartime existence certainly did not offer many opportunities for looters in Germany I or during any of the three United Kingdom evacuations; and we regard it as unlikely that looting took place even during the serious crises of Germany II, Japan, and Warsaw II, situations where military and/or civil authorities still maintained a reasonable level of control.

Chapter 7

Conclusions, Implications, and Unanswered Questions

In this final chapter we seek out the larger lessons and implications of the various events described and compared in earlier sections of the study. This process involves a critical assessment of the twenty-two preexisting hypotheses concerning evacuation behavior in the face of actual or expected disasters set forth in the introductory chapter and, beyond that, a series of reflections on a number of theoretical and empirical questions that have risen in the course of our investigation. We also note in passing some of the items our analysis of the historical record suggests for a further research agenda, and comment on the relevance of this record in coping with major emergencies in the future.

THE EXISTING HYPOTHESES TESTED

In Table 7-1 we offer our best judgment as to whether the available data: (1) confirm, either strongly or modestly, each of twenty hypotheses; (2) contradict the hypotheses, again strongly or weakly; or (3) are inadequate, irrelevant, or conducive to a neutral verdict. The two remaining hypotheses do not lend themselves to tabular treatment, but are discussed in the text. The reader should recall that the hypotheses are numbered in order of decreasing inherent plausibility (at least as they appeared to us initially) and/or documentary confirmation. Some of the questions covered below have already appeared in our comparative analysis in the preceding chapter, but are approached here from a somewhat different angle.

1. *The propensity to evacuate, or the likelihood of being advised to*

Table 7-1. Hypothetical and Actual Evacuation Behavior Compared

Degree of Support

XX: Strongly supports. X: Supports. 0: Evidence neutral or irrelevant.
#: Contradicts. ##: Strongly contradicts. n.d.: No data. +: Emergency personnel.

Event	1 Propensity to evacuate varies inversely with distance to disaster	2 Distance-decay principle applies	3 Evacuees move in rational direction	4 Evacuation risks less than remaining in situation
Floods, Storms				
Ohio River Flood	X	X	X	XX
Winnipeg	XX	XX	X	XX
Gulf Coast Hurricanes	X	XX	X	X
Belize	0	X	X	X
Darwin	0	##	X	X
Earthquakes, Volcanic Eruptions				
Skopje	X	X	X	X
Anchorage	n.d.	#	X	X
Managua	0	X	X	X
La Soufrière	X	X	X	0
El Asnam	n.d.	X	X	X

War-Related				
Warsaw I	X	XX	X	0
Warsaw II	0	X	0	XX
United Kingdom I	X	#	X	X
United Kingdom IIa	X	X	X	0
United Kingdom IIb	X	X	X	X
France I	X	#	XX	0
France II	X	0	XX	#
USSR	X	X	XX	XX
Leningrad	0	X	XX	XX
Germany I	X	#	X	X
Germany II	X	X	X	X
Japan	X	X	X	XX
Industrial				
Three Mile Island	XX	XX	XX	0
Mississauga	XX	XX	X	X
Bhopal I	X	X	#	0
Bhopal II	n.d.	X	X	##
Chernobyl (Kiev)	X(X)	X(X)	X(X)	XX(X)

continued

Degree of Support

XX: Strongly supports. X: Supports. 0: Evidence neutral or irrelevant.
#: Contradicts. ##: Strongly contradicts. n.d.: No data. +: Emergency personnel.

Event	5 Choice of destination affected by personal/social history	6 Voluntary evacuation delayed by attachment to home/locality	7 Evacuees return as quickly as possible	8 Convergent behavior observed	10 Nuclear families evacuate as unit
Floods, Storms					
Ohio River Flood	n.d.	X	X	+	X
Winnipeg	X	X	X	X	X
Gulf Coast Hurricanes	X	XX	X	X	X
Belize	n.d.	n.d.	X	+	n.d.
Darwin	X	X	0	X	0
Earthquakes, Volcanic Eruptions					
Skopje	X	X	X	+	X
Anchorage	XX	#?	X	XX	#
Managua	XX	n.d.	0	+	X
La Soufrière	X	0	X	+	X
El Asnam	n.d.	n.d.	X	+	X

War-Related					
Warsaw I	X	X	X	#[1]	#
Warsaw II	X	0	XX	0	X
United Kingdom I	XX	#	n.d.	#	n.d.
United Kingdom IIa	0	XX	XX	#	##
United Kingdom IIb	0	XX	XX	#	##
France I	X	0	X	#	n.d.
France II	XX	#	XX	#	X
USSR	0	n.d.	X	#[1]	X
Leningrad	0	#	X	#	X
Germany I	0	n.d.	X	#	#
Germany II	0	X	X	##	X
Japan	X	X	X	##	0
Industrial					
Three Mile Island	X	#	XX	X	X
Mississauga	X?	0	XX	+	XX
Bhopal I	X	#	n.d.	+	X
Bhopal II	X	#	n.d.	##	X?
Chernobyl[1] (Kiev)	0(X)	X(n.d.)	0(X)	+(#)	XX(#)

[1]Military units entering the city in preparation for defense, and evacuees from other places entering the city.

Degree of Support

XX: Strongly supports. X: Supports. 0: Evidence neutral or irrelevant.
#: Contradicts. ##: Strongly contradicts. n.d.: No data. +: Emergency personnel.

Event	11 Women, children, inform more likely to evacuate than able-bodied men	12 Families with children more likely to evacuate	13 Elderly less likely to evacuate	14 Positive correlation between SES and propensity to evacuate
Floods, Storms				
Ohio River Flood	X	X	#	0
Winnipeg	X	X	#	0
Gulf Coast Hurricanes	X	X	X	0
Belize	n.d.	n.d.	n.d.	X?
Darwin	X	X	#	0
Earthquakes, Volcanic Eruptions				
Skopje	X	X	n.d.	n.d.
Anchorage	X	X	n.d.	X?
Managua	0	X	n.d.	X?
La Soufrière	X	X	n.d.	0
El Asnam	X	n.d.	n.d.	n.d.

War-Related				
Warsaw I	#	X	X	X
Warsaw II	0	0	0	0
United Kingdom I	X	n.d.	0?	XX
United Kingdom IIa	XX	X	X	#
United Kingdom IIb	XX	X	X	#
France I	X	X	X	X?
France II	0	#	n.d.	X?
USSR	X	X	X	X²
Leningrad	X	X	X	X
Germany I	X	X	X	X
Germany II	X	X	X	X
Japan	X	X	X	X?
Industrial				
Three Mile Island	X	X	X	X
Mississauga	0	0	X	0
Bhopal I	n.d.	n.d.	n.d.	#
Bhopal II	X	n.d.	n.d.	X?
Chernobyl (Kiev)	0(X)	0(X)	0(X)	0(X?)

²Except for front zone.

Degree of Support

XX: Strongly supports. X: Supports. 0: Evidence neutral or irrelevant.
#: Contradicts. ##: Strongly contradicts. n.d.: No data. +: Emergency personnel.

Event	15 Evacuation effectiveness function of socio-technical infrastructure	16 Evacuation facilitates normal redistribution	17 No long-term demographic effects on impacted communities	18 Previous disaster experience conductive to evacuate
Floods, Storms				
Ohio River Flood	X	#	X	X?
Winnipeg	X	#	X	X
Gulf Coast Hurricanes	X	#	X	X
Belize	X	X?	#	#
Darwin	XX	X	X	0
Earthquakes, Volcanic Eruptions				
Skopje	X	X	#	#
Anchorage	X	X	X	#?
Managua	X	X	#	X?
La Soufrière	XX	n.d.	X	XX
El Asnam	X	0	n.d.	X

War-Related				
Warsaw I	0	#	#	X
Warsaw II	X	#	##	XX
United Kingdom I	X	#	X	X
United Kingdom IIa	X	#	X	X
United Kingdom IIb	X	#	X	#
France I	0	#	X	X
France II	X	#	X	X[3]
USSR	XX	XX	#	X
Leningrad	X	#	##	X
Germany I	X	#	X	0
Germany II	X	X	X	0
Japan	X	#	X	0
Industrial				
Three Mile Island	X	#	X	0
Mississauga	XX	#	X	X
Bhopal I	X	#	n.d.	0
Bhopal II	X	#	n.d.	XX
Chernobyl (Kiev)	X(X)	#(#)	#(X)	0(X)

[3]Belgium: XX.

Degree of Support

XX: Strongly supports. X: Supports. 0: Evidence neutral or irrelevant.
#: Contradicts. ##: Strongly contradicts. n.d.: No data. +: Emergency personnel.

Event	19 Panic evacuation unknown or rare	20 Evacuation behavior invariant with respect to class of disaster	22 Evacuation behavior invariant with respect to ethnic group
Floods, Storms			
Ohio River Flood	X	X	n.d.
Winnipeg	X	X	X
Gulf Coast Hurricanes	X	X	n.d.
Belize	#?	n.d.	#?
Darwin	X	X	n.d.
Earthquakes, Volcanic Eruptions			
Skopje	#	X	#
Anchorage	X	X	n.d.
Managua	#?	X	0
La Soufrière	#	X	0
El Asnam	#	X	0

War-Related			
Warsaw I	#	#	#
Warsaw II	X	X	X
United Kingdom I	#	#	o
United Kingdom IIa	X	#	o
United Kingdom IIb	X	#	o
France I	X	X	X
France II	##	#	X
USSR	#	X	#
Leningrad	XX	X	XX
Germany I	X	X	o
Germany II	#	X?	o
Japan	#	#	o
Industrial			
Three Mile Island	#	##	n.d.
Mississauga	X	X	X
Bhopal I	##	#	n.d.
Bhopal II	##	##	n.d.
Chernobyl (Kiev)	#(#)	X(#)	0(0)

evacuate, varies inversely with actual or perceived distance from the site of a disaster.

The available evidence (for twenty-four of our twenty-seven events) lends considerable credibility to this commonsensical notion. The fact that confirmation is especially robust in three particularly well documented cases—Three Mile Island, Mississauga, and Winnipeg—bolsters confidence in the general rule that individuals and administrators calculate spatial risks in a rational manner and act accordingly. Moreover, the neutral cases do not invalidate this conclusion. When disaster struck Belize, Darwin, Managua, Warsaw II, and Leningrad, virtually the entire metropolitan area was afflicted, and there was no ready means to gauge differing levels of risk within the endangered zone. All we need add is that the principle in question is particularly salient when there is a single point source for the disaster, as in industrial accidents or volcanic eruptions, or when the disaster is linear in character as is generally true for advancing hostile armies, most floods, and many storms.

2. *The distance-decay principle generally applies to movements of evacuees, so that the number temporarily residing at a given point will be inversely proportional to distance from disaster site or zone of actual or perceived danger.*

Here we have another self-evident proposition one would expect to be amply ratified by real-world experience. Unfortunately, the picture emerging from the actual events is not nearly as straightforward as might be anticipated. It is true enough that the friction of distance (and cost) did prevail in the majority of events for which we have any sort of account of dispersal patterns. Indeed, in some cases, such as Germany II, and probably Japan, many workers took up residence in suburban localities and commuted daily to their workplace. But in at least four cases—Darwin, Anchorage, United Kingdom I, and France I—there was a decided tendency for evacuees to maximize, rather than minimize, distance from the disaster zone. We also have reason to believe that such were the intentions of many, perhaps most, of those fleeing southward during l'Exode, but, as luck would have it, they were overtaken by events in mid-flight.[1] Furthermore, although we have concluded that the evidence generally supports the hypothesis when considering Leningrad, USSR, and Germany I and II, we also have some indications that a large minority of the dislocated chose the most remote refuge available. Indeed the proposed principle seems weakest in the category of war-related evacuations. In any event, our four counter-examples suffice to cast serious doubt upon the general validity of the hypothesis, and, in turn, such a possible negation has important implications for general mobility theory that we take up at a later point.

3. *Evacuees tend to move in whatever direction(s) are believed to minimize or cancel the effects of the disaster.*

It would be most surprising if historical fact failed to validate such a statement. And indeed, as the evidence suggests, the evacuating individuals and households or the official decision makers guiding them did reach logical conclusions as to the safest, or at least safer, directions in which to travel. Furthermore, in all but one instance, the perceived direction(s) was also the correct one—further proof of the essential rationality of the persons involved. The one anomalous case is that of Bhopal I, when many, probably most, of the justifiably panic-stricken residents fled along the same general southward path followed by the wind-driven lethal cloud of gas. Many failed to outrun the cloud. Had they been less agitated, these evacuees would have been better served if they had moved at right angles to the wind direction, or even back toward the Union Carbide plant. But, allowing for the extraordinary circumstances and massive confusion during the darkness of the early morning hours, we must still assume that the victims in question *believed* they were acting rationally. Thus we regard the hypothesis as being well confirmed.

4. *The risk of death or injury during evacuation is less than that incurred by remaining in place during the disaster period.*

The mass of evidence supports the logic of evacuation as a strategy for minimizing death and injury during periods of disaster. The immediate question, it must be emphasized, is physical survival or well-being. The calculation of the social and economic costs of evacuating as opposed to those of remaining *in situ* is an entirely separate issue, one to be dealt with at a later point.

We can identify only two counter-examples: the case of France II and, even more emphatically, that of Bhopal II. In the former event, it is likely, even in lieu of hard data, that a significant number of evacuees from northern France and the Low Countries perished en route from bombing and strafing, traffic mishaps, and, possibly, the rigors of travel under nearly the worst possible circumstances. To a lesser degree, the same fate must have befallen some of the persons engaged in Bhopal II. In both cases, the panic-stricken wayfarers would almost certainly have suffered less physical trauma by staying home. In rather similar fashion, the participants in La Soufrière, Warsaw I, United Kingdom IIa, and, possibly, France I involved themselves in needless exercises since, on balance, it is probable their prospects for survival were not enhanced by flight. But such exceptions are at worst irrelevant and do not falsify the general proposition.

We have placed Three Mile Island in the neutral category because the controversy over the immediate and long-term health effects of the accidentally released radiation remains unsettled—and because the exodus produced no traffic deaths or injuries. The final apparent anomaly, that of Bhopal I, is also classified as neutral in light of the fact that many of those rushing out of the city, possibly into the path of the gas cloud and into the dangerous chaos of clogged highways, may have been living in neighborhoods not directly affected by the accident. Taking the event as a whole, whether the lives and injuries averted by evacuation were equal to, or greater than, the casualties of the evacuation (including, again, those persons who followed the cloud) is a question we will never be able to answer satisfactorily.

In summary, then, we find ourselves in essential agreement with the findings of Hans and Sell (1974) who analyzed all evacuations in the United States between 1960 and 1973 involving twenty or more persons (and resulting from natural disasters and industrial accidents). The only qualification we would attach to their conclusion that the evacuation strategy is benign and effective in conserving lives is that the outcome may be quite different in situations where excessive panic prevails, or when evacuation in itself may be hazardous, as, for example, in the face of hostile military activity.

5. *Social relationships and previous travel experience can markedly affect choice of destination by the evacuee.*

The evidence strongly confirms the propensity of evacuees to seek out familiar persons and places for their temporary abodes. At least such is the pattern when all or most of the evacuees enjoy freedom of choice. It is likely that in two events for which we have no relevant data—Belize and El Asnam—just such a situation prevailed. Among the documented cases, the evidence is especially persuasive for Anchorage, Managua, and United Kingdom I. Moreover, given a range of options, the great majority of evacuees shun the discomforts and impersonality of official shelters or avail themselves of such facilities for the briefest of periods.

But the qualification is crucial. The hypothesis is irrelevant when the movements of evacuees are planned and managed by governmental authorities. The most extreme examples of such regimentation would be United Kingdom IIa and IIb, Germany I, and Chernobyl. On the other hand, there are intermediate cases where the journeys are government-assisted but where families and individuals were given some latitude in selecting destinations, as happened in Darwin and La Soufrière. In general, then, the hypothesis holds to the degree that officials do not monopolize the decision-making process.

6. *Whatever the nature of the emergency, the great majority of human beings are inherently reluctant to leave their home localities voluntarily. Consequently, voluntary evacuations tend to be small and/ or later than would be reasonable, or officially desired, given the actual or expected magnitude of a disaster.*

There is so much evidence to buttress this assertion that, on first considering it, comment may seem unnecessary. In the great majority of events studied here and many other evacuations as well, the crisis managers have had considerable difficulty in convincing enough of the population at risk to depart in timely and voluntary fashion (Hans and Sell 1974:48). "When warned adequately of approaching natural disasters, approximately 50 percent of the threatened population will evacuate upon receipt of official advisories" (Drabek 1986b:103). What seems to be at issue is not simply inertia or occasional skepticism about the reality of danger but rather a positive emotional attachment to home, neighborhood, friends, and relatives, a perception of safety in familiar surroundings, and the availability of support systems in addition to economic factors. Perhaps nowhere is the strength of this rootedness better illustrated than in the history of United Kingdom IIa and IIb. Similarly, in the cases of Germany II and Japan it was only when the stricken cities had become virtually uninhabitable that massive out-movements finally began. And even in the direst of circumstances, as in Chernobyl or besieged Stalingrad, a few diehard resisters managed to elude detection and eviction.

But the general rule enunciated above was dramatically violated in at least six instances. In the cases of Leningrad and Bhopal the immediacy of the threat was so great and overwhelming that the only problem was finding means for removing huge masses of eager evacuees rapidly enough. In other events, where hysteria tended to prevail— United Kingdom I, France II, and Bhopal II—loyalty to hearth and home was weaker than the impulse to flee. The Three Mile Island situation resembled that of Bhopal II in that dread of the unknown was more potent a factor than attachment to familiar surroundings. Indeed, in the former event, more persons evacuated from a much wider zone than was deemed necessary or prudent in the official guidelines. The moral, then, is that the hypothesis can be accepted only with serious reservations. Normal attachment to one's locality can be canceled by any of the following or a combination thereof: (1) the immediacy of catastrophe; (2) a significant level of panic occasioned by an actual or anticipated disaster; and (3) anxiety about unfamiliar, unprecedented forms of physical danger.

7. *Evacuees will return home as quickly as they are able to do so physically and administratively.*

This hypothesis, which is obviously closely akin to the preceding one, is abundantly verified by the available information. Moreover, the powerful urge to return homeward as soon as the danger has abated seems to prevail regardless of the degree to which the volume and timing of the evacuation was more or less, or later, than desired by the authorities. We find only six qualified exceptions to the rule. Many of the persons leaving Anchorage and Darwin did not return for the simple reason that they did not regard themselves as permanent residents and, in any event, had intended to migrate elsewhere in the fairly near future. The fact that much of central Managua was left in ruins, and remains so to this day, means that a large percentage of the evacuees were obliged to take up permanent residence elsewhere. This was also the case in Warsaw II, at least temporarily, because of the virtually total destruction of the city. The case of Chernobyl is quite special in that the proximate area has been rendered uninhabitable for an indefinite period. Finally, in the case of Leningrad, the bureaucratic problems encountered in procuring the needed official permission to return kept many former residents away permanently.

8. *Disasters usually generate some convergence toward the disaster zone as well as evacuation from it.*

This statement is akin to Everett Lee's claim that "For every major migration stream, a counterstream develops" (1966:55). But although the rule may hold to some extent in the case of evacuations, we find that such opposing movements are different in character from those encountered in ordinary migrations. As we have already seen, with few exceptions, evacuees reverse direction and move back to their homes as rapidly as possible. But, in addition, a number of evacuations have generated convergence toward the disaster site on the part of nonresidents who generally remain only for short periods (Fritz and Mathewson 1957). As Table 6-10 indicates, floods, earthquakes, volcanic eruptions, and some industrial accidents can trigger in-movements by relief workers, technicians, the military, and the curious. But our listing also demonstrates the fact that, with the marginal exceptions of Warsaw I and Leningrad, when some refugees entered the city from the west and southwest respectively, or other events when troops enter a city in order to defend it, cities undergoing war-related evacuations are hardly likely to attract visitors from elsewhere. This may be the only instance in which we can draw a sharp distinction between war-related events and those engendered by natural disasters and industrial accidents. In any case, the volume of convergence (by outsiders) is much less than the outward and inward movements of residents. Our reason for including the phenomenon in this study is its possible relevance to general mobility theory.

9. *Causative factors having to do with evacuation and the various attributes of such movements are associated in multivariate fashion, so that rarely, if ever, do we find a simple, direct correlation between any single variable and evacuation behavior.*

The nature of our data—and the hypothesis—is such that we cannot subject this proposition to any methical test. However, our subjective judgment is that the statement is true. In dealing with such complex phenomena as mass evacuations, it is altogether plausible that there are many intertwining pathways between cause and effect.

10. *Nuclear families tend to evacuate as a unit.*

This proposition has been regarded as axiomatic by American students of disaster and evacuation, and our cross-cultural data set generally tends to confirm it. The exceptions, and they are important, are to be found where strong central authorities have deemed it wise to move mothers and children to presumably safe locations, as occurred in Germany I and United Kingdom IIa and IIb, or where individual families decided on their own to separate their offspring from danger zones, as happened in United Kingdom I or in Kiev and other Ukrainian cities as a result of the Chernobyl disaster. The special circumstances of Anchorage and Warsaw I were such that in the former women and children dominated the stream of evacuees while younger males were overrepresented in the Warsaw I exodus. It is worth noting that this tendency for the entire family to act as a unit seems to prevail whatever the type of disaster in question or the level of socioeconomic attainment of the community.

11. *Women, children, and the infirm are more likely to evacuate than able-bodied males of working age.*

12. *Families with children are more likely to evacuate than childless families or single individuals.*

These two propositions are so closely related that it makes sense to consider them jointly. It is also relatively easy to evaluate them. Although the available data are far less abundant and detailed than one would desire, they appear to sustain both hypotheses in all but a few cases. Those exceptions are explained by special circumstances: the removal of entire populations indiscriminately, as happened in Warsaw II, France II, USSR, Managua, and Mississauga, or situations favoring the departure of males, for example, Warsaw I.

13. *The elderly tend to be less likely to evacuate than is the case with younger persons.*

Here again we have an intuitively obvious proposition but also one for which the statistical underpinnings are meager. Such evidence as we do have (it is particularly persuasive for Three Mile Island and Mississauga) generally supports the proposition that the elderly are less inclined to evacuate in emergency situations, just as they are less likely to engage in other forms of mobility, and have relatively poor physical or financial means for implementing any such desire. The apparent exceptions—Winnipeg and Darwin—are only weakly negative. In a number of other cases, the hypothesis is irrelevant because the exodus involved virtually the entire population. We would expect a partial negation of the hypothesis in situations where many of the elderly are institutionalized and their movements are decided by administrators. This may be the explanation for the expeditious transfer of the elderly in Winnipeg.

14. *A positive correlation exists between socioeconomic status within the community and the propensity to evacuate.*

Such a statement may have little relevance, again, when entire communities are shifted, as happened in Warsaw II, La Soufrière, Chernobyl, and Mississauga, or nearly so in the case of Darwin. The most emphatic confirmation of the rule is the self-generated exodus of the relatively well-to-do or their offspring in United Kingdom I, while the same sort of tendency was evident in the government-managed Leningrad exodus. We also find positive evidence in the documentation for Three Mile Island and Warsaw I, and in surveys of prospective behavior among Long Island, N.Y. residents (Johnson 1985:409), and good reason to speculate that such selectivity prevailed in Anchorage and a number of other events. On the other hand, the cases of United Kingdom IIa and IIb and Bhopal I strongly challenge the hypothesis. In the former instances, the nature of the operation was such that the lower strata of society were much overrepresented, while the Bhopal disaster happened to have had its greatest impact on the poorer neighborhoods of the city.

The microgeography of the impacted communities must also be considered in dealing with the hypothesis. Lowlying areas susceptible to flooding tend to be populated by less affluent households. Similarly, the more fortunate members of society do not normally reside next to railroad rights-of-way or heavy industrial plants with the potential for dangerous accidents having spatially invasive effects. On the other hand, it is mostly the well-to-do who can afford to live seasonally or otherwise along or near those sea coasts most exposed to hurricanes and flooding.

Our conclusion must be that the principle in question for the most part operates only weakly and frequently not at all, given the available information. Obviously this is a fertile topic for future study. Retrospective surveys of evacuated populations could certainly help clarify the matter.

15. *The effectiveness of an evacuation is a function of preplanning, quantity and quality of administrative or managerial resources, and the capacities of the communication and transport systems.*

In this hypothesis we confront directly for the first time the possible relationship between attributes of a country or region. The infrastructure implied by the above statement and the sophistication of disaster planning and preparation are clearly associated with the general developmental status. What do we find? Leaving aside Warsaw I and France II, we conclude that our proposition is pretty firmly established. In the case of the two exceptions, we are dealing with situations of political disarray and widespread panic in which the adequacy of preplanning and the quality of the physical and managerial infrastructure were not especially significant issues.

On the positive side, the most convincing testimony for the soundness of the hypothesis may come from Darwin, Mississauga, and La Soufrière. Although Guadeloupe is far down the ranks of the world's countries in terms of level of socioeconomic attainment, it has been the beneficiary of the largess of a European regime and, during the prolonged agony of 1976, was the focus of considerable scientific, technical, and administrative expertise. At the other extreme, the inhabitants of Belize, El Asnam, Managua, and Bhopal were obliged to fend for themselves and encountered many problems under rather chaotic circumstances. In the case of the latter two, the existence of reasonably good surface transport facilities did not guarantee an orderly, effective exodus. Bhopal I strongly underscores the critical importance of organization and preparedness—on the part of both corporate and governmental agencies. On the other hand, the best-laid plans can go awry, as illustrated by the essential futility of the government's efforts in United Kingdom IIa and IIb and the near-paralysis of the decision-making process in Three Mile Island. In general, however, we cannot escape the moral that the financial, technical, organizational, and other resources of a community have a considerable bearing on the effectiveness of emergency evacuations.

The questions posed here should be a prime item on the agenda for any future cross-national analysis of evacuation behavior. We can anticipate more events and better data in the future.

16. *Emergency evacuations simply facilitate or accelerate redistributional trends already under way that would have been consummated eventually even in the absence of any disaster.*

On balance, the evidence for any such assertion is mixed and unconvincing. The only one of our events that weighs in emphatically on behalf of the hypothesis is the Soviet evacuation that began in 1941. Indeed the hastening of a preexisting, officially sponsored, and, to some degree, spontaneous eastward shift in the population of the USSR may be the only silver lining in an otherwise dismal historical episode. There is also less dramatic substantiation in the cases of Darwin and Anchorage. Their evacuations may not have affected the long-term demographic evolution of the cities, but it did advance the schedules of many residents who would have become outbound migrants at some later date. We can also speculate about the possibility that their wartime evacuations speeded up locational shifts within Poland and Germany and, just conceivably, that seismic disasters hastened changes in the population maps of Nicaragua, Belize, and Skopje already in progress. But in all these instances we lack the rigorous analyses to prove or discard any such contention.

What is certain, on the contrary, is the minimal or nonexistent effect of evacuation over the long term upon the spatial patterning of Ohio River communities, those along the Gulf Coast, Winnipeg, Mississauga, the Three Mile Island locality, and, presumably, Guadeloupe, or at a broader scale, Great Britain, France, Japan, and no doubt Italy as well.

17. *Evacuations have no discernible long-term effects on the demographic characteristics of the population at risk or those of the host area.*

The proposition is obviously closely associated with the preceding one, and indeed largely contradicts Hypothesis 16. It follows, then, that we should be on more solid ground here than with the belief that evacuations facilitate redistributional trends already under way. And we do discover that, with the major exceptions of Poland, the Soviet Union, and Chernobyl and the less striking cases of Belize, Skopje, and Managua, it is impossible to detect the impacts any of our evacuations may have had on either the distribution or composition of present-day populations. At best the emergency movements simply interrupted or temporarily reversed ongoing changes in such countries as France and Japan. In the cases of Poland and Germany, the other population changes generated by World War II and its immediate aftermath were so vast and pervasive that it is difficult, perhaps impossible, to isolate whatever lasting effects their short-lived urban evacuations may have had. Our best guess, however, is that they cannot be detected.

18. *Prior experience with similar disasters, whether in the area in question or elsewhere, increases the probability that an individual or family will evacuate.*

Or, we might add, that the responsible authorities will be better equipped to cope with emergencies. This general proposition does survive critical scrutiny, but with some informative exceptions. Indeed Drabek (1986b:107) concludes that the relationship between past experience and subsequent evacuation is far from straightforward.

The strongest support for the proposition comes from La Soufrière and Bhopal II, for in both instances the communities vividly recalled previous catastrophes and evacuated expeditiously in anticipation of disasters that never quite came to pass. Something of a "disaster culture" has also developed along the Ohio River Valley and Gulf Coast, one that made evacuation an acceptable strategy to the residents. Earthquake-prone Managua may be another case in point, but the possibility remains undocumented.

Recollections of the invasion and/or bombings of World War I certainly facilitated France I and II, United Kingdom I, Warsaw I, Leningrad, and USSR, while the Germans and Japanese had no such wartime experiences to fall back on, a fact that may have delayed their major evacuations until the last possible moment.

Learning through experience on the part of the authorities, whether immediate or vicarious, was probably also conducive to the success of the Winnipeg and Mississauga evacuations. On the other hand, it is rather hard to understand why Belize, Skopje, Anchorage, and El Asnam were so poorly prepared to handle disasters of a rather familiar type. However, the most striking negation of the hypothesis is clearly United Kingdom IIb. So unhappy with their experiences in United Kingdom IIa were so many of its participants that it became quite difficult to persuade many to repeat the journey even in the face of serious urban bombing campaigns by the Luftwaffe.

19. *Panic evacuations have never been observed or are extremely rare.*

We have already rather thoroughly demolished this belief in the preceding chapter. All that needs to be added here is that in only eleven of our twenty-seven cases are we reasonably confident that no significant degree of panic was to be observed. Where panic did occur, we attribute it to the unfamiliarity of the specific type of disaster, the sheer magitude of the threat as experienced or anticipated, or organizational ineptitude, or some combination thereof.

20. *Evacuation behavior is essentially invariant with respect to class of disaster, that is, other things being equal, human beings will respond in very much the same way when faced with evacuation decisions whatever form the disaster might take.*

21. *War-related evacuations have little in common with peacetime evacuations caused by technological or natural disasters.*

Although Hypothesis 21 does not lend itself to tabular presentation, it is obvious that these two propositions are intimately related. The notion of the invariance of disaster behavior (the war-related cases implicitly omitted) has become accepted doctrine among most mainstream students in North America, but our findings from an analysis of twenty-seven varied events are such that we must reject this almost axiomatic belief.

The case for invariance is soundest for the evacuations caused by natural disasters, since there are many points of similarity among these events. But we can also extend membership in this group to Warsaw II, France I, Germany I, the Soviet events, Mississauga, and Chernobyl. This basic reasons for such commonalities would seem to be either effective administrative control or familiarity with the type of disaster in question or some combination of these two factors.

But we can identify at least nine events that, in our opinion, differ in some basic fashion from the evacuations that do conform to some standard model of behavior. The most fully documented is Three Mile Island, in which an unexpected event of a totally unfamiliar nature precipitated a unique pattern of evacuation. In itself this one case effectively refutes Hypothesis 20. Somewhat akin to TMI are the equally aberrant stories of Bhopal I and II and Kiev and, presumably, other Ukrainian communities following the Chernobyl debacle. To this company we must also add such war-related cases as Warsaw I, the British evacuations, and France II, episodes that fail to conform to the standard evacuation model. Although some war-related evacuations do resemble those inspired by natural disasters that have become routinized over time, there is enough deviance in Germany II and Japan to make us reluctant to bracket them with the former.

As far as Hypothesis 21 is concerned, then, we conclude that, as a group, our eleven war-related events do not display any collective coherence in terms of evacuation attributes. On the other hand, we have detected enough points of resemblance among specific war-related evacuations, for example, France I, Germany I, and Leningrad, and those of a nonmilitary character that it makes no sense to exclude them from a comprehensive survey of evacuation behavior.

22. *Evacuation behavior is essentially invariant among ethnic groups within a given country or among the inhabitants of different countries if allowances are made for differences in demographic, social, economic, and other standard variables.*

This final hypothesis is as interesting as any but is also especially troublesome to evaluate. Since we have here two related propositions, that is, the degree of variability in evacuation behavior related to ethnicity *within* a country on the one hand and possible differences in such behavior *among* different countries based on cultural or ethnic differentials on the other, a logical procedure is to treat these two notions separately.

In at least eighteen of our twenty-seven events, the populations at risk were so nearly homogeneous in terms of ethnic identity and hence value systems and derivative attitudes that the hypothesis is irrelevant. In those cases where ethnic diversity is to be reckoned with, we must make a further distinction between situations where governmental authority mandates differential management of various ethnic groups and those in which differences in behavior are caused spontaneously by the ethnicity-specific proclivities of the participants themselves.

The event that most clearly illustrates the point is the Ohio River Flood, when the Red Cross and other agencies insisted upon segregating black from caucasian evacuees, but where it is conceivable that those members of the two groups who were acting upon their own initiative might in any case have followed different patterns of movement and timing. Given the substantial changes in interracial relations in the United States in recent decades, at least at official levels, one would expect to find less overt discrimination in the handling of the Gulf Coast evacuations. Nevertheless the possibility of black/white differentials remains there too. The available documentation does not allow any judgment on this question since these studies take little notice of socioeconomic variables and ignore racial matters. It is unfortunate that, despite the title "Minority Citizens in Disasters," Perry and Mushkatel (1986) do so little to address such matters.

Perhaps the clearest example of ethnic factors at work at both the governmental and household level is to be found in the evacuation and resettlement associated with the Skopje disaster. In the case of Darwin, we know that the officers in charge considered special treatment for the aboriginal minority residing in the city, even though they failed to execute any such intentions. Although we lack specific information, it is inherently unlikely that many of these aborigines drove or flew great distances from their homes as did so many of their caucasian neighbors. Unfortunately, we also lack documentation as to whether the several distinct ethnic/racial groups inhabiting Belize behaved in similar fashion when they were assaulted by Hurricane Hattie.

Given the chaotic conditions of Warsaw I and the spottiness of the statistics, we can only speculate that the large Jewish population of that metropolis may have been more eager to depart than its gentile citizens, and perhaps less willing to return, but that would seem to be a logical supposition. Among the evacuating populations considered in this study none were more polyglot than those of the western Soviet Union. Scattered and incomplete though they be, our data do hint that there were discernible differentials in the propensity to evacuate among Ukrainians, Great Russians, Poles, Jews, Moldavians, Ruthenians, Lithuanians, and an abundance of other ethnic entities. Complicating the analysis of the USSR situation is the fact that some of the impacted ethnic groups (notably the Moldavians and those in the Baltic Republics) had only recently been unilaterally incorporated into the Soviet Union and were unhappy with their subsequent treatment. Consequently, there was some reluctance to move into the interior, and some persons even welcomed the invaders.

Despite the paucity of relevant cases and the weakness of pertinent data for those that do merit inspection, there does seem to be sufficient evidence to undermine any claim of uniformity of evacuation behavior among different ethnic groups sharing a single metropolitan area. However, when it comes to evaluating the role of *international* cultural or ethnic differences in shaping evacuation behavior rather than those operating at the intrametropolitan scale, the task is immensely more problematic. Quite simply, there is no ready-made method for canceling out all the many other important variables, the historical, environmental, political, and infrastructural as well as the standard socioeconomic and demographic variety and isolating the workings of any specifically cultural factor. Indulging in counter-factual historical geography is not a great help. We can try, with little luck, to imagine what might have happened if, for example, the Three Mile Island area had been inhabited by Japanese, Hindu, Algerian, or French families instead of Pennsylvanians and whether they would have reacted much differently. Or, to make the thought experiment somewhat more realistic, we might envision a future Chernobylian mishap in some European or Asian setting (a far from incredible scenario), and think about the form such an evacuation might take.

A somewhat more manageable type of speculation would simulate an event paralleling United Kingdom IIa or IIB, France I, or Germany I in a multinational country such as Yugoslavia or India. Remembering how awkward the situation had been for both evacuees and hosts in the Great Britain of 1939–45, when the persons in question shared the same general culture, however widely class values and mores may have differed and clashed, would even such an uneasy accommodation be feasible if much of the population of Calcutta or Zagreb were to be dispersed to the further reaches of their respective countries with no regard to ethnic identities in the event of a military or other huge emergency?

Although we are inclined to subscribe to the salience of the ethnic factor, we must make do for the time being with the unsatisfactory conclusion that the evidence currently available fails to provide the means for any sort of useful test of Hypothesis 22. On the other hand, the data accumulated on nonethnic issues do persuade us that it is quite imprudent to assume any universality for the findings derived from North American or Western European experience, quite apart from the effects of differing cultural predilections. The political, organizational, economic, and infrastructural conditions prevailing in such advanced societies create possibilities for managing disasters that are difficult to duplicate in less fortunate regions.

IMMEDIATE FINDINGS SUMMARIZED

In this section we present a few higher-order generalizations that have become apparent to us in the empirical analysis of our twenty-seven evacuation events but that may have been obscured and thus overlooked by the reader in the course of rather detailed discussion in the preceding pages.

First of all, we believe the results of the analysis have amply justified the basic research strategy. The decision to include every substantial, documentable evacuation regardless of location, the character of the disaster that caused flight, or date of occurrence has created a unique body of evidence bearing on the essential nature of the phenomenon and a set of original questions still to be addressed and answered. We could not have begun to deal with preexisting questions or assess the validity of accepted doctrine if we had confined ourselves to a single portion of the world or to only one or two classes of disaster. We find interesting commonalities as well as differences in the behavior of metropolitan populations living in widely separated, sharply contrasting habitats and belonging to distinctly different cultural worlds.

In the same vein, we have identified a number of contrasts, but also many similarities, within and between various classes of disasters, and enough of the latter to convince us of the value of treating the entire social response to disasters as an essentially unitary enterprise. It has been especially rewarding to ascertain that the attributes of war-related evacuations, which have been routinely ignored in other general studies, overlap those triggered by natural catastrophes and industrial accidents. In short, we are persuaded that however essential it is to have thorough accounts of individual events or sets of closely related ones, it is counterproductive to limit the methodical scrutiny of evacuations and other disaster-related matters to a single region, period, or type of calamity if we are to gain genuine understanding of the larger issues.

One of the safer generalizations—indeed it borders on truism—to be extracted from the observed events is that the behavior of participants is not only rational, at least within the limits of available information and experience, but also in keeping with general sociological, demographic, and geographic principles. But an important addendum must be attached to such a statement, namely, that these general principles may be subject to some revision in the light of evacuation experiences. We are also stretching the definition of rationality beyond its customary limits to include panic flight, which, in some circumstances, may be the only sensible option. Put another way, despite the extreme character of the event, the social order is not violated nor its rules repealed when a substantial portion, or all, of a city's inhabitants are temporarily relocated. Furthermore, the evacuees act in accordance with the laws of social psychology and those of human mobility (about which more later), even though we could not fully spell out either code in the absence of such extraordinary real-world experiments, a view first promulgated by Eichenbaum (1970). Thus we can regard the emergency evacuation of cities as falling within the general realm of spatial mobility and adhering to a set of still dimly perceived covering laws that embrace both "normal" and "abnormal" movements.

Another more immediate general finding is the impracticality of prolonged evacuation. If we adopt a strict definition of evacuation and thus eliminate the minority of evacuees who might be classified as premature migrants (as seems to have been the case with a number of persons leaving Darwin and perhaps Anchorage) and also those persons who were obliged to alter status from that of evacuee to refugee (a fate befalling some of the Polish, French, and German citizens evacuating during World War II), or those who became migrants because of economic opportunity or marriage in what was to have been a temporary residence, or the destruction of their former home, the sojourn in temporary quarters was generally as brief as possible. The reasons are not difficult to identify. The economic and psychological costs, for both the relocated and their hosts, and the strain on the logistics of daily existence, are heavy in the short run and intolerable over an extended period. Thus we find evacuees returning to familiar surroundings most often in a matter of days or weeks, seldom after many months or years—and usually after leaving home as late as possible.

The major exceptions have been those situations where the home territory was enemy-occupied over a protracted period and the self-imposed exile, lasting five years or more, of relatively well-to-do English men, women, and children during World War II. The western Soviet case is the prime example of the former but somewhat marginal given the official prewar and subsequent encouragement of eastward migration. The Chernobyl case is also exceptional, even though the former residents of the irradiated zone had every hope and intention of returning. But it is important to point out that the financial burden of permanently resettling so many households has been considerable, and it is doubtful that the Soviet government can subsidize many more such forced migrations. We must also note that young children, who, of course, have little choice as to residence, may undergo lengthy separation from their normal habitat, as happened to those involved in Germany I and United Kingdom I, IIa, and IIb. Even granting these various exceptions, however, we must conclude that long-term evacuation of large numbers of adults or entire families has not been a viable option in the past and is an equally unattractive policy for future emergencies.

The next general finding is one we had not fully anticipated. It appears that despite the enormous immediate disruption of normal life

entailed in mass evacuations, the demographic and geographic effects
are almost always temporary. These traumatic events are clearly
important in and of themselves, but they leave few or no longer-term
traces in the mappable landscape or population structure. At most,
emergency evacuations can simply accelerate or intensify changes that
were already under way. The quite singular exception to this rule is, of
course, Chernobyl and its seemingly permanently depopulated environs. We can only speculate that this event may be the precursor of an
eventual series of such indefinitely prolonged dislocations, and that
major nuclear power station accidents in the future may radically revise
our theoretical notions concerning evacuation. At the micro level, we
must also note the persistent emptiness of Managua's once congested
central district, a legacy of economic constraints and political ineptitude in the months and years following the earthquake. It appears to
be another isolated case.

Any generalization about the transience of the effects of evacuation
must take into account the possibility, best exemplified by Warsaw II
and Germany II, that emergency evacuations can be enfolded within,
and entangled with, larger war-related redistribution and restructuring
of populations. For example, do we attribute the deficit of adult males
in a given locality to war losses or evacuation, or some combination of
the two factors? Nevertheless it is striking to what extent the predisaster populations of the affected cities have reconstituted themselves.
Thus, despite the influx of refugees from the east, "In 1946, 92 percent
of Düsseldorf's total population, 91 percent of Hamburg's population,
and 94 percent of Berlin's population had lived in these cities before
the war" (Bernert and Iklé 1952:138). In any event, it is well-nigh
impossible to ascribe with confidence any changes occurring in the
postdisaster settlement patterns of metropolitan areas either directly
or indirectly to these temporary relocations, with the somewhat marginal exceptions of Skopje and Managua. It is conceivable, of course,
that exposure to new localities, and the resulting favorable or unfavor-
able impressions, may have some impact on subsequent migratory
decisions by the evacuees, but any such hypothesis would be extremely difficult to test. As for the demographic impact of evacuation,
aside from its effect on mortality, injury, or illness during the emergency period, it is hard to imagine any consequences for fertility, age
and sex structure, marital or household characteristics, or any of the
other standard demographic variables.

A further term, one that is more in the nature of an observation than
a finding, has to do with the role of official authority in the management

of evacuations. Without denigrating the importance of individual and household perceptions and decisions, in every one of our events, with the possible exception of United Kingdom I, governmental agencies at the local, provincial, national, and even international level have played important, often decisive roles in the planning or execution of these emergency transfers or coping with their results. We mention this obvious fact here because we may have accorded it insufficient attention in previous sections. It also happens to be a fact that complicates the cross-national approach. There is no simple way to adjust for differences in political cultures and institutions among various countries or to quantify such a variable, but there can be little doubt that it is significant in the responses to actual or anticipated disasters. Continuing in this self-critical mode, we suggest that the question of the relative weight of private vs. official forces be addressed more directly and rigorously in future analyses conducted at the international scale.

SOME LARGER QUESTIONS

Up to this point we have confined ourselves to those aspects of emergency evacuations of cities that are of particular concern to geographers and demographers. But such issues unavoidably merge into some broader themes and questions that are appropriate for this final section of the study. The most obvious of these items is the simple matter of whether the evacuation strategy in general, or, more specifically, the strategy as practiced in the set of events we have been able to deal with, has proved effective in achieving its primary objective: the saving of human lives and a reduction in the number of physical injuries.

The answer, obviously, must be based on conjecture, as it is a comparison between casualties actually experienced and the hypothetical number that would have been recorded if the evacuees had remained *in situ*. For some of our events, this type of calculation can be made with a fair degree of confidence. Thus we can rather closely approximate the numbers of British, German, Japanese, and Leningrad evacuees who would have suffered death or injury through enemy bombing or shelling (or, in the Leningrad case, through starvation) in their regular residences and workplaces by applying the known rates registered for the residual populations. We might even be able to refine such exercises down to the neighborhood level. Similarly, it would be relatively easy to compute the number of persons who would have

drowned or been incapacitated by flood waters or waves and wind in
the Ohio River cities, Winnipeg, and the Gulf Coast communities.

There is much greater difficulty in estimating how many casualties
were averted in situations such as those encountered in Bhopal I and
Chernobyl—or in Kiev and other Ukrainian and Belorussian communities—because of the lack of details concerning the concentration and
path of the lethal agents as well as the location and movements of the
population at risk. But we can be reasonably certain that evacuation
was beneficial in these events. It is equally difficult, or impossible, to
approximate the number of persons who avoided injury or even death
by leaving damaged structures in El Asnam, Anchorage, Belize, Darwin, Managua, or Skopje, but, again, it seems safe to assume a positive
result.

In Table 7-2 we have indicated our best judgment as to whether or
not evacuation fulfilled its most urgent purpose of minimizing casualties. In nineteen of twenty-eight events (if we regard Kiev as a separate
item), we conclude that evacuation did achieve this end, in greater or
lesser degree. The numbers in question range from the very small (as
in Mississauga or Darwin, where some may argue that no one was
saved) to the possible millions in the Soviet case. The verdict, then,
must be that on balance the evacuation strategy has been beneficial.

But we dare not ignore the remaining events. In at least four cases—
Belize, Anchorage, France I, La Soufrière, and, possibly, Warsaw
II[2]—the evidence is too meager or ambiguous for clear judgment, or it
is likely that evacuation had no effect either positive or negative. The
Three Mile Island exodus is especially hard to evaluate because, as
noted earlier, controversy still rages over the question of whether
those who stayed behind received a radiation dosage sufficient to cause
delayed adverse effects. In at least three other cases—Warsaw I,
France II, and Bhopal II—the evidence suggests that the hazards of
the journeys in question probably exceeded the risk of death or injury
that would have been incurred by remaining in place.

Although we believe that more often than not evacuation does serve
to reduce deaths and whatever bodily insults the population at risk
may suffer from a disaster, immediately or after some delay, there are
other important considerations to enter into the equation before reaching a well-rounded decision on the value of evacuations. Specifically,
what are the economic and psychic costs of such episodes in addition
to the value of lives saved and injuries averted? Although it may seem
cold-blooded to engage in this type of cost-benefit analysis, it is

Table 7-2. Effectiveness of Evacuation in Saving Lives and Reducing Injury

Degree of Effectiveness

XX: Important positive effect. X: Slight positive effect. 0: Effect neutral and/or evidence ambiguous.
#: Probable increase in death and injury.

Floods Storms		Earthquakes, Volcanic Eruptions		War-Related		Industrial	
Ohio River Flood	XX	Skopje	X	Warsaw I	#	Three Mile Island	0
Winnipeg	XX	Anchorage	0	Warsaw II	X	Mississauga	X
Gulf Coast Hurricanes	XX	Managua	X?	United Kingdom I	X	Bhopal I	X
Belize	0	La Soufrière	0	United Kingdom IIa	X	Bhopal II	#
Darwin	X	El Asnam	X	United Kingdom IIb	X	Chernobyl	XX
				France I	0	(Kiev)	X?
				France II	#		
				USSR	XX		
				Leningrad	XX		
				Germany I	X		
				Germany II	XX		
				Japan	XX		

essential to generate such information if the evacuation strategy is to be compared with other modes of disaster management.

To the best of our knowledge, only one such calculation has ever been executed, that for Three Mile Island (Hu and Slaysman 1981), in large part because of formidable methodological and data problems. On the positive, or benefit, side of the ledger, placing a dollar value on the hypothetical saving in lives and injuries is no simple matter. Although actuaries have worked out the value of a human life in most so-called advanced countries (a value that changes over time), we would need to know the age, gender, occupation, and other particulars concerning the persons who might have perished or been impaired in lieu of evacuation. Equally challenging is any realistic estimate of the medical and hospital costs that would have been incurred had the population rejected the evacuation option. As far as other costs are concerned, the computations can be equally complicated. What are the direct monetary costs of the journey, whether borne by the evacuees themselves or some official agency? How large is the bill for temporary lodging, food, and various services for evacuees, hosts, or whoever may be subsidizing the sojourn? How great a financial drain in terms of lost wages and all forms of economic product that are not made up subsequently?

Much more intangible, but perhaps no less important, are the psychic costs of an evacuation for both evacuees and hosts. There are items we cannot ignore even though there is no known way to translate them into monetary terms. What can be noted, though, is the subsequent price in terms of resistance to official decisions and directives when a given evacuation turns out to have been needless or of dubious benefit. Such examples as La Soufrière and United Kingdom IIa come to mind.

Plainly, then, we are incapable of answering the question as to whether evacuations are generally cost-effective. A case-by-case approach is the only viable strategy, and at best we can offer only guesses about certain individual events. Thus there cannot be much dispute that some of the major wartime evacuations—Leningrad, USSR, Germany II, and Japan, and Chernobyl as well—were paying propositions however huge the expenditures involved. On the other hand, one may argue plausibly for either side of the argument in cases such as Mississauga, Three Mile Island, and some of the Gulf Coast hurricanes. If any general moral is to be drawn from the preceding discussion, it is that there is no consistent answer to the question of value of evacuations, whether as measured in human lives and suffering or on the accountant's balance sheet. Variability from event to event is enormous.

Another extremely weighty item is the consideration that during the course of the century the universe of disasters has increasingly come to form a single interactive system. (The thought that it is improbable that this study could have been conceived and initiated before the 1980s testifies to the recency of this situation.) Some of the reasons for the interrelatedness of the events in question (with or without evacuation) are obvious: advances in communication technology; the rising incidence of certain classes of disasters; the appearance of local, national, and international bureaucracies, along with a corps of experts, supposedly equipped to deal with such emergencies; and the development of professional societies and journals devoted to the subject. What we are articulating is the notion that awareness of, and knowledge about, a particular disaster has come to affect subsequent behavior not just locally but also frequently nationally and even internationally, that a learning process is at work within the system.

At this point we must finally confront an issue previously evaded and one that has perennially bedeviled students of human society: how to deal with unique events. Although historians are necessarily reconciled to uniqueness, it is a problem that creates much discomfort for demographers and many geographers, along with most other social scientists who aspire to scientific rigor. The position we adopt here is that enunciated by sociologist Robert Nisbet:

> If, as is so often argued today . . . events, "unique events" as they are called, are not amenable to the systematic needs of social theory, so much the worse for the theory. The objective, after all, is not the illumination of concept and theory. It is the illumination of reality as mind and sense reveal this reality. (Nisbet 1969:279)

In this study, the issue goes well beyond the difficulty of forming generalizations from a small and varied sample. Several of the events included here are unique in one or more senses of that term. At least three—TMI, Chernobyl, and Bhopal—can be classified as unprecedented in character and also uniquely important in the way they have transformed, indeed radically reshaped, our perceptual landscape worldwide. Other disasters have been remarkable for sheer magnitude rather than novelty of type, but have also profoundly affected subsequent attitudes and actions. Examples include the Ohio River Flood of 1937, Hurricane Audrey in 1957, and the Mount Pelée eruption of 1902.

Another variety of uniqueness is historical in character. Although this may be wishful thinking, we regard it as unlikely that the blanket bombing of urban populations using *conventional* explosives will be a feature of any future international conflict. (Chemical and biological forms of warfare are separate issues.) Be that as it may, the World War II evacuation experiences of Great Britain, Germany, and Japan amount, in the aggregate, to a historically unique phenomenon in terms of magnitude, if not kind.[3]

Pursuing this train of thought, it would be useful to classify the events considered here, and disasters in general, into two categories: those that are unique by reason of exceptional impact or unfamiliarity of type; and "routine" disasters, those that tend to be repetitive or are commonplace in character. The recent series of Gulf Coast (and South Atlantic Coast) hurricanes are obvious examples of the latter genre, but one might also include the rather less frequent but damaging earthquakes in seismically active zones and floods in certain high-risk valleys, all of which are capable of spawning evacuations. Indeed, small-scale, localized evacuations caused by train derailments, river barge mishaps (e.g., Duclos et al. 1987), and various industrial accidents have become almost weekly occurrences in the United States, and local emergency officials in the more affluent nations have acquired a good deal of expertise in handling them from their own experiences and those of others.

But experience, or group memories, of earlier disasters does not always lead to optimal, or even sensible, behavior. Recollections of World War I were responsible for the madness of l'Exode and, it must be added, those rather dubious exercises we call United Kingdom IIa and IIb. Similarly, it is debatable whether Bhopal II was the proper reaction to Bhopal I. We postpone comment on the possible lessons for the future implied by Three Mile Island, Chernobyl, and the Bhopal disasters; but this is the appropriate point to note that the "cry wolf syndrome" may frustrate the plans and intentions of emergency managers. Thus the absence of any serious hostile activity in the British skies during the first several months of World War II clearly sabotaged the effectiveness of United Kingdom IIa, while the debacle of La Soufrière may make the public less receptive to any future volcanic alert in the Lesser Antilles. If the universe of disasters is an increasingly interactive system, as we are fully convinced, the web of shared communications and the channels of cause and effect are knotted in complex ways that are not readily untangled.

POSSIBLE CONTRIBUTIONS TO POPULATION THEORY

We come next to a primary objective of this study: an assessment of the contribution of the evacuation experience to theoretical concepts in demography and population geography. The concern at this point is less with the immediate value of the empirical findings than with their deeper implications. Our general conclusion is that the data we have assembled are indeed relevant to the formation of basic theory. As Belcher and Bates (1983:118) put it, "Because so much movement is compressed within such a short time span, a disaster provides the specialist in migration with a natural laboratory in which to study the phenomenon." However, at this still rather rudimentary stage in the development of a new field of study, we can postulate only a few relatively firm ideas, and must offer more questions than answers. But these are truly important questions.

Turning to specific items, the fact that emergency evacuations, large and small, have been occurring with some frequency means that there is no avoiding the task of setting such spatial movements in their rightful locus within that complex, multidimensional universe of phenomena we call human territorial mobility. And such inclusion must necessarily modify the ways we perceive and conceptualize the totality of this important scholarly project (Chapman 1987). In the process of giving evacuation its proper due, there are two questions to be disposed of: how to relate it to other modes of mobility; and how to cope with its several dimensions.

It has become increasingly apparent in recent years that the circulation of human beings is just as legitimate a topic of inquiry as presumably permanent migrations, that indeed the two forms of movement are overlapping bands along a single continuum. Furthermore, there is no question that evacuees, as we have defined them (and have distinguished as best we can from refugees) are circulators. But we also find that in any realistic classificatory scheme one must allow for the possibility that circumstances can shift a mover from one category to another, or that the classifications of a given movement may differ as the perceptions of the concerned actors may vary. Evacuees may become refugees (usually against their will), or homeless persons, turn into "normal" migrants, or be regarded as a subspecies of commuters. In fact, much "night-time evacuation" became routine in many German cities subject to frequent bombing (Bernert and Iklé 1952:137); and the same sort of daily round trip was common in wartime Japan and in Great Britain, where it was called "trekking." In any case, because of its potentially polymorphous nature, evacuation straddles the boundaries between circulation and migration and between other modes of movement. Perhaps more effectively than any other subset of the larger phenomenon it fortifies the contention that human mobility in all its endless variety constitutes a seamless whole.

Like all other forms of human mobility, evacuation must be measured along more than one dimension, an approach evidently pioneered by William Petersen (1975). With respect to some attributes, such as magnitude, duration, direction, distance, and degree of external control, evacuation overlaps one or more other types of movement. For example, evacuees may fall along a scale of independence of action anywhere from total freedom of choice to absolute compulsion, just as is true for various forms of labor migration. Consequently we can hardly label evacuation unequivocally as compulsory movement. But each mobility type has at least one characteristic uniquely its own. In the case of evacuation, there are two: intentionality and motivation. What makes the evacuee's situation distinctive and sets it apart from other forms of circulation is the understanding that the return trip will be made as expeditiously as possible to complete what may well be a once-in-a-lifetime episode.

In other modes of mobility, if we confine ourselves to the basic question of remaining or moving, one usually detects the strong presence of at least two of five possible motives, namely: livelihood considerations; the quest for pleasure; social obligations; innate individual psychological predispositions; and physical survival. Furthermore, the analyst often has great difficulty in disentangling the relevant factors and gauging their relative weights. In emergency evacuations, however, the single overriding factor driving the participants is the instinct for survival. In some instances, of course, it may be modulated by the psychological makeup of the population at risk, but only to a minor extent, and in some events may not figure at all. Consequently, of all varieties of mobility, evacuation may be the easiest to explain and describe, assuming adequate data.

The noneconomic character of evacuations is a crucial point that bears reiteration. In varying degrees, monetary calculations enter significantly into virtually all other forms of mobility decisions, that is, whether to stay or go, be they regular migrations, commuting, vacations, tourism, pilgrimages, retirement moves, pioneer settlement, the slave trade, intra-urban shifts of residence, or home-to-campus journeys by college students. (The majority of marital migrations *may* be the only interesting exception.) But the economic burden seldom enters the consciousness of potential evacuees faced with the prospect of personal extinction, and, one assumes, it is far from uppermost in the minds of officials in the midst of an emergency. After the basic decision has been made, cost factors may surface in the choice of destination or mode of transport, but with less force than in other types of travel. Here we are treating decisions made in the heat of battle, so to speak, not the sort of calm, rational deliberation concerning the cost-effectiveness of evacuations we suggested earlier as important in long-term policy formulation. And, of course, there is always the possibility of overreaction.

Setting aside these observations on matters definitional and motivational, what have we gained in terms of fresh theoretical knowledge? The answer must be two pregnant ideas. The first is not entirely original, but our evidence lends it some much-needed support. It has become apparent, if one views emergency evacuations—along with pleasure and retirement travel, the circulation of students and pilgrims, and various movements driven by social factors—as essential components of the total universe of territorial mobility, that the economistic models that have been so much in vogue for the better part of a century to describe and explain this large, many-sided phenomenon are quite incomplete and defective. As the preceding paragraphs have maintained, the economic factor may be paramount in some types of mobility but absent or trivial in others—and, in general, may well be declining in relative salience in recent decades. In any event, it is only one of a family of explanatory or causative factors, and must be treated as such in any comprehensive theory covering human movements in terrestrial space.

We are not about to set forth any such ambitious schema; it is beyond our capabilities and, we dare say, that of other students of the subject given the current state of knowledge. We simply wish to emphasize again the complexity of human mobility and the fact that noneconomic factors, along with the economic, are crucial components in shaping the patterns in question.

It is also important to stress the great and growing importance of information, whether personal or collective, in analyzing spatial movements. In the case of emergency evacuations, knowledge about comparable past events in one's locality or elsewhere, news about the actual or impending disaster, information about possible destinations, means of travel, and possible alternatives to evacuation, all such forms of intelligence feed into decisions reached by individuals and officials. They certainly do not act blindly or altogether instinctively, and that consideration must be factored into whatever general model of human mobility we arrive at eventually. In this consideration we can offer a specific suggestion: that it would be worthwhile to conduct longitudinal surveys over some decades to determine in what ways the migration and circulation behavior of veterans of major evacuations may be modified (or not modified) by their experiences during past emergencies when they are compared to some suitable control group.

Our second, possibly major, idea is clearly related to the first. It has to do with the validity of the distance-decay principle that undergirds the gravity model, a doctrine that has figured so prominently in modern economic and population geography. This is the notion that the friction of distance (and the closely associated costs of time and money) almost fully explains the dispersion of people and other objects outward from a given place. In more general terms, the gravity model describes the interaction between two or more places on the basis of population size and physical distance raised to some appropriate power. As we have already seen, the majority of the events covered in this study confirm the doctrine. But the existence of some exceptions may prompt us to question its general validity; indeed even a single documented counterexample could suffice to falsify any such social law.

May we suggest that it is time for a major overhaul of the distance-decay principle and consequent revisions of the gravity model? It makes sense to believe that, insofar as human beings make rational decisions in their spatial behavior, they seek to maximize or minimize (as the case may be), or at least satisfice, one or more items. In the case of most "normal" migrations, and most journeys to school, church, commercial establishments, and various service offices, a dominant consideration is usually travel distance, in an effort to minimize time, effort, and expenditures, although other factors certainly can enter into the equation. But there are many other instances in which little thought is given to convenience or to shortening the journey; indeed there may be a deliberate effort to move as far away, or keep moving as long, as is practical.

Aside from the "aberrant" evacuations, examples of such nonminimizing migratory or circulating behavior include: much retirement migration; many tourist, vacation, and convention journeys; the quest for certain rare and costly goods or services; pioneer colonization; many refugee movements; teenage "cruising"; mineral prospecting; and wrongdoers fleeing the police. Furthermore, in selecting colleges a large minority of North American students deliberately end up on a campus at a considerable remove from the parental home, and nowadays distance matters little or not at all in the career moves of upwardly mobile business executives, academics, and other professionals. It is also becoming increasingly evident that the length of the journey to work is only one, and not necessarily the most decisive, element in choosing one's next residence within a metropolitan area. To cite another trivial but pertinent example, given the option and means, many residents of high-rise apartment buildings would prefer living on an upper floor or even in the penthouse, even though the location increases the time and vertical distance consumed in daily travel. We should also remind the reader once more of the doughnut effect so often observed in the spatial disposition of evacuees.

What explains these exceptions to the distance-decay principle? The migrants and circulators in question are clearly trying to optimize, or at least enhance, something other than convenience (to use a short-hand term for the expenditure of money, time and effort). Their objective may be to improve the quality of life in nonmaterial as well as material ways, or to attain peace of mind, or to seek out economic opportunities that by their nature are remotely located, or simply to savor fleeting pleasures. In the case of evacuees, and refugees as well, the quest is for physical safety and comfort. The point of this discussion is that the motives and controlling factors that mold the spatial patterns of human movements are almost always plural. It is exceptional to find no more than a single variable at work. Physical distance between origin and destination may be overall the most important and obvious factor, but others enter the picture and may even exceed or negate the gravitational effect of distance. If we are ever to achieve a reasonably satisfactory, comprehensive model, or theory, of human mobility, it must take into account a multiplicity of forces acting to determine where, how, when, and how many of what sorts of human beings move about the face of the earth. It is a difficult challenge, but not an impossible one.

IMPLICATIONS FOR THE FUTURE

How likely is it that metropolitan communities will continue to resort to mass evacuations in times of emergency in the future? And how effective will this strategy prove to be?

The first question is much easier to treat than the latter. For two obvious reasons, there is a virtual certainty that the incidence of natural and human disasters affecting urban populations will be greater in coming decades than it has been in the past. First, barring some truly horrendous catastrophe, the human population of this planet will continue to grow at a substantial rate far into the next century, and the upsurge in urban numbers will be especially vigorous occurring as it does and will at a worldwide rate far exceeding the rural increment. Many of these expanding metropolises are located on sites susceptible to floods, storms, earthquakes, and volcanic eruption; and virtually all are subject to the risk of major accidents (à la Mississauga) involving freight trains, trucks, or waterborne traffic. The problem will be exacerbated by the development of new industrial processes generating lethal or noxious substances. As Brigadier I. G. C. Gilmore has so aptly stated,

> . . . the effects of disasters which give rise to the question of whether to evacuate or stay put are likely to increase with the passage of time, because the population continues to rise in disaster-prone regions, and advances in technology continue to produce greater man-made hazards, or to upset nature's ecological balance. (Gilmore 1980:193)

Within certain countries of the First World there has been a decided tendency toward the thinning out of metropolitan populations as suburbanization and exurbanization have progressed. These lower densities mean that disasters of whatever kind may have a less severe impact, but in most of the rest of the world urban concentrations have been increasing, and so too the susceptibility to disaster.

We must note in passing that the next few decades may prove, or disprove, the actuality of a major global warming trend, one that could raise sea levels a matter of meters rather than just centimeters. If such a calamity comes to pass, many large metropolises, such as London, Amsterdam, Calcutta, Leningrad, and New Orleans among a host of others, will face the prospect of choosing between prohibitively costly protective measures and removal to higher ground. But the latter strategy falls into the category of relocation rather than the type of temporary evacuation dealt with here.

Another near-certainty about the future is that when a major disaster disables an urban area or a large section thereof, an appreciable portion of its population will evacuate. The exodus could be spontaneous or it could be organized and directed by officialdom, or there may be some combination of these two modes. As this study has indicated, evacuation has generally succeeded in its immediate objective of preserving life, and this fact has become part of the conventional wisdom. We have also noted that there is much less certainty about the cost-effectiveness of the strategy in economic terms, but no political juris-diction has performed the required calculations, and few have planned and prepared other comprehensive methods of disaster mitigation. Consequently, when the emergency does materialize, political pres-sures, as well as simple human emotion, will usually prevail and make evacuation the only acceptable alternative.

Such findings as we have been able to establish apply best to more or less traditional types of disaster—those of natural origin and those related to conventional warfare. As was suggested previously, one variety of disaster, the massive aerial bombardment of cities using conventional explosives, may be unlikely to recur, although the possi-bility remains of evacuation in the face of occupation by advancing armies. In any event, we can feel relatively comfortable about envi-sioning the shape of future scenarios triggered by these familiar causes by extrapolating from past experiences—but with one very large fly in the ointment.

As noted earlier, the science and art of weather prognostication have made remarkable strides over the past few decades, and we can expect further refinements in coming years. Consequently, emergency man-agers now know which communities, or sections thereof, should be evacuated when and for how long, and citizens of such cities as Darwin and Winnipeg have learned how dangerous it is to ignore the advisories of meteorologists and hydrologists. But it can also be perilous to rely too blindly on the forecasts of experts. Although significant advances in sciences of seismology and volcanology have resulted in efforts to predict catastrophic events, they have met with limited success thus far. We can be reasonably confident that there will be some improve-ment in the predictive capabilities of the experts, but the margin for error will remain quite wide for many years. This fact places emer-gency managers in an excruciating position, especially since it is unlikely that elected officials governing cities in earthquake-prone areas can afford the political risk of not preplanning an emergency management plan.

Try to imagine the plight of decision makers in Los Angeles and other Southern California communities if they were to be informed of the 50 percent probability of a truly devastating earthquake within the next month. (Incidentally, seismologists are convinced that such an event is virtually certain during the next few decades.) Assume that a plan is available to evacuate several million inhabitants, that it is carried out somehow, but then that no unusual geophysical event takes place. (In a limited way, something like such a scenario was played out in the New Madrid, Missouri region during December 1990.) Not only would the economic cost have been enormous, along with the social trauma, but the political repercussions would be horrendous. Even more seriously, the next warning of impending catastrophe might prove to be accurate but the rate of citizen cooperation could be fatally inadequate. On a much more modest scale, we have seen at least the first part of such a scenario played out in the La Soufrière event. What will happen in Guadeloupe the next time the volcano threatens to blow itself to bits? An interesting sidelight on this issue is the reluctance to evacuate on the part of those Mississaugans who happen to have been participants in the rather frustrating British evacuations during World War II.

We are left with a small, but perplexing, family of disasters that renders both prognostication and mangagement quite problematic. It includes industrial accidents, such as those at Three Mile Island, Bhopal, and Chernobyl, where the lethal agent is unfamiliar and/or difficult or impossible to sense, in contrast to such visible or familiar substances as chlorine or ammonia. In cases when the confrontation is with the unknown, the behavior of the population at risk is not at all predictable by the rules of more ordinary emergencies. Furthermore, we have not *yet* accumulated sufficient experience to formulate a new set of rules.

The Three Mile Island and Chernobyl events, not to mention the catastrophic nuclear accident in western Siberia in 1957 that was hushed up until recently, are especially troublesome in their implications for the future. All three disasters revealed managerial ineptitude: the inability or unwillingness of the responsible officials to implement promptly such evacuation plans as had existed on paper, along with confusion or conflict among various layers of governmental and corporate authority. It is difficult to be optimistic about the prospects for improvement on this score when, not if, future accidents occur at nuclear power plants resulting in the release of substantial quantities of radioactivity. Despite official assurances, future disasters are inevitable, but, of course, as is true for any sort of industrial accident, the time and place cannot be anticipated.

The geographic pattern of evacuation in Chernobyl-type events also departs from the norms documented for other industrial disasters and those created by the forces of nature. Spontaneous evacuation occurs well beyond the zone in which there is any immediate danger to life or health, even though it may be unwise to disregard the long-term effects of minor intakes of radioactive materials over extended areas. In any case, we will have many individuals acting on the basis of fears and uncertainties that may not be justified by the physical facts, that is, overreaction rather than the underreaction that usually makes life difficult for emergency managers. Despite Ronald Perry's claims to the contrary (1985:16, 20, 60, 65), it is difficult to see how we can fit human responses to accidents of a nuclear character into a standard general model of evacuation behavior by simply acknowledging the "emotional" dimension. At a certain point, quantitative differences create qualitative distinctiveness.

It is interesting to note that the evacuation problem has become a major nightmare for the nuclear power industry, first in the United States, subsequently in the Soviet Union, and potentially in other countries as well. Indeed this is the problem that may eventually nail the coffin shut on Long Island's Shoreham plant (Johnson and Ziegler 1983), and delayed the start-up of New Hampshire's Seabrook plant for several years. In both those locations, the combination of dense proximate populations with constricted evacuation corridors of questionable capacity has made massive evacuation an implausible proposition. If there is any silver lining in the Three Mile Island and Chernobyl incidents, it is that there was an abundance of good exit routes for the former and a relatively thin population nearby for the latter.

THE EVACUATION STRATEGY IN FUTURE NUCLEAR CONFLICTS

The final question to be addressed in this study is by far the most momentous: What does the history of emergency evacuation have to tell us about the efficacy of the strategy in the event of nuclear warfare? To our chagrin, the short answer must be little or nothing, at least directly. Furthermore, logical inference renders a negative verdict.

The atomic bombing of Hiroshima and Nagasaki in 1945 is, of course, the only historical precedent we have to exploit, but it is minimally informative. Neither city had advance knowledge of the attack or of its innovative character, and there was no anticipatory evacuation. Moreover, in each case it was a single device dropped on a single target. The minority of survivors who were ambulatory or movable were able to find refuge and medical assistance in other localities that were still functioning after a fashion. The pattern of evacuation did not differ drastically from that experienced by other heavily bombed Japanese cities.

We regret having to confess the virtual uselessness of historical example in the one situation where the need for foreknowledge is most pressing. Thus evaluating the potential utility of evacuation in nuclear conflicts means falling back on conjecture and reliance on logical argument.[4]

The outlook for the survival of the urban victims of nuclear warfare by means of evacuation or other means today and in the foreseeable future is radically different from the World War II experience—and much less favorable. If we were ever to be so unfortunate as to witness a nuclear exchange involving any of the half-dozen or so countries with the capabilities for long-distance assault, multiple warheads would be delivered at or near a multiplicity of urban, military, and industrial targets within a short span of time. Furthermore, over the past forty-odd years there has been enormous technical progress in the design and production of nuclear weapons and delivery systems. The present-day larger, more sophisticated devices are some orders of magnitude more powerful than the primitive bombs detonated over Japan. (For example, it is quite conceivable that a single well-placed hydrogen bomb could incapacitate almost the entire population of Israel.) In addition to the immediate destruction caused by blast, heat, and radiation on or near the ground, there is every likelihood that the EMP (electromagnetic pulse) Effect generated by a single blast in the upper atmosphere could knock out virtually all civilian and the great bulk of military electronic communications, thus rendering any organized evacuation scheme extremely difficult to carry out.

Would it be possible to defend or save metropolitan populations from nuclear attack? Since there is no effective active military defense against airborne nuclear weapons—or those transported by surface means for that matter—nor is there much likelihood of any, only two relatively passive options have received serious attention: underground shelters and mass evacuation. The difficulty with the former, aside from the crushing cost of providing livable quarters for some weeks or months for many tens of millions of persons, is that there is no assurance of long-term or even immediate survival. Only the deepest of shelters would protect their residents from roasting or asphyxiation if a bomb were to strike anywhere in the neighborhood. Evidently neutralist, non-nuclear Switzerland has been the only country thus far with sufficient wealth, technology, and political will to provide under-ground refuges for its population. But even assuming that the Swiss, and some American, Soviet, Chinese, British, French, and other subterranean creatures were to live through the first critical days and weeks, there is the depressing possibility that the world to which they eventually emerge would be unlivable. To the lingering radiation, destruction of physical facilities and social infrastructure, and quick extermination of much plant and animal life, one must add the strong probability of a nuclear winter that would radically disrupt the food-producing system and other vital elements of the ecosystem.

The same ultimate fate would befall the participants of a successful mass evacuation. But what are the prospects that such a maneuver could be executed in the first place for not just one but for a large array of cities in the face of an imminent nuclear attack? The question has been addressed in as nearly a definitive manner as one could hope by Leaning and Keyes (1984), and the result is a thorough debunking of any such program as espoused, for example, for France (Fautrière 1955). The essential argument is that the evacuation strategy is foolish on at least two basic counts. First the logistics are simply unworkable. The simultaneous evacuation of virtually the entire metropolitan population of the United States, Soviet Union, Great Britain, or any other potential target country entails impossible demands on the transportation system and calls for a flawless (but untested) apparatus of social control en route to and within a vast, nonexistent array of reception centers, a prospect that falls within the realm of social science fiction. Second, the observation of the readily observable implementation of mass evacuation plans by a potential adversary during a period of serious international tension might very well precipitate a preemptive strike, and thus bring about the very holocaust one seeks to avert.

It is conceivable, but just barely, that a single large metropolitan center might engineer the rapid removal of all its unpanicky inhabitants in order to avoid their destruction by nuclear weapons, an evacuation presumably performed *before* the delivery and detonation of the nuclear devices. But it is inconceivable that this could happen, say, for the entirety of the Northeastern Megalopolis in the United States, an exercise that would involve transferring everyone from Boston, Providence, Hartford, New York City, New Jersey, Philadelphia, Wilmington, Baltimore, Washington, and many lesser places to a set of imaginary sanctuaries in two or three days. Interestingly enough, a full-scale practice drill involving a large fraction of a city's population has never been staged anywhere. Nor is it likely given the magnitude of the economic, social, and political costs. A few surprise drills involving only key governmental personnel have yielded ludicrous results.

If the evacuation strategy was applied, with varying degrees of success, in Germany, Japan, France, Great Britain, Poland, the Soviet Union, and other countries during World War II, the situation then was quite different from today's. Only one or a few cities were bombed on any given day, and various forms of aid could be supplied from other cities. When evacuation did take place, it was generally spread over a period of weeks or months during or after the enemy attack. To have any chance of succeeding, evacuation in anticipation of nuclear attack would have to be performed hastily *before* the critical moment, not during or after the event, a truly fatal constraint.

Moreover, settlement patterns of the 1940s have changed greatly in the years since. In general, the absolute and relative numbers of city dwellers in the more likely target countries have grown considerably, while the populations of the small towns and countryside have either stagnated or declined. It may have been feasible, but only just, to squeeze most of metropolitan Japan into the countryside in 1944–45. Today such a transfer would be unthinkable. And, to pursue another even more mind-boggling example, and accepting the heroic assumption that rural America had not become dangerously irradiated after a wide-ranging nuclear assault, just where could one stow metropolitan California for the duration within the southwestern quadrant of the United States, not to mention Phoenix, Tucson, Las Vegas, Albuquerque, and other urban agglomerations?

The analogy with World War II becomes even more far-fetched when we consider the possibility that evacuation might have to become long-lasting or even permanent. German, Japanese, and British evacuees could return to their battered cities and begin reconstructing them rather promptly; but such a homecoming may be out of the question if the urban site has become intensely irradiated—the Chernobyl unpleasantness squared and cubed! Even if we imagine a much more cheerful scenario, namely that evacuation did take place successfully and that because of some adroit last-minute diplomacy war has been averted, would a repetition of the experience be possible whenever the next crisis boiled up?

If there is any grand moral to be drawn from this study, and the events past and prospective that have concerned us, it is not an entirely cheerful one: that the application of history and social science to the amelioration of human misery may be a meritorious exercise but something feasible only within modest limits—limits that are almost certainly more constricted than the human capacity for folly.

NOTES

1. Somewhat comparable is the history of the evacuation of Leningrad's children. Initially they were removed to the suburbs and other nearby localities; but with the approach of the invading army they returned to the city proper.

2. Given the extent to which the city and its infrastructure had been wiped out, it is plausible that the sum of death and suffering would have been substantially greater if the Germans had not insisted on removing the inhabitants of Warsaw. On the other hand, the blessings of evacuation were dubious for those who were sent to concentration camps.

3. We are well aware of other relatively recent war-related evacuations into as well as out of cities—events that surely merit methodical study. We have, for example, the partial emptying of major urban centers in Kampuchea, Iraq, Iran, and Lebanon during the conflicts of the 1970s and 1980s and, conversely, the influx of rural folk into the metropolises of Vietnam and Afghanistan during the recent troubled history of these two countries. Large though these movements may have been, they do not begin to match the enormity of the European and Japanese evacuations during World War II. We must note in passing that the question of which is deemed safer in time of war—the city or the countryside—poses an interesting challenge to the social or demographic historian.

4. Historical examples of calamity and recovery not only fall short of evoking a realistic image of survival after nuclear war, but the very act of looking to history for information and advice can in itself mislead. The destruction of human beings in Hiroshima and Nagasaki radically exceeded all we had previously learned about disaster effects. Yet Hiroshima and Nagasaki are no more than a transition between prenuclear disaster and that which we face from contemporary nuclear weapons. Nothing we have known begins to suggest the dimensions of such a holocaust. But in our recognition of these dimensions of destruction—of the possibility of a nuclear "end"—lies the beginning of the wisdom we may draw upon to prevent it from taking place. (Leaning and Keyes 1984:300)

Bibliography

A. BOOKS, ARTICLES, OFFICIAL DOCUMENTS

Adamowicz, Aleś, and Danił Granin. 1988. *Księga Blokady* [The Book of the Blockade]. Warsaw: Państwowy Instytut Wydawniczy. [Polish translation, 2d ed. from the Russian original *Blokadnaya Kniga*]

Aguirre, Benigno. 1983. "Evacuation as Population Mobility." *International Journal of Mass Emergencies and Disasters* 1(3):415–37.

Alexander, David. 1981. "Disaster in Southern Italy November 1980." *Geographical Magazine* 53(9):553–61.

————. 1984. "Housing Crisis after Natural Disaster. The Aftermath of the November 1980 Southern Italian Earthquake." *Geoforum* 15(4):489–516.

Ambraseys, N. N. 1966. "Seismic Environment. The Skopje Earthquake of July 1963." *Revue de l'Union Internationale de Secours* 5:1–20.

American Red Cross. 1938. *The Ohio-Mississippi Valley Flood Disaster of 1937. Report of Relief Operations*. Washington, D.C.

————. 1962a. *A Special Report on the Evacuation of the Texas Louisiana Gulf Coast in Advance of Hurricane Carla*. Washington, D.C.

————. 1962b. *Hurricane Carla: Report of the American National Red Cross*. Washington, D.C.

Amoroux, Henri. 1961. *La Vie des Français sous l'Occupation*. Paris: Librairie Arthème Fayard.

Anderson, William A. 1969. *Disaster and Organizational Change: A Study of the Long-Term Consequences in Anchorage of the 1964 Alaska Earthquake*. Columbus: Ohio State University, Disaster Research Center.

Appleman, Roy E. 1961. *United States Army in the Korean War. South To the Naktong, North to the Yalu*. Washington: Department of the Army, Office of the Chief of Military History.

Bähr, Jürgen. 1980. "Managua (Nicaragua)—zur Stadtentwicklung seit dem Erdbeben von 1972." *Die Erde* 111:1–19.

Baker, Earl J., John C. Brigham, J. Anthony Paredes, and Donald D. Smith. 1976. *The Social Impact of Hurricane Eloise on Panama City, Florida.* Technical Paper No. 1, Sea Grant Program, Immediate Response Project. Tallahassee: Florida State University.

Barnes, Kent, et al. 1979. *Human Responses by Impacted Populations to the Three Mile Island Nuclear Reactor Accident: An Initial Assessment.* New Brunswick, N.J.: Rutgers University, Department of Environmental Resources. [Unpublished paper].

Bartelski, Leslaw M. 1968. *Walczaca Warszawa* [Fighting Warsaw]. Warsaw: Książka i Wiedza.

Bartlett, Glen S., Peter S. Houts, Linda K. Byrnes, and Robert W. Miller. 1983. "The Near Disaster at Three Mile Island." *Mass Emergencies and Disasters* 1(1):19–42.

Bartoszewski, Władysław. 1959. "Wrzesień Warszawy 1939" [September 1939 in Warsaw], 99–114 in: *Warszawski Kalendarz Illustrowany 1959.* Warsaw: Państwowe Wydawnictwo Naukowe.

Bates, F. L., C. W. Fogelman, V. J. Parenton, R. H. Pittman, and G. S. Tracy. 1963. *The Social and Psychological Consequences of a Natural Disaster: A Longitudinal Study of Hurricane Audrey.* Disaster Study Number 18, Publication 1081. Washington: National Academy of Sciences/National Research Council.

Bates, F. L., W. T. Farrell, and J. K. Glittenberg. 1977. *A Longitudinal and Cross Cultural Study of the Post Impact Phases of a Major National Disaster (The February 1976 Guatemalan Earthquake).* Athens: University of Georgia. [Unsolicited research proposal to the National Science Foundation]

Bayerisches Statistisches Amt. 1947. "Bevölkerung," 20–23 in: *Statistisches Jahrbuch für Bayern 1947.* München: Bayerisches Statistisches Amt.

Beczkowicz, Zygmunt. 1972. "Samopomoc Społeczeństwa Warszawy we Wrześniu 1939" [Self-Help Organization in Warsaw, September 1939], 287–99 in: Skaradziński, Bohdan, and Zdzisław Szpakowski, eds., *Wrzesień 1939: Z Problemów Najnowszej Historii.* Warsaw: Biblioteka Więzi.

Belcher, John C., and Frederick L. Bates. 1983. "Aftermath of Natural Disasters: Coping through Residential Mobility." *Disasters* 7(2):118–28.

Berenstein, T., and A. Rutkowski. 1958. "Liczba Ludności Żydowskiej i Obszar Przez Nią Zamieszkiwany w Warszawie w Latach Okupacji Hitlerowskiej" [Size of Jewish Population and Area of Its Residence in Warsaw during the Hitlerite Occupation]. *Biuletyn, Żydowski Instytut Historyczny,* no. 26: 73–114.

"Bericht des vom Senat des Freien und Hansestadt Hamburg berufenes Sachverständigenausschusses zur Untersuchung des Ablaufs der Flutkatastrophe. Hamburg, 5.6.1962 (1962)." *Mitteilung des Senats an die Bürgerschaft*, no. 198. Hamburg.

Bernert, Eleanor H., and Fred C. Iklé. 1952. "Evacuation and Cohesion of Urban Groups." *American Journal of Sociology* 58:133–38.

Biddell, A. J. Drexel. 1976. *Poland and the Coming of the Second World War. The Diplomatic Papers of A.J. Drexel Biddell, Jr., United States Ambassador to Poland 1937–1939*. Columbus: Ohio University Press.

Blašković, V. 1967. *Ekonomska Geografija Jugoslavije*, 2d ed. Zagreb: Informator.

Bonacina, Giorgio. 1970. *Obiettivo: Italia. I Bombardamenti Aerei delle Città Italiane dal 1940 al 1945*. Milano: U. Mursia.

Booth, Edmund. 1985. "The Chile Earthquake of March 1985." *Disasters* 9(3):190–96.

Bowden, M. J. 1982. "Geographical Changes in Cities Following Disaster," 114–26 in: Baker, A. R. H., and M. Billings, eds., *Period & Place: Research in Historical Geography*. Cambridge: Cambridge University Press.

Bowonder, B., Jeanne X. Kasperson, and Roger E. Kasperson. 1985. "Avoiding Future Bhopals." *Environment* 27(7):31–37.

Boyd, William. 1944. *Evacuation in Scotland: A Record of Events and Experiments*. Bickley, Kent: University of London Press.

Brookfield, Harold C. 1984. Personal Communication. July 17.

Brunn, Stanley, D., James H. Johnson, Jr., and Donald J. Ziegler. 1979. *Final Report on a Social Survey of Three Mile Island Area Residents*. East Lansing: Michigan State University, Department of Geography. [Unpublished paper]

Burton, Ian, Robert W. Kates, and Gilbert F. White. 1978. *The Environment as Hazard*. New York: Oxford University Press.

Burton, Ian, et al. 1981. *The Mississauga Evacuation. Final Report to the Ontario Ministry of the Solicitor General*. Toronto: University of Toronto, Institute for Environmental Studies.

Byrnes, Kevin Francis. 1977. *The Migratory Response to a Natural Earthquake: the 1972 Managuan Earthquake*. Master's thesis, Michigan State University, Department of Geography, East Lansing.

Calder, Angus. 1969. *The People's War: Britain—1939–1945*. New York: Pantheon.

Canada, Department of Resources and Development. 1953. *Report on Investigations into Measures for the Reduction of the Flood Hazards in the Greater Winnipeg Area*. Ottawa: Department of Resources and Development, Water Resources Division.

Canadian Red Cross Society. 1980. *Report on the Emergency Evacuation of the City of Mississauga, Ontario, Sunday, November 11 to Sunday, November 18, 1979.* Toronto: Ontario's Emergency Services, The Canadian Red Cross Society, Ontario Division.

Canadian Red Cross Society, Manitoba Division. 1950. *"Call 320," A Documentary Record of the 1950 Flood and Red Cross Activities in the Disaster.* Winnipeg: Hignell.

Carter, T. Michael, Stephanie Kendall, and John P. Clark. 1983. "Household Response to Warnings." *Mass Emergencies and Disasters* 1(1):95–104.

Carton de Wiart, Adrian. 1950. *Happy Odyssey.* London: Cape.

Carydis, Panayotis, G., et al. 1982. *The Central Greece Earthquake February–March 1981: A Reconnaissance and Engineering Report.* Washington: National Academy Press.

Chamberlain, E. R., L. Doube, G. Milne, M. Rolls, and J. S. Western. 1981. *The Experience of Cyclone Tracy.* Canberra: Australian Government Publishing Service.

Chapman, Murray. 1987. "Population Movement Studied at Microscale: Experience and Extrapolation." *Geoforum* 15:347–65.

Chen Yong, Kun-Ling Tsoi, Chen Feibi, Gao Zhenhuan, Zou Qija, and Chen Zhangli. 1988. *The Great Tangshan Earthquake of 1976: An Anatomy of Disaster.* Oxford:Pergamon.

Chenault, William W., Gary D. Hilbert, and Seth D. Reichlin. 1979. *Evacuation Planning the TMI Accident.* McLean, Va.: Human Sciences Research.

Ciborowski, Adolf. 1967. "Some Aspects of Town Reconstruction (Warsaw and Skopje)." *Impact* 17(11):31–48.

———. 1982. *Physical Development Planning for Human Settlements in Disaster-Prone Areas; Report Prepared for the United Nations Center for Human Settlements.* Warsaw: Warsaw Technical University, Department of Architecture.

———. 1983. Personal Communication August 10.

Cieplewicz, Mieczysław, ed. 1969. *Obrona Warszawy w 1939 r.-Wybór Dokumentów Wojskowych* [Defense of Warsaw in 1939: Selection of Military Documents]. Warsaw: Wojskowy Instytut Historyczny.

Clark, Reginald Harold. 1950. *Notes on Red River Floods, with Particular Reference to the Flood of 1950.* Winnipeg: Manitoba Department of Mines and Natural Resources.

Clarke, John I. et al., eds. 1989. *Population and Disaster.* Oxford: Blackwell.

Cornell, James. 1976. *The Great International Disaster Book.* New York: Scribner's.

Cruz Roja Nicaraguense. 1973. *Memorias de la Emergencia de Managua con*

Motivo del Terremoto del 23 de Diciembre de 1972. Managua: Cruz Roja Nicaraguense.

Cutter, Susan, and Kent Barnes. 1982a. "Evacuation Behavior and Three Mile Island." *International Journal of Disaster Studies* 6(2):116–24.

———. 1982b. *Three Mile Island: Risk Assessment and Coping Responses of Local Residents: A Summary Report.* Rutgers Geography Discussion Paper No. 20. New Brunswick, N.J.: Rutgers University.

Dacy, Douglas, C., and Howard M. Kunreuther. 1969. *The Economics of Natural Disasters: Implications for Federal Policy.* New York: Free Press.

Daniels, Gordon. 1975. "The Great Tokyo Air Raid, 9–10 March 1945," 113–31 in: Beasley, W. G., ed., *Modern Japan: Aspects of History, Literature and Society.* Berkeley and Los Angeles: University of California Press.

Davies, Norman. 1977. *Poland, Past and Present: A Selected Bibliography of Works in English.* Newtonville, Mass.: Oriental Research Partners.

Davis, Ian. 1975. "Skopje Rebuilt: Reconstruction Following the 1963 Earthquake." *Architectural Design* (Nov.):660–63.

———. 1977. "Emergency Shelter." *Disasters* 1:23–40.

Davis, I. R. 1973. *Managua December 23rd, 1972: The Provision of Shelter in the Aftermath of Natural Disasters: Report on Housing Strategy, December 1972–September 1973.* London: University College London, School of Environmental Studies.

"Dokumentarischer Bericht über die totale Evakuierung der ostfranzöischen Departements am 2. September 1939 (1956–57). *Ziviler Luftschutz* 20:316–37; 21:47–48, 72.

Donnermeyer, Joseph F. 1975. *Forced Migration: A Bibliography on the Sociology of Population Displacement and Resettlement.* Exchange Bibliography No. 880. Monticello, Ill.: Council of Planning Librarians.

Drabek, Thomas E. 1986a. "Social Problems in Disaster: Family Evacuation." *Social Problems* 16:336–49.

———. 1986b. *Human System Responses to Disaster: An Inventory of Sociological Findings.* New York: Springer-Verlag.

Drabek, Thomas E., Harriet L. Tamminga, Thomas S. Kilijanek, and Christopher R. Adams. 1981. *Managing Multiorganizational Emergency Responses: Emergent Search and Rescue Networks in Natural Disaster and Remote Area Settings.* Program on Technology, Environment and Man, Monograph #33. Boulder, Colo.: University of Colorado, Institute of Behavioral Science.

Drozdowski, Marian Marek. 1975. *Alarm dla Warszawy: Ludność Cywilna w Obronie Stolicy we Wrześniu 1939* [Alarm for Warsaw: Civilian Population in the Defense of the Capital in September 1939], 3d ed. Warsaw: Wiedza Powszechna.

————. 1976. *Stefan Starzyński Prezydent Warszawy* [Stefan Starzyński, Mayor of Warsaw]. Warsaw: Państwowy Instytut Wydawniczy.

————. 1989. Personal Communication June 2.

Drozdowski, Marian Marek, and Andrzej Zahorski. 1975. *Historia Warszawy* [History of Warsaw], 2d ed. Warsaw: Państwowe Wydawnictwo Naukowe.

Duclos, P., L. Sanderson, F. E. Thompson, B. Brackin, and S. Binder. 1987. "Community Evacuation Following a Chlorine Release, Mississippi." *Disasters* 11(4):286–89.

Dynes, Russell R., et al. 1979. *Report of the Emergency Preparedness and Response Task Force*. The President's Commission on the Accident at Three Mile Island. Washington: GPO.

Eichenbaum, Jack. 1970. "Some Anomalous Views of Migration." Paper presented at Annual Meeting of Association of American Geographers, San Francisco.

Emergency Planning Canada. 1979. *Report on Mississauga Train Derailment and Evacuation*. Toronto.

Erickson, John. 1975. *The Road to Stalingrad: Stalin's War with Germany*. *Volume 1*. New York: Harper and Row.

Eustace, W. S. 1977. "Hurricane Hattie." *Belizean Studies* 5(5):7–18.

"Die Evakuierten in Schleswig-Holstein." 1956. *Statistische Monatshefte Schleswig-Holstein* 8:54–56.

Fautrière, Jean. 1955. "La Dispersion et l'Évacuation de la Population Civile. Bases Topographiques et Démographiques." *Revue International de la Croix-Rouge* 32:169–83.

Federal Republic of Germany (FRG), Bundesministerium für Vertriebene, Flüchtlinge und Kriegsgeschädigte. 1956. *Die Betreuung der Vertriebene, Flüchtlinge, Zugewanderten, Evakuierten, Kriegssachgeschädigten, Heimkehrere, Kriegsgefangenen, Heimatlosen Ausländer, Ausländischen politischen Flüchtlinge, Rückgeführten Personen, Auswanderer*. Bonn.

————. 1958–64. *Dokumente deutscher Kriegschäden*, 5 vols. Bonn.

Fineman, Mark. 1984. "Indian City Falls Prey to Its Fears." *Philadelphia Inquirer*, Dec. 15:1A, 2A.

Fischer, Lorenz. 1952. "Die Rückkehrwilligkeit Evakuierter und ihre statistische Erfassung. Methodenkritische Bemerkungen zu der Zählung von 1951." *Allgemeines Statistisches Archiv* 36:256–62.

Fisher, Jack. 1964. "The Reconstruction of Skopje." *Journal of American Institute of Planners* 30:46–48.

Fitz Gibbon, Constantine. 1957. *The Blitz*. London: Allan Wingate.

Fitzpatrick, S. 1985. "Postwar Soviet Society: The return to 'Normalcy,'

1945–1953," 129–56 in: Linz, Susan J., ed., *The Impact of World War II on the Soviet Union.* Totowa, N.J.: Rowman and Allanheld.

Flynn, Cynthia Bullock. 1979. *Three Mile Island Telephone Survey: Preliminary Report on Procedures and Findings.* NUREG/CR-1093. Tempe, Ariz.: Mountain West Research, Inc.

———. 1982. "Reactions of Local Residents to the Accident at Three Mile Island," 49–61 in: Sills, David L., C. P. Wolf, and Vivien B. Shelanski, eds., *Accident at Three Mile Island: The Human Dimensions.* Boulder, Colo.: Westview Press.

Flynn, C. B., and J. A. Chalmers. 1980. *The Social and Economic Effects of the Accident at Three Mile Island: Findings to Date.* NUREG-CR-1215. Washington: National Research Council.

Fogarty, M. P. 1945. *Prospects of the Industrial Areas of Great Britain.* London: Methuen

Fokin, N. A., et al., eds. 1961. *Istoria Velikoy Otechestviennoy Voyny Sovetskogo Soyuza 1941–1945* [History of the Great Patriotic War of the Soviet Union, 1941–1945], vol. 2. Moscow: Voyennoye Izdatelstvo.

Forrest, Thomas R. 1965. *Hurricane Betsy, 1965: A Selective Analysis of Organizational Response in the New Orleans Area.* Historical and Comparative Disaster Series, no. 5. Columbus: Ohio State University, Disaster Research Center.

Foucher, Michel. 1982. "Esquisse d'une Géographie Humaine des Risques Naturels." *Hérodote*, no. 24:40–67.

Fournier d'Albe, E. M., and Stavros Agnanostopoulos. n.d. *The Events of July 1978 in Thessaloniki, Greece.* Geneva: United Nations Disaster Relief Organization.

Fricke, Werner. 1976. *Bevölkerung und Raum eines Ballungsgebietes seit der Industrialisierung. Eine geographische Analyse des Modellgebietes Rhein-Neckar.* Hannover: Hermann Schroedel Verlag.

Fritz, Charles E., and J. H. Mathewson. 1957. *Convergence Behavior in Disasters: A Problem in Social Control.* Disaster Study Number 9 (NAS/NRC Publ. 476). Washington: National Academy of Sciences—National Research Council.

Fuller, Clark W. 1975. *People and Hurricanes: A Study of Attitudes in Belize.* Master's thesis, Ohio University, Athens.

Gamble, H. B., and R. H. Downing. 1981. *Effects of the Accident at Three Mile Island on Residential Values and Sales.* University Park: Pennsylvania State University, Institute for Research on Land and Water Resources.

Geipel, Robert. 1982. *Disaster and Reconstruction: The Friuli (Italy) Earthquakes of 1976.* London: George Allen & Unwin.

324   Bibliography

Gentileschi, Maria Luisa. 1983. Personal Communication July 4.

Gerber, Eugène. 1941. *Die französische Flüchtlingstragödie*. Berlin: Deutsche Informationsstelle.

Germany. Nationalsozialistische Deutsche Arbeiterpartei (NSDAP), Reichsleitung, Hauptamt für Volkswohlfahrt. 1943. *"Erweiterte Kinderlandverschickung" und Umquartierung aus Luftschutzgründen und wegen Fliegerschäden*. Rundschreiben Nr. 123/43. Berlin, and subsequent reports 1944–45. [Manuscript in Bundesarchiv, Koblenz NS 37/1010]

Germany. Statistisches Reichsamt. 1942. "Fläche und Bevölkerung der grösseren Verwaltungsbezirke 1939 und 1943." *Statistisches Jahrbuch für das Deutsche Reich 1941/42*. Berlin.

Gerrare, Wirt (William Oliver Grener). 1903. *The Story of Moscow*. London: J. M. Dent & Co.

Gilbert, Martin. 1982. *Atlas of the Holocaust*. London: Michael Joseph.

Gilmore, Brigadier I. G. C. 1980. "Evacuate or Stay Put?" 189–200 in: Oliver, John, ed., *Response to Disaster*. James Cook University of North Queensland.

Ginesy, Robert. 1948. *La Seconde Guerre Mondiale et les Déplacements de Populations: Les Organismes de Protection*. Paris: A. Pedone.

Goldhaber, Marilyn K., and James E. Lehman. 1982. "Crisis Evacuation during Three Mile Island Nuclear Accident: The TMI Population Registry." Paper presented at the Annual Meeting of the American Public Health Association, Montreal.

Goldhaber, Marilyn K., Peter S. Houts, and Renee DiSabella. 1983. "Moving After the Crisis: A Prospective Study of Three Mile Island Area Population Mobility." *Environment and Behavior* 15(1):93–120.

Gore, Rick. 1984. "A Prayer for Pozzuoli." *National Geographic* 165:615–25.

Gould, Peter R. 1988. "Tracing Chernobyl's Fallout." *Earth and Mineral Sciences* [Pennsylvania State University] 57(4):57–65.

Gouré, Leon. 1962. *The Siege of Leningrad*. Stanford: Stanford University Press.

Grange, Samuel G. M. 1981. *Report on the Mississauga Railway Accident Inquiry, Conducted by the Honorable Mr. Justice Samuel G. M. Grange*. Ottawa: Ministry of Supply and Services.

Grazia, Alfred de. 1985. *A Cloud over Bhopal: Causes, Consequences and Constructive Solutions*. Bombay: Kalos Foundation.

Great Britain, Home Department. 1938. *Report of Committee on Evacuation*. London.

Gregg, A. R. 1968. *British Honduras*. London: H. M. Stationery Office.

Guadeloupe, Information Service. 1977. *Volcan de la Soufrière en Guadeloupe: Les Événements de 1976*. N.p.

Guadeloupe, Prefecture. 1977. *Volcan de la Soufrière*. N.p. [mimeographed]

Guillain, Robert. 1947. *Le Peuple Japonais et la Guerre: Choses Vues 1939–1946*. Paris: René Julliard.

Haas, J. Eugene, Harold C. Cochrane, and Donald G. Eddy. 1974. *The Consequences of Large-Scale Evacuation Following Disaster: The Darwin, Australia Cyclone Disaster of December 25, 1974*. Working Paper 27. Boulder: University of Colorado, Institute of Behavioral Sciences.

"Die Hamburger Evakuierten." 1947. *Hamburg in Zahlen*. No. 8 (October).

Hamman, Henry, and Stuart Parrott. 1987. *Mayday at Chernobyl: One Year On, the Facts Revealed*. London: Hodder and Stoughton Paperbacks.

Hampe, Eric. 1963. *Die zivile Luftschutz in Zweiten Weltkrieg*. Frankfurt an Main: Bernard & Graefe-Verlag für Wehrwesen.

Hans, Joseph M., Jr., and Thomas C. Sell. 1974. *Evacuation Risks—An Evaluation*. Las Vegas, Nev.: U.S. Environmental Protection Agency, Office of Radiation Programs.

Hanson, Joanna K. M. 1978. *The Civilian Population and the Warsaw Uprising of 1944*. Cambridge: Cambridge University Press.

Havens, Thomas R. H. 1978. *Valley of Darkness: The Japanese People and World War Two*. New York: W.W. Norton.

Havey, M. C., et al. 1980. *Derailment: The Mississauga Miracle*. Toronto: Queens Printer for Ontario.

Heer, David M. 1965. *After Nuclear Attack: A Demographic Inquiry*. New York: Praeger.

———. 1978. "Effects of Warfare on Demographic Variables," 475–82 in: *International Population Conference, Mexico 1977: Proceedings*. Liège: International Union for the Scientific Study of Population.

Hewitt, Kenneth. n.d. *Air War and the Destruction of Urban Places*. Research Paper Series No. 8244. Waterloo, Ont.: Wilfred Laurier University, Department of Geography.

———. 1983a. "Place Annihilation: Area Bombing and the Fate of Urban Places." *Annals of the Association of American Geographers* 73:257–84.

———. 1983b. "Seismic Risk and Mountain Environments: The Role of Surface Conditions in Earthquake Disaster." *Mountain Research and Development* 3(1):27–44.

———. 1987. "The Social Space of Terror: Towards a Civil Interpretation of Total War." *Environment and Planning D: Society and Space* 5:445–74.

Hire, Jean De la. 1940. *Le Crime des Evacuations: Les Horreurs Que Nous Avons Vues*. Paris: Tallandier.

Hirose, Hirotada. 1979. "Volcanic Eruption and Local Politics in Japan: A Case Study." *Mass Emergencies* 4:53–62.

Hu, The-wei, and Kenneth S. Slaysman. 1981. *Health-Related Economic Costs of the Three Mile Island Accident.* University Park: Pennsylvania State University, Institute for Policy Research and Evaluation.

Huff, M., and H. B. Carroll. 1962. "Hurricane Carla at Galveston." *Southwestern Historical Quarterly* 65:293–309.

Hugo, Graeme J. 1984. "The Demographic Impact of Famine: A Review," 7–31 in: Currey, B., and G. Hugo, *Famine as a Geographical Phenomenon.* Dordrecht: D. Reidel.

Hultåker. (n.d.) *Evakuera.* Disaster Studies 2. Uppsala, Sweden: Uppsala University, Department of Sociology.

Iklé, Fred Charles. 1950a. *The Impact of War upon the Spacing of Urban Population.* Ph.D. dissertation, University of Chicago.

———. 1950b. "Reconstruction and Population Densities of War Damaged Cities." *Journal of American Institute of Planners* 16:131–39.

———. 1951. "The Effects of War Destruction upon the Ecology of Cities." *Social Forces* 29:383–91.

———. 1958. *The Social Impact of Bomb Destruction.* Norman: University of Oklahoma Press.

Iklé, Fred Charles, and Harry V. Kincaid. 1956. *Social Aspects of Wartime Evacuation of American Cities with Particular Emphasis on Long-Term Housing and Re-Employment.* Disaster Study No. 4. Washington: National Academy of Sciences and National Research Council.

Instytut Historii Polskiej Akademii Nauk. 1964. *Cywilna Obrona Warszawy we Wrześniu 1939 r.* [Civil Defense of Warsaw in September 1939]. Warsaw: Państwowe Wydawnictwo Naukowe.

International Committee of the Red Cross. 1974. *ICRC Action in Cyprus.* Geneva.

International Labour Office. 1957. *International Migration 1945–1957.* Geneva.

Isaacs, Susan, ed. 1941. *The Cambridge Evacuation Survey: A Wartime Study in Social Welfare and Education.* London: Methuen.

Janis, Irving L. 1951. *Air War and Emotional Stress: Psychological Studies of Bombing and Civilian Defense.* New York: McGraw-Hill.

Jaruzelski, Jerzy. 1982. "Pierwsze Dni Września (z Raportu Ambasadora USA w Warszawie)" [First Days of September Based on the Report of U.S. Ambassador to Warsaw]. *Kronika Warszawy* No. 2/50:25–44.

Johnson, James H., Jr. 1985. "A Model of Evacuation Decision-Making in a Nuclear Reactor Emergency." *Geographical Review* 75:405–18.

Johnson, James J., Jr., and Donald J. Ziegler. 1983. "Distinguishing Human

Responses to Radiological Emergencies." *Economic Geography* 59:386–402.

Jones, Barclay G., and Miha Tomaževič, eds. 1982. *Social and Economic Aspects of Earthquakes: Proceedings of the Third International Conference: The Social and Economic Aspects of Earthquakes and Planning to Mitigate Their Impacts Held at Bled, Yugoslavia, June 29–July 2, 1981.* Ithaca, N.Y.: Cornell University, Program in Urban and Regional Studies.

Jones, E. L. 1981. *The European Miracle: Environments, Economies, and Geopolitics in the History of Europe and Asia.* Cambridge: Cambridge University Press.

Joseph, Dov. 1960. *The Faithful City: The Siege of Jerusalem, 1948.* New York: Simon and Schuster.

Julka, B. (n.d.) *Bhopal Gas Tragedy* (A Report). N.p. [mimeographed]

Kaiser, W. (n.d.) "Die Evakuierten in Landesbezirk Baden," 39–43 in: *Die Flüchtlinge und Evakuierten im Landesbezirk Baden.* Karlsruhe: Badisches Statistisches Bundesamt.

Kalbog, Chaitanya. 1984. "Troops Patrol Bhopal after 150,000 Flee." *Washington Post*, Dec. 15:1.

Kamalov, Kh. Kh., et al. 1966. *900 Gieroicheskikh Dniei* [900 Heroic Days]. Moscow and Leningrad: Nauka.

Kamaluddin, A. F. M. 1985. "Refugee Problems in Bangladesh," 221–36 in: Kosiński, Leszek A., and K. Maudood Elahi, eds., *Population Redistribution and Development in South Asia.* Dordrecht: D. Reidel.

Kamm, Henry. 1983. "Along the Bay of Naples, Tremors Get To Be a Habit." New York *Times*, Sept. 8:I, 2–3.

Karakos, A., I. Papdimitriou, and S. Pavlides. 1983. "An Preliminary Investigation of Socio-Economic Problems Following the 1978 Thessaloniki (Greece) Earthquake. *Disasters* 7(3):210–14.

Karasev, A. V. 1951. "Leningrad v Period Blokady (1941–1943 gg)" [Leningrad during the Siege Period, 1941–1943]. *Istoria SSSR* 2:3–32.

———. 1959. *Leningradtsy v Gody Blokady* [People of Leningrad in the Years of the Siege]. Moscow: Izdatelstvo Akademii Nauk.

Kates, Robert W., J. Eugene Haas, Daniel J. Amaral, Robert A. Olson, Reyes Ramos, and Richard Olson. 1973. "Human Impact of the Managua Earthquake." *Science* 182:981–90.

Katz, Arthur M. 1982. *Life After Nuclear War: The Economic and Social Impacts of Nuclear Attacks on the United States.* Cambridge, Mass.: Ballinger.

Kawabe, Hiroshi. 1982. "General Remarks on the History of Urban Population in Japan," in: Kohno, Yoshikatsu, ed., *The General Issues on the City and the Autonomy.* Tokyo: Research Committee for Tokyo City Government. [in Japanese]

Keegan, John, ed. 1989. *The Times Atlas of the Second World War.* New York: Harper & Row.

Kennedy, Will C. 1982. *Organizational Activity and the Military in Disaster Operations in Chile in a 1965 Earthquake: A Historical Case Study.* Preliminary Paper 80. Columbus: Ohio State University, Disaster Research Center.

Kersten, Krystyna. 1974. *Repatriacja Ludności Polskiej po II Wojnie Światowej* [Repatriation of Polish Population after World War II]. Wrocław: Ossolineum.

Killian, Lewis M. 1954. *Evacuation of Panama City Before "Hurricane Florence."* Washington: National Academy of Science, Committee on Disaster Studies.

Klemin, A. S., ed. 1981. *Eshelon za Eshelonom* [Transports Following Transports]. Moscow: Voyennoye Izdatelstvo Ministerstva Oborony.

Koch-Erpach, R. 1951. "Zur Rückführung der Evakuierten." *Veröffentlichungen aus dem Institut für Raumforschung* 46/51:6–8.

Korboński, Stefan. 1978. *The Polish Underground State: A Guide to the Underground, 1939–1945.* East European Monograph Series No. XXXIX. New York: Columbia University Press.

Kornrumpf, Martin. 1951. "Das Problem der Rückführung der Evakuierung: Zur Erfassung der rückkehrwilligen evakuierten durch das Bundeswohnungsministerium." *Europäische Forschungs Gruppe, Mitteilungen,* no. 2:39–41.

Kovalchuk, V. M. 1975. *Leningrad i Bolshaia Zemlia: Istoria Ladozhskoi Komunikatsii Blokirovannogo Leningrada v 1941–1943 gg.* [Leningrad and the Greater World: History of Ladoga Communication from Blockaded Leningrad in 1941–1943]. Leningrad: Nauka.

Kramer, John M. 1986. "Chernobyl and Eastern Europe." *Problems of Communism* 36(6):40–58.

Krawchenko, Bohdan. 1985. *Social Change and National Consciousness in Twentieth-Century Ukraine.* St. Antony's Macmillan Series. London: Macmillan.

Kraybill, Donald B. 1979. *Three Mile Island: Local Residents Speak Out. A Public Opinion Poll.* Elizabeth, Pa.: Elizabethtown College, Social Research Center.

Kraybill, Donald B., Daniel Buckly, and Rick Zmuda. 1979. "Demographic and Attitudinal Characteristics of TMI Evacuees." Paper presented at Annual Meeting of the Pennsylvania Sociological Society, Philadelphia.

Kreps, G. A. 1984. "Sociological Inquiry and Disaster Research." *Annual Review of Sociology* 10:309–30.

Kuester, Inge, and Stewart Forsyth. 1985. "Rabaul Eruption Risk; Population Awareness and Preparedness Survey." *Disasters* 9(3):179–82.

Kulischer, Eugene M. 1943. *The Displacement of Population in Europe.* Montreal: International Labour Office.

———. 1948. *Europe on the Move: War and Population Changes, 1917–47.* New York: Columbia University Press.

Kumanev, G. A. 1963. *Sovetske Zheleznodorozhniki v Gody Velikoi Otechestvennoi Voyny* [Soviet Railwaymen During the Great Patriotic War]. Moscow: Izdatelstvo Akademii Nauk.

———. 1976. *Na Sluzhbe Fronta i Tyla: Zheleznodorozhnyi Transport Nakanunie i v Gody Velikoi Otechestvennoi Voyny 1938–1945* [In the Service of the Front and Rear: Railroad Transport Before and During the Great Patriotic War, 1938–1945]. Moscow: Nauka.

Kunreuther, Howard, and Elissandra S. Fiore. 1966. *The Alaska Earthquake: A Case Study in the Economics of Disaster.* Washington: Institute for Defense Analysis.

Kunz, E. F. 1973. "The Refugee in Flight: Kinetic Models and Forms of Displacement." *International Migration Review* 7(2):125–46.

Lagadec, Patrick. 1982. *Major Technological Risk: An Assessment of Industrial Disasters.* Oxford: Pergamon.

Lagrange, Maurice. 1977. "Le Rapatriement des Réfugiés après l'Exode (Juillet-Setembre 1940). *Revue d'Histoire de la Deuxième Guerre Mondiale,* no. 107:39–52.

Lamprecht, Heinz. 1949. *Die Bevölkerungsumschichtung in Nordrhein-Westfalen.* Dortmunder Schriften zur Sozialforschung. Dortmund.

Landau, L. 1962. *Kronika Lat Wojny i Okupacji, Tom I. Wrzesień 1939-Listopad 1940* [Chronicle of War and Occupation, vol. 1, September 1939–November 1940]. Warsaw: Państwowe Wydawnictwo Naukowe.

Larass, Claus. 1983. *Der Zug der Kinder. KLV-Die Evakuierung 5 millionen Deutscher Kinder im 2. Weltkrieg.* München: Meyster.

Laurens, André. 1980. "Populations Réfugiées et Déplacées en Arège de 1939 à 1945." *Revue d'Histoire de la Deuxième Guerre Mondiale,* no. 119:45–59.

Leaning, Jennifer, and Langley Keyes, eds. 1984. *The Counterfeit Ark: Crisis Relocation for Nuclear War.* Cambridge, Mass.: Ballinger.

Lee, Everett S. 1966. "A Theory of Migration." *Demography* 3:47–57.

Leeds, Arline, ed. 1983. *El Asnam, Algeria Earthquake October 10, 1980: A Reconnaissance and Engineering Report.* Washington: National Academy of Sciences, Committee on Natural Disasters.

Lehigh University, Institute of Research. 1953. *Impact of Air Attack in World War II: Selected Data for Civil Defense Planning, Division I: Physical*

Damage to Structures, Facilities, and Persons. Volume I: Summary of Civil Defense Experience. Bethlehem, Pa.

Leighton, Alexander H. 1949. *Human Relations in a Changing World: Observations on the Use of the Social Sciences*. New York: E. P. Dutton.

Leitch, Donald G. 1950. "Soviet Housing Administration and the War-time Evacuation." *American Slavic and East European Review* 9(3):180–90.

Leonard, Ralph. 1985. "Mass Evacuation Disasters." *Journal of Emergency Medicine* 2:279–85.

Lieberman, S. R. 1985. "Management in the USSR: The Wartime System of Administration and Control," 59–76 in: Linz, S. J., ed., *The Impact of World War II on the Soviet Union*. Totowa, N.J.: Rowman and Allanheld.

Lindell, Michael K., and Ronald W. Perry. 1982. "Protective Action Recommendations: How Would the Public Respond?" *Transactions of the American Nuclear Society* 41:423–24.

Linz, S. J., ed. 1985. *The Impact of World War II on the Soviet Union*. Totowa, N.J.: Rowman and Allanheld.

Lipowski, Adam. 1970. "Procesy Demograficzne w Warszawie w Latach 1945–1949" [Demographic Processes in Warsaw, 1945–1949]. *Warszawa Stolica Polski Ludowej*, Studia Warszawskie 5(1):317–40.

Liverman, Diana M., and John P. Wilson. 1981. "The Mississauga Train Derailment and Evacuation, 10–16 November, 1979." *Canadian Geographer* 25:365–75.

Lorimer, Frank. 1946. *The Population of the Soviet Union: History and Prospects*. Geneva: League of Nations.

Lowrie, Donald A. 1963. *The Hunted Children*. New York: W.W. Norton.

Madajczyk, Czesław, ed. 1974. *Ludność Cywilna w Powstaniu Warszawskim* [Civilian Population in the Warsaw Uprising]. 3 vols. Warsaw: Państwowy Instytut Wydawniczy.

Maier, Laus A., et al., eds. 1979. *Das Deutsche Reich und der Zweite Weltkrieg*, vol. 2. Stuttgart: Deutsche Verlags-Anstalt.

Malecki, H. J. 1947. "Das Flüchtlingsproblem in Niedersachsen," *Neues Archiv für Landes und Volkskunde von Niedersachsen*, no. 1:45–80.

Mallin, Jay. 1974. *The Great Managua Earthquake*. Charlotteville, N.Y.: SamHar Press.

Manitoba Emergency Planning Committee. 1950. *Blackboy Emergency Plan, First Draft, May 13, 1950*. Winnipeg.

Marples, David W. 1986a. *Chernobyl and Nuclear Power in the USSR*. Edmonton: Canadian Institute for Ukrainian Studies.

———. 1986b. "Chernobyl and Ukraine." *Problems of Communism* 35(6):17–27.

Marshall, Richard D. 1976. *Engineering Aspects of Cyclone Tracy, Darwin, Australia 1974.* NBS Building Science Series 86. Washington: National Bureau of Standards.

McLuckie, Benjamin F. 1970. *A Study of Functional Response to Stress in Three Societies.* Ph.D. dissertation, Ohio State University, Columbus.

————. 1977. *Italy, Japan and the United States: Effects of Centralization on Disaster Responses 1964–1969.* Historical and Comparative Disaster Series. Columbus: Ohio State University, Disaster Research Center.

Metaxa, A., Th. Mpalli, M. Triantaphylou, and V. Kaleura. 1979. "Psychological Observations on the Population of Thessaloniki after the Earthquake of 20th June 1978." *Neurologia and Psychiatria* 2(1–4):4–16. [in Greek]

Meyer, A. 1958. "L'Exode: Mai–Juin 40." *Revue d'Histoire de la Deuxième Guerre Mondiale*, no. 31:85–87.

Meynen, Emil, ed. 1958. "Bevölkerungsentwicklung der Grossstädte Deutschlands von 1820–1956." *Geographisches Taschenbuch 1958–59.* Wiesbaden: Franz Steiner Verlag.

Meynier, André. 1950. *Les Déplacements de la Population vers la Bretagne en 1939–1940.* Travaux du Laboratoire de Géographie de l'Université de Rennes no. 14. Rennes: Les Nourittures Terrestres.

Mirowski, Włodzimierz 1968. *Migracje do Warszawy* [Migration to Warsaw]. Wrocław: Zkład Narodowy im Ossolińskich.

Misiunas, J. Romuald, and Rein Taagepera. 1983. *The Baltic States, Years of Independence, 1940–1980.* Berkeley and Los Angeles: University of California Press.

Misztal, S. 1984. Trzęsienie Zierni w Rejonie El Asnam (Algeria) w dniu 10.x.1980 r. [Earthquake in El Asnam Region (Algeria) on October 10, 1980]. Manuscript made available by the author.

Mitchell, James K. 1989. "Where Might the International Decade for Natural Disaster Reduction Concentrate Its Activities: A Comparative Analysis of Disaster Data Sets." Paper presented at the 85th Annual Meeting of the Association of American Geographers, Baltimore, March 19–22.

Moore, Harry Estill, Frederick L. Bates, Marvin V. Lyman, and Vernon J. Parenton. 1963. *Before the Wind: A Study of the Response to Hurricane Carla.* NAS-NRC Publ. 1095, Disaster Study Number 19. Washington: National Academy of Sciences and National Research Council.

Morehouse, Ward, and M. Srun Subramaniam. 1986. *The Bhopal Tragedy.* New York: Council on International and Public Affairs.

Müller-Miny, Heinrich. 1959. "Katastrophe und Landschaft: Ein Beitrag zur Kulturlandschaftsforschung am Beispiel griechischer und deutscher Landschaft." *Berichte zur Deutschen Landeskunde* 23:95–124.

Multilingual Demographic Dictionary. 1982. 2d ed. Liège: Ordina.

Myers, P. F., and A. A. Campbell. 1954. *The Population of Yugoslavia.* International Populations Statistics Reports, Series P-90, No. 5. Washington: U.S. Bureau of the Census.

NAS/NRC Committee on Disaster Studies. 1955. *Studies in Holland Flood Disaster 1953,* 4 vols. Washington: National Academy of Sciences and National Research Council.

National Research Council, Committee on the Alaska Earthquake. 1970. *The Great Alaska Earthquake of 1964: Human Ecology.* Washington: National Academy of Sciences.

Neigoldberg, V. Ya. 1965. *Rechnoi Transport v. Gody Velikoi Otechestvennoi Voyny* [River Transport in the Years of the Great Patriotic War]. Moscow: Transport.

New York Public Library, The Research Libraries, Reference Department. 1977. *Subject Catalog of the World War II Collection,* 3 vols. Boston: G. K. Hall.

Nisbet, Robert. 1969. *Social Change and History.* Oxford: Oxford University Press.

Ogasawara, Yoshikatsu. 1947, 1948. "A Study Concerning Population Migration around the Time of the End of WWII." *Journal of Social Geography* No. 1 and No. 4. [in Japanese]

Okazaki, Ayanori. 1949. *Effects of the Late War upon the Population of Japan.* Tokyo: Research Institute of Population Problems.

Ollier, Nicole. 1970. *L'Exode sur les Routes de l'An 40.* Paris: Éditions Robert Laffont.

Osorio, Ivan. 1976. "Managua Rebuilds a City from Earthquake Ruins." *Geographical Magazine* 48:460–64.

Padley, Richard, and Margaret Cole, eds. 1940. *Evacuation Survey: A Report to the Fabian Society.* London: George Routledge & Sons.

Palacio, Joseph O. 1982. "Post-Hurricane Resettlement in Belize," 121–35 in: Hansen, Art, and Anthony Oliver Smith, eds., *Involuntary Migration and Resettlement: The Problems and Responses of Dislocated People.* Boulder, Colo.: Westview Press.

Perry, Ronald W. 1979. "Evacuation Decision-Making in Natural Disasters." *Mass Emergencies* 4:25–38.

―――. 1981. *Citizen Evacuation in Response to Nuclear and Nonnuclear Threats.* Final Report from F.E.M.A. under Contract No. EMCO-C-0296. Seattle: Battelle Human Affairs Research Center.

―――. 1983. "Population Evacuation in Volcanic Eruptions, Floods and Nuclear Power Plant Accidents: Some Elementary Considerations." *Journal of Community Psychology* 11:36–47.

————. 1985. *Comprehensive Emergency Management: Evacuating Threatened Populations*. Greenwich, Conn.: JAI Press.

Perry, Ronald W., Michael K. Kindell, and Marjorie R. Greene. 1981. *Evacuation Planning in Emergency Management*. Lexington, Mass.: Lexington Books.

Perry, Ronald W., and Alvin H. Mushkatel. 1984. *Disaster Management: Warning Response and Community Relocation*. Westport, Conn.: Quorum Books.

————. 1986. *Minority Citizens in Disasters*. Athens: University of Georgia Press.

Petersen, William. 1975. *Population*. 3d ed. New York: Macmillan.

Polyakov, Yu. A., et al., eds. 1966. *Eshelony Idut na Vostok: Iz Istorii Perebazirovanya Proizvoditelnykh Sil SSSR v 1941–42 gg* [Transports Are Going East: From the History of Redistribution of Productive Forces of the USSR in 1941–42]. Moscow: Nauka.

Poniatowski, Zdzisław, and Ryszard Zelwiański. 1972. *Wojnę Przeżył co Czwarty* [Every Fourth Person Survived the War]. Warsaw: Iskry.

Popovski, Jovan. 1964. *Skopje 1963*. Zagreb: Ognjen Prica.

Porwit, Jarian. 1959. *Obrona Warszawy Wrzesień 1939* [Defense of Warsaw, September 1939]. Warsaw: Czytelnik.

Pospelov, P. N., ed. 1974. *Sovetski Tyl v Velikoy Otechestviennoy Voynie* [The Soviet Rear in the Great Patriotic War]. 2 vols. Moscow: Mysl.

Proudfoot, Malcom J. 1956. *European Refugees: 1939–52: A Study in Forced Population Movement*. Evanston, Ill.: Northwestern University Press.

Quarantelli, E. L. 1954. "The Nature and Conditions of Panic." *American Journal of Sociology* 60: 267–75.

————. 1960. "Images of Withdrawal Behavior in Disasters: Some Basic Misconceptions." *Social Problems* 8(1):68–79.

————. 1970. "A Selected Annotated Bibliography of Social Science Studies on Disasters." *American Behavioral Scientist* 13:452–56.

————. 1979. "Some Needed Cross-Cultural Studies of Emergency Time Disaster Behavior: A First Step." *Disasters* 3:307–14.

————. 1980. *Evacuation Behavior and Problems: Findings and Implications for the Research Literature*. Columbus, Ohio: Disaster Research Center.

Quarantelli, E. L., with David C. Hutchinson and Brenda D. Philips. 1983. *Evacuation Behavior: Case Study of the Taft, Louisiana Tank Explosion Incident*. Miscellaneous Report 34. Columbus: Ohio State University, Disaster Research Center.

Ramberg, Bennet. 1986–87. "Learning from Chernobyl." *Foreign Affairs* 65(2):304–28.

Rana, Bhola. 1984. "Bhopal Survivors Demand More Aid." Philadelphia *Inquirer*, Dec. 20:13A.

Rasky, Frank. 1961. *Great Canadian Disasters*. Toronto: Longmans Green.

Ratyńska, Barbara. 1982. *Ludność i Gospodarka Warszawy i Okręgu pod Okupacią Hitlerowską* [Population and Economy of the City and Region of Warsaw under Nazi Occupation]. Warsaw: Książka i Wiedza.

Rawski, Tadeusz, Zdzisław Stąpor, and Jan Zamojski. 1966. *Wojna Wyzwoleńcza Narodu Polskiego w Latach 1939–1945* [Liberation War of the Polish Nation, 1939–1945], 2d ed. Warsaw: Wojskowy Instytut Historyczny.

Reinhold, Robert. 1984. "More Gas Is Found at Plant in India." New York *Times*, Dec. 22:4.

Robertson, Sara, ed. 1986. "Chronology 1986—The Soviet Union and Eastern Europe." *Foreign Affairs* 65(3):667–68.

Roth, Robert. 1970. "Cross-Cultural Perspectives on Disaster Response." *American Behavioral Scientist* 13:440–51.

Routh, Stephen D. 1983. *An Examination of Non-Radiological Risks in Nuclear Reactor Accidents*. M.S. thesis, Pennsylvania State University, University Park.

"Zur Rückführung der Evakuierten." 1951. *Institut für Raumforschung Bonn, Informationen*, no. 51:6–8.

Rumpf, Hans. 1962. *The Bombing of Germany*. New York: Holt, Rinehart and Winston.

Sakowska, Ruta. 1975. *Ludzie z Dzielnicy Zamkniętej: Żydzi Warszawie w Okresie Hitlerowskiej Okupacji, Październik 1939–Marzec 1943* [People of the Closed District. Jews in Warsaw during the Nazi Occupation, October 1939–March 1943]. Warsaw: Państwowe Wydawnictwo Naukowe.

Salisbury, Harrison E. 1969. *The 900 Days: The Siege of Leningrad*. New York: Harper & Row.

Samsonov, A. M. 1958. *Velikaya Bitva pod Moskvoy 1941–42* [The Great Moscow Battle 1941–42]. Moscow: Akademia Nauk SSSR.

Sauvy, Alfred. 1978. *La Vie Économique de Français de 1939 à 1945*. Paris: Flammarion.

———. 1983. "Evacuation de Grand Villes en France en Cas d'Urgence." Personal Communication June 30.

Scanlon, Joseph. 1980. *The Peel Regional Police Force and the Mississauga Evacuation: How a Police Force Reacted to a Major Chemical Emergency*. N.p.: Canadian Police College.

———. 1983. "Review of The Mississauga Evacuation Final Report." *Mass Emergencies and Disasters* 1(2):345–51.

Schmidle, A. D. 1957. "Evakuierung in Vergangenheit und Zukunft." *Ziviler Luftschutz* 21:187–93.

Segbers, Klaus. 1987. *Die Sowjetunion im Zweiten Weltkrieg. Die Mobilisierung von Verwaltung, Wirtschaft und Gesellschaft im "Grossen Vaterländischen Krieg" 1941–1943*. Studien zur Zeitsgeschichte 24. Munich: R. Oldenbourg Verlag.

Senese, Donna M. 1988. "The Roles and Status of Women in World War II Germany." Paper presented at the Annual Meeting of the Association of American Geographers, Phoenix, Arizona.

Shabad, Theodore. 1986. "Geographic Aspects of the Chernobyl Nuclear Accident." *Soviet Geography* 27:504–26.

Shrestha, Nanda R. 1988. "A Structural Perspective on Labour Migration in Underdeveloped Countries." *Progress in Human Geography* 12:179–207.

Shtchegolev, J. M. 1959. "Uchastye Evakuirovannogo Naselenya v Kolkhoznom Proizvodstve Zapadnoy Sibiri v Gody Velikoi Otechestvennoy Voyny" [Participation of Evacuated Population in the Production of Kolkozes in Western Siberia during the Great Patriotic War]. *Istoria SSSR* 3(2):139–45.

Silver, Ray L. 1987. *Fallout from Chernobyl*. Toronto: Deneau.

Simon, Sacha. 1964. *Moscou*. Paris: Librairie Arthème Fayard.

Sloane, D. Louise, Janette M. Roseneder, and Marily J. Hernandex. 1974. *Winnipeg: A Centennial Bibliography*. Winnipeg: Armstrong Printers.

"Southern Italy's Earthquake." 1981. *UNDRO News*, March 1.

Stanford Research Institute. 1953. *Final report. Impact of Air Attack in World War II: Selected Data for Civil Defense Planning. Division III: Social Organization, Behavior, and Morale under Stress of Bombing. Volume 2: Organization and Adequacy of Civilian Defenses*. SRI Project 669. Stanford, Calif.

Stannard, Bruce. 1984. "Rabaul Trembles as Fears of Big Bang Grow." *The Bulletin* [Sydney], February 28:44–51.

Steinberg, Heinz Günter. 1978. *Bevölkerungsentwicklung des Ruhrgebietes im 19. und 20. Jahrhundert*. Düsseldorfer Geographische Schriften 11. Düsseldorf: Geographisches Institut der Universität Düsseldorf.

Stevens, William K. 1984. "Indians Flee City As Chemical Plant Plans to Restart." New York *Times*, Dec. 14:A1, A10.

Stratta, James L. 1981. *Earthquake in Campania-Basilicata, Italy, November 23, 1980*. Washington: National Academy Press.

Stretton, Alan B. 1975. *Darwin Disaster: Cyclone Tracy. Report by Director-General, Natural Disasters Organization of the Darwin Relief Operations, 25 December 1974–3 January 1975*. Canberra: Australian Government Publishing Service.

————. 1976. *The Furious Days: The Relief of Darwin*. Sydney: Collins.

————. 1979. "Ten Lessons from the Darwin Disaster," 503–07 in Heathcote, R. L., and B. S. Thom, eds., *Natural Hazards in Australia*. Canberra: Australian Academy of Science.

Strope, Walmer E., John F. Evaney, and Jiri Nehnevajsa. 1977. "Importance of Preparatory Measures in Disaster Evacuations." *Mass Emergencies* 2(1):1–17.

Strope, Walmer E., Clark D. Henderson, and Charles T. Rainey. 1977. *Draft Guidance for Crisis Relocation in Highly Urbanized Areas*. CPG-2-8-17. Washington: Defense Civil Preparedness Agency.

Strzelecki, Edward. 1972. "Uwagi i Wnioski na Temat Pierwszego Prowizorycznego Zestawienia Wyników Spisu 15. v. 1945 r. Szkic Dyskusyjny" [Comments and Conclusions re. First Provisional Compilation of Census Results, May 15, 1945. Discussion Draft]. *Warszawa Stolica Polski Ludowej, Studia Warszawskie II*.

Strzelecki, Zbigniew, ed. 1984. *Społeczno-ekonomiczne Problemy Migracji Ludności Warszawy i Pragi* [Socio-economic Problems of Migration in Warsaw and Prague]. Szkoła Główna Planowania i Statystyki, Monografie i Opracowania 135, Warsaw.

Strzembosz, Tomasz. 1983. *Akcje Zbrojne Podziemnej Warszawy 1939–1944* [Armed Actions of the Underground in Warsaw, 1939–1944]. Warsaw: Państwowy Instytut Wydawniczy.

Swenson, Bennett. 1937. "Floods in the United States January and February 1937." *Monthly Weather Review* 65:71–86.

Szarota, Tomasz. 1988. *Okupowanej Warszawy Dzień Powszedni* [Daily Life in Occupied Warsaw]. Warsaw: Czytelnik.

Szczypiorski, Adam. 1976. "Mieszkania i Ludność Warszawy w Czasie Wojny i Hitlerowskiej Okupacji" [Housing and Population of Warsaw During the War and Nazi Occupation]. *Studia Demograficzne* 46:27–41.

Taeuber, Irene B. 1958. *The Population of Japan*. Princeton: Princeton University Press.

Tasch, Dieter. 1983. *Hannover in Bombenkrieg 1943–1945*. Hannover: Hannoversche Allgemeine Zeitung.

Thomas, Hugh. 1977. *The Spanish Civil War*, rev. ed. New York: Harper & Row.

Thornton, Judith. 1986. "Chernobyl and Soviet Energy." *Problems of Communism* 35(6):1–27.

Thrift, Nigel, and Dean Forbes. 1986. *The Price of War: Urbanization in Vietnam 1954–85*. London: Allen and Unwin.

Titmuss, Richard M. 1950. *Problems of Social Policy*. London: H.M.S.O. and Longmans, Green.

Tokuhata, George K., and Edward Digon. 1985. *Cancer Mortality and Morbidity (Incidence) around TMI.* Harrisburg: Pennsylvania Department of Health.

Treadwell, Mattie E. 1962. *Hurrican Carla—September 3–14, 1961.* Office of Civil Defense, Region 5, Denton, Texas. Washington: GPO.

Twomey, Steve. 1984. "The Little Town atop the Volcano: Inch by Inch, Closer and Closer." Philadelphia *Inquirer*, Sept. 21:2–A.

United Nations Development Programme. 1970. *Skopje Resurgent: The Story of a United Nations Special Fund Town Planning Project.* New York: United Nations.

United Nations Statistical Office. 1963. *Demographic Yearbook 1963.* New York.

U.S. Agency for International Development. (n.d.). *Disaster Relief. Case Report: Nicaragua-Earthquake December 1972.* Washington.

U.S. Agency for International Development, Office of U.S. Foreign Disaster Assistance. 1983a. *Disaster History: Significant Data on Major Disasters Worldwide, 1900–Present.* Washington.

———. 1983b. *Annual Report FY 1983.* Washington.

U.S. Army Engineer District, Mobile, Ala. (n.d.). *Report on Hurricane Camille 14–22 August 1969.* Mobile.

U.S. Congress, House of Representatives, Committee on Agriculture. 1963. *Skopje, Yugoslavia, Earthquake Tragedy.* Washington.

U.S. National Oceanic and Atmospheric Administration. 1973. *Some Devastating North Atlantic Hurricanes of the 20th Century.* Washington.

U.S. Nuclear Regulatory Commission. 1987. *Report on the Accident at the Chernobyl Nuclear Power Station.* NUREG 1250. Washington.

U.S. Strategic Bombing Survey. 1947a. *Civilian Defense Division. Final Report.* European War, Civilian Defense Division, Report 40. Washington.

———. 1947b. *Cologne Field Report.* Washington.

———. 1947c. *Hamburg Field Report. Volume I—Text.* Washington.

———. 1947d. *Hanover Field Report.* European War, Civilian Defense Division, Report 43. Washington.

———. 1947e. *Field Report Covering Air-Raid Protection and Allied Subjects in Kobe Japan.* Civilian Defense Division, Report No. 7. Washington.

———. 1947f. *Field Report Covering Air-Raid Protection and Allied Subjects in Kyoto, Japan.* Pacific War, Civilian Defense Division, Report No. 6. Washington.

———. 1947g. *The Effects of Air Attack on Japanese Urban Economy. Summary Report.* Pacific War, Urban Areas Division, Report 55. Washington.

————. 1947h. *The Effects of Air Attack on the City of Nagoya.* Urban Areas Division. Washington.

————. 1947i. *The Effects of Strategic Bombing on Japanese Morale.* Pacific War, Civilian Studies, Report 14. Washington.

————. 1947j. *Final Report Covering Air-Raid Protection and Allied Subjects in Japan.* Pacific War, Civilian Studies, No. 11. Washington.

Unrein, Hans. 1953. *Die Bevölkerungsentwicklung in Thüringen 1910–1949. Eine regionale Studie.* Inaugural-Dissertation. Jena: Friedrich-Schiller Universität.

Urbanik, Thomas, II. 1978. "Texas Hurricane Evacuation Study." *Texas Transportation Researcher* 14(4):6–7.

Urlanis, B. C. 1971. *War and Population.* Moscow: Progress Publishers.

Vanssay, B. de. 1979. *Les Événements de 1976 en Guadeloupe: Apparition d'une Sub-Culture de Désastre.* Thèse de Doctorat de 3e Cycle. Université Antilles Guyane, École des Hautes Études en Sciences Sociales, Université Paris 5.

Vanwelkenhuyzen, Jean, and Jacques Dumont. 1983. *1940. Le Grand Exode.* Bruxelles: RTBF Éditions.

Vidalenc, Jean. 1951. "L'Exode de 1940. Méthodes et Premiers Résultats d'une Enquête." *Revue d'Histoire de la Deuxième Guerre Mondiale,* no. 3:51–55.

————. 1957. *L'Exode de Mai–Juin 1940.* Paris: Presses Universitaires de France.

Vinci, Felice. 1944. *Un' Inchiesta sugli Sfollati.* Università degli Studi di Milano, Studi dell'Istituto di Scienze Economiche e Statistiche. Milano: Gualdoni.

Voight, Barry. 1988. "Countdown to Catastrophe." *Earth and Mineral Sciences* [Pennsylvania State University] 57(2):17–30.

Voigt, Hans. 1950. *Die Veränderung der Grossstadt Kiel durch den Luftkrieg: Eine siedlungs- und wirtschaftsgeographische Untersuchung.* Schriften des Geographischen Instituts der Universität Kiel, Band XIII, Heft 2. Kiel.

Voznesenskiy, H. 1968. *Stroiteli Frontu* [Construction Workers for the Front]. Moscow.

————. 1971. *Vsemirno-Istoricheskaya Pobeda Sovetskogo Naroda 1941–1945* [Global-Historical Victory of the Soviet Nation 1941–1945]. Moscow.

Walters, K. J. 1977. *Darwin: Australia's First Cyclone Resistant City.* Darwin: Darwin Community College Printing Dept.

Webber, D. L. 1976. "Darwin Cyclone: An Exploration of Disaster Behavior." *Australian Journal of Social Issues* 11:54–63.

van Wehrt, Rudolf. 1941. *Frankreich auf der Flucht: Ein Erlebnisbericht aus dramatischen Tagen.* Oldenburg: Gerhard Stalling.

Weisman, Steven R. 1985. Personal Communication May 25.

Western, J. S. 1980. "Caring for the Community in Disaster Situations: The Short-Term Aspects," 119–32 in Oliver, John, ed., *Response to Disaster.* James Cook University of North Queensland: Center for Disaster Studies.

Western, J. S., and L. Doube. 1978. "Stress and Cyclone Tracy," 377–401 in: G. Pickup, ed., *Natural Hazards Management in North Australia.* Proceedings arising from 2nd NARU Seminar, Darwin, N.T. 11–14 September 1978, N.p.

Western, John S., and Gordon Milne. 1979. "Some Social Effects of a Natural Hazard: Darwin Residents and Cyclone Tracy," 488–502 in: Heathcote, R. L., and B. S. Thom, eds., *Natural Hazards in Australia.* Canberra: Australian Academy of Science.

White, Anthony G. 1976. *Earthquakes and Cities: A Selected Bibliography.* Exchange Bibliography No. 1109. Monticello, Ill.: Council of Planning Librarians.

White, Gilbert F., and J. Eugene Haas. 1975. *Assessment of Research on Natural Hazards.* Cambridge, Mass.: MIT Press.

Wilkinson, Kenneth, P., and Peggy J. Ross. 1970. *Citizens' Responses to Hurricane Camille.* Report 35. State College, Miss.: Mississippi State University, Social Science Research Center.

Windhan, Gerald O., Ellen I. Posey, Peggy J. Ross, and Barbara G. Spencer. 1977. *Reactions to Storm Threat During Hurricane Eloise.* Report 51. State College, Miss.: Mississippi State University, Social Science Research Center.

Wright, James D., Peter H. Rossi, Sonia R. Wright, and Eleanor Weber-Burdin. 1979. *After the Clean-Up: Long-Range Effects of Natural Disasters.* Beverly Hills, Calif.: Sage Publications.

Young, P., ed. 1974. *Atlas of the Second World War.* New York: Putnam's Sons.

Yugoslavia, Federal Statistical Office. 1968. *Statistical Pocketbook of Yugoslavia.* Beograd.

Zahrelli Gas Kand Sangharsh Morcha 1985. *A Report of Activities til 14.1.85.* Bhopal. [mimeographed]

Ziegler, Donald J., Stanley D. Brunn, and James H. Johnson, Jr. 1981. "Evacuation from a Nuclear Technological Disaster." *Geographical Review* 71:1–16.

Ziegler, Donald J., and James H. Johnson, Jr. 1984. "Evacuation Behavior in Response to Nuclear Power Plant Accidents." *Professional Geographer* 36:207–15.

Ziegler, Donald J., James H. Johnson, Jr., and Stanley D. Brunn. 1983. *Technological Hazards*. Resource Publications in Geography. Washington: Association of American Geographers.

B. PERIODICALS

Corriere Milanese (Milan)

Current Digest of the Soviet Press

The Globe and Mail (Toronto)

The Hindu

Hindustan Times

Indian Express

Informator (Zagreb)

Le Monde (Paris)

Nai Duniya (India)

National Herald (India)

New York *Times*

Ogonyok (Moscow)

Philadelphia *Inquirer*

Times of India

The Week (Kerala State)

Winnipeg *Tribune*

Worcester [Mass.] *Evening Gazette*

Index

About the Authors

Professor Emeritus Wilbur Zelinsky has been teaching geography at the Pennsylvania State University since 1963 after earlier appointments at the University of Georgia and Southern Illinois University. Among other activities, he served as president of the Association of American Geographers in 1972–73. Within the field of population studies his interests have focused on questions of population distribution and mobility. He has also published a wide variety of items dealing with the cultural and social geography of North America, and is currently concerned with transnationalization of late twentieth-century society.

Professor Leszek A. Kosiński is professor of geography at the University of Alberta, Edmonton, Canada, and presently serves as a secretary-general and treasurer of the International Geographical Union and member of the Executive of the International Social Science Council. Polish-born and educated, he taught at various American universities before migrating to Canada in 1968. His research interests have concentrated on population mobility in Europe and other parts of the world. The author/editor of eighteen books and over a hundred articles published in fifteen countries in ten different languages, Professor Kosiński personally experienced evacuation of Warsaw following the 1944 uprising.

In this landmark study, two eminent geographers present the first comparative cross-national analysis of emergency evacuations engendered by every sort of disaster: military, natural, and industrial. Zelinsky and Kosiński have selected 27 evacuations of cities due to actual or anticipated emergencies during the past 50 years, from the Ohio River Flood of 1937 to the Chernobyl nuclear accident in 1986.

The Emergency Evacuation of Cities deals with an unprecedented range of places throughout the world—urban communities at various levels of socioeconomic development and over the longest span of time feasible. The authors analyze, compare, and contrast these extraordinary events, testing a series of hypotheses in an effort to learn what light historical experience can shed on areas of scholarly and practical concern. The central focus is on the demographic and geographical aspects of these experiences and how the empirical record of human behavior during such nonroutine events can contribute to the enrichment of general mobility theory and to more sensible emergency planning by national and local communities.